OUR MOST TROUBLING MADNESS

ETHNOGRAPHIC STUDIES IN SUBJECTIVITY

T. M. Luhrmann, Editor

1. *Forget Colonialism? Sacrifice and the Art of Memory in Madagascar,* by Jennifer Cole

2. *Sensory Biographies: Lives and Deaths among Nepal's Yolmo Buddhists,* by Robert R. Desjarlais

3. *Culture and the Senses: Bodily Ways of Knowing in an African Community,* by Kathryn Linn Geurts

4. *Becoming Sinners: Christianity and Moral Torment in a Papua New Guinea Society,* by Joel Robbins

5. *Jesus in Our Wombs: Embodying Modernity in a Mexican Convent,* by Rebecca J. Lester

6. *The Too-Good Wife: Alcohol, Codependency, and the Politics of Nurturance in Postwar Japan,* by Amy Borovoy

7. *Subjectivity: Ethnographic Investigations,* edited by João Biehl, Byron J. Good, and Arthur Kleinman

8. *Postcolonial Disorders,* edited by Mary-Jo DelVecchio Good, Sandra Teresa Hyde, Sarah Pinto, and Byron J. Good

9. *Under a Watchful Eye: Self, Power, and Intimacy in Amazonia,* by Harry Walker

10. *Unsettled: Denial and Belonging among White Kenyans,* by Janet McIntosh

11. *Our Most Troubling Madness: Case Studies in Schizophrenia across Cultures,* edited by T. M. Luhrmann and Jocelyn Marrow

OUR MOST TROUBLING

MADNESS

CASE STUDIES IN SCHIZOPHRENIA
ACROSS CULTURES

Edited by T. M. Luhrmann *and* Jocelyn Marrow

UNIVERSITY OF CALIFORNIA PRESS

University of California Press, one of the most distinguished university presses in the United States, enriches lives around the world by advancing scholarship in the humanities, social sciences, and natural sciences. Its activities are supported by the UC Press Foundation and by philanthropic contributions from individuals and institutions. For more information, visit www.ucpress.edu.

University of California Press
Oakland, California

Library of Congress Cataloging-in-Publication Data

Names: Luhrmann, T.M. (Tanya M.), 1959– editor,
    contributor. | Marrow, Jocelyn, editor, contributor.
Title: Our most troubling madness : case studies in
    schizophrenia across cultures / [edited by] T. M. Luhrmann
    and Jocelyn Marrow.
Other titles: Ethnographic studies in subjectivity ; 11.
Description: Oakland, California : University of California
    Press, [2016] | Series: Ethnographic studies in subjectivity ;
    11 | Includes bibliographical references and index.
Identifiers: LCCN 2016006838 | ISBN 9780520291089
    (cloth : alk. paper) | ISBN 9780520291096 (pbk.) |
    ISBN 9780520964945 (ebook)
Subjects: LCSH: LCSH: Schizophrenia—Cross-cultural
    studies. | Schizophrenia—Case studies.
Classification: LCC RC514 .O93 2016 | DDC 616.89/8—dc23
LC record available at http://lccn.loc.gov/2016006838

25   24   23   22   21   20   19   18   17   16
10   9   8   7   6   5   4   3   2   1

For all those who struggle to make a life with serious psychotic disorder

CONTENTS

List of Illustrations   *ix*

Foreword   *xi*
Kim Hopper

Acknowledgments   *xv*

Introduction   *1*
T. M. Luhrmann

1. *"I'm Schizophrenic!"*: How Diagnosis Can Change Identity
   in the United States   27
   T. M. Luhrmann

2. Diagnostic Neutrality in Psychiatric Treatment
   in North India   42
   Amy June Sousa

3. Vulnerable Transitions in a World of Kin: In the Shadow
   of Good Wifeliness in North India   56
   Jocelyn Marrow

4. Work and Respect in Chennai   71
   Giulia Mazza

5. Racism and Immigration: An African-Caribbean Woman
   in London   86
   Johanne Eliacin

6. Voices That Are More Benign: The Experience of Auditory
    Hallucinations in Chennai   99
    T. M. Luhrmann and R. Padmavati

7. Demonic Voices: One Man's Experience of God, Witches,
    and Psychosis in Accra, Ghana   113
    Damien Droney

8. Madness Experienced as Faith: Temple Healing
    in North India   127
    Anubha Sood

9. Faith Interpreted as Madness: Religion, Poverty, and
    Psychiatry in the Life of a Romanian Woman   139
    Jack R. Friedman

10. The Culture of the Institutional Circuit in the United States   153
    T. M. Luhrmann

11. Return to Baseline: A Woman with Acute-Onset, Non-affective
    Remitting Psychosis in Thailand   167
    Julia Cassaniti

12. A Fragile Recovery in the United States   180
    Neely A. L. Myers

    Conclusion   197
    Jocelyn Marrow and T. M. Luhrmann
    Notes   223
    Bibliography   241
    Contributors   265
    Index   269

ILLUSTRATIONS

1. John Hood's drawing of schizophrenia / 32

2. In India, patients attend appointments with family / 48

3. A young married woman on the Ghats of Varanasi / 57

4. A banyan tree / 72

5. A woman alone on the streets of Mumbai / 78

6. Accra General Psychiatric Hospital (sign and waiting area) / 117

7. A page from Sunita's notebook / 132

8. A poverty-striken woman in Romania / 144

9. A woman with psychosis on a street in Chicago / 157

10. Zaney's drawing of her social world / 162

11. Thai spirit house / 171

12. A member's cartoon drawing of the Center / 181

13. Rules governing life on the street (window and doors) / 190

FOREWORD

KIM HOPPER

The world is unjust, and this is why acknowledging injustice is vital for recovery.
—Philip Thomas and Eleanor Longden[1]

This observation—by a social psychiatrist and a peer/service user with formidable voice-wrangling skills herself—may seem out of place in a volume self-described as clinical ethnography. After all, what's explored in this work is the hard labor of managing psychosis; its remit is the everyday and experience-near, faithful to the instabilities and uncertainties of recovery (and, for that matter, anthropological tradecraft). But such a project can't help but raise the prior question of how it is that disabling distress of this sort is differentially distributed. And, more to the point here, it can't ignore the embedding contexts that make possible the makeshift healing labors—accidental, incomplete, still in flux, variously understood, and fragile though they may be. "Recovery," for which we aim, is an odd-job term: an analytic construct in search of precision and a claims-making vehicle in search of leverage or purchase. The analytic construct directs our attention to complexity: by what range of contrivances have variously situated people fashioned viable lives during or after psychosis? And, when not conscripted by neoliberal mischief, the claim-making vehicle invites us to forge the long-overdue linkage to social determinants made elsewhere in public health. The signal achievement of *Our Most Troubling Madness*—drawing upon extended case studies of comparative ethnographic inquiry to challenge what passes for "treatment as usual" in the West—may be that it reckons with both.

The dozen case studies assembled here offer a much-needed corrective to decades of tantalizing, methodologically fraught, and often fruitless debates over "outcomes elsewhere." In what amounts to a wide-ranging friend-of-the-court brief, submitted by a crop of mostly young anthropologists under the steady hand of a wise near-elder, this book asks how healing occurs, with what vagaries in course and thoroughness in reach, and what—over time, across multiple venues and audiences, drawing from a broad range of contingencies and allies—healing actually entails in practice. The tone in diplomacy-speak is "constructive engagement." A choir of tempered voices is convened to press the claim that better understanding of how culture shapes prospects of recovery *there* will have implications for treatment *here*—a claim demonstrated rather than asserted throughout most of this volume, and brought forward with steel and well-earned indignation in the concluding chapter.

Tellingly, the accountings presented here are less concerned with discrete, measured outcomes than with closely worked portrayals of troubled lives taking shape over time and across place. They explore how time and familiarity find their way into "symptom" load and "disability"; what it takes/means to make productive sense of madness and how shifts in idiom can assist that process; the varied guises and suspect terms under which relief and respite may be found; the importance (which peers have insisted on for years) of "experientially similar others" in providing succor and counsel; the distinction between managing well even if, by others' lights, one is "really sick"; how local/individual explanatory models weigh competing registers of shame and respectability; how clinicians can work fruitfully with those models; how hearing voices can exact a grueling apprenticeship that, if "successfully" completed, can confer a contemporary version of having weathered sixteenth-century spiritual exercises of "discernment"; the durable virtues of patience and the *longue durée*. They also confront something often missing from standard clinical accounts: frank recognition that the achievements of recovery are partial and provisional, subject to the buffetings of fate, accidents of circumstance, and the slow crawl of time. Our own stocktaking efforts introduce their own measures of indeterminacy; even the most faithfully executed ethnography is, at best, partial and provisional. (As we are repeatedly reminded, the stories recounted here are fractured, incomplete, riddled with gaps and inconsistencies, polyphonic in the telling.) If schizophrenia is shaped by culture, recovery is also. The semantic nod to "madness" reminds us, first, that despite the classification debates that occupy psychiatry, naming is social practice in everyday life, not professional dicta; and second, that collaborative work with those working in alternative or oppositional endeavors may be difficult and painful, but no less urgent for that.

Our Most Troubling Madness is a clarion call (with the requisite scholarly imprimatur and earmarks) to abandon the sheltering conventions of our time that would relieve all but established neuro-technicians of responsibility for dealing with "brain disorders." Instead, taking its cue from the yield of far-ranging inquiries, it sets recovery as a de facto social project. The only real question is whether to be an informed participant or a clueless bystander.

Actually, no. There's another question: What stands in the way of such eminently reasonable reform? To address that question, to position ourselves to make what we learn about such inertial resistance useful, we will need a different kind of ethnography. These are parlous times for mental health reform in the United States. For every flicker of progress, flotillas of counterpoint are on hand: cost-containment, "good enough" outcome measures pared down to bovine passivity, Pharma-driven research, a public told repeatedly to rhyme mental illness with violence, and a systemic failure to recognize the material necessities of full social participation. Luhrmann is surely right to insist that we have "data and theory to contribute," but for the campaign shaping up on this terrain, we will need to reach beyond the "classics" of "kinship, class, personhood, poverty, meaning"—crucial though they may be. The sort of "anthropology of viable alternatives" I have in mind will need to deal with the rude machinery of bureaucracies and budgets, regulations and reimbursement schemes, embittered politics and backstage maneuvering. It must inquire into the vexed clemencies of family recruitment. It will have to contend with public mental health's notorious institutional isolation. It will need to suss out what it takes for new approaches to break into the therapeutic "formulary," an imprimatur that ensures legitimacy and longevity along with reimbursement. And, should fresh options present themselves, if only as provisional social experiments, it will need to be ready to document the invariably messy story of their implementation, ideally offering that reportage for use in making midcourse corrections.

For that, the sort of "engaged anthropology" so winningly on display here—anthropology with a happily divided soul, faithful to the ethnographic project *and* committed to the pragmatic struggle to translate its implications—may be exactly what's needed.

ACKNOWLEDGMENTS

We would like to express deep and abiding thanks to those who allowed us into their lives (some of the names that follow are pseudonyms) and who so generously shared their stories with us, and to the many institutions that allowed us to do research with their clients: John Hood, and those around him; Meeta, Veena, Anisha, and their families and doctors; Priyanka, her families, and her doctors (Sanghamitra Sarkar, M.A.; Professor Anjoo Sharan Upadhyaya, Ph.D.; and Professor Indira Sharma, M.D., Banaras Hindu University); Madhu and the Banyan staff, including Vandana Gopikumar; Violet, her community, and her doctors; Sita and her family and the Schizophrenia Research Foundation (SCARF India); Charles, and Akwasi Osei (the director) and the staff of the Accra General Psychiatric Hospital; Sunita, the women of Balaji Temple, and the Sri Balaji Temple Trust, Mehndipur, Dausa; Alexandra, her friends and her doctors, and Mugur Ciumageanu, Anca Sevcenco, Nadina Visan, and Mihai Avadanei; Zaney and the women and staff of Sarah's Circle and the Uptown neighborhood; Poi and Uten Mahamid and Thongsuk Mongkhon; and Meg, the staff at the Center, Sue Estroff, Sydney Hans, and Beth Angell.

Tanya Marie Luhrmann and Jocelyn Marrow also thank Kim Hopper—as always, the good angel of our project; Alexa Hagerty for her help with the final stages of the manuscript; our editor Reed Malcolm and the remarkable University of California Press staff; and the many scholars who have encouraged and sustained us throughout the course of putting this book together.

T.M. Luhrmann's research in Uptown was supported by the National Institutes of Health (NIH R34 MH090441) and in India by a grant from the Institute for Social Science Research at Stanford University; Jocelyn Marrow's field research was supported by a Junior Fellowship from the American Institute of Indian Studies and a Fulbright-Hays Doctoral Dissertation Research Abroad Award; Julia Cassaniti was supported by a Century Fellowship at the University of Chicago and by a Fulbright-Hays Doctoral Dissertation Research Abroad Award; Johanne Eliacin's fieldwork in London was supported by a National Science Foundation (NSF) Dissertation Improvement Grant in Cultural Anthropology, a Nicholson Long-Term Dissertation Fellowship from the Nicholson Center for British Studies at the University of Chicago, travel grants from the Center for the Study of Race, Politics, and Culture, and an NIH/National Institute of Mental Health (NIMH) Mental Health Dissertation Research Grant (R36 MH081727–02); Jack Friedman's research was supported by funding from the U.S. Fulbright Senior Scholars Program and an NIMH T32 Training Grant in "Culture and Mental Health" administered through the University of Chicago's Department of Comparative Human Development; Neely Myers's field research was supported by a University of Chicago Trustees' Fellowship; Anubha Sood's research was supported by an NSF Dissertation Improvement Grant and by the Wenner-Gren Foundation's Doctoral Dissertation Award; and Amy Sousa's field research was supported by a Fulbright-Hays Doctoral Dissertation Research Abroad Award and by the Woodrow Wilson Foundation.

Introduction

T. M. LUHRMANN

Schizophrenia is and is not a thing in the world.[1] To borrow a phrase from Steve Shapin, there is no such thing as schizophrenia, and this is its ethnography.[2] There are few medical labels that have been so firmly rejected—and for some good reasons. There is no specific genetic marker for the illness. It has no clear-cut trajectory, though most who experience it probably never return to the way they were before things went wrong. It has no unique symptoms—no symptoms specific to this disorder and not found in other disorders. The man who distinguished schizophrenia from bipolar disorder, Emil Kraepelin, did so on the basis of schizophrenia's progressively degenerative course—and now many argue that recovery from schizophrenia is possible. The man who gave the disorder its name, Eugen Bleuler, did not list hallucinations among his identifying features of the disorder—and these days, hallucinated voices are often assumed to be its primary symptom.[3] Schizophrenia may have been with us forever, but there are those who believe that the illness only emerged in the nineteenth century.[4] The difference between people who best fit the description of schizophrenia and those who similarly best fit the description of bipolar disorder or depression is striking—and yet more people seem to lie in the broad, gray, murky boundaries. The difficulty of finding specific neuroscientific markers for this (or, for that matter, any other) psychiatric illness has led the National Institute of Mental Health (NIMH), in recent years, to refuse to fund research based on diagnostic categories.[5]

And yet there certainly is a real and terrible disorder, the most devastating of all the psychiatric illnesses, that at its most severe has clearly recognizable features and is found in nearly every corner of the world. In the modern era the disorder has consistently been understood as a combination of several groups of symptoms: first, the so-called positive symptoms of psychosis—the radical break with reality signaled by delusions, hallucinations, and incoherent speech; second, the so-called negative symptoms of emotional withdrawal, signaled by an unexpressive face and voice tone, often called "flat affect," and mismatched emotion-cognition displays, like giggling when talking about something sad; and third, the so-called symptoms of cognitive dysfunction, signaled when someone's life at work or at home seriously falls apart for a significant length of time. People with schizophrenia often hear voices talking to them, commanding them, sneering at them, cajoling them, sometimes so loudly it can be hard for them to hear anyone else, and the voices can continue for decades. The illness is terrifyingly common, claiming roughly one in a hundred people pretty much everywhere we have looked.[6]

This book examines the way this terrible madness is shaped by its social context: how life is lived with this madness in different settings, and what it is about those settings that alters the course of the illness, its outcome, and even the structure of its symptoms. We will call this madness "schizophrenia," recognizing that the term is contested and its boundaries complicated, because the term points to the severe, persistent break with reality that is recognized around the world and is also identified in each of our case studies. It is a term with invisible scare quotes, but no other word does its job.

The question of how this madness is shaped by its social setting is a much bigger one than it was even a decade ago. Until recently, schizophrenia was perhaps our best example—our poster child—for the "bio-bio-bio" model of psychiatric illness: genetic cause, brain alteration, pharmacologic treatment.[7] The embrace of its fundamentally organic nature had arisen from new scientific research that swept in a biological psychiatry. The triumphant rethinking of psychiatric illness was heralded by books like Nancy Andreasen's *The Broken Brain: The Biological Revolution in Psychiatry*, which took schizophrenia as its focus and as the best evidence for the disease-like nature of serious mental illness.[8] The 1990s became NIMH's "Decade of the Brain." Psychiatry was to be wrested away from its decades-long dependence on psychoanalysis and established as a field of medicine like any other.

That has happened. Psychiatry is no longer the field it was when psychoanalysis dominated the way psychiatrists thought. Most disorders are understood as diseases, and most of them are treated with medication. But in recent years psychiatric disorders have become less culture free, *less* biological, if by "biological" we mean that they are understood to arise from our genes and to unfold independently from our social world. Increasingly we know that our genes interact with our environment and that this *epigenetic* interaction deeply shapes our lives.[9] This is true even of our most terrible madness. In the case of schizophrenia, we now have direct evidence that people are more likely to fall ill with schizophrenia in some social settings than in others, and more likely to recover in some social settings than in others. We know from the empirical research carried out by the new social epidemiology that something about the social world gets under the skin. The puzzle is to figure out what it is.

There is a new role for anthropology in the science of schizophrenia. Psychiatric science has learned—epidemiologically, empirically, quantitatively—that our social world makes a difference. But the highly structured, specific-variable analytic methods of standard psychiatric science cannot tell us what it is about culture that has that impact. Anthropology can. At least, the careful observation enabled by rich ethnography allows us to see in more detail what kinds of social and cultural features may make a difference to a life lived with schizophrenia.

This volume presents twelve case studies that help illustrate some of the variability in the social experience of schizophrenia. We sought cases that best illustrate the main hypotheses about the different experience of schizophrenia in the West and outside the West. Most of the authors are psychiatric anthropologists, that breed of ethnographer who takes mental illness as a central focus. Each was asked to tell the story of one person in the particular culture they studied who represents something important about the experience of schizophreniform disorder in that setting.

To be clear, the authors did not themselves conduct formal diagnostic interviews with their subjects. In each case, however, the author met the subject in a context in which caseworkers, clinicians, or the subjects themselves volunteered a diagnosis of schizophrenia or schizophreniform disorder (e.g., schizoaffective disorder). In all cases it was clear that the subject experienced "positive symptoms" like hallucinations or delusions; that the subject's life had been seriously disrupted by their illness; and that they had struggled with the symptoms for more than six months. These are, in broad brushstrokes, the *DSM* criteria for schizophrenia. There is no question that each of our subjects has been very ill with a serious psychotic disorder.

There is, inevitably, a catch-as-catch-can quality to these case studies. Few anthropologists focus exclusively on schizophrenia. We reached out to find people already working in the field who would have contact with possible cases.

Most of our cases come from the United States or from India, because the well-known findings that schizophrenia has a more benign course in India than it does in the West have led many anthropologists to look at schizophrenia in India. Our overrepresentation of work in India allows us to examine closely the factors that might account for this better outcome.

We also have more case studies about women. This is an accident based on our own gender—most of the contributors to this book are women. It is easier in many societies—and certainly in India—for female ethnographers to form close relationships with women. This accident may serve us well. Women are somewhat less likely than men to fall ill with schizophrenia: globally the incidence rate is roughly 1.4 men to 1 woman.[10] An emphasis on women may help us to see more clearly the social conditions that make someone vulnerable. And by looking primarily at women, we are at least comparing like with like.

We use our case studies to look closely at some basic problems in culture and schizophrenia: diagnosis and social identity; vulnerable transition points that may help trigger illness; a kind of psychosis, more common outside the West, in which people return to baseline after madness; immigrants who are more at risk of illness; a more benign voice-hearing experience; supernaturalist explanations of psychosis; the harsh institutional circuit that many with schizophrenia encounter in the United States; and recovery. At the end, we draw conclusions from these case studies and from other ethnographies, including an excellent collection by Janis Jenkins and Robert Barrett, *Schizophrenia, Culture, and Subjectivity,* that precedes us in the field. We believe that if we understood culture's impact more deeply, it could change the way we treat schizophrenia. That's particularly important because it turns out that schizophrenia is probably more common in a Western setting, and certainly more caustic.[11]

We call this approach "clinical ethnography."[12] All of us were trained first and foremost as ethnographers. But many of us have had substantial clinical training (and Johanne Eliacin became fully licensed as a clinical psychologist while obtaining her scholarly degree). We read the psychiatric literature as well as the anthropological literature. We do not see our job, first and foremost, as criticizing mental health professionals as observers. We see ourselves as working alongside mental health and medical professionals to understand the illnesses humans confront and to contribute to the process of helping ease their distress. We begin with the epidemiological puzzles and set out to research the patterns of local meaning that may help explain them.

There has been a shift in the way many anthropologists have been thinking about psychiatry in the past decade—away from a skeptical, even dismissive approach to clinicians to a more clinically engaged research process. These engaged anthropologists are more empathic with the struggles faced by clinicians, more collaborative with scientists and clinicians, more likely to publish in medical journals as well as in anthropology journals, and often more medically sophisticated. They are more likely to work in the trenches alongside clinicians.[13] In a recent essay, Rob Whitley calls this approach "no opposition without proposition." He argues that psychiatric anthropologists should not only provide a meaningful critique of practices and beliefs within psychiatry, and not only illuminate the sociocultural, familial, and clinical contexts of illness, but also serve as a positive catalyst for change.[14] This is an engaged anthropology "in" medicine, as well as an anthropology "of" medicine. That is what we set out to accomplish here.

But first, we begin with an overview of our most troubling madness.

In the years when Benjamin Franklin defended the creation of the new America and Jean-Jacques Rousseau and others wrote tracts that set out the conditions for a just society, madness was imagined as a disease fomented by a world choking under the weight of its own civilization.[15] On his way to building his argument about the social contract, Rousseau invented a state of nature—part hypothetical, part based on travelers' tales—that he saw as a state of grace and possibility. The real Europe around him he took to be corrupt and decadent, and he thought that it drove men mad. In *Emile*, he wrote that "Everything degenerates in the hands of man." The nineteenth century—with the sense of social fragility after the French revolution, the rapid urbanization and social turmoil of the industrial revolution, the rising awareness of other ways of life through colonial expansion—led many European intellectuals to the conviction that European society was in trouble and decaying from within. In his end-of-the-century best seller, *Degeneration*, the Parisian Max Nordau pronounced that "We stand now in the midst of a severe mental epidemic; of a sort of black death of degeneration and hysteria."[16]

As the nineteenth century turned into the twentieth, Émile Durkheim used statistics and census data to demonstrate, in *Suicide*, that as social cohesion loosened, more people killed themselves. In his models, primitive people were so socially cohesive that they barely had any individuality at all. He thought that in such densely interdependent groups people might kill themselves for altruistic reasons, like World War II kamikaze pilots who deliberately crashed their bomb-loaded planes into enemy warships. But they would not kill themselves from anomie. I remember a class in graduate school in which our lecturer, sketching out Durkheim's theory on the blackboard, drew moderns as a crowd of stick figures with little round heads and primitives as one large oval head with dozens of little stick bodies poking out beneath. No one in that society, in this way of thinking, should ever have been psychiatrically ill.

That sensibility lingered on in Claude Lévi-Strauss, who in *Tristes Tropiques* wrote of a Europe suffocating "like some ageing animal whose thickening hide has formed an impermeable crust and, by no longer allowing the skin to breathe, is hastening the ageing process." The Amazonian Nambikwara, by contrast, he thought of as free. One evening, gazing at ocher-smeared families around a campfire, Lévi-Strauss wrote that an observer "can see in all of them an immense kindness, a profoundly carefree attitude, a naïve and charming animal satisfaction and—binding these various feelings together—something which might be called the most truthful and moving expression of human love."[17]

This happy vision was shattered by long-term fieldwork. It became clear that people like the Nambikwara did struggle with mental illness, and indeed with the same mental illnesses (in some broad sense) as those in the West. And yet it would also become clear, over time, that there was in fact something to these romantic views, although the contrast had been vastly overstated.

In the early twentieth century the colonial encounter had, of course, banished the myth of the Noble Savage—"gloriously glowing in rude but radiant physical health"[18]—but it had not entirely demolished the sense that fragile nerves and melancholy were the products of civilization.[19] Indeed, early anthropological reports seemed to confirm this. In 1929, C. G. Seligman, an anthropologist and physician, argued that serious mental illness did not exist in New Guinea, except where people had been deeply westernized.[20] This incensed a young British woman who came to Ghana in the 1930s and noticed a series of new shrines she thought were treating mental illness.

[T]here still lingers the idea that mental stress and mental illness are the prerogative of "over civilized" societies: that the simple savage may have Ancylostomiasis but cannot have Anxiety: that he may, in his innocence, believe his neighbour to be making bad magic against him, but he still sleeps like a top.[21]

M. J. Field could write. She returned home but came back to Ghana after the war, by that point trained as a psychiatrist, and settled in as an observer at a rural shrine. She recorded over 2,500 supplications. Most of these were about infertility and business trouble, but some seemed to be about serious psychiatric trouble.[22] She took remarkably detailed notes about those cases. At the end of her work, when drought and rising bus prices meant that fewer people were coming to the shrine, she went looking for what she called *chronic schizophrenia*—a term the British used more narrowly than Americans did[23]—and found forty-one individuals in twelve Ashanti country towns and villages with a population of 4,283 (in the 1948 census). These people, often located for her by a tribal elder, were obviously mad, talking *basu-basu*—for example, "an unkempt woman, with a baby on her back, dancing, singing, laughing and shouting."[24]

Field's *Search for Security* is a remarkable book, both because of its trenchant asides—"the latter Christian prophets owe their extinction to the poverty of their understanding and personality and the consequent inanity of their prophesying"[25]—and the unparalleled detail of her data. (She offers 144 examples of the mottos painted on the sides of local taxis.) She had no trouble recognizing in Ghana the serious psychiatric disorders she saw in her own society, although not all of the Ghanaians she thought were medically ill were seen as such by their fellow villagers. Nearly every person she thought could be diagnosed with depression came to the shrine accusing themselves of being witches.

> Patients suffering from severe depression are, the world over, unshakably convinced of their own worthlessness and wickedness and irrationally accuse themselves of having committed every unforgivable sin. In Africa the worst sin they can imagine is witchcraft, and they insist that they have abundantly committed it.[26]

Field thought that local ideas about witchcraft could not have been sustained by these shrewd and common-sensical people without the rich evidence of those repeated confessions.

Her observations about schizophrenia are striking, and increasingly they are supported by later work. She thought that the basic rates were about the same as they were in Britain, but that they were higher for those who were literate, not because such people had complicated conflicts about being both traditional and Western, but because of frustrated aspirations—because the hard work of becoming literate often led to little economic gain.[27] We now know that poverty and racism do increase the risk of psychotic illness. She sometimes saw a kind of psychosis in which people became suddenly and dramatically ill—and then just got better. We now know that there is a condition—non-affective acute remitting psychosis—that behaves this way, and that it is more common outside the West. She thought that the work demanded by farming—not only physical but intermittent, so that there were often unoccupied men sitting around the village—made it easier for a man with schizophrenia to pass as normal. She noticed that a third of the women with chronic schizophrenia became ill after menopause but that the stress of marriage could precipitate the illness. And she thought that on the whole, people with schizophrenia were better off in these villages, where they were known and cared for by relatives, than they would be in urban hospitals. This was not because rural Ghana was a place of timeless tranquility.[28] It was because in rural areas, people knew who the ill were, knew whether they would be violent, and tolerated them as part of the social world. The treatments did not always look kind. She saw people shackled to logs and locked in houses. But ill people stayed with those who knew them.[29]

A few years later a research team—headed by Alexander Leighton, a psychiatrist from Cornell, and Adeoye Lambo, the medical superintendent in the district where the study was done (and later a psychiatrist at University College, Ibadan, Nigeria)—came up with similar results, though in less detail. They set out to replicate in Yoruba country the same epidemiological survey that Leighton had done in his famous Stirling County study, which had found—as Durkheim had predicted—that people in more socially integrated communities were less ill.[30] Using the same diagnostic handbook, they found that while the general pattern of symptoms were quite similar in both settings—"we have not come upon any symptom patterns that are recognized by the Yoruba and are not recognized in [American] psychiatry"[31]—the overall level of impairment rose as one went from a rural African village (15%) to an African town (19%) and thence to Stirling County (33%). The Yoruba really did suffer from recognizable mental illness, but modernization seemed to make things worse.[32] This work also affirmed the observations of Field and of the anthropologist Robert Edgerton (in his study of psychosis in four African communities) that what mattered in a rural African setting was behavior, not inner experience.[33] In African villages, people were identified with serious mental illness when they shouted, stripped naked, and ran into the bush—not because they reported hallucinations. To be sure, the voices may well have told them to do these things. But it was the behavior, not the voices, that concerned their peers.

These views were not, however, the dominant perspective on schizophrenia within anthropology. These were the years when psychoanalysis dominated psychiatry, and to some extent anthropology, in the United States. In the 1930s Margaret Mead, Ruth Benedict, Edward Sapir, Gregory Bateson, Ralph Linton, and others ran in psychoanalytic circles. They were part of an interdisciplinary seminar at Columbia with psychoanalysts like Abram Kardiner that continued for years.[34] From a psychoanalytic perspective, schizophrenia was a reaction to social experience—not a disease. Even if one conceded some organic process, there were no absolute standards against which people could be declared ill or out of place. What defined people as abnormal was what counted as normal, and that judgment was social and relative. As Ruth Benedict asserted in "Anthropology and the Abnormal," "one of the most striking facts that emerge from a study of widely varying cultures is the ease with which our abnormals function in other cultures."[35] Many anthropologists—and many romantic readers of anthropology—wanted to argue that people with the odd hallucinatory experiences the West called "schizophrenia" would thrive in a less modern setting as shamans. They would not even be identified as ill. Some protested that such a shaman would still be sick; as George Devereux, the most vehement of these voices, said, "Briefly stated, my position is that the shaman is mentally deranged."[36] But he was arguing against a dominant position.

You still hear this argument that "our" schizophrenia is "their" shamanism. Compassionate clinicians, trying to make bad news sound better, sometimes tell patients that their ability to see and hear what others do not would be highly valued in other societies. Patients sometimes reach out to the idea of shamanism to make sense of their own sensory experiences or to repair an identity spoiled by the diagnosis—as John Hood does, in a case presented later in this volume. In general, those claims are wrong. In 1983 Richard Noll pointed out that what shamans experience is quite different from what those with schizophrenia experience. The shamanic "state" is willed, is often prosocial (the shaman saves souls and dances with spirits), and accords with local expectations of behavior appropriate for shamans. None of these is typically true of people with schizophrenia.[37] In fact, the shaman must make it clear that he is *not* mad.[38] Shamanism is now understood more as a dissociative process, a trance practice more akin to speaking in tongues and spirit possession than to psychosis. It is nonetheless also true that the relationship between dissociation and psychosis has now become one of the most vexed questions in the study of psychosis and spirituality, as some of our case studies illustrate.[39]

Meanwhile, the way schizophrenia was understood during the mid-twentieth century would become famous as the most notorious misuse of psychoanalytic theory in American psychiatry. When psychoanalysis dominated American psychiatry, back before the biomedical revolution (roughly from World War II until the 1980s), the dominant American psychiatric perspective on schizophrenia held that the condition was the result of the patient's own emotional conflict. Such patients (it was thought) were unable to reconcile intense feelings of longing for intimacy with their fear of closeness. Neglect in early childhood and their subsequent intense resentment, fury, and violence drove them into an autistic self-preoccupation from which they yearned for contact but were too terrified to reach out for it. As Frieda Fromm-Reichmann—one of the most famous therapists of schizophrenia and the model for the fictional analyst in I Never Promised You a Rose Garden—wrote, "the schizophrenic's partial emotional regression and his withdrawal from the outside world into an autistic private world, with its specific thought processes and modes of feeling and expression, is motivated by his fear of repetitional rejection, his distrust of others, and equally so by his own retaliative hostility, which he abhors, as well as the deep anxiety promoted by this hatred."[40]

Often, clinicians blamed the mother for delivering conflicting messages of hope and rejection. She was "schizophrenogenic": her own ambivalence paralyzed her child and drove him or her into the clinical impasse of the illness. The phrase was Fromm-Reichmann's, although she appears to have used it only once in her own work: "the schizophrenic is painfully distrustful and resentful of other people, because of the severe early warp and rejection that he has encountered in important people of his infancy and childhood, as a rule, mainly in a schizophrenogenic mother."[41] As the theory developed, schizophrenia became the endpoint of dominating, overprotective, but basically rejecting mothers who actually drove their children crazy. A 1949 article by Trude Tietze, a Viennese-educated psychiatrist, illustrates the genre well. Tietze interviewed the mothers of twenty-five hospitalized adult patients diagnosed with schizophrenia and concluded that they were the cause of their sons' disturbance. "Once their superficial smiling front was broken through, one was appalled at the emotional emptiness one found. There was a lack of genuine warmth. . . . It is this intuition or empathy with the child that appears to be missing or inadequately developed."[42]

By the 1960s it was standard practice in American psychiatry to regard the mother as the cause of the child's psychosis.[43] So entrenched did this view become that scholars made the most remarkable statements. One author wondered, in a particularly condemnatory essay describing those with schizophrenia as having been reared with "subtle malignancy," whether schizophrenia as it is known today would exist "if women were impersonally impregnated and gave birth to infants who were reared by state nurses in a communal setting."[44] The willingness of relatives to pay for hospital care was thought to arise from the guilt they felt for their role in the patient's suffering. *The Mental Hospital*, the classic 1954 study of one of the best psychoanalytic hospitals, contains this remark: "In some cases it would be reasonably adequate to describe the ideal relative as a person who appeared, gave the history precisely, accurately and directly, and disappeared forever, except for paying his bills—by mail."[45]

While, from a psychoanalytic perspective, all relationships are fraught by conflict, these relationships between a mother and her schizophrenic child were thought to be particularly torn. Gregory Bateson famously characterized their presumed destructive ambivalence as a "double bind." The characteristic experience of schizophrenia, he argued, was one in which a mother would approach with a loving invitation; the child would respond, reaching out to give her a hug; the mother would flinch from the embrace; the child would withdraw; and the mother would then say, "Don't you love me?" "The child is punished for discriminating accurately what she is expressing, and he is punished for discriminating inaccurately—he is caught in a double bind."[46] The patient then becomes unable to assign what Bateson called "the correct communicational mode" to utterances. Bateson inferred the schizophrenic double bind from his observation that patients with schizophrenia often confused the literal with the metaphorical, but also from his own theory of communicational frames. That theory argued that communications have meaning in a context: an aggressive gesture after the indication "This is play" ("Let's play pirates") has a meaning quite different from that aggressive gesture in a nonplay frame. He thought that people developed schizophrenia because when they were caught in a double bind—hug me, don't touch me—frame sorting was emotionally impossible, and so they conflated communicative frames, the literal and the metaphorical, the explicit and the implied.

It was precisely because these patients seemed so conflicted, so incoherent, so sick, that psychiatrists found them to be the most interesting and most compelling patients of the era. In one of the most famous hospitals of the time, Mass Mental, the Massachusetts Mental Health Center where many future psychiatric leaders were trained in the 1950s and 1960s, to use psychoanalysis to treat people with schizophrenia became the ultimate professional challenge.[47] Perhaps the most dominant figure at Mass Mental in its heyday was Elvin Semrad, the legendary director of psychiatric residency. He took seriously Freud's dictum that psychoanalysis was a cure through love, and he taught that a doctor's ability to cure came from his ability to care. He taught that care meant to be able to sit with the patient and to bear with him the pain that the patient feared so much that he chose madness over recognition. To Semrad, a schizophrenic patient was the most exciting patient, the tough, difficult patient who made the doctor a "real" doctor because to connect emotionally with such a patient was so hard. As he wrote, "In order to engage a schizophrenic patient in therapy, the therapist's basic attitude must be an acceptance of the patient as he is—of his aims in life, his values and his modes of operating, even when they are different and very often at odds with his own. Loving the patient as he is, in his state of decompensation [his psychosis] is the therapist's primary concern in approaching the patient."[48] Not everyone agreed. Even at Mass Mental, at least some young psychiatrists concluded that these patients were struggling with a brain disorder, and left them alone. "It was nonsense," someone said to me thirty years after the fact. "You couldn't do anything with them."[49]

In the 1970s, for many reasons, psychiatry moved away from psychoanalysis. More and more people began using medical insurance, and insurers resisted reimbursing care for a condition that didn't resemble a disease. At the time, psychiatrists often treated diagnosis as an afterthought. Researchers began to demonstrate that different clinics gave different diagnoses to the same patient.[50] In a spectacularly embarrassing study published in *Science*, a Stanford psychologist revealed that twelve different hospitals, each with a trained medical team, had given diagnoses of schizophrenia to people who weren't ill at all, but said they'd heard a voice saying "thud."[51] R. D. Laing, a psychiatrist, had already published his *The Divided Self* (1960), in which he explained that psychiatric symptoms made sense: they were reasonable attempts to communicate anguish. Thomas Szasz, also a psychiatrist, had published *The Myth of Mental Illness* (1961), in which he argued that there were no mental illnesses—that schizophrenia (for example) simply wasn't real in the way that cancer was real. Michel Foucault's passionate *Madness and Civilization*, which argued that psychiatry was modern society's attempt to corral and control inner experience, had been available in English since 1964. The anti-psychiatry movement was in full swing. The profession was in real danger of losing all credibility.

Psychiatry fought back. In 1980 the American Psychiatric Association published the *Diagnostic and Statistical Manual of Mental Disorders*, third edition, more commonly called "*DSM-III*." The two previous *DSMs* had been slight, spiral-bound notebooks not taken too seriously by clinicians. In those earlier volumes the diagnostic ancestors of the current psychiatric labels are clearly marked—but they are adjectives, not nouns. There is a "schizophrenic reaction," not "schizophrenia." The language is distinctly psychoanalytic. The "psycho-neurotic disorders," for instance, are "anxiety reaction," "obsessive-compulsive reaction," and "depressive reaction" rather than (as in *DSM-III*) "generalized anxiety disorder," "obsessive compulsive disorder," and "major depression." The 1952 manual (the first one) described all these problems this way: "The chief characteristic of these disorders is 'anxiety,' which may be directly felt and expressed or which may be unconsciously and automatically controlled by the utilization of various psychological defense mechanisms."[52]

DSM-III was a fat book. There were many more diagnoses, they were more precisely detailed, and they were presented with a panoply of science. The psychodynamics had been expunged. In their place stood clear-cut (well, more than before) lists of criteria, often with inclusion rules: five of the following nine, eight of the next sixteen. If a patient met the criteria, the patient had a mental illness. If the patient did not, she or he did not. The patient's personal history—his or her ambivalence, toilet training, basic trust, dependency, whatever—was irrelevant. From the vantage point of *DSM-III*, it didn't matter how the patient had become ill or why. What mattered was whether the patient met the necessary number of criteria, which could be determined (more or less) by a short interview. All of a sudden, there was a sharp, clean dividing line between mental health and illness.

And that line was determined by science. These diagnoses were based on what anyone could observe or determine in an initial interview (more or less—actually, using the manual required considerable skill), and the committee that came up with the lists of criteria went to great lengths to demonstrate that different people would give the same diagnosis to the same patient. There was push-back. In a bracing book called *The Selling of DSM*, two social scientists accused Robert Spitzer, the leader of the task force that came up with the manual, of snowing the field with illusory statistics.[53] They undoubtedly had a piece of the truth. And yet, it is also clear that the new categories actually were more specific than the older ones. Here is the *DSM-II* overview of schizophrenia:

> This large category includes a group of disorders manifested by characteristic disturbances of thinking, mood and behavior. Disturbances in thinking are marked by alterations of concept formation which may lead to misinterpretation of reality and sometimes to delusions and hallucination, which frequently appear psychologically self-protective. Corollary mood changes include ambivalent, constricted and inappropriate emotional responsiveness and loss of empathy with others. Behavior may be withdrawn, regressive and bizarre. The schizophrenias, in which the mental status is attributed primarily to a *thought* disorder, are to be distinguished from the *Major affective illnesses* . . . which are dominated by a *mood* disorder. The *Paranoid states* . . . are distinguished from schizophrenia by the narrowness of their distortions of reality and by the absence of other psychotic symptoms.

And schizophrenia, "simple type":

> This psychosis is characterized chiefly by a slow and insidious reduction of external attachments and interests and by apathy and indifference leading to impoverishment of interpersonal relations, mental deterioration, and adjustment on a lower level of functioning.

Now consider this one from *DSM-III*:

DIAGNOSTIC CRITERIA FOR A SCHIZOPHRENIC DISORDER

A. At least one of the following during a phase of the illness:
   (1) bizarre delusions (content is patently absurd and has no possible basis in fact), such as delusions of being controlled, through broadcasting, thought insertion, or thought withdrawal
   (2) somatic, grandiose, religious, nihilistic or other delusions without persecutory or jealous content if accompanied by hallucinations of any type
   (3) delusions with persecutory or jealous content if accompanied by hallucinations of any type
   (4) auditory hallucinations in which either a voice keeps up a running commentary on the individual's behavior or thoughts, or two or more voices converse with each other

(5) auditory hallucination on several occasions with content or more than one or two words, having no apparent relation to depression or elation

(6) incoherence, marked loosening of associations, markedly illogical thinking, or marked poverty of content of speech if associated with at least one of the following:

    a. blunted, flat or inappropriate content

    b. delusions or hallucinations

    c. catatonic or other grossly disorganized behavior

B. Deterioration from a previous level of functioning in such areas as work, social relations, and self-care.

C. Duration: Continuous signs of the illness for at least six months at some time during the person's life, with some signs of the illness at present. The six month period must include an active phase during which there were symptoms from A, with or without a prodromal phase, as defined below.[54]

Then there were lists of symptoms for the prodromal and residual phases of the illness, and some inclusion and exclusion criteria.

It is clear that the *DSM-III* definition narrowed the gate for the diagnosis. Before 1980, people who might later be diagnosed with post-traumatic stress disorder or multiple personality disorder or, for that matter, borderline personality disorder—now all thought to have their origin in trauma, and all new diagnoses in *DSM-III*—could easily be diagnosed with schizophrenia. After 1980, "schizophrenia" would be reserved for people who were the most sick.

Ethnographic work contributed to this effort by demonstrating that severe madness—schizophrenia—appeared with the same patterns of symptoms (delusions, hallucinations, and significant long-term impairment in functioning) in non-Western settings and was recognized as madness (and not shamanism) in those settings. In 1976, in an article in *Science*, Jane Murphy took on then-popular "labeling theory," which often invoked Benedict's essay on the relativity of the normal/abnormal distinction. Labeling theory argued that what was labeled as mental illness in any particular setting was merely a deviation from the normal; that the norms differed in different groups; and that people so identified internalized the disapproval and rejection of others in their group, and so habituated and perpetuated the stigmatizing behavior.[55] The brain, in short, had nothing to do with psychiatric illness. Murphy presented fieldwork among Yupik-speaking Eskimos on an island in the Bering

homes following hospitalization.[67] While some early observers argued that these kinds of hostile comments might generate a schizophrenic "response," these days many observers believe that expressed emotion represents a consequence, rather than a cause, of schizophrenia.[68]

And now there is epidemiological evidence, mostly from Europe, that social factors increase the incidence of the diagnosed illness. Sophisticated studies, using the new, narrow, post-*DSM-III* diagnostic category or its equivalent, have shown that schizophrenia is associated with the social class of one's father (and presumably of one's birth), the risk increasing as the class declines.[69] It is associated as well with urban living.[70] The risk increases with what is called "ethnic density": the incidence of schizophrenia among nonwhite people rises as their presence in their neighborhood begins to fall. If your skin is dark, your risk for schizophrenia rises as your neighborhood whitens, whether you live in the United States or in London.[71] Most strikingly, the risk of schizophrenia for immigrants to the United Kingdom rises sharply, an effect that—like these other effects—has now been shown in so many papers by so many researchers and with such methodological care that it cannot be explained away by clinicians' racial bias.[72] Those who arrive in England from the Caribbean or whose parents were born in the Caribbean have a much higher incidence (number of new cases within a specific period) of schizophrenia and of other psychotic disorders than whites, even adjusting for social class and age.[73] Black Africans who immigrate to England have a similarly elevated risk, while South and East Asians have an elevated risk but a lower one.[74]

This is not genetics: the risk of schizophrenia in the countries of origin seems to be no higher than it is for whites in Europe.[75] It is not that only sick people migrate: the effect holds for Surinamese patients in the Netherlands, where nearly half the population of Surinam has arrived.[76] And the risk actually increases for the second generation of these immigrants.[77] Again: the anthropologist's temptation is to look for clinical bias. But the sheer number of these studies, combined with the powerful evidence that social status affects health, should lead us to look not just for bias, but for the way that discrimination gets under the skin. As the editors of *Society and Psychosis* have remarked, with these findings psychiatry has "rediscovered its roots."[78] Social conditions and experiences over the life course really count, even in the development of what seems to be among the most organic of psychiatric disorders. [79]

So it should not be surprising that cultural difference shapes the course and outcome of schizophrenia in developing and developed countries. In a

TABLE I   EPIDEMIOLOGICALLY IDENTIFIED RISK FACTORS

Immigration	Risk is particularly high for immigrants to Europe from predominantly dark-skinned countries; risk is higher for second generation than for first generation; risk is independent of social class
Economic social adversity in childhood	Risk increases with parental unemployment, single-parent household, adults on social welfare benefits
Socioeconomic status	Risk increases with lower socioeconomic status at birth and even at parent's birth
Urban living	Risk increases with urban dwelling and seems to increase the longer time is spent in cities
Ethnic density	Risk increases as ethnic density declines
Social adversity in childhood	Risk increases with physical, emotional, and sexual childhood abuse

1973 World Health Organization (WHO) study, the "International Pilot Study of Schizophrenia" (or IPSS), researchers had found that two years after initial contact and identification, patients looked better in Africa and India than they did in sites scattered throughout the West. But the results were decades old, some of the data were dubious, people were identified at different stages of their illness, and clinicians had used an older and more capacious pre-*DSM-III* definition of schizophrenia. So the study was redone, this time with a treated incidence sample (the DOSMeD). That is, researchers set out to actively identify people presenting for the first time with the symptoms of serious psychotic disorder not only at mental health services, but also at primary care settings, police stations, jails and prisons, traditional healers, and religious shrines. There were twelve research sites in ten countries, a stricter diagnostic category, a clearer method, and a more careful analysis.[80] At the two-year follow-up, patients in developing countries had experienced significantly longer periods of unimpaired functioning, and complete clinical remission was far more common (although proportions of continuous unremitting illness were similar).

Results from a major reanalysis of both studies (along with several other study cohorts, from India, China, and Germany) were reported in 2001 (the ISoS).[81] A fuller account, under the editorship of the anthropologist Kim Hopper, was published in 2007. It involved original data collection with well over a thousand new interviews, eight hundred of which were with people who had been followed since their first episode of illness. The team used a rigorous method of case identification, common data-collection instruments, and common analytic strategies across ten countries and fourteen sites. The results held up, despite the concerns, the criticisms, and the limitations of the data. No matter whether you look at symptoms, disability, clinical profile, or the ability to do productive work, roughly 50 percent more people do well after a diagnosis of schizophrenia in the developing world than they do in the developed world.[82]

But the "developing world" in this third reanalysis and study (the ISoS) was mostly India, and in particular two centers: Chandigarh in the north, which took part in the early WHO surveys; and Chennai in the south, which did not but had comparable data. The Chennai data are particularly impressive, not only because the researchers are consistent, the follow-up rates are excellent, and the diagnostic criteria are strict, but also because Chennai is not a romantic rural paradise. It is, as Hopper remarks, the "great, teeming, postcolonial, sectarian-riven complicated place that is India" at its most urban and chaotic.[83] Researchers identified ninety first-contact and first-episode patients who met ICD 9 criteria for schizophrenia (International Classification of Diseases; these are much like the *DSM-III* criteria, except that the period of disturbance need last only one month and not six). Ten years later, 76 patients remained in the sample (nine had died, four by suicide). Two-thirds of them were symptom free, and they remained symptom free and medication free even ten years after that, twenty years after first contact.[84] This was significantly higher than the overall rate for the ISoS study. (The most striking news here, to be clear, was the high rate of recovery in all groups, including those in the developed world.)[85]

Because of this focus on India in the third study and reanalysis, some still challenge the claim that schizophrenia has a better prognosis in the developing world.[86] Yet the observation that people with schizophrenia have an easier time of it outside the West has long been present in the ethnographic literature. M. J. Field thought that it was easier to be a person with schizophrenia in rural Africa than in London: people were less afraid of the ill person (because they knew him or her personally), and a man who didn't work seemed less out of place in an agricultural community. Field was not alone. The great anthropologist Meyer Fortes and his wife Doris Mayer, a psychiatrist, returned to his field site in Ghana thirty years after his first visit. He thought that more of the Tallensi were seriously psychiatrically ill than on his first visit (when he remembered almost no one who was mad), but his wife was more impressed that the psychoses seemed more benign than the ones she saw in Britain.[87] Nancy Waxler found that in Sri Lanka, psychoses seemed to be shorter-lived and more easily cured.[88]

There does appear to be a higher percentage of people in developing countries who do not really have schizophrenia, as it is commonly understood, but a form of psychosis from which people recover and return to baseline functioning.[89] Non-affective acute remitting psychosis (NARP), an illness characterized by acute onset and complete remission, resembles schizophrenia enough that a clinician might diagnose it as schizophrenia. Patients become suddenly and acutely psychotic, and then just get better. (Field noticed such patients among her Ashanti sample.) Moreover, it has also become clear that there are far more psychotic-like experiences, for example hallucinations, in the apparently normal population than we realized, and that the rates of these phenomena vary from culture to culture.[90] It may be more acceptable to respond to stress with psychotic hallucinations outside of a Western setting.

At the same time, NARP and brief psychotic reactions do not explain the WHO results. They do not explain the Chennai data, and investigators found that in the WHO studies, some of the developing-country patients who looked worst at the beginning were among the group that looked best at the end. "The more pointed challenge posed by 'non-affective acute remitting psychosis' . . . also failed to pan out."[91] Hopper and Wanderling concluded from their reanalysis that NARP was indeed more common among the cases labeled schizophrenic in the developing than in the developed world.[92] Nonetheless, when subjects who experienced single-episode psychosis were dropped from the analysis entirely, the recovery rates dropped—but still favored the developing world.

So it does seem as if the WHO results are due to what we might call, following Janis Jenkins and Martin Karno, the "black box" of culture—the immensely complicated ways that people live in their skins in different social settings.[93] Hopper points out that in the discussions around the outcome differences, "culture" almost always refers to non-Western settings: as he remarks, "'culture' has been a mock-elegant way of referring to 'there' as opposed to 'here.'"[94]

Why should people with schizophrenia and other serious psychoses do better in India? Among the factors most commonly discussed are these:

a. In India, the family remains fully involved in the treatment, unlike in America.[95]

b. In India, unlike in America, ascribed family roles are important to one's social status and sense of self; patients do not have to be primary bread-winners or primary caretakers to be considered valuable members of the household; people may live in joint families.[96]

c. In India, unskilled and semiskilled work, such as agriculture and home-based artisan piecework, may be less stressful and less demanding than entry-level jobs in America, which are often in fast-paced, high-social-contact settings like McDonald's.[97]

d. In India, fewer families exhibit expressed emotion than in America.[98]

e. In India, while psychiatrists diagnose schizophrenia in patients, they do not use the label in interacting with the patients and the patients do not use the label for themselves.[99]

f. In India, the auditory hallucinations of persons with serious psychotic disorder may be more benign.[100]

g. In India, there are subtle psychological features that may shape an individual's reactivity: psychotic hallucinations may seem more similar to standard religious practice than they do in America; there may be a different understanding of self-coherence; there may be a different degree of stigma attached to mental illness as, for example, compared to divorce; there may be different expectations of professional achievement; and there may be different degrees of comfort with allopathic medicine.[101]

In a 1997 review of decades of ethnographic work, Byron Good argued that the following four hypotheses deserve particular attention:[102]

a. *The local cultural interpretation of mental illness.* Is the illness understood to be inevitably chronic? A broken part of the essential self? Or a passing storm?

b. *The presence of an extended family.* Is there another breadwinner? Are there other people at home to help? And is help provided, or is the person locked in a back room and kept from inquisitive eyes to preserve the family's honor?

c. *Industrial-age labor vs. agricultural or nonwage labor.* Can the ill person work? Can he or she contribute? In a world in which wages reward performance, someone with illness will be less easy to employ.

d. *The basic social environment.* The difference in living conditions—urban squalor as opposed to the traditional family home—may ultimately be more important to outcome than any actual treatment provided.

There is another interpretation, not widely discussed in the psychiatric literature of this debate but perhaps equally important: that the normative treatment for schizophrenia in American culture may significantly make things worse, and possibly even turn psychotic reactivity (the possibility of a brief psychotic reaction) into chronic clienthood, and that it does so by repeatedly creating the conditions for demoralization and despair, and for what we will call "social defeat." In other words, the culture "here" may be as important as the cultural other "there."

So the deep problem of the variable vulnerability to schizophrenia is embedded in the classic issues of anthropology: kinship, class, personhood, poverty, meaning. We have data and theory to contribute. And by attending to the ways in which central anthropological concerns about kinship, care, relationality, and cultural notions of selfhood and personhood shape the way that illness is identified, experienced, and treated, we hope to make it clear that schizophrenia cannot be understood fully without its cultural context.

Epidemiologists track numbers. Ethnographers use the only method that can reliably and validly identify the features of the social world that are real and salient for subjects. Our aim in this volume is to present case studies that give detail and depth to these hypotheses about our most troubling madness. We hope that by doing so, we will provide the material to help us tease out the complex ways in which culture shapes illness—and, perhaps, eventually nudge the treatment of serious mental illness toward an easier outcome. We believe that understanding the culture in which schizophrenia unfolds may have clear and consequential implications for treatment. We hope to show that here.

"*I'm* Schizophrenic!"

How Diagnosis Can Change Identity in the United States

T. M. LUHRMANN

One of the challenges of living with schizophrenia in the United States is the clear identity conferred by the diagnostic label itself. To receive care in a society so acutely aware of individual rights is to receive an explicit diagnosis. A patient has the right to know. But the label "schizophrenia" is often toxic for those who acquire it. It creates not only what Erving Goffman called a "spoiled identity" but an identity framed in opposition to the nonlabeled social world. Tanya (T. M.) met John Hood in San Diego.

———

When I met John Hood in 1998, he had just received San Diego County's Mental Health Person of the Year award for his contributions to the mental health community.[1] It was the first time the award had been given to someone diagnosed with schizophrenia. I could see why people would want to acknowledge him. Tall and lanky, John had a big personality, and he was a great spokesperson for the "consumer's perspective"—the point of view of someone who used mental health services. He served in a range of local mental health organizations, represented consumers for national organizations (Alternatives, the National Alliance for the Mentally Ill), and periodically flew to Sacramento to speak to the California Board of Mental Health. The year after his award, John gave the speech introducing that year's winner, a mental health advocate (who did not have schizophrenia). It was clearly the best speech of the night—relaxed, confident, funny, full of to-the-point stories—and the seven hundred people in the audience fell about laughing more than once. John recalled that Richard, the man he was introducing, had been assigned as the patient advocate for some poor guy who wanted out of his three-day involuntary hold at the hospital. When Richard arrived at the hearing, John said, he saw that the patient had his ear to the wall. So Richard put his ear to the wall, too. After a while, the judge said to Richard, "Do you hear anything?" Richard said no. Then the judge said to the patient, "Do you hear anything?" The patient said, "No, and I've been here for three days." Later Richard got up to speak and said, "All those stories were true." Then he said that when he and John had gone to Sacramento to speak with the Board of Mental Health, he was exhausted at the end of the meeting and John was chipper. So John put his arm around Richard and said, "I feel sorry for you. You think so carefully about what you are going to say, and you choose your words, and you worry about the effect of what you say on the relationships you have with people. I can say anything I want. *I'm* schizophrenic!"

John Mack Hood III—he liked all his names—grew up in Southern California. He said that even in kindergarten he had been withdrawn, not "socially appropriate," a term he learned from the mental-health-treatment world.

> Then, at the end of sixth grade, I said to myself, I will be a heavyweight. I will go out and make friends with the most popular people in school. And I did. It worked. I still wasn't able to deal with reality, in the psychological sense. But I was elected to be the Boys Federation representative from my homeroom and the Red Cross representative from my homeroom, even the homeroom representative from my homeroom. I did some wild stuff. I skinned a cat in physiology and pinned it to the door of a young, beautiful English teacher. I became notorious for that.[2]

The year John graduated from high school, his family moved to London so that his father could pursue a doctoral degree at University College. John stayed behind and got a job at a gas station in Colorado. He lived in the attic above the station. The attic had no shower, so John didn't shower. It didn't occur to him to find one elsewhere, and he had no friends to point out that he stank. He lasted three months before he came down with a horrible rash and ended up in the emergency room. Looking back, he could see that this was the beginning of getting ill—what a psychiatrist would call the "prodromal" stage, the months that precede the explosion of psychotic symptoms clinicians call the first "break" with reality, when patients typically become hospitalized for the first time. "All this stuff is pathological in some sense, but the real symptoms, when I became aware of them as symptoms, came later."

John did moderately well that year as a freshman at the new University of California in San Diego, up in La Jolla by the beach. It was the middle of the sixties and he threw his lot in with the counterculture. More than three decades later, the counterculture was still his reference point. I'd given him a tape recorder and a pile of cassettes so that he could talk to me even when I was not present. He taped more than a hundred hours of material, often late at night, often without his dentures, so that the words are blurred and rounded. On cassette after cassette, as he muses about his childhood, his friends, his illness, and his daily life, he interprets his stories through the music of that time.

> It was Sunday today, or yesterday, and I was at great peace. I listened to Bob Dylan's 1966 Prince Albert Hall in London concert, and it was a two CD set and I have it on tape. I listened to it and it just brought me into contact with how I understood every word he was saying. It makes me realize the song "Like a Rolling Stone" is as much a learning experience for me as it ever was. *You know something's happening but you don't know what it is, do you, Mr. Jones?* I see that I really am a Mr. Jones and that I don't know what's happening, the bottom line.[3]

John looked like a hippie even at the end of the millennium. His hair was long, he had a beard, and he wore an embroidered Muslim skull cap. He gave me an armful of paperback books on the sixties to read, because he thought I'd never understand him without understanding those times. He made cassettes for me of the music he loved, music that was playing every time I went to visit. He told me that one of Neil Young's records explained his life. "If I could have made an adjustment within the counterculture, I would have been okay. The counterculture kept me stabilized that first year." It seems to have been clear to him, by the end of his first year of college, that he wasn't going to make it in the mainstream.

The summer after his freshman year, he went to live with his parents in London. On his way from California, he stopped in New York for a night. In a cheap hotel room he shared with a stranger, he felt his mind take off. "It whirled and it would not stop." Nevertheless, he arrived in England without incident. It was a bad summer, lonely and isolated. He knew no one and argued constantly with his parents, who were frightened by the drugs he was taking and horrified by his long hair, his clothes, and his hippie lifestyle. He came back to California that autumn, but he had never signed up for a college room—he may not have been enrolled—so he camped out in friends' rooms.

Someone made an appointment for him to see a psychiatrist to talk about "the workings of the mind." The night before the appointment, John stayed up all night and wrote page after page about his own philosophy of mind. "I expected that *I* would teach *him*." During the appointment, the psychiatrist asked him whether he would like to stay that night in the hospital, and John agreed because "after all, I was homeless."

Since then John has been hospitalized about a dozen times, although he had not been hospitalized for over a decade at the time I met him. He had taken antipsychotic medication for three decades. He told me that he had never heard voices, but he heard the walls creak loudly and repeatedly. Small sounds would capture his attention so that they stood out against the backdrop of the everyday, vivid and demanding and threatening. "Creaks" was the best term he was able to produce to describe them. He felt that these creaks were punitive. "I am obsessed, as I am to this day, by the idea that there is a super-natural force that makes creaks in the walls, and that they are God telling me what I am doing wrong. There is a real creak. You might not notice it, but it is there." He would see streetlights turn on and off, or see shifts in the light's intensity, and to him these shifts were dense with meaning. It was as if some small sensory event that a normal person might register and ignore somehow swelled in importance for him and became insistent, so that he could not turn away. John would see people signal that they were attacking him and defending themselves against him by scratching their chins or their ears, or shifting position and leaning on their elbows. He called this the "social game."

I never saw John react to these moments, the way you can see sometimes that people hear voices when they turn and look or get so distracted they lose the conversational thread. The most apparent evidence of his illness was that he would shift from everyday common sense into flagrant delusion. He recorded this on a cassette in November 2000:

> Well, it's now quarter to eleven. It's the eleventh or something like that. It's Friday night and I've already slept for the night. I'll probably sleep early in the morning like two. It's hard to say when I get tired. I thought I'd talk about my political politics. It's controversial to a lot of other people, and they had different feelings about it. We're right in the middle of recounting Florida's votes, and I actually ran for president this time, this year, the year 2000. It's November 2000. This is the election I was running for president.

And then he'd shift back—in this case, to describing his day at work. Next on this cassette he said, "Anyways, I was going back to my story, it's sounding a bit like . . . where they could lock you up in an insane asylum for no reason whatsoever." John knew that he had ideas that were part of what he called a "delusional system," but he also felt that what he experienced was true. He felt this intensely—the realness impressed itself upon him and he could not shake it.

It is not uncommon for people with serious psychotic disorder to feel that they are committed simultaneously to different epistemic frames. They often know that some of their thoughts and sensations are symptoms of a mental illness, and yet they also feel that those thoughts and sensations are accurate perceptions of their world. At the beginning of the illness, the person may not identify these new events as "symptoms." They are part of the new horrors of her life. Pulsations beat upon her skull, or people begin to sneer and hiss at her, or her mind becomes no longer safe and the world is made of porous air. Some clinicians argue that many delusions arise from the patient's need to make sense of these unnerving thoughts and sensations—that people decide they are victims of alien invasion or government spying because they can think of no other way to interpret what they experience, and then the delusions become entrenched because the thoughts or pulsations or voices don't stop.

John moved between these different perspectives throughout the time I knew him, laughing at ideas he called delusional and yet treating as real the parallel universe in which they made sense and in which supernatural events seemed to take place around him all the time. In a sheaf of notes for a speech in 1998, he wrote, "From an early part of my life and during my mental illness, I studied very hard to be a Wizard and even though our society has no criteria for Wizards, Warlocks, Witches, Prophets, Saints, etc. that does not mean that mental health clients may not relate well to these types of people." He sometimes thought of himself as the risen Christ, although he did so with self-teasing irony. "I thought there was this job, a good clean job, which was the Second Coming, and I thought I fulfilled the conditions for it, even though I don't believe in biblical prophecy or anything like that. So I saw myself as able to have more authority and power than was appropriate. That was delusional." But he called himself a shaman throughout our conversations, and he was clear that if he had been born in India he would have been called a holy man. In London, that was what the psychiatrist had told his parents.

For about a year, maybe a little longer, I met with John several times a month. I'd drive down to the sketchy neighborhood where he lived independently in a one-bedroom apartment. There were posters thumbtacked to the

FIGURE 1. John Hood drew this to represent the experience of someone with schizophrenia.

walls and a couple of dilapidated couches. There was a beautiful portrait of him that he had commissioned from one of his friends for $300—an oil-painted mosaic of a photograph she had reproduced many times and lacquered, so that John seemed to multiply across its surface. A table shelf in the corner held dozens of pill bottles, those standard-issue orange plastic containers with white lids. The fridge held little besides beer and Coke, and the air was usually thick with cigarette smoke, but the kitchen and living room were tidy. The yard was mostly cracked clay with struggling grass, and the air always seemed to be hot and dry. Still, John invariably wore a blazer and a hat. We would sit and talk about music and schizophrenia and the mental health system. Once, when I commented that he lived in a complex world, he said that that was exactly the point. "I have a very complicated truth, which no one can figure out, and I work with it in a dynamic kind of way. The bottom line is that the system is so complicated that it had got me through a lot of binds."

Sometimes John talked about these multiple frames as "two worlds": the world of being a shaman, and the world of being a normal working person. "I'm starting to see more how I have two sorts of consciousness that are alive. You know, I have work." He understood that there were ways of talking and acting that were appropriate to the normal world, the clinical world, the world his parents lived in. "I can talk in the clinical jargon that's very orthodox and what's considered standard normal clinical talk. I can talk about it in an intellectual standard way."

"Shamanism" was everything else. His dreams. His sense that he needed to know more about Jungian psychology. The wild, odd ideas he associated with his madness. "When I go out, I can go crazy if someone is babbling at me for twenty minutes. I feel like I'm going crazy. Then I bring peace back to myself and swim in the consciousness of mystic union." He talked to me about astral journeys and his "shadow side" and about an angel that perched on his bed once when he was sick and told him to take his medication. In a long tape he made for me in June 2000, he began by talking about shamanism and then shifted into a contrast between the sophisticated psychoanalyst who knew about the unconscious—"a combination of a philosophical system coupled with a behavioral science and what I would consider a more shamanistic technique"—and the idiocies of modern biomedical psychiatry. And then he paused. "Sigmund Freud wouldn't touch me with a ten-foot pole. He never would have touched a person who was diagnosed with a psychotic paranoid schizophrenia."

This was John's terrible dilemma. It was hard for him not to despise the life trajectory that had taken him out of the upper middle class into shabby housing and public assistance. His talk of shamanism was one way to make sense of the otherness and to make it seem like an advantage, a gift, which most people did not understand. But he didn't really think he was better off. Mostly, he made sense of the difference by identifying it as a failure created by his social world. "We are cultural heretics," he explained. "We are probably the most hated people on the planet."

There is no question that the most terrifying part of schizophrenia is the sense that one's mind is slipping beyond one's grasp, unreliable and out of control. In some fundamental sense, that shock must be common to those who experience schizophrenia, regardless of their social community or the cultural expectations with which they live. Our inner voice, our thoughts, our sensations: these are the most intimate of human experiences, and to feel them alter must be profoundly disturbing. In some ways John recognized that he had an organic process in the brain that had profoundly changed his mental experience. He repeatedly called himself ill. But he blamed his sense of being flawed on the social fact that there was a biomedical model and a biomedical psychiatry, and throughout the time I knew him, he managed his sense of dual realities through a vehement rejection of what he took to be the social expectations of a normal person.

John hated the idea that he had a "diseased brain."

> I'm on the California Board of Mental Health, as a consumer. When we come around for introductions, what I say is, "My name is John Hood, and I have a diseased brain"—and they all laugh. Can you imagine how insulting it would be if you turned to me and said, "I'm *sorry* you have a diseased brain?" When it gets right down to it, the medical model is an *insult* to me. To say that I have a diseased brain: it does not validate me.

From this point of view, it is not the putatively diseased brain that is the problem. It is the idea that you have a diseased brain that destroys you. "When it comes down to it, there's no greater stigma than the client thinking that his mind is diseased."

He despised himself for taking medication.

> It makes you hate yourself so much more because you take medication. They say, there's nothing wrong with me except I have to take these damn pills, that's what's messing me up. It's the most stigmatized group in the country. That you need pills in order to function. I can see guilt on my mother's face even to this day when I pull a pill out of my pocket and eat it.

He often used the verb "eat" to describe taking medication.[4] The word captures the basic-as-bread role medication played in his life: that it was not ancillary or cosmetic or corrective, but that without it, he was not right.

And he saw the label "schizophrenia" as the sign that he was set apart and different and bad. "When I talk to people, I have to say, 'I am a person with schizophrenia,' and I don't like that. I'm not 'with' anything. I have severe functional impairments when it comes to certain aspects of living. I'm not 'with' anything. I'm me." One afternoon when I was at his apartment, I tried to understand why the word had such a caustic quality for him. He had a friend over, a woman who was also diagnosed with schizophrenia. "When people say that you are schizophrenic, what does that mean?" I asked her. "Well," she responded drily, "it means that *they're* not schizophrenic."

In the past few decades, people who call themselves "consumers" or "psychiatric survivors" or "ex-patients" have sprung up as groups around the country. Most take a strong stand against diagnosis and mandated medication. They see themselves as fighting for the rights of mental health patients, and they have become a potent political force in mental health across the country. It was because of their political authority that someone like John could have a seat on the California Board of Mental Health. Many of these groups set out to reverse the stigma of being "crazy" and to wear it like a badge. That, of course, also underscores the differences they try to erase: abnormal versus normal, mad versus sane, us versus them.

In the end, this may have been what undid John. He had built his identity on not being one of "them"—the normals. He was mad, he was crazy, he was a shaman. But shortly before John was named Mental Health Person of the Year, he became a "peer counselor" in the local county psychiatric hospital. The post was newly invented and, thus, ill defined. The clinical staff thought that it would help soften the hard line between normal and abnormal for inpatients to have someone who had recovered (more or less) work on the inpatient wards. These positions have become more common around the country in recent decades as the Recovery Movement has become more dominant. Most people assume that the positions are good not only for the peer counselors' clients but for the counselors themselves.[5]

But the job was hard on John. I went there with him one afternoon. There were some twenty patients in each of two units, one short-term and one for longer stays. The patients were quite ill. The place reeked because few of them bathed. I had a long conversation with someone who explained that we were on a spaceship and that she had been artificially born out of an egg created by people on the unit. John ran several different groups—those sessions that pepper the days of inpatient units and provide activities for otherwise long hours. In one group, he showed a *Beverly Hillbillies* episode and asked people what the plot was and what it meant. In another group, he played music from the 1960s and '70s and asked people whether they had ever been as happy or as sad as the songs described. He seemed comfortable.

And he loved the job. He loved having a pass that allowed him to enter the hospital as staff, and having keys that would open locked doors. He thought he was good in the role.

> I remember, there was this wonderful woman, younger than me, she was asked the very first day to take me around and show me what goes on there. She took me to her first group, and I hadn't met anyone yet. Then I started discovering some of the clients I had been locked up with at mental hospitals, or in board and care facilities, we all had the same friends and we had some real stories to swap. So I get on the unit and Michelle introduces me and in about ten minutes not only am I contributing heavily to the group but pretty soon I am running the group. It evolved so quickly. This is really what I like doing.

But he also felt like a double agent. He felt that he worked as a staff person and was treated as a staff person—"but clearly, I am considered mad by our society." Because he was mad, he was like the patients, and he hated the authoritarian oppression that he fought so hard against as a consumer. Yet he felt that he had the authority of the staff in turn.

> I've got those double-locked doors in my life when I do my major double agent work and negotiations, and it is clear what the two sides are. I have the staff and I have the clients, and I trade secrets with each and I can't get caught doing it. You gain confidences and rapport and take them on as a personal friend, find out what their strength and weaknesses are, where they might crack, what they might do. You can use that information in the way you think is best. . . . But when you are a double agent, you don't know if the other person already knows, and you never know how much of the truth they are telling you.

He talked about being a double agent again and again in the cassette tapes he made for me. There are long passages about how much he accomplished on the unit, and how important his work was. The time I visited his job with him, at the end of the day he told me that he had made 250 crucial interventions. But the cassettes are also full of guilt and betrayal. He had crossed over. He didn't like it.

In some ways, the straddling of the irrational and the rational, the mad and the sane, is inherent to mental health services. Any clinician engages both with the autonomous rational decision-maker and the crazy person in each encounter with a client. In *Everyday Ethics*, the anthropologist Paul Brodwin describes the pain clinicians feel in managing the straddle. They want to treat clients like themselves—as more or less freely choosing adults—and yet their mandate is to get them to comply with decisions that other people have made for them. They have an impossible job. "Operating at the boom rungs of a strained system, they cannot conceivably give clients what they need [safe housing, refrigerators and televisions, drug-free friends]. Yet they must impose services that clients explicitly do not want."[6]

That is the challenge of mental illness. The ill person is, and is not, what we call "competent"—able to assess the world and respond to it in a way that others around them deem normal. The less competent a person is in the eyes of others, the more those others will take over for them. To "care" can mean to take over someone else's autonomy, yet most clinicians go into the profession to restore autonomy to people in pain. The way a clinician makes a call can feel like a judgment on his or her own humanity.

For John Hood, the decision to be the authority over someone else's mind felt as intolerable as confronting the stark reality that other people were willing to judge him mad. I thought he used his countercultural sensibility to negotiate his unease with being the authority, just as he had used it to manage his unease with being mad. To be a "cultural heretic" was to reject both roles. So he would bring his Beatles and his Grateful Dead into the clinic to play to his clients, and to see if he could get them to love it as much as he did. But it was an awkward patch.

Whatever initiated the descent, by 1999 people began to say that John was "doing less well." He seemed less stable, more prone to outbursts. His talk became more jagged and wandered farther afield. He began talking about going off his medication. There were days when he was foggier than usual. I started meeting him in the afternoon rather than the morning, because he seemed more alert later in the day. He was involved with a client-run drop-in center called the Meeting Place, and around this time the center collapsed because no one was paying the rent or utilities. Some of the clients had located a health provider willing to support the center, but only on the condition that a nonclient would be in charge, and the clients had agreed. John became furious. He felt that the values of the center had been violated, and that the clients could not acquire the sense of self-worth the Meeting Place had fostered if it was no longer client run. He felt they had turned it from a place to encourage growth into an adult kindergarten.

It was also around this time that John became a Jehovah's Witness. Some of their members had come to his door to proselytize, and John decided they had their finger on the truth. He began to go to meetings and to argue with their elders, and his apartment became noticeably full of their books and pamphlets. Sometimes I wondered whether he saw his conversion as a perverse joke on the people who had converted him. John was still working at the hospital, and he set out to save a client on the unit whom, he said, the staff did not want to deal with because the client was too violent. He signed up a string of Jehovah's Witnesses to see this man and marched them in and out of the hospital. He wanted me to see the man too, but I refused. I'd already met the man on the unit and he had scared me, because he leered at me, and I knew he had hurt someone badly. I had never been frightened of John before, but that afternoon I was. He suddenly straightened in his chair and began stabbing the air with his finger, shouting at me that a book I had written was so one-sided it was ridiculous, and that I never described him as a shaman. I told him to calm down and then he yelled at me some more and then suddenly said, "You want me to calm down? I'm calm!" and he sat back and shut up like a petulant child.

Now John started calling me at home, which he had never done before. He called because he wanted thousands of dollars to buy the house next door, because a friend of his was getting evicted from it. He called because he wanted me to buy him a machine so that he could copy tapes he wanted me to see. He was beginning to have more trouble at work. That month I sat next to his boss at some mental health event in the hospital, and she said that she was worried about him. She thought he had cut way back on his medication, and she told me that the woman from next door who had been evicted was now sleeping on his couch. She thought the woman was using drugs. Then she sighed: "Every day I come in here, and I look at the vending machines in the courtyard [beyond the locked gate to the unit] and I wonder what it's like to look at the vending machine and to know that you can't get to it to get a coke." She'd tried to leave the gate to the courtyard unlocked for a while, but then someone had tried to hang himself in the space, and the hospital wouldn't let that experiment continue.

And then I left town for a while—it was summer—and when I came back a month later, John was in a hospital way out in the east county. This meant he would lose his house. People on disability payments often lose their income when they are hospitalized. John was behind on the rent anyway, and his landlord wanted him out. That week I talked to the man John had introduced as his successor as Mental Health Person of the Year. Richard didn't know the details of how John had ended up in the hospital, but he had been over at the house shortly beforehand. He brought John some Taco Bell to remind him of the times they'd spent together, when they would go to Taco Bell and "solve the problems of the universe." John stood in the front yard eating it like an animal, and Richard said that it broke his heart, because John seemed so ill that Richard worried he might never recover. And yet just a few weeks earlier John had been to a meeting with him when consumers were going up to the microphone, one after another, to make statements. John got up and said, "For some reason I can't get this Beatles song out of my head." And then he sang the first verse of "Nowhere Man," which ends with the phrase "making all these nowhere plans for nobody." The audience cracked up.

I moved from California that autumn, before John left the hospital. The next time I saw him was in the spring of 2001. He was living in an old hotel that had been turned into supported housing for people with psychiatric disabilities. He was still charming and effusive, but his words no longer made as much sense. He lived in half of a room, decently sized but dirty. He still had a bunch of books, including one I'd written (partly about him), and lots of tapes, and his portrait, and a mess of clothes. On the porch there was an enormous hookah, or water pipe. We sat out there in the heat, swathed in strong tobacco, John unnerved by my presence after so many months, angry and distant but talking loudly and insistently all the time. "God stinks," he said at one point.

I didn't come out to San Diego again for several years. During that time I would get packets from John—long, scrawled letters with drawings and metaphysical reflections. I wrote back, but more briefly. In 2005, I returned to the city and decided to find him.

I drove out to El Cajon to meet him in a settlement way south of the main city. I was about an hour late (I got lost), but when I arrived John was standing on the street waiting for me, in sunglasses (which he took off for our meal, mostly) and an old man's spiffy getup: an olive felt fedora, a shirt neatly buttoned with a bolo tie, and a gazillion necklaces with various significant items hanging from them—a Mary icon, a sacred tooth, a wedding ring he said he'd offered to someone who refused him. He was getting married again, he said, to two black women who worked at Volunteers for America, and he would move to Africa with them. He invited me to visit.

It was indescribably sad. Still, he looked good—even dapper. He carried a pack of playing cards from Hawaiian Airlines, and said he liked cards but didn't play them because he'd read the Bhagavad Gita, and everything had gone wrong from a game of cards. (Close enough, I thought to myself.) He referred to himself several times as a Muslim cleric. He said that he no longer heard his creaks. Then he said that it wasn't that the creaks had stopped, but that he had stopped giving them significance—he no longer allowed his thoughts to follow them.

He'd been homeless in the years since we last met. He didn't like the old hotel, so one day he just left and slept on the street. Homelessness is hard, he said, because you have to be vigilant all the time and you are constantly in search of food. But there was a freedom he really liked. You wake when you like, sleep when you like, say what you want. It was safer than some of the hotels he also slept in, because in hotels there are corridors and people can rough you up. But then he immediately said that he'd been attacked three times in one day on the street. He ended up with a staph infection in his hand that had not healed for months. He talked about what hard work it was to be on the street, how you constantly were looking for food, stuff, how getting stuff made it harder too because then you had to protect it. He eventually left El Cajon as well because police swept out the area he slept in and swept away his stuff. In fact, even when he was "in" El Cajon he seemed to come and go. He went down to Mexico and stayed in what he called a brothel (it was a cheap hotel), which he said his case manager had arranged.

Remarkably, he seemed to have had contact with his caseworker, on and off, during all this time. He said that he kept that connection because he wanted services, but his caseworker couldn't give him any. That is, he wanted money and food. But his caseworker wouldn't do that. The only real services, he said, came from the church, which fed him. The caseworker would say things like "Be here in three weeks." John said, "You can't make plans like that. Who knew where you would be in three weeks?" But eventually John left the street because his caseworker told him to be somewhere at a certain time, and he did so and went into the office, he said, and he was really hungry and he saw another person's candy bar in a drawer and he took it. At least, that's the way he remembered it. He said, "You know, I was delusional back then." And then two police squad cars came, and an ambulance, and a whole SWAT team (as he remembered it), and he ended up in the hospital for three months, which he said he hated. When he left, he went to a locked facility in Alpine. Then he was transferred to El Cajon. He said he didn't know how much longer he could last there.

He did eventually find a placement in a care facility for persons with serious mental illness. About ten years later he sent me a packet of drawings with a phone number, and we spoke. He said he had a place to live, and friends, and that everything was okay. But the clarity that had once been so striking was gone. I couldn't follow much of what he said.

He lives there still.

Diagnostic Neutrality in Psychiatric Treatment in North India

AMY JUNE SOUSA

In India, doctors deemphasize diagnoses and the biomedical specifics of what are essentially grave conditions, like schizophrenia. They don't talk about diagnoses or treat diagnoses as important, at least when interacting with their patients. As a result, they leave many possible ways to imagine the future intact. This may widen the range of possibilities for living in the present. Amy met Meeta and the others when she conducted fieldwork in Lucknow in 2008.

————

Meeta describes her illness as tension in her head: there is a pressure in her forehead that produces a pain in the space between her eyebrows; some days the pain is so intense that she has a hard time seeing. Meeta is young, not older than twenty, and hauntingly thin. Her collarbones poke through her thread-bare cotton *kurta*, which hardly protects her on this damp December morning. But Meeta says she is not cold, she was standing in the sun earlier, she's okay. I ask if her illness has a name. "Yes," she replies. Using English words, she says, "mental problem." She looks to her father, who shakes his head in agreement and repeats, "mental problem." But her psychiatrist describes the situation somewhat differently: "Meeta is a schizophrenic, she has hallucinations and she is tubercular and I can't believe her parents let her leave home without a sweater."

Discrepancies between doctors' and families' accounts of mental illness were common in the hospitals and clinics where I conducted this research. I regularly asked people the name of their illness. They responded that the mind was "not right" or, simply, that the illness didn't have a name. Many reported that intoxicants (nash), rather than sickness, drove them to the hospital. Other times, people would simply list off physical and affective symptoms. Another response, less frequent but regular, was "depression," the word spoken in English by people who didn't speak English otherwise. Many were familiar with the term depression and used it as a catchall for mental health problems in general. After hearing people's explanations, I often asked permission to look at their outpatient medical records. Invariably, I saw a variety of codes from the International Classification of Diseases (ICD) scribbled in them: "F20" for schizophrenia, "F31" for bipolar affective disorder, "F42" for obsessive-compulsive disorder, and so forth. The patients and their families didn't realize that these letters and numbers indicated that their ailments did, in fact, have names.[1]

In North Indian psychiatric settings, doctors and their patients view mental illness through distinctive lenses. Psychiatrists regard detailed biomedical information as inessential to the care they deliver. There is little time to discuss medical explanations, and doctors prefer not to interfere with families' own interpretations of mental illness. When doctors do choose to discuss a diagnosis with a family, they try to emphasize a condition's treatability. This lack of diagnostic focus, which I will call "diagnostic neutrality," is a treatment tool that psychiatrists use, often unwittingly. By deemphasizing diagnoses, doctors prevent the development of negative stereotypes that encumber social recovery in other cultural contexts. In this way, diagnostic neutrality may thwart social processes that have transformed schizophrenia into a devastating diagnosis elsewhere.

The North Indian families who participated in this research did not treat relatives with schizophrenia as though they had immutable biological conditions. They imagined schizophrenia as a cluster of symptoms that would remit with medication and time—as not who a person is, but rather a condition a person temporarily has. This provided some element of optimism as families went about the business of caring for their ill relatives and planning a future free from mental illness. It also left patients less vulnerable to despondency: they didn't frame their condition as intractable.

"She is different than me. She can't get better." This is how Anisha compared herself to her elder sister, Veena. Anisha repeated this comparison frequently during my visits to the Somdev Chaturvedi household in Lucknow, especially when Veena drifted in and out of the sitting room. Veena was completely silent: she floated around the house like a specter, disheveled, staring but never speaking. Veena had not spoken for years—amounting, on the day I met her, to decades of silence. She was nearly fifty. The sisters' mother told me that Veena mysteriously became silent when she was a teenager: "She was sharp-minded and active. And then some force took complete control over her." After all that time, Mrs. Chaturvedi still grappled with what possibly could have happened. She said, "A pundit told me that sometimes spirits live on flowers and if you pick that flower the spirit will take over your mind and body. Maybe she picked a flower on that day [she stopped speaking] and it captured her soul." During another visit, she suggested that Veena's silence indicated a household affliction: "Some people say that there is a curse on our house. Everything just turns out bad for our family, even though we keep praying, even though we do the *pujas*—so many pujas."

Veena spent her days at home, pacing from room to room, watching television, and resting. Her affect was disturbing and zombie-like: she smirked oddly and unprovoked; she brought her face close to mine and stared, then shook her unkempt body and backed away. These were the moments when Anisha would remind me that she and her sister were different. Anisha was right—she and her sister were quite different. Anisha talked at length, too much according to her mother and brother, while Veena was voiceless. Anisha cooked and cleaned alongside her sister-in-law. She bathed and lined her eyes with *kohl* and dressed in the morning. Veena, as Anisha explained contemptuously, couldn't do anything, not even wash her own body. What Anisha did not know was that she and her sister were the same in one way: both had been diagnosed with schizophrenia.

Since she was a teenager, Veena had spent time in and out of government mental hospitals in Delhi and Agra. She tried innumerable drug treatments and received electroconvulsive therapy. Yet Veena's illness and her silence prevailed. The Chaturvedi family came to accept what a psychiatrist in Delhi once told them: "Veena is in the fifty percent that can't get better." Veena's brother (the functional head of the household since their father had died) said in response to this, "Why put her in a hospital? If she can't get better, then she might as well stay at home." Mrs. Chaturvedi added, "Anyway, people don't get better sitting around hospitals." So, for the past several years, Veena had spent her days at home.

Anisha had never spent time in a psychiatric hospital, and her life followed a fairly conventional trajectory until her mid-twenties. Prior to her marriage, she received treatment for symptoms of malaise that included chronic body aches, feelings of suffocation, and a persistent feeling of being unsafe. It wasn't until after marrying, just over a decade ago, and moving in with her in-laws that her symptoms intensified. It was around the same time that she and her family learned that her middle sister was burned to death in a kitchen fire at her in-laws' house in rural Bihar. Anisha said, "She was burned to death in the fire. She didn't make it out alive." The circumstances surrounding the fire were mysterious. Her brother-in-law was also injured by the flames. He severely burned his hand and underwent numerous operations, spending a small fortune to repair it. According to Anisha, the husband burned his hand setting her sister ablaze. According to Mrs. Chaturvedi, he burned his hand trying to save his wife. The long history of these sorts of "accidents" in North India sadly lends weight to Anisha's side of the story. Anisha enjoyed reminiscing about her beloved sister and sharing photographs of her, something her mother strongly discouraged.

Not long after moving in with her in-laws, and after her sister's death, Anisha began to suspect that her husband would kill her. This portion of Anisha's history remains unclear, but it seems that her suspicions were fueled in equal parts by the horror of her sister's death, her increasingly paranoid delusions, and actual domestic violence. At some point she was prescribed antipsychotic medication, but Anisha recalled that her ex-husband fought against her use of them. She said that her in-laws preferred to "treat" her condition with beatings and blows to her head with sticks. Their hostility may have exacerbated her symptoms, which in turn incited more abuse. The result seems to have been a vicious circle that ultimately led to the disintegration of Anisha's marriage and her sanity.

Terrified that her sister's fate also awaited her, one day Anisha opened the closet, took out whatever she could carry, and fled to her maternal home. Her parents were not empathic. Despite the death of their middle daughter, Mr. and Mrs. Chaturvedi continued to believe that running away from one's husband was deplorable. So, after a few weeks of rest, the Chaturvedis forced Anisha to go back to him. Unsurprisingly, Anisha was not welcomed at her in-laws' home. But quite to her astonishment, all traces of her had been removed from the premises and her husband already had a new wife. Outraged and humiliated, she returned to her parents' home, where she had been living for a decade when I met her.

After returning to her maternal home, Anisha's condition continued to deteriorate. She became obsessed with thoughts that her own family would hurt her and even wanted to kill her. In recalling that time, Anisha pointed to her head and said that these thoughts crowded her mind; they tormented her and would not let her alone. Mrs. Chaturvedi explained that Anisha would read the newspaper, focus on crime stories, and become obsessed that the villains would come find her. Mrs. Chaturvedi laughed and, pointing at Anisha's young nephews running in the sitting room, exclaimed that "Even babies were enemies!" Anisha laughed along with her, chortling at the person she had been.

Though Anisha was relaxed on the day she laughed at the thought of babies as her adversaries, her paranoia was far from a distant memory. There were times when I visited and she would be full of fear and anger. In those moments she would repeat, over and over, phrases like "They all talk about me. They say I talk crap" and "At least I survived. I got out before they killed me." She seemed haunted by the death of her sister.

Now that she was fully immersed in life with her natal family, she had managed to find a peace that was not possible in the home of her in-laws. Anisha's story is not so uncommon in India. Women with schizophrenia and other serious mental illnesses are often divorced or rejected by their spouses.[2] These very same women who are excluded from household chores and deemed unfit for marriage by their in-laws may go on to function well if they return to their maternal families, despite schizophrenia. When among her in-laws, Anisha was labeled "crazy"; with her own family, she was simply another member of the household.

On my first visit to the Somdev Chaturvedi residence, I asked for the name of Veena's illness. First, Anisha said she thought it was called "depression" (using the English word). She and her mother thought about this for a bit before agreeing that, actually, it was not depression. Then, struggling with the pronunciation, Mrs. Chaturvedi said something that sounded like "shizo," prompting me to ask if Veena had schizophrenia. Anisha and her mother both nodded their heads yes—that was the name of her illness. I then asked Anisha what the name of her own illness was. She replied that she didn't know the name. Mrs. Chaturvedi thought for a few moments, shook her head, and said that Anisha's illness didn't have a name.

I asked permission to see Anisha's outpatient record book. Her mother scurried off to retrieve it. The booklet's cover was plastered over with a colorful picture of Ganesha. As I opened it, I felt Anisha and Mrs. Chaturvedi's eyes watching me intensely. Written on the first page was "F20," the ICD-10 code for schizophrenia. Under the diagnosis was the following list of symptoms, written in English: "previous hearing voices, abuses, suspiciousness, disturbances, auditory hallucinations." Anisha's psychiatrist had kept her on a fairly uniform and straightforward medication regime since she began treatment in 1999. She took the first-generation antipsychotic pimozide and the anxiolytic lorazepam. Anisha complied with treatment and took her medications daily.

The Chaturvedis didn't know what diagnostic codes were, nor did they speak or read English. The outpatient booklet was, of course, a reminder of Anisha's illness, the pills they had to buy, and their periodic journeys to the psychiatric hospital. Beyond this, the information contained within that little booklet did little to influence how the Chaturvedis interpreted and dealt with Anisha's illness or how Anisha herself coped. Now the open booklet on my lap threatened to interfere. Sensing that I might comprehend something in the book that she didn't, Anisha asked, "Do you understand my illness?" Misunderstanding, I thought she was asking if I understood what she was going through, if I was sympathetic to her struggles. When I empathized with her situation, she just stared at me, annoyed. Then, slowly, in very clear Hindi to be sure I comprehended, she said, "Please explain what is wrong with me. Do you know if my illness has a name?" Not knowing what to say, I stammered, "Chemicals in your brain combined with difficulties in your life and caused the problem. It's not the type of thing that has a name." Anisha and her mother just nodded.

In a short minute, I had to make a choice: whether to continue to conceal the name of Anisha's illness from her or to tell her that the doctors considered her illness to be the same one that her sister had. The ways in which ill persons and their families imagine the future give character to their strivings and ambitions, shaping the choices they make and how they navigate the domain of everyday life.[3] If Anisha and her mother had come to associate Anisha's diagnosis with Veena's, their whole perspective on the future might have changed. The word *schizophrenia* had little relevance in the Chaturvedi household until I drew attention to it by helping Anisha and her mother recollect the name of Veena's illness. Once out in the open, the diagnosis would gain solemnity through its association with Veena, who was dramatically ill. If extended to Anisha, the diagnosis could directly challenge her conviction that Veena was different than her and possibly induce dread and anger. So

FIGURE 2. In India, patients typically come to their appointments with family members. (*Photo: Amy Sousa*)

I chose to do what the Indian doctor had done—I did not give her condition a name.

Moreover, Anisha's diagnosis was really of little practical value to her and her family. Anisha and Veena were so perceptibly different that their shared diagnosis had little relevance in their daily lives. And indeed, their conditions illustrate the breadth of psychiatric categories. Individuals who fall within a single diagnostic parameter often have eclectic clinical presentations. This is especially true for schizophrenia, a syndrome notable for its multiple subtypes and the range of symptoms, course, and trajectory it encompasses. We talk about schizophrenia as a single disease, but in fact, recent research suggests that the illness likely consists of a group of disorders with heterogeneous etiologies, rather than one circumscribed disease entity.[4] That schizophrenia manifests itself differently and to different ends in different people was the daily reality of the Chaturvedi household.

Veena appeared to suffer from catatonic schizophrenia. This subtype is rare in the West today, but still present in the Indian clinics where I conducted research.[5] Catatonic schizophrenia is marked by striking disturbances in motor function. These can include everything from mutism, as in Veena's case, to severe stupor, to repetitive or mimetic behaviors, to extreme excitement on par with delirious mania.[6] The classic and most dramatic presentation of catatonia is posturing (catalepsy). The ill person gets "stuck" in an often odd and uncomfortable position for hours on end. This is the manifestation of catatonia most often pictured in psychiatry textbooks, usually in black-and-white photos taken by Emil Kraepelin in the early twentieth century. In these images people are frozen in bizarre stances: limbs in the air; faces tilted theatrically to the sky; mouths grimacing. Veena's bodily comportment was rigid and certainly peculiar, but it was a far cry from these depictions. Some of her impaired motor faculties were likely a side effect of long-term antipsychotic use and a history of institutionalization. Veena's mutism was her most prominent catatonic symptom. It had been with her since the onset of her illness. Her silence was also her most mysterious symptom. We can only conjecture what—if anything—provoked it.

Anisha, on the other hand, had a different set of troubles. Her persistent beliefs that people intended her harm, and her earlier psychosis, established the basis of her diagnosis of paranoid schizophrenia. Her symptoms seemed to be clearly exacerbated by psychosocial factors. Her history leaves one to wonder if she even would have become sick if she had had a more understanding husband, a living middle sister, and an elder sister who didn't become terrifyingly ill when Anisha was just a child.[7] And despite her tumultuous past, Anisha's prognosis was better than that of people diagnosed with other subtypes of schizophrenia and those whose illness had an earlier onset. People with paranoid schizophrenia tend to show less regression of their mental faculties and less impairment to emotional response and behavior than other subtypes of the illness and, consequently, experience better long-term outcomes.[8] This was evident with Anisha, who met several criteria for recovery when I met her. Recovery, defined broadly, is not only the remittance of symptoms, but also the process by which people are able to lead productive lives that include working, learning, and participating in their communities.[9] There is, of course, one major caveat. In India, a woman of Anisha's age should not be reliant upon the resources of her maternal family, which, in her case, were provided by her brother's income and her father's pension. She should be an active member of her husband's family and busy caring for children of her own. Anisha's illness and hostile in-laws derailed her from those traditional tracks. But her natal family carved out a role for her and she cooked, cleaned, and helped care for Veena.

Anisha and her family hadn't abandoned the possibility that she would eventually be 100 percent well. They hoped that maybe she would be able to marry again one day. Anisha's psychiatrist gave the Chaturvedis no reason to expect otherwise. There was no need for them to anticipate a future inevitably marked by the deterioration of Anisha's health. This contrasts with the attitude the Chaturvedis held toward Veena, which was one of resignation. They would always wonder why she became so ill, yet they ultimately accepted the reality of her condition. Years of failed treatments had earned Veena the dismal privilege of spending her days silently wandering from room to room. Anisha's and Veena's circumstances required very different attitudes and approaches to care.

The Chaturvedis, like so many other families I met, attended to the observable symptoms of mental illness rather than to diagnostic terminology. Consequently, Anisha didn't have to think of herself as someone who "can't get better" just because she had the same diagnosis as her sister, whose illness would not relent. Instead, Anisha saw herself as someone who succumbs to fear and gets overwhelmed by thoughts she can't control. She considered herself vulnerable in a world where in-laws can turn murderous. And, more than anything else, she felt a grave sense of loss when she reflected on all the experiences she never had. Her life was not easy. Yet this did not prevent her from believing in a better future. And, as someone who might get better, Anisha had to contribute to the household and account for her actions. The very demands her family made of her were ultimately rehabilitative.

Kemal Ahmed was a single adult male in his early thirties. He was tall and thin, with a head of thick, disheveled hair that hadn't been washed for many days. He came to the hospital accompanied by his parents and a family friend. There, they consulted with Dr. Rao, a senior psychiatrist. Kemal's family was middle class, and his father was a civil servant. The family friend was a former journalist who once wrote about the Indian health-care system; having her along made Kemal's parents feel more confident. They explained that Kemal's problems began over a decade ago, before the age of twenty, and despite many efforts at treatment there had never been any real improvement. Kemal's mother described his current condition as follows:

> He doesn't brush his teeth. Once in a while he takes a bath only. Last month he was talking about dying a lot. He tried to shoot himself with an air gun. He is sad, he is continuously sad. He says he is sad. He used to be friendly. At least he would

talk to the neighborhood children and give them treats and play with our dogs and be kind to animals. Now all of that is ended.

Speaking for the first time, Kemal's father added that his son didn't sleep, he paced. All night Kemal walked back and forth across the house, and during the daylight hours he cloistered himself in his small, dark room. The family was also concerned with Kemal's increased disorientation, his garbled mumbles, and the way he talked to himself.

Dr. Rao listened to all this quietly. Then he asked only if Kemal had any addictions and if he was ever violent or aggressive. They replied that Kemal smoked about forty cigarettes a day and had a mild temper. Dr. Rao then turned to Kemal. What follows are the only words that Kemal spoke during the entire appointment, and he did so with great difficulty. His head shook nervously and his speech was slurred.

> Dr. Rao: Kemal, how do you feel?
> Kemal: I should have come here first.
> Dr. Rao: But, anyway you came here today. How do you feel?
> Kemal: Drawn into the ground.
> Dr. Rao: Is there any reason why you say you don't want to live?
> Kemal: [after pausing a long moment] The medication. My whole life was a mistake.
> Dr. Rao: [shaking his head] Sometimes we all feel like that, but if we think about it too much then it is a problem.

Kemal was obviously confused and disoriented. It was unclear what he was thinking or trying to express. His father then pulled out a small bag brimming over with packets of pills. The father explained that he purchased these from a doctor in a nearby district. Dr. Rao looked at all these medications and shook his head in disgust. He said that 50 percent of the problem was the medicine. He explained:

> Most of these medications have the habit of sedating and pulling you down from the inside. Kemal has to be pacing up and down because he has this restlessness that comes from the inside. He is not interested in pacing all night but he has to do it. In the next ten days you will see improvement. His will to live has gone down, but it will improve. I am giving only two medicines plus one more.

Dr. Rao prescribed a medication regime typical of many people I knew who were receiving treatment for schizophrenia in India. This regime included a first-generation antipsychotic and a prophylactic to prevent side effects such as tremors, slurred speech, and Parkinsonism. When he arrived, Kemal already seemed to be suffering from some of these symptoms, as well as from the common side effect of akathisia, which is characterized by a feeling of restlessness and the need to move around constantly. Whatever medications were in the father's bag (I never was able to find out) put Kemal in a restless stupor.

In addition to the antipsychotic and prophylactic, Dr. Rao wrote a prescription for an anti-anxiety medication to be taken three times per day, but only for ten days. He also prescribed an optional sleeping medicine to be administered only if Kemal couldn't sleep. So, in reality, four medicines were prescribed rather than the "two plus one" promised by Dr. Rao. By placing emphasis on two medications rather than the actual four he prescribed, Dr. Rao played down the complexity of Kemal's condition—with the intention of comforting the Ahmeds, it seemed.

The appointment ended on a positive note with Dr. Rao's vote of confidence that in ten days there would be a big improvement. This is actually Dr. Rao's signature line. He typically promises families that after a specific number of days they will see tremendous improvement, and ten is his favorite number. He instructed the family to give him a call after a month and concluded the appointment by saying, "Kemal doesn't have to come to the clinic for every appointment. You [referring to his parents] can come in on his behalf." In response, Kemal's mother exclaimed, "This is great!" Everybody seemed happy with this approach to treatment, and they left the office in oddly good spirits. I say "oddly" good spirits because during this appointment Dr. Rao also wrote "F20" in thick black letters on the very first page of Kemal's brand-new outpatient record booklet. Kemal had received an official diagnosis of schizophrenia. In a different context, this could fill a family with despair. Instead, the Ahmeds said, "This is great." They smiled, and they felt a renewed sense of optimism.

This clinical encounter could easily be critiqued as paternalistic or patronizing. Dr. Rao used his own judgment to decide what the Ahmeds should know about their son's condition. He didn't take the time to fully explain the nature of Kemal's illness, and he quickly moved the Ahmeds out the door so he could treat the more than fifty families waiting in line behind them. It is not uncommon for an Indian doctor to see ten patients in an hour. In this sense, we could say that Dr. Rao gave the Ahmeds illusory hope, dispensed for his own convenience. I myself thought this way when I began my fieldwork. However, as I observed hundreds of appointments and built relationships with families, I began to think differently. I started to understand that downplaying the severity of illness and deemphasizing diagnoses can instantiate respect—rather than paternalism—in North Indian clinics. Respect is the ability to see others as sources of moral worth and as deserving of sympathetic identification. The diagnostic neutrality of Indian clinics is an instantiation of respect insofar as it works against the categorization of the patient as irrevocably different. Diagnostic neutrality means that diagnosis does not provide a means of self-identification in addition to one's family, religion, social class, and employment—categories that are all valued in this setting. The outward behaviors of mental illness already create schisms within families. An approach to care that minimizes obvious differences, instead of focusing on or labeling these differences, may help the mentally ill remain identified with their families and integrated in domestic life, even if they are the household's most eccentric members. This, in turn, may guard against exclusion and feelings of worthlessness, which are bad not only for recovery, but for human flourishing in general.

A final example to demonstrate the value of diagnostic neutrality takes us to a private psychiatric hospital on the outskirts of town, where a middle-class woman in her late fifties came in to see Dr. Kapur. This lady's husband, a retired army colonel whom I will simply call "the Colonel," had been diagnosed with paranoid schizophrenia long ago. At home, the Colonel was a tyrant. He relished regimentation, presumably a throwback to his years in the army, and he imagined that he ran his home like the barracks. Although his present state of mind didn't afford him the clarity to maintain order in any measurable way, his family largely endured his behavior.

As soon as the Colonel's wife entered Dr. Kapur's office, she immediately started making apologies; all she had managed to bring with her today, she said, was a ripped-out page from her husband's outpatient booklet. The Colonel, she explained, hid his booklet in the hopes that this would prevent anybody from seeking out treatment on his behalf. Undeterred by these antics, his wife found the booklet, ripped out the latest page, and returned the book to its hiding spot. She then slipped out the back door when no one was looking. At today's appointment, Dr. Kapur listened carefully to the woman's detailed description of the Colonel's behaviors and his symptoms before deciding to increase his dose of the antipsychotic risperidone. For her part, Dr. Kapur was more than happy to treat the Colonel by proxy. The last time he had come to the hospital he had tried to kick, and consequently was bitten by a street dog. Then he refused to take any antirabies medication.

When I asked if the Colonel ever ate his medications by his own volition, Dr. Kapur shook her head—"No way." As if holding a pestle in her right hand, she made a motion like she was grinding something in the palm of her left hand. She then brought her right fingertips to her mouth in the gesture of eating. What this pantomime meant was that the Colonel's wife ground up the antipsychotic pills, which came in an odorless and tasteless formulation, and mixed them into whole wheat flour. She then carefully added water and kneaded and rolled this specially fortified flour into flatbreads (roti or chapati), which she quickly cooked on the griddle before serving to the Colonel each and every night. Indian foodstuffs happen to be particularly good for concealing antipsychotic medications. Pungent spices mask hints of contamination, and psychotropic molecules easily melt into the dough of the breads typically served with North Indian meals. *Parathas*, layered wheat flatbreads laden with ghee or oil, have a reputation for being especially good conduits. As one doctor explained, even someone who is highly paranoid and in the throes of psychosis, who will only come out of her room when everyone else is asleep, will not be able to resist "nice room-temperature parathas left sitting on the kitchen table for several hours." In this way, late-night kitchen raids become prime opportunities for medicating noncompliant patients. In the case of the Colonel, this approach enabled him to continue living at home under the auspices of a family who indulged his military status.

What all these examples demonstrate is how, in the cultural setting of vernacular-speaking middle-class North India, families find their own ways to integrate mentally ill relatives into domestic life—ways that are often intuitive, tactile, pragmatic, and not guided by biomedical information. This entails making practical and symbolic alterations to daily life. Thus, Anisha was permitted to rejoin her maternal family and participated in domestic duties. While the family didn't actively engage Veena, they had carved out a place for her in the household. Likewise, the Colonel was free to command his troops, who were actually his extended family, so long as he ate his chapatis every night. Kemal, too, was deeply enmeshed in family life, but in a very different way. The Ahmeds let Kemal be, much as the Chaturvedis did Veena. However, the important distinction is that the Ahmeds believed that their son, as they remembered him before his illness, would reemerge. The family coped with his illness largely by tailoring their own lifestyle to it. Rather than begging him to leave his room during the day, his mother dutifully placed food by his door. If Kemal's nocturnal ways left his parents sleepless, they napped in the afternoon. By keeping Kemal close, the Ahmeds contained his psychopathology, shielding it from the gaze of the wider community. Whether or not this protection eased the trajectory of his illness, it did provide Kemal a safe and supportive environment to live in.

Diagnostic neutrality weakens the link between mental illness and identity formation. It is a way of practicing psychiatry that does not encourage patients and their families to accept biomedicine's underlying rationalities, categories, and ways of knowing. This prevents psychiatry from interfering with explanatory models and social structures, already in place, that are more appropriate for interpreting and managing mental illness in this context. The result is a style of treatment that is at once deeply embedded in the biomedical model, on account of its heavy reliance on pharmaceuticals, but also distanced in the way that it marginalizes biomedical explanations. As a result, schizophrenia is neither a way to be a person in North India, nor a way to identify oneself as a person.

Vulnerable Transitions in a World of Kin

In the Shadow of Good Wifeliness in North India

JOCELYN MARROW

Schizophrenia unfolds within a social world. What stresses a vulnerable individual, what matters as a symptom of illness, how the illness is understood, and who becomes responsible for treating it—all these matters are interpreted within community. In North India, that is the world of family and kin. The event that precipitated young Priyanka's episode of psychosis was the notoriously stressful transition in every rural North Indian woman's life at the time of her marriage and relocation into the domestic world of her new in-laws. As Priyanka fell ill, what mattered was the way she violated the expectations of right behavior with her new kin. The management of her illness would involve a complex negotiation in which Priyanka, her parents, and her in-laws made sense of her illness in different ways in order to get the best response (from each one's perspective) from the other actors in this social drama. Jocelyn met Priyanka when doing fieldwork in a hospital in Varanasi near the end of April 2002.

———

Even under the best of circumstances, a newly married Indian woman who is just beginning to live with her in-laws experiences stress to a degree previously unfamiliar to her. In her new marital home, she is restricted in speech and behavior. Her movements outside the household are monitored carefully and with suspicion, if not entirely forbidden. She must veil and behave demurely in front of her husband's elders and avoid speaking to any elder male household members as much as possible. She frequently finds that the opportunity to talk with her husband is available only at night, after the rest of the household has gone to sleep; in front of the elders, even small demonstrations of affection

FIGURE 3. A young married woman sits alone on the Ghats of Varanasi. While many young women such as Priyanka look forward to becoming wives and mothers, the transition to life with their new husbands and families may be difficult and cause distress. (*Photo: iStock*)

toward him—a loving smile, an extra sweet on his plate—are forbidden. And she feels far, far away from the comfort of her own parents, siblings, and girlfriends, regardless of the actual distance between her natal and conjugal homes.

In her new marital home she is subjected to scrutiny, and usually to criticism. While her speech and behavior are greatly restricted, members of her new household and their visitors feel free to remark upon her physical appearance in great detail; they will also evaluate the goods she brought from her parents as her trousseau and dowry. Finally, the extent of her skills and efforts as a worker is minutely observed. Invariably, she will be the object of constant direction and correction, because her conjugal family's food preferences and styles of running the household are different than those of her natal family, and she must be taught to accommodate the tastes and preferences of her new family.

She enters her new family as its least important member. Eventually, once she has sons—and, even more, when her sons have brides of their own—she will become a person of comparatively great power. But for now, she must learn to meet the expectations of this small community and become a dutiful and quietly responsive member of it.

Every young bride worries about pleasing her in-laws and her new husband and is mindful that if they don't like her they may make her life miserable. Most young women don't become ill enough upon marriage to warrant outside help, even under the worst of circumstances. And yet it is remarkable how much mutual suspicion, worry, and feelings of harassment there are in the experience of even the healthiest bride, and how common is the conviction that one is being persecuted by one's in-laws. Many of the details regarding Priyanka's worries that I gathered from interviewing Priyanka, her natal and conjugal family members, and her doctors were not false. But she didn't act like other young brides. Under the stress of scrutiny and harassment, she began to weep angrily and loudly, to speak aggressively toward those to whom she ought to defer, and to isolate herself from the family members to whom she should be trying to assimilate. She sat by herself and mumbled. She presented, then, a formidable problem to the families—her parents and her husband's parents—who had responsibilities toward her.

When I met Priyanka during her stay at the inpatient unit of Banaras Hindu University's Department of Psychiatry, she was twenty-two years old and had been married for three years. Even so, she had only begun to live with her husband and his family in their village a little more than two months before. In this region of North India (northeastern Uttar Pradesh), weddings are often solemnized a few years before the bride moves in to live with her husband.[1] The departure of the bride to her husband's home for her first period of residence is referred to as the *gauna*. The period of time the young married woman spends in her in-laws' home immediately following her gauna is particularly delicate. It is a time of discovery for all in the conjugal household—interpersonal, sexual, and emotional. The new wife and daughter-in-law strives to make a good impression on the members of her new household, at the same time attempting to limit the extent to which she will be subordinated, if not exploited. It is a balancing act for the young wife. She must gain approval of demanding familial superiors while engaging in subtle, yet not blatantly inappropriate, maneuvering to fulfill some of her own desires.

This notoriously stressful period of the young woman's life was acknowledged as such by many of my Varanasi contacts. After marriage, a young woman finds herself among a group of strangers upon whom she must depend for her well-being. She misses her parents and natal kin terribly, and her fear and anxiety are intensified by the fact that she has probably never spent a single night before her marriage away from familiar relatives. After marriage, she must become sexually active, and her lack of knowledge about sexuality—and the pressure she feels from her conjugal family to engage in intercourse with a young man she barely knows—may lead to painful coitus, and thence to more anxiety and fear. As an unmarried daughter, she learned how to perform domestic work, but it is likely that her natal family members were relatively indulgent regarding how consistently or thoroughly she did her housework. As a young wife, she must not shirk even the heaviest and dirtiest tasks that will be assigned to her as the person with the lowest status in the household. The Indian mental health professionals I knew cited this time of a woman's life as the period during which she is most likely to experience depression, a somatoform disorder, or a psychotic break.

At the same time, these mental health professionals complained that it is not uncommon for the families of girls suffering chronic psychotic disorders or intellectual disabilities to knowingly deceive grooms' families by failing to disclose potential brides' mental illnesses or deficits before their weddings. One psychiatrist told me that sometimes natal kin will bring a newly married young woman to the hospital during a relapse of illness and beg the consultant psychiatrist not to tell the conjugal family that she is a returning patient. In Priyanka's case, neither the professional staff at the hospital nor Priyanka's natal kin disclosed to me that she had suffered a similar illness before her gauna. However, at one point, Priyanka's mother-in-law voiced a doubt that it was not likely that Priyanka had become so severely ill only in the brief couple of days after her gauna.

Priyanka's first stay at her new household was difficult from the beginning. Her mother-in-law reported that she had been crying continuously since the day after her arrival. According to her father-in-law, they noticed that something was wrong with Priyanka after they began the preparations for his own daughter's impending gauna. His daughter's departure was to follow Priyanka's arrival—the latter arrived on the seventeenth of February, and the former's departure for her husband's home was scheduled for the twentieth. Priyanka's conjugal family was getting together the gifts they would give their own daughter to take to her *susural* (conjugal household). Priyanka's father-in-law explained to me, "I don't know how she got this idea, but she became suspicious that we were going to give *her* things to *my* daughter."

As is customary among village families who have a new resident daughter-in-law, visitors—relatives, well-wishers, work associates, and neighbors—stopped by the house of the new bride to inspect her and the goods that she brought with her. Therefore, Priyanka's mother-in-law had been in possession of the key to Priyanka's shiny new Godrej cupboard since Priyanka's arrival, and was showing visitors the items contained within. Suspicious that her trousseau would be given to her sister-in-law, Priyanka demanded the key to the Godrej from her mother-in-law. She received it and then refused to give it back, insisting that her husband had advised her not to return it to his mother.

"Indeed," Priyanka's father-in-law conceded to me, "we were going to give Priyanka's new cupboard to our own daughter for her gauna—our house is very small and we do not have room for it here. Once Priyanka relocates to Allahabad to stay permanently with her husband near his workplace, we will buy her a Godrej for her things there." This was one of those moments when it became clear that the line between psychotic paranoia and reality could be thin in this stressful time.

And yet: her husband, Sandesh, set out to explain to me that there was more than heightened suspicion in her behavior. He said that Priyanka's pillow-talk was "crazy" the second night after her arrival. He told me that she "said things to me that no wife should say to her husband." She made accusations against his parents and threatened to punish him if he were to "pain her heart." She told him that he would "suffer" if he were not good to her, because "no one will be here to cook for you." Sandesh said that she tried to strangle him that night.

According to her in-laws, her odd behavior escalated the next day. She began to isolate herself, to sit in a room alone and cry. Her father-in-law instructed her that she should not pronounce her husband's name, but she continued to refer to Sandesh by his name. (It is considered rude for wives to refer to their husbands by their given name. People believe that each time a wife pronounces her husband's name she subtracts months or years from his longevity.) As is also the local custom, Priyanka's brothers visited her in her conjugal household on the fourth or fifth day after her gauna. Priyanka's father-in-law reported that she told her brothers that her mother-in-law did not like her, and that she was not happy. Her brothers began to worry that she was in trouble. Her father-in-law remembered that one brother sat with his head in his hands after talking with Priyanka, a posture he took to mean "Oh my God, why is she doing this?" After the visit, she began to sleep irregularly and to sit alone and talk to herself. Priyanka noticed a gun in the house and became afraid. Her mother-in-law chided her, "Why are you afraid of this? Do you think we will keep a gun to kill you?"

At this point, Priyanka's father-in-law summoned the rest of her natal family to come and see her condition and intervene. From his point of view, the problem was that she was isolating herself, behaving disruptively, and—probably most serious—refusing to work. Her mother, brother, and sister-in-law arrived to see her. It is not uncommon for the conjugal family to demand that the natal family intervene in the initial stage of the cohabitation when things are tense; it is their expected job to help soothe the marriage and ensure its success. Marriage is perhaps the most important social achievement for most Indians. It is sometimes said to be more stigmatizing to have a marriage end in divorce than to have serious mental illness.[2]

It is also the job of the natal family to insist that everything will be fine. And indeed, when they visited Priyanka, she spoke and laughed with them as if she were perfectly fine—at least, they said they did not believe she was having difficulties. The father-in-law asked them to take her back with them so they could observe her condition over time, but her natal kin refused.

There was more than the stress of a new marriage in play. Priyanka's husband had a job as a foreman (*mistry*) in Allahabad. He had planned to spend only two weeks with his new wife before returning to work. This is the fate of many lower-middle-class North Indian wives these days, and it is often the custom that the new wife will stay behind in her unfamiliar conjugal home while the young man works elsewhere. As the date he was to return approached, Priyanka began to insist that she be allowed to go to Allahabad with her husband. Her in-laws protested that he could not provide a nice home for her in Allahabad yet—he lived in a single room—and therefore she could not accompany him. When Sandesh left for Allahabad in the first week of April, Priyanka began to cry uncontrollably.

I learned this story of Priyanka's illness entirely from her father-in-law, mother-in-law, and husband. As they told it, they emphasized the aspects of Priyanka's suffering that were disruptive to the smooth functioning of their household and that violated their sense of appropriate behavior for a hard-working and decorous daughter-in-law and wife. For Priyanka's conjugal family, it was evident that there was something wrong with her because of her persistent and willful flouting of family roles and expectations. She refused to work. She was completely uninterested in household chores. Her mother-in-law compared her own (elder) married daughter to Priyanka: "Even though my daughter used to sleep the whole day in her *maike* [natal home], in her *susural* [conjugal home] she works and is doing well." Referring to Priyanka, she continued: "I do not understand her. She wants me to serve her. She wants me to prepare food and feed her so that she can sleep the whole day. I will not tolerate this. She spends the whole day sleeping in her room. When I come and ask her to help me prepare food, she says she cannot do it."

Priyanka was in the hospital by the time they told me these things. Her husband complained again that she had said things to him that "no wife should say to her husband." He accused her of talking to him without respect and with anger, suspiciousness, and threats. When my female research assistant tried to explain to Sandesh that Priyanka was in trouble, he became indignant: "Trouble—*I'm* in trouble!" His mother chimed in: "She thinks that she should be able to talk with her husband in front of his male friends; as soon as he comes in the house, she rushes to him, even if he is with other men. She cannot do that."

This emphasis on behavior, rather than on psychotic symptoms, is characteristic of families in India. In her book on mentally ill women in contemporary Delhi (many of whom were diagnosed with psychotic disorders), Renu Addlakha demonstrates that it is when women's behavior exceeds what is role-appropriate that it becomes defined as a problem requiring intervention of some kind. For example, she describes one woman diagnosed with schizoaffective disorder whose presenting problem[3] was written in her chart as suffering from "not doing housework" and "not observing personal hygiene for the last six years." The psychiatric exam, meanwhile, identified "excessive talking, singing, and evidence of grandiosity"—symptoms much more in line with international standards of illness classification.[4] For many families, it is the violation of the norms of femininity that is identified as mental illness. I witnessed a middle-aged husband plead with the resident psychiatrist writing his wife's intake, "There is no peace [*shanti*] in my house, Doctor Sahib! Please give her some kind of medicine so that there will be peace." In that case, it was not clear to me that there was a real mental illness in play. This "ill" wife's "symptoms" of expressing her anger through fighting with him and cursing at him under her breath only became manifest after twenty-nine years of marriage, hours after she was insulted by him by being beaten with shoes. Anthropologists have described this behavior-based style of diagnosis as driven by "nuisance value."[5]

The lay identification of madness differs from that of psychiatrically trained practitioners in placing little value on subjective symptoms of psychosis. In international and U.S. psychiatric nosologies, the identification of psychosis presumes that most individuals suffer from prominent hallucinations or delusions.[6] Yet while I heard hundreds of cases of psychosis presented at the Department of Psychiatry, there was not one case in which the patient's problem was initially described by family attendants as involving hallucinations or delusions, although further exploration of symptoms by the professional staff often revealed hallucinations or delusions. Women's presenting problems tended to refer to their violation of gender roles: not doing housework, behaving indecorously, not maintaining hygiene. Men's illnesses were also identified by aberrant behavior and speech. A typical lay description of a male suffering psychosis was that "He runs all over the place (*idhaar udhaar bhaagta he*). He insults people (*gaali deta*) and his speech makes no sense (*anaap-sanaap bolta he; at-fat bolta he; ut-phatang bolta he; bakwas bolta he*)."

It seemed clear that Priyanka was indeed suffering from psychosis. Dr. Gulaal, the resident in charge of Priyanka's case at the Department of Psychiatry, explained to me that she was diagnosed with paranoid schizophrenia because she was delusional when she first arrived at the hospital: she believed that her in-laws were conspiring against her parents. I did not meet Priyanka until she had already been treated at the hospital for ten days. She had been undergoing electroconvulsive therapy and seemed to have responded positively to the treatment. Any delusions had abated; she did not verbalize any apparently delusional beliefs when I spoke with her. Even so, she appeared withdrawn, distraught, and fearful.

After a few visits to Priyanka's bedside at the hospital, I met her mother, who defined Priyanka's problems differently than her in-laws. Indeed, she defended her daughter. In front of Priyanka's mother-in-law, she excused Priyanka's behavior as due to homesickness: "She has so much affection for us—*mayajaal* with us. I have been trying to make her understand that she will have to stay with her in-laws and her husband."

The mother-in-law replied, "From the first day she complained about us."

Priyanka's mother explained politely that those comments did not represent her daughter's true feelings: "Please understand that physically and mentally she is not okay."

The mother-in-law countered that when Priyanka saw a gun in their house, she became terrified.

The mother tried to explain: "It is not like that; she is afraid of everything. She hears the mooing of a water buffalo and I need to make her understand that it will not hurt her."

The mother-in-law replied, "Since she entered our house she has been behaving this way. How is it that in two days she has become like this?"

The mother explained, "She is not well; this is why she behaves this way."

Beneath the surface of this back-and-forth lay a none-too-veiled complaint: if Priyanka's family knew that she was mentally ill when she married, they had, in effect, violated their family obligation of offering a decent bride. But if Priyanka had become temporarily ill because she was sensitive, if the shock of a new home—perhaps with inconsiderate family members—had unsettled her, why then, it was the conjugal family's responsibility to accept her and to help her behave more responsibly.

There was also the issue of black magic. In qualitative interviews with young, urban South Indian men experiencing a first episode of psychosis, Ellen Corin and her coauthors found that supernatural fear was a pervasive subjective experience of early psychosis.[7] Some subjects felt that they had been subjected to black magic or evil spirits. In Bangladesh, "pervasive draining fear," in folk ontologies, carries the risk that the fearful person's soul will be scared away by an invading spirit or ghost. There, "magical fright" is thought to be useful to possessing spirits, who are able to take advantage of states of fear and confusion in order to enter the body.[8]

In fact, Priyanka's in-laws' first efforts to manage her illness involved attempts to exorcise the evil spirits they assumed were possessing Priyanka. At night she had been speaking crazily (*anaap-sanaap*) and behaving "as if she were not even human," trying to strangle her husband and referring to him by name, which suggested to her conjugal family that there was something not human invading her mind and will. A female *tantrik* near Sasaram, in the state of Bihar, said she was possessed of something devilish (*shaitani chiz*), but that she ought to be treated with biomedicine. A priest of a Hanuman temple in Allahabad confirmed the tantrik's diagnosis and treatment recommendations.

For Priyanka, the sense of persecution was certainly real, and it highlights the enormous emotional challenge that many new brides face in this world of arranged marriages and clear social expectations for the bride's behavior. A well-known Bengali psychiatrist, Ajita Chakraborty, writes that she increasingly sees depressive and paranoid symptoms coexisting or alternating in the presentations of a notable segment of young housewives brought to her Kolkata clinic, who describe feeling persecuted by conjugal family members.[9] She reports that some of these young housewives "cross the threshold and become psychotic, but at what stage and why the resentment and the blaming becomes a delusion is debatable." Unable to manage the new stresses, roles, and demands that are placed upon them after marriage, they feel "helplessness, a sense of inadequacy, hopelessness, anger and resentment."[10] Presumably, many of the young housewives are actually subjected to hostility, close surveillance, and critique by their conjugal relatives to a greater or lesser extent during this notoriously emotionally, psychologically, and physically difficult time of life, which scholars have likened to a "domestic . . . version of military boot camp" in its insistence on discipline, endurance, and subordination.[11]

Priyanka felt caught within a hostile world. Even her in-laws' narrative of the days following her arrival at their household suggests they behaved in ways that could have given Priyanka the sense that she was indeed in a hostile world. Recall that her father-in-law cited Priyanka's suspicion that he would give her things to his own daughter for her gauna as evidence of Priyanka's illness, and then went on to admit that her suspicion was entirely correct—he was planning on giving her new cupboard to his daughter. Later, when I spoke about this with the consultant psychiatrist in charge of Priyanka's case, she was adamant that Priyanka's in-laws had no legal, or even customary, entitlement to the items gifted to Priyanka by her parents at her gauna. Still, it is not uncommon, nor unexpected, that in-laws will behave self-servingly with their daughters-in-law and take advantage of their dependent and lowly status in any way they wish. Daughters-in-law, if they protest any theft or misbehavior at all, must find a way to do so without jeopardizing their own futures by provoking their conjugal families' anger, retaliation, rejection, or violence.

Priyanka's mother attributed her daughter's distress to the harsh behavior of her in-laws. She explained to me, in front of the mother-in-law, that the latter was "always very rough and rude with [Priyanka]. She says things to her harshly that could be said gently." The mother-in-law protested this:

> The way she says to me "No, I am not able to do the cooking" is very rough and rude, and I feel hurt. I don't want to be hurt anymore. Since she has come to my house two months ago, I have fed her with my own hand, but she has behaved very badly. If she would have behaved nicely, I would be ready to wash her sanitary napkins. I am not such a rough and rude lady—I looked after my elder brother-in-law in the village when he fell ill. So I am not so hard-hearted. But she makes me like this.

Yet Priyanka's mother continued: "Always the mother-in-law speaks harshly; my daughter has mental problems, but she doesn't care about that. She could say things gently—ask her to prepare food gently—but she won't do that."

Learning that there were no immediate plans for her to live with her husband in Allahabad increased Priyanka's distress. Wives residing in their conjugal households without their husbands sometimes regard their situation as akin to being held hostage as a domestic drudge, without any potential ally to turn to in the face of mistreatment.[12] New brides expect that sexual and affectionate ties will convert their husbands into their allies in domestic settings hostile to their interests.[13] In the absence of her husband, Priyanka's experience of her conjugal household might well have been very bleak.

It is worth reflecting upon the meaning, in this family drama, of Priyanka's appearance. She was breathtakingly beautiful: slender, tall, unusually fair, with perfect features. In contrast, her new husband was relatively dark and average-looking. With so much aesthetic capital in her favor, Priyanka may have assumed that most young men would not give her up all that easily, and so she was willing to gamble with the early demand to separate their nuclear household from his parents' household. Even so, all this took place in a social world in which stories circulate about young brides who are murdered, tortured, or forced to commit suicide by their in-laws as a result of their dissatisfaction with the new bride or her dowry. These stories are sometimes true. It seemed reasonable that Priyanka might fear her in-laws. Clearly she was aware that they were not pleased with her; in fact they had become her adversaries in the two months before she entered the hospital. The sad reality of daughter-in-law murder suggests that her fear at seeing the gun in her in-laws' home may not have been delusional. Her mother-in-law, telling this story, gave shape to Priyanka's fear in a way that might have been heard to constitute a threat: "Do you think we will keep a gun to kill you?"

For many years anthropologists have observed that people with psychosis, for whom there is a terrifying ambiguity to the realness of the world, are caught within double binds.[14] Priyanka was caught in the snares of one, though it was never entirely clear to me how much reality there was to her fears. But from Priyanka's perspective, if she was afraid, she was called delusional; yet if she was not suspiciously vigilant, she risked theft or perhaps death. And by the time I met everyone in the hospital, ill-will on both sides seemed to be spiraling out of control in the household, with Priyanka and her in-laws each escalating the expression of their displeasure and anger.

Scholars have remarked on how hospital stays in India serve as a place of retreat from interpersonal tension in the family, in which alliances can be bolstered and reconfigured and support marshaled for struggling members.[15]

Priyanka's hospital stay did seem to function that way. There she was able to receive support from her mother and natal kin, and impartial intervention from the professional staff for her problems with her in-laws. Should Priyanka have returned to her natal home at the time she was struggling with them, her early return would have stigmatized her as a failed wife and daughter-in-law. On the other hand, Priyanka's mother and natal kin could not comfortably visit with her at her conjugal home; it is considered impolite for a wife's family to take any hospitality—even a glass of water—from her conjugal family. The hospital provided a liminal space in which mother and mother-in-law could dialogue, express their respective concerns, and hopefully come to some resolution regarding how to manage their charge's problems.

This in fact is understood as part of the hospital's responsibility. The professional staff at the Department of Psychiatry considered it their duty to intervene in family problems for the benefit of the patient. In Priyanka's case, her doctors emphasized to her conjugal family that she was suffering from an illness, and that her inappropriate behavior as a wife and daughter-in-law was not a moral failing. They repeatedly explained that her incapacitation was outside of her control, and that she should be given the love and care due an ill family member. On the other hand, they encouraged Priyanka to work—to assist her family attendants, especially her mother-in-law, with preparing meals and cleaning up. Once I observed a nurse come by Priyanka's bed to take her temperature several hours after an administration of electroconvulsive therapy. Priyanka was kneading dough alongside her mother-in-law, who was cutting vegetables. The nurse praised her: "Oh, you are working—good! Make some rotis!"

Priyanka, for her part, actively worked to assign her suffering meaning in ways that differed from the interpretations of her in-laws, her mother, and her doctors. She tantalized her audiences with a claim that there was something deep in her heart that was paining her. She repeatedly referred to a "matter of the heart" (*dil ki baat*) causing her suffering. Over five visits I had with her, she was never explicit about the details of this "matter of the heart." Yet in the context in which it came to light, it was not difficult for me to guess (as she would have understood). Priyanka drew upon the well-known tropes of lovesickness and broken-heartedness to explain, and hopefully receive sympathy for, her distress and "madness."

The first time we met Priyanka and her conjugal family, her father-in-law had encouraged my research assistant to find out the substance of this "matter of the heart" to which she repeatedly referred. Entering her hospital room, my assistant was greeted by Priyanka, who touched her feet and told her to sit. Priyanka's husband suddenly announced that he was leaving. He picked up his bag. Priyanka began to cry loudly, "Call him back, call him back!" Priyanka's mother-in-law went after her son. When he returned, he said to my assistant, "Big sister (*didi*), did you call me?" She answered that it was Priyanka who had called him.

Priyanka then asked Sandesh, "You are going?"

He replied to my assistant, "My train is at one." My assistant asked where he was going. "Baksar." His wife rushed to him and touched his feet. After a few minutes, he got up to leave. Priyanka grabbed his wrist and he pushed her away. She began to cry.

Sandesh told my research assistant that she ought to ask Priyanka about the matter of her heart. He added that he would not be back for two weeks. Priyanka rushed to touch his feet again, and when he left, she began to scream and cry. She threw herself on the bed and pulled the end of her sari over her head. She remained face-down on the bed, crying silently. The sight of her, ornamented with all the signs of marital auspiciousness (*solah shringar*)—a new bright red sari, rows of red bangles on her arms, red vermillion liberally applied to the part of her carefully combed hair—yet thrown down and weeping on the bed, was a singularly dramatic picture of a young, fragile, broken heart.

Then my research assistant asked again about her *dil ki baat*. Priyanka replied that her in-laws knew what it was. The mother-in-law irritably retorted, "How can we know if you don't tell us?" Priyanka and her mother-in-law began to argue, with Priyanka still face-down on the bed—a bundle of bright red sari. Priyanka insisted, "He left without speaking to me."

The mother-in-law replied, "Why should he speak to you? You've never behaved nicely to him! You are crying all the time." She continued, complaining that Priyanka had been crying since she arrived. Clearly, continued her mother-in-law, she did not like her in-laws and did not want to live with them.

Priyanka cut in, "That is not true! I just want to live with my husband." That plea for her husband's presence would be her refrain through her hospital stay. Days later, Sandesh visited Priyanka's bedside again. Priyanka served him a glass of water, which he accepted, but he still refused to speak to her. Sorrowful about her husband's rejection, she cried continually in the days following—her eyes watery and her voice quavering.

In India, there is a widely shared trope of love as suffering—loving attachment as *maya*, and love-in-separation as *viraha*. Maya, in its most literal sense, means illusion; however, in context it refers specifically to the feelings of love, longing, and attachment as illusory and, ultimately, as the cause of human suffering.[16] Viraha is the feeling that comes when one loses the person one loves. Viraha is described in folk and classical texts as a type of sickness—usually more symptomatically similar to consumption or hysteria than to psychosis, but sickness nonetheless.[17] Priyanka seemed to believe that her pain ought to be comprehensible to, and received sympathetically by, those around her; they should have understood that she became sick because of her strong but unfulfilled attachment to her husband. She made it clear that she needed him for her well-being. This was the "matter" of her "heart"—that she was pining for an emotionally and spatially distant husband.

The narrative of a woman's subjective experience of the pain of separation from her husband appears again and again in North Indian folklore and folk songs and in contemporary artistic and mass media such as novels and films.[18] The expression of lovesickness ought to evoke compassion and pity from observers.[19] Further, in Ayurvedic and popular nosologies, lovesickness leads to madness (*stri-paagal*; literally, "women's madness"). It is a "Hindu social stereotype," that "of a love-story coming to a bad end."[20] While the stereotypical lovelorn woman's behavior is more hysterical than psychotic,[21] Priyanka stretched and manipulated the meanings and signs that circulate with the ubiquitous North Indian figure of the dedicated, self-sacrificing, lovesick wife to include herself among this noble lineage of heroically suffering women. To her parents, her in-laws, and the hospital staff, she indicated as clearly as she could that her illness was due to her husband's rejection and separation.

Priyanka's hospital stay occurred in the shadow of "good wifeliness." By this I mean that what it is to be a good wife was constantly referenced by her in-laws, husband, and even (to a lesser extent) the professional staff. She was said, explicitly and implicitly, to have behaved inadequately as a wife. Her mother and mother-in-law used the hospital as neutral territory to confront each other with their different interpretations of the cause of this inadequacy: her mother blamed the mother-in-law's harshness; the mother-in-law blamed the daughter-in-law's unwillingness to be a good wife. The professional staff insisted that Priyanka was failing her domestic role because of her illness; they argued that with proper, solicitous care and medical treatment the failure could be reversed. And Priyanka asserted that any improper behavior was due to her "heart," broken by the rejection of the man whom she had married.

Four days after my last meeting with Priyanka, she was discharged from the hospital into the care of her natal family. I was never able to visit her again. As far as I know, she didn't return to the hospital during the following eighteen months, and I'd like to believe that her capacity to shape the meaning of her illness was evidence of her resilience and boded well for her recovery. While at her most psychically and emotionally fragile, she communicated a coherent and culturally plausible alternative to the accounts of doctors, in-laws, and parents. She was not an inadequate wife because of a brain disease, a bad marital environment, or moral failings, as they each argued in turn. Instead— tentatively deploying the trope of love-as-suffering—she was such a singularly loving wife that, even after a few months of living side-by-side with her husband, the threat of separation from him had broken her heart and driven her insane. She suggested that rather than being inadequate, she was excellent— and that the symptoms of her suffering ought to be understood as proof of her devotion.

Biomedical etiology, diagnosis, and treatment are dominant—but not hegemonic—in the cultural milieu of vernacular-speaking North India. The origin and cure that Priyanka hinted at with the talk of her "matter of the heart" is a culturally robust alternative explanation for her distress. I can only hope that in turning away from a view of herself as lacking or inadequate, she was able find the inner strength to manage the pain of her matter of the heart, while negotiating a return to a role in her new family.

Work and Respect in Chennai

GIULIA MAZZA

India is home to more than 60 percent of the slum dwellers in the world, but few of them are homeless, even when they stay on the street. Urban families without a place to live will settle into a square of city pavement with a kitchen area and sleeping place, and others will respect their space. Relatively few of those who are mentally ill live without their families. Yet some do, either because they have been abandoned or because they fled. The Banyan is a nongovernmental organization founded in 1993 to rescue poor, abandoned, homeless women with mental health issues. Since its inception, the Banyan has treated over two thousand persons with mental illness. They bring in women who are often too incapacitated to remember their own names and care for them, treat them, and teach them to work. They provide food, clothing, shelter, medication, general health care, therapeutic activities, and occupational training—all for free. They have been able to return over a thousand of them to their natal homes. The Banyan's remarkable success arises in part from the way these families understand the problems created by illness: first and foremost as failure to work, not as an inner experience with symptoms of distressing voices. Giulia met Madhu in the spring of 2010.

I picked Madhu out easily from the row of women sitting in the hallway. She was unusually tall for an Indian woman, with a broad, pock-marked face framed by slightly greasy hair with streaks of gray in it, gathered in a hasty ponytail. Her large stomach bulged under a burgundy *salwar kameez* tunic, unadorned except for a bit of frumpy purple lace. She rose and smiled shyly

FIGURE 4. The banyan tree is said to be like the Indian joint family. Each branch grows roots that support the main trunk. (*Photo: T. M. Luhrmann*)

when I went up and introduced myself, and we agreed to get a cup of chai from the vendor across the street—I had by that time learned that any social interaction of some importance takes place while sipping that sweet, milky tea. During the short walk over, I noticed that her bare feet were cut and cracked, but she didn't seem bothered by them. She chattered cheerfully about what she had had for breakfast and what could be expected for lunch.

Madhu struggled with schizophrenia. Her family had tried to help her recover a few times, in the hope that she would once again be able to participate in family life and contribute to the work of the household. These attempts were not successful, and fifteen years before I met Madhu, her family, unable to cope with the strain, had abandoned her on the street to fend for herself. She had wandered across India since then, by way of trains boarded more or less at random, sometimes finding shelter in temples and mental hospitals, sometimes not. When she didn't find work, she would beg for food and money on the street. After perhaps five years (the chronology isn't quite clear) she was spotted by Banyan staff and taken in for care.

When a woman like Madhu comes into the Banyan, she is placed in a capacious urban dormitory. She is washed, deloused, and given medication and therapy. Those who are there seem happy and grateful to have clean clothes and safety. When a woman is ready, the Banyan seeks out her natal family (rather than her in-laws) and then accompanies her to sometimes distant regions. There they negotiate with family members and the village *panchayat* (council) to keep the woman, and they make sure that she has a steady supply of psychopharmaceuticals. They ensure that she will be able to work—to sew, clean, and cook—when they bring her back to the family, so that they can show that she will contribute. The Banyan knows that many of these families will accept the woman back and care for her only if she can be a productive member of the household.

But sometimes relatives refuse to take their family member back into the fold. That was true for Madhu. She was then sent to a small facility in the rural fishing village of Kovalam. Geared toward long-term residency and surrounded by gardens, the living center is a more low-key, relaxed environment than the crowded urban setting. It was there that I met Madhu. She spoke fluent English, and we spoke for three sessions of ninety minutes each.

Talking to Madhu was not a simple task. Getting someone to tell you her life story is, under any circumstances, a delicate process. Memory is reconstructed, not merely recalled. In my conversations with Madhu, however, everyday distortion was dramatically exacerbated. Her sentences were meandering and fragmented. I walked away from the first interview with a splitting migraine that did not let up for hours. The effort to keep track of the multiple strains at play in the story—her version of events, my theories about those events, and the business of steering the interview—had been immense.

The effects of time and psychosis on Madhu's memory were considerable, and without the benefit of contact with her family, it was difficult to corroborate much of her past. Some parts of her story were credible, some incredible, and many existed in an ambiguous area in between. There were, however, a handful of facts that seemed clear: Madhu was rejected by her family when she became ill, and for years she led a wanderer's life at the fringes of society, before being rescued by the Banyan. She shared her story in a fantastically frustrating, surprisingly eloquent voice; I regret that I cannot convey its distinctive sound here, its quiet, raspy, singsong quality. Since Madhu was the only source I had access to, the following account is very much from her perspective, directed occasionally by my own inferences when her narrative strays into uncertain ground.

When I met her, Madhu was thirty-eight years old. She had been born in Pune, a midsized city on the western coast of India. She described a golden childhood of financial ease and freedom that seemed too good to be true. The third of four children, she said that her family lived in a well-heeled neighborhood reserved for officers and their families. Madhu stressed that she was a healthy child who loved the English-speaking schools she attended: "When I was small, that time I never get any infection, never any current, any those boils, when, *tho* [so], I never get any sick, any psychology. Then I was studying nicely. My daddy told me one time, 'What, what you doing *beta* [little one]?' 'What, daddy, I'm studying.'"

Back then her complexion had not yet been darkened by relentless exposure to the sun, she said. She used to be fair-skinned, with a long, thick braid that ran down her back, crowned with a bow to match her school uniform. She remembered that she was plump even then. Her schoolmates would taunt her for it, calling her "fatty" and pinching her. She told me that she didn't hold grudges, though. She chuckled when she talked about "all this stupidity."

In her memory Madhu's parents were perfect. Mr. Bhat, an officer, doted on his daughter and showered her with praise for her industriousness, in school and around the house. He was always insisting that she stop tutoring younger children and focus on her own studies, even if he was proud of the money she made doing it. Mrs. Bhat was a stylish, somewhat distant woman who wore Western clothes and spent her days at the races or the local ladies' club. Madhu remembered that Mrs. Bhat didn't even know how to wear a sari, the traditional garment favored by women in India, preferring freshly pressed jeans instead. Mrs. Bhat threw money around liberally, lending great sums to whoever asked. The couple was wealthy, elite, and glamorous.

The third key adult figure that Madhu described was a woman she called Kamla. When asked about her mother, the first name Madhu mentioned was Kamla. Then she corrected herself, and said that Kamla was a servant in the household of Mr. and Mrs. Bhat, her parents. But she called her "mommy"; she remembered cooking dal and roti with her; and she remarked that Kamla had arranged her marriage. Kamla was the one who would accompany Madhu on the long train journey to a temple, in search of a cure for her "mad girl"; she is the one who would visit Madhu, when that cure failed, at an asylum where Madhu briefly worked and lived.

At first I really thought that Kamla was just a beloved nanny to whom Madhu was unusually attached. Yet despite her good English, Madhu did not seem middle class. In subsequent interviews, Madhu said that she, too, was a servant. I suspect that Kamla was, in fact, Madhu's real mother, and that mother and daughter worked as servants in the wealthy Bhat household. As a young girl, Madhu existed on the edges of this world and in the shadows of its elite inhabitants; it would not be surprising that she might want to cross into the sun and stand as an equal among them, through memories transformed and enhanced by psychosis.

Madhu remembered how, as she got older, her "parents" left her more and more often in the servants' quarters, while they spent longer stretches of time at the club before moving in there completely. Madhu did not follow them: "They left me to Kamla." When she talked about why, she talked about work. Madhu thought it might have been because she was no longer useful around the house: "I also don't know. They say, I don't know to work, they say, Kamla told, I work. I say, OK *baba* [slang, "buddy"]. Very nicely I got. I do work, I do vessel also . . . you wash clothes, the madam told me. OK. Then madam also poor, then they give forty rupees per month [less than $1 U.S.]. I said, OK baba, I told, three days I came, I stay here, and mommy is staying there, I don't know. I am, I am, maybe I forgot. . . ."

Still, Madhu was unusually well educated for being a servant's daughter. I found her English quite impressive, especially considering she didn't get a chance to practice it very often. Someone seemed to have invested substantially in her schooling. Madhu seemed to think it was Mr. Bhat's idea. Whatever the case, Madhu went to school and loved to learn.

There is no doubt some truth to Madhu's version of her youth. The upper-class Bhats probably did exist and were a part of her childhood; Madhu probably was a bright and talented student. But in the world constructed by her psychosis, these bits of reality from the past became better. Thus, the Bhats were not her mother's employers but her own loving, glamorous parents; and Madhu accumulated thousands of rupees tutoring younger children, pleasing her proud papa. She also claimed to have earned a slew of degrees, including multiple bachelor's, master's, and even an M.B.B.S—the Indian equivalent of an undergraduate M.D. Like many people I met in India, Madhu believed that education was the key to a better life. She told me that she wanted to study hard so that she could work.

It is unclear when Madhu's voices began: she hinted that it may have started as early as her teenage years. More consistently, however, she placed the onset sometime after her marriage, which makes sense: the age fits (early twenties), and the stress of marriage and child rearing may have triggered symptoms.

Madhu described the voices in great detail. She believed they were real and external, but somehow within her as well: "They outside also, in my mind also." She had never seen the speakers, for they were careful to always remain behind her back, but they sometimes spoke through her mouth. My own sense was that though Madhu believed the voices were really "out there in the world," she understood that they were also experiences she alone was privy to.

Yet she connected the voices to her illness only indirectly. Thus, though the voices might drive her "mad" by distracting and harassing her, she didn't construe them as a symptom of "madness." That is, she never said anything to the effect of "I hear voices, therefore I am mad." Instead, she talked about her illness as chronic listlessness and inability to work. *Those* were her symptoms. From Madhu's point of view, then, the dynamics of her illness might be summarized in the following way: "I hear voices which distract me from my daily activities in a chronic way; I am chronically distracted; therefore I am mad."

Madhu reported a variety of voice-hearing experiences. One category of voices was relatively benign, consisting of important political figures who sought her help. For example, Sonia Gandhi, the current Congress party leader of India, beseeched Madhu to feed starving children. Madhu referred to these assignments collectively as her "world stop work" and felt that she had been invested by these figures with control over global affairs and responsibility toward the poor and vulnerable, sometimes as Prime Minister of the World (or South Africa, depending). Like her higher-education delusions, this fantasy communicated that Madhu felt capable and worthy of more than what society expected; lowly housework was not for her, but rather "writing work, full Prime Minister job."

The second category of voices was more sinister. These Madhu referred to as "spirits" and *bhut pret* ("ghosts") who originated from Pune, her birthplace. There were scores of such spirits and they plagued her constantly, teasing her about her weight, stealing food, hounding her for money she didn't have, and keeping her awake at night. They would catch her from behind and corner her in the bathroom, demanding she open her dress and have sex with them or they would bite off bits of her body. On bad days, there was simply no escaping their harassment:

> I do my work, and they put me, knife they put. Knife they put. Talk with us, give me that, give me this, give me that. This I want, this, open your dress, open, open this full dress, give me, I want to do sex with you. . . . I can't get up, I can't walk, I can't sit, I can't eat, eating time, this hand, they took away like this, "We want to eat," that plate gone, and they ate. And this, they say, "Don't eat more," I say, they took and they eat, what I eat? . . . When I come to bathroom, they come, when I go wash this all, and then I go to wash my clothes, they come, taking bath, they come, wash clothes, I wash clothes, I take bath . . . they are there only with me.

Among this nameless horde, two spirits were more well defined. One of these was a nameless ghostly Baba, a Hindu temple priest, who routinely terrorized Madhu by threatening to rob her, wound her, and kill her with a knife. The other, named Harlene, was the leader of the spirits. Madhu said she knew the corporeal Harlene when they both lived in Pune and Harlene's family employed Madhu and her mother as servants. Harlene was everything a young Madhu might aspire to: she had a master's degree from a famous Chennai university, and the rare privilege of having fallen in love with her parents' choice of husband before the marriage was arranged. Madhu believed that, about four years before I met her, Harlene had followed her to Chennai in order to hinder her "world stop work" and claim Chennai as her own territory, threatening to kill Madhu if she did not comply.

Madhu had mixed feelings about the spirits. Considering the severity of their threats and the toll they took on her daily life, I expected her to be uniformly terrified; but this was not so. At times she discussed the spirits in helplessness, awe, and fear; at other times, she made light of them, dismissing

FIGURE 5. Madhu was alone on the streets of Mumbai, as this woman is, before she found her way to Chennai. (*Photo: T. M. Luhrmann*)

their cruel antics as "stupidity" and "nonsense" with an indulgent "kids will be kids" tone. Madhu even joked that Harlene, the most fearsome leader of the spirits, was nothing but a "bloody bum," and giggled that she was "fat" and "ugly"! I was surprised to discover that, in fact, the spirits were not always out to get Madhu—occasionally, they would "think nice" of her, claiming that they worked in her favor, and affectionately pet her on the head. But mostly they were mean.

Though Madhu had not been able to successfully drive out the spirits, she sometimes employed a strategy of appeasement: for example, she would try to soothe Harlene by reminding her that she, Madhu, was neither as rich nor as powerful as the spirit leader, that she was a humble "mental patient" who merely desired to sit quietly and go about her business in peace. When the spirit Baba threatened to cut off her leg, Madhu reasoned with him that then she would become *langdi*, a cripple, and how would she survive then? Madhu also seemed willing to compromise: she once joked with me that the spirits should at least keep away while she did important work, like writing, studying, and talking to me. However, Madhu was adamant on one point—that the spirits must leave her alone once she returned home to Pune and allow her to attend properly to her children and household.

It seemed that the voices were not yet clamoring loudly when Madhu had an arranged marriage at the age of seventeen with Rakesh, a man ten years her elder with two children from his first wife. Rakesh was handsome and fair-skinned, she said. He worked in the construction business—a good match. Madhu was impressed, but she worried that she didn't have enough dowry to get married and that her family's finances would suffer as a result. She went into great detail describing the various encounters between the two families, including the lavish meals she herself prepared, but she said little about the marriage. She told me that it was a happy marriage, and that Rakesh was a good husband to her. Eventually she bore four children, whom she always talked about with a great deal of tenderness and longing. When I asked her how old her firstborn was, she indicated with her hand that he was as tall as me—but said he was five. She had not seen them in over ten years.

Her account suggested that while Madhu was probably struggling with some symptoms of her illness as a young mother, she managed to keep the household running well enough. Then (she explained) tragedy struck. One day, she was preparing dinner with the help of the elder children while the babies slept in the next room. Her brother-in-law appeared. She said he was acting oddly—he refused to eat and insisted that Madhu get cleaned up. He washed her himself, all the while reassuring her that he was like a father to her. He had her change out of her green sari into a green salwar kameez suit. She was very particular about this color detail.

As her brother-in-law threw a few belongings in a purse, Madhu asked him again and again what had happened. At first, he told her only that he was taking her to her natal home, but he eventually said that Rakesh had been involved in a fight, that he had been knifed in the stomach, and that he was dead. Madhu told me that her first thought was for her children. Her brother-in-law reassured her that he and his wife would take care of them while she was gone, that it was getting late, that she should hurry up. In tears, she kissed the children one by one and was taken away.

> Madhu: I said now, cry, what is this, my children . . . they make me lose. They make like this, na. They make me lose, then I don't know . . .
>
> Giulia: Lose your mind?
>
> Madhu: Ha [Yes], they make my mind lose.

Madhu replayed this scene for me again and again, every time we spoke. Details changed, but the anguish—the helpless confusion, the sense of being wrenched away from everything she held dear and of losing her mind in the process—remained constant in each retelling.

Madhu could not remember how long she sat in her mother's house—maybe two months, maybe two years. "Mental problem means . . . I am failed for, in tenth, two years. Failed two years. I am not studying, not study, yes study . . . this, any . . . any tensions come. This why Rakesh is not talking to me, why they sending me to my mommy's house." In one version, Madhu's troubles were triggered by the death of her husband, but in another, Rakesh himself sent Madhu away.

At any rate, Madhu was clear by then that she was "mad gone." She described this state alternately as "tension," "psychology," and "having mind." When asked to explain what she meant by this, she referred to her inability or unwillingness to work: "Mad means, I sit there . . . they told me, 'She is not working in the house' . . . I was not working that time, not studying, not working that time, not make-upping my all, things, washing clothes not I am, combing my hair not I am . . . I am just lazily . . . lazy, lazy girl." Note the clear association of madness with not working: an inability to perform the duties expected of her, whether they be study or work. This is characteristically South Asian. Admittedly, "dysfunction" is central to the *DSM* diagnosis of schizophrenia, but many Americans imagine schizophrenia as defined by its positive symptoms: voices and delusions. In the South Asian context, madness is first and foremost an inability to work and to be proper. That was why Madhu included in her list of symptoms her indifference to her appearance: she wore no makeup, she refused to comb her hair.

She also made it clear that there was a social cause of her illness. At times, it is true, she seemed totally bewildered at the arbitrary way people were struck down: "I don't know, how all, how people go mental, what . . . this girl mental, this girl is nice. I can't make it out so soonly." Yet mostly she seemed certain that mental illness was caused by other people, like a curse. Madhu suspected that her own illness was brought on by her spiteful sister-in-law, who envied Madhu her brood of healthy sons.

The chronology of what happened next was very muddled, but it seemed that Madhu must have left her home and begun wandering. She seemed first to have headed toward a Hindu temple in the city of Pune itself, where she made some money cleaning latrines and slept in the adjoining simple structure that accommodated pilgrims overnight. After a fantastical detour to Switzerland, New Zealand, and the United States (by train, no less), Madhu crossed into another state, Bengal. She said she was taken in by the sisters of Mother Teresa, who cared for her a while before accompanying her back to Pune. Madhu went to Pune to find her natal family. She said that they were relieved to see her, but they were not willing to have her living at home. She remembered her brother filling out an application that got her accepted at Ayodhya, a charitable organization nearby where Madhu could perform tasks like chopping vegetables and washing dishes in exchange for food and shelter. It was a place, she said, for "mad people."

She also remembered that no one ever came to visit her except for Kamla, who spent time with her every day and even worked alongside her. Though Madhu didn't dislike Ayodhya, she felt abandoned and ashamed: "Alone . . . self-conscious. Conscious I feel," she admitted. Kamla, too, seemed to have been dissatisfied with the situation, perhaps because she didn't notice any improvement in Madhu's condition, or perhaps because she thought it cruel that her daughter lived so close to home, yet not at home. Or perhaps Kamla too felt keenly the shame of neighbors gossiping about her daughter. For whatever reason, Madhu said that Kamla decided that it was time to try something different, and the family pooled their money to finance a pilgrimage for Kamla and Madhu to a far-off healing temple in Bihar. Madhu said that her family reassured her that the Baba would tell her "what to do and what to know," and that "Baba will make you nice, then you work."

An overnight train brought Madhu and her mother to the temple, but they were not immediately granted an audience with the Baba. Days passed. Madhu grew increasingly more nervous. She refused to eat. She got "tension." On the morning they were finally invited to see the Baba, Madhu remembered preparing herself carefully for the encounter: she had Kamla plait her long hair, apply red *kumkum* powder down the part, the mark of a married woman, and apply a red *bindi* to her forehead. As she climbed the temple steps to the place where she was to be cured, a *chakkar* (dizziness) came upon her, and she felt as if the steps were being dragged from underneath her. She told me that she rushed down the stairs in a blind panic and leapt into an auto-rickshaw, ordering the driver to go in any direction away from the temple. Madhu's travels took her once more to the other side of the country, to an area on the outskirts of Mumbai. She knew no one and had no place to go—so she sat on the sidewalk and begged.

Madhu did not say much about this time in her life. It was not clear how long she was homeless or how exactly she survived. Occasionally some kind shopkeeper would give her scraps of food, but Madhu also resorted to rooting through garbage, for the coins strangers tossed at her were hardly enough to buy a cup of tea. She would sometimes sleep on the side of the road itself, but she favored bus stops and train stations for the shelter they provided and the crowds of people from whom she could beg money. The streets of urban India are overwhelming: choked with traffic, pollution, and noise, swarming with people and livestock, saturated with a million smells compounded by the heat. They flood with monsoon rains; in the dry season, they are a cloud of dust. I cannot imagine what it must have been like for Madhu, lost and frightened, to navigate this chaos. If she had not already slipped away from reality, this onslaught on the senses might have driven her to it.

Amid this sea of people and frenetic activity, Madhu felt painfully alone. For most Indians, the idea of being separated from their families is the worst kind of nightmare: while the web of extended family can be a tangle of demands and control, it is also a powerful support system. For Madhu, this indifference was the worst thing about being homeless—no clean clothes, food, or water, no one to talk to, no one to care: "I sit only . . . God only knows how I ate, how I recover, how I recover from that."

It is shocking how easily a human being can fade into the background of a busy street. There was a bridge near the hostel where I lived in Chennai, and I crossed it twice a day, holding my breath to keep out the awful stench of the river that mucked along below. I carefully avoided the heaps of trash as well, which were sometimes on fire and at other times were being plundered by goats. One night, I saw a heap move in the darkness, as if the pile of rags and plastic bags and bits of paper had come to life. Overcoming my terror, I looked closer: there were five people there, quietly rummaging through the garbage, keeping some for themselves and sorting the rest into bags. I later learned that they worked and slept on the bridge every night but disappeared by morning, like a dream.

Madhu insisted that men didn't "do sex things" with her while she was homeless. Some of her anecdotes suggested otherwise. She said that a man in a train station ordered her to marry his dark, unattractive son; when she refused, he beat her, then offered her food. Afterward, the man indicated that she could go sleep near a pile of garbage, but she was chased away by an angry mob. Another time, she was alone in a train car with a man. After she told him she was very hungry, he came over and sat next to her, offered her a packet of cookies, and called her "darling" while holding her hand. The next thing she remembered was an "accident," that somehow she fell or was pushed off the train. I had noticed an injury, on the top of her hand, the moment I met her: it was a nasty wound, scarred over as if it had been burned.

Then again, not everything about living on the road was bad. Sometimes kind students at the bus depot would explain to Madhu which bus to take, and sometimes people gave her food. She liked the freedom from demands: "Best thing is . . . living on the road, no work, this, nice way we beg and eat, this is nice. No tension I got . . . not working, just sitting still." Madhu never adequately explained how she made her way as far south as Chennai. In her cryptic, elegant way, she said, "From there, I am here." When the Banyan's rescue team found her on the street, Madhu recalled, they had the following exchange:

> I'm sitting here, and she [the head social worker] came in the car. And she told, "Come here, who are you." I said, "Madhu Bhat." "Why you are here?" I said, "I am here, my mother left me, I am here sitting and begging and eating." "Uh, you want to come with us? Ashram [a place of spiritual and cultural activity] is there, Banyan is there." I never knew Banyan means what, I never knew that. I never knew that all. Then she said, "Come, come. Come here, sit in car, we are taking you." Then I came here.

By the time I met her, Madhu had come a long way. She invariably described Kovalam as "nice," sounding grateful and contented when she talked about her time there. She liked being safe and she liked the routine: waking up at a certain hour, washing herself, keeping her belongings (possessing belongings!) in her own personal cubby. And she could work. She was paid for her work, money she could use to buy biscuits. This made her happy.

She had a remarkably positive outlook. She harbored practically no resentment toward her family. She was looking forward to seeing them all again, especially her children, whom she always mentioned with great longing. She also believed that Rakesh might still be alive, and grew bashful when talking about their reunion, like a young bride. In the days before I left India, the Banyan had begun planning another trip back to Pune to reunite her with her family. They were confident that now that Madhu could work, her family would take her back.

Madhu was clear that she had made a full recovery and that she was ready to return home and lead a productive family life. She compared herself favorably

to other women living at Kovalam, who were still "mad": they talked to themselves, laughed too loud, drooled, and refused to eat. Their behavior was disruptive and socially inappropriate; in comparison, Madhu's was respectful and
socially appropriate: "I recently talk with people, laugh with people, nicely I
behave." The greatest evidence of her recovery, however, from her point of view,
was her capacity to work. Madhu proudly announced that she was now able to
complete all her chores to the satisfaction of the Banyan's staff. In the same
conversation, though, she said that Kamla had visited her in the night with a
swarm of daughters, all identical and all mad, whose murmuring had chased
away her sleep.

It was precisely this blurred boundary between truth and delusion that
made it so difficult for me to reconstruct Madhu's past: one moment she would
be making perfect sense, and then an elephant would suddenly appear in the
narrative, carrying her aloft and feeding her milk from his trunk, the transition accomplished smoothly and with complete confidence. I found myself
straining to keep track of this boundary, marking it down with hallucinations
and fantasies, tracing the family history and notions of illness that directed
its path. I wanted desperately to differentiate the real from the imaginary, to
separate the healthy from the ill, so that I could "get my story right," and even,
yes, "get" Madhu herself.

After finishing the third interview, Madhu and I headed across the street
for one last cup of chai. Like all small towns around midday, the place was
deserted, and every sound rang out in the stillness: crows, a baby crying, the
tinkle of bells clustered at the tip of an ox's curving horns. Then a rhythmic
clanging of drums and metal began, and Madhu guided me to its source, a
tiny roadside temple. I found myself suddenly immersed in ritual: I cupped
my hands to receive the milk the Baba offered, and, following Madhu's lead,
smoothed the rest over my head. The Baba then ceremoniously poured the
rest of the milk and handfuls of marigolds over stone figures of the rat Mooshika, attendant of the god Ganesha, and the rounded lingam, a representation
of the god Shiva. A stern woman rinsed the sculpted surfaces, and the yellow
petals eddied in a swirl of milk and water on the ground.

I watched them, transfixed and slightly uneasy—I was out of my element,
far from the familiarity of the conference room. There, the pace of the interview had been set by my questions; here, it was the drum and the bell and the
Baba's chanting. Then Madhu took my hand and led me before the Baba, who
held a small tray of colored powders and a burning lamp. After he had traced

a few lines on Madhu's forehead with the powder, she used both hands to gather the smoke from the lamp and direct it over her head. Next in line, I submitted obediently to the powder, but then hesitated, uncertain how to perform the actions required. Without missing a beat, Madhu moved in beside me and gently, lovingly, swept the smoke over my head. In that moment, I felt that the "boundary" I had been so preoccupied with had been obliterated, that the Madhu smiling down at me was whole, clear, present. Where she had been clouded, now she was luminous.

Racism and Immigration

An African-Caribbean Woman in London

JOHANNE ELIACIN

Arguably the most important discovery in the recent social epidemiology of schizo-phrenia is that the illness does not occur at a fixed rate across the globe as research-ers used to believe, but at variable rates. One of the best-documented cases is among the African-Caribbean community in Britain, where the risk for schizophrenia is as high as fifteen times the rate for the local white community. Rates among the African-Caribbean British are much more elevated than rates among African-Caribbeans living in Jamaica. This essay argues that there are five features of social experience within the community that may contribute to these increased rates: social inequality, racism, social fragmentation, increasingly fragile cultural identity, and community "expressed emotion." Johanne met Violet during her long-term ethno-graphic study of the African-Caribbean British community.

––––––

When I first met Violet, a single mother of Jamaican origins in her late forties, she had been hospitalized for several months at a psychiatric hospital in North London. It was her third hospitalization since she had been diagnosed with schizophrenia about twenty years before. This time, the police had brought her to the hospital with her family's approval when they had found her disori-ented, wandering the streets with bare feet, and provoking fights with strang-ers. With a small frame and barely five feet tall, Violet looked more like an easy target for harassment in the rough, gang-infested neighborhood of London than a fierce woman who terrorized bystanders on the streets. But she was that, nonetheless.

She was also not unique. On the psychiatric ward of the North London hospital, Violet was one of dozens of African-Caribbeans diagnosed with schizophrenia. African-Caribbeans constitute the majority of psychiatric inpatients at this hospital and many others throughout London. They are thought to be the victims of a growing mental health crisis in Great Britain, in which a significant number of individuals of African-Caribbean descent develop schizophrenia—or, more broadly, psychosis—at a rate up to fifteen times higher than the white British population.[1]

As is the fate of many with schizophrenia, Violet's life was marked by psychiatric hospitalizations, debilitating symptoms, and emotional turmoil. Yet her illness experiences were distinctively shaped by her life as an African-Caribbean immigrant in England. That history had shaped her understanding of schizophrenia and her explanation of why she fell ill. Violet thought that the high rates of schizophrenia within her community had been caused by racial discrimination. But she also saw the social world of her community as playing a role. She thought of schizophrenia as a symptom of the empty, broken community that racial discrimination had created and that her community needed to repair.

I conducted two years of ethnographic fieldwork in London among African-Caribbeans diagnosed with schizophrenia, relatives of patients, and members of this community who did not have a diagnosis of schizophrenia. From many conversations and hundreds of hours of observations, I saw five features of this complex social world that I thought contributed to the increased rate of schizophrenia: the experiences of racism, social inequality, social fragmentation, rapid social changes that overwhelm fragile cultural identities, and community expressed emotion. I believe that they produce a toxic environment of "social defeat" that induces psychological stress and vulnerabilities in genetically predisposed individuals.[2] These factors are not unique to African-Caribbean British or to the development of schizophrenia. However, in combination, they produce a social environment that seems as if it must be detrimental to the mental health of those who live within it. These five risk factors serve as a background for understanding Violet's social world as a black woman of Caribbean descent in England. Woven throughout her story, they provide a framework for examining the daily realities of African-Caribbean British who live with schizophrenia.

THE RISK FACTORS

Social Inequality

Although some members of the African-Caribbean community are integrated into the British middle class, significant socioeconomic disadvantages continue to persist in the Caribbean community; and in the areas of health and education, the social conditions of this group are deteriorating. Their social position is characterized by incomplete integration and the continuous struggle for equal rights and opportunities. The socioeconomic problems faced by African-Caribbeans in Britain are further exacerbated by the "disillusionment" of many second- and third-generation African-Caribbeans with British society. Like their parents, the younger generations straddle two worlds, yet they report greater feelings of loss and uprootedness than their parents.[3] British-born African-Caribbeans are reported to experience more social deprivation than their Caribbean-born parents, and they have higher risks of schizophrenia and higher rates of suicide.[4] In the United Kingdom, studies have shown that psychosis is associated, even more strongly than physical health, with income-related inequality; people who are more disadvantaged are at greater risk of psychosis.[5] The risk is even greater for those who live in poor areas and in disintegrating inner-city areas.[6]

The Stress of Racism

The history of African-Caribbeans in England is marked by enduring racism in all aspects of British life. Discriminatory policies and overt, covert, and institutional forms of racism contribute to a hostile environment and social inequalities for African-Caribbeans. During my fieldwork, participants often described the relationship between race and schizophrenia in terms of "stress," by which they meant that racism causes stress, which leads to physiological and emotional changes, which in turn increase the risk of schizophrenia. They were highly aware of the social inequalities and disparities in their community. They often spoke to me of the historical and structural inequalities that have shaped their social trajectory in Britain, among them discriminatory employment and housing policies and police brutality. Moreover, the participants in my study explicitly linked their perception of socioeconomic disparities, their sense that they were treated unfairly, and their frustration with their own failed expectations to schizophrenia. They emphasized that these factors had a direct impact on their mental health and, for that matter, on the way community members perceived those who were ill and on the way ill people responded to their treatment.

Social Fragmentation

African-Caribbeans in London frequently described their community as "fragmented," as "broken and lost." They argued that the basic structures, such as extensive family networks and partnerships, that were once constitutive of Caribbean community were now disintegrating. These narratives of fragmentation not only reflected their everyday life, but served to construct and reproduce a sense of themselves as fragmented. Thinking about themselves as broken, they learned to describe and remember their lives through the lens of fragmentation.

Rapid Social Change and an Increasingly Fragile Cultural Identity

As a result of migration and varied sociohistorical and cultural processes, the Caribbean community in London is rapidly changing. Many of these changes have undermined the community's ability to buffer their stress, by depleting their sociocultural resources and erasing their coping mechanisms. Not only are their extended families fragmented, but their nuclear family systems are disintegrating. A remarkably high percentage of community members live alone. Many people have, in effect, left the community and assimilated into the British mainstream. As a result, this generation of African-Caribbeans in England express great anxiety over losing their sense of who they are.

Community Expressed Emotion

Community expressed emotion is a term I draw from the theories of expressed emotion and the "double bind."[7] Research studies have shown that when people with schizophrenia return home from the hospital, those whose caretakers express critical or hostile emotions are more likely to relapse. The classic "double bind" scholarship argued that patterns of communication that created the sense of being trapped or defeated could lead to illness in the first place. I found in the African-Caribbean community a pattern of hostile, critical emotion, not limited to the family or even the specific program of post-hospitalization care, but permeating all levels of social interaction of the patient. I offer the framework of "community expressed emotion" to conceptualize the emotional tone I saw in the Caribbean community. I do not make these observations to criticize the community, but to capture the widespread criticism and intense experience of shame and anger that its members often experience as a group and that are reinforced and mirrored within their interpersonal relationships, within the community, and in their families. To live in such an environment, I believe, is to experience oneself as ashamed, broken, and having fragile ties to a shared cultural identity.

Violet's narrative of schizophrenia touched on all five of the risk factors I identified. As she spoke to me, she described family fragmentation, social deprivation, racial stress, and a constant experience of defeat in everyday social settings. Her story gives us a window to her internal world and to the experiences of African-Caribbeans afflicted with schizophrenia in England—their losses and their attempts to make meaning of a devastating psychiatric illness.

During my first visits with Violet, she had been in the hospital for several months and was in the process of rebounding from her recent psychotic episode. She was eager and ready to leave the hospital. She no longer held the delusion that her psychiatrist had impregnated her with twins. She recognized her adult daughter who visited her on the ward. She did not think anymore that her daughter was still a toddler and that she had left her all alone and vulnerable at home. She was able to differentiate her false beliefs from reality. She no longer spent her day sobbing in isolation, the image of a "mad" woman, unkempt and aggressive.

In fact, in our first interview, dressed casually and adorned with makeup, Violet looked refreshed, even graceful. Sitting with me in the small lounge at the hospital with the TV running incessantly in the background, Violet described comfortably, in a soft voice, the time when she was "ill," when she was "not herself":

> I did not like the illness and the way it makes me do things and wander the streets, and shouting. I never used to do that, you know [when I was well]. I left the house and went down the street and I would be shouting and saying things to people, which I never do. So, when I remember back, like now, when I remember back, it's frightening to say I could get hurt by going out there interfering with complete strangers. It frightens me, and I don't like it. . . .
>
> [When I was ill], I got up in the mornings, I just dressed and wandered the streets. I remember I went in a McDonald's, went upstairs. I don't know how I got outside near the roof. I left my slippers there, came back and walked bare footed in the streets. . . . You know, as I said, I did things like that because the medication wasn't working. . . . I realized in hindsight here [the hospital] is better because at least you are inside and the nurses, they keep an eye on you. You don't have to go outside and say, make a fool of yourself to the neighbors or whatever.

This conversation was the beginning of a series of interviews spanning more than a year, in which we discussed her experience of living with chronic mental illness.

Violet was well aware that she had been diagnosed with schizophrenia. Indeed, she knew she had been living with the symptoms of schizophrenia for nearly twenty years. Many psychiatrists had treated her. Many friends had talked about it with her. The high rate of schizophrenia within her community was common knowledge. Yet Violet never referred to herself as "schizophrenic" or as having schizophrenia. She referred to her emotional struggles simply as "the illness," a neutral term for the mysterious disease or, in her view, an entity that "takes over her," her physical ability, will, and cognition. She avoided the term *schizophrenia* not because she didn't know it but because it meant too much. In the world of psychiatry that she had become a part of over the years of her treatment and hospitalizations, schizophrenia is viewed as the worst kind of madness. While the treatment and prognosis for schizophrenia have improved drastically in the past few decades, helping many patients to live independent and productive lives, the diagnosis is still interpreted by many as a life sentence. But in Violet's world and her African-Caribbean community in England, the diagnosis also stands for a lifetime of emotional and physical struggles; it is an expression of social exclusion and a symbol of racial discrimination. She said that being diagnosed could even make you ill:

> I don't know if you notice, for most black persons with mental illness, the first thing the doctors, they all say, "You're schizophrenic"; it's a known fact—as I said, you know, with my case . . . as soon as my sister took me to my doctor, and they were explaining to him what happened to me, he said straightaway I was schizophrenic. He said it straightaway, straightaway! So, what I am saying is that even if I wasn't at the time, although I was a little depressed [because] I was crying and everything. . . . So, before I knew it they took me to a place in Barnet, and I was put on medication. Even if I wasn't fully ill, over the years with the amount of medication you get, it would definitely drive you that way . . . I mean before you get to that stage, [you could] get a little counseling and without putting you on medication. Once you [are] on it, it gets in the system and your body gets used to it and you can't do without it. I thought maybe I would be able to come off medication and you know, sort myself out. But, I realized, even as I get older it's in my system so long, the body can't do without it, I need it.
>
> The doctors, they don't understand black people. . . . Say for instance you might be talking and you raise your voice, they might say it is a sign of madness. . . . A person might be on the street in argument with somebody or whatever, shouting, the police come, they bring you here, [to the hospital] you see? . . . There's nothing wrong with the person . . . but they are not going to believe you [because] they *assume* your mental state. . . . Before you know it you're in here and that is it.[8]

Violet says many things here. She says that doctors simply presume that black people are likely to have schizophrenia. She says that African-Caribbeans in Britain are misdiagnosed with schizophrenia because white clinicians do not understand African-Caribbean culture. She questions the usefulness of medications, claiming that patients are often overmedicated and that the powerful antipsychotics cultivate a dependency akin to addiction. She thinks that police are too involved in psychiatric admissions, and that they interpret cultural behaviors like gesturing as threats. And she thinks that along the way, all these misinterpretations and misjudgments can make a scared person fall sick with the illness even if they weren't ill up to that point.

These are important issues; I heard them again and again from community members. The debate about the elevated rates of schizophrenia among individuals of Caribbean descent has been on the British national stage for decades and still garners sustained press. While I was in the field, at least once a month there was a research article or some kind of news coverage about this topic in the media. In the community, almost everyone I spoke to knew about the schizophrenia crisis and had an opinion about its cause that inevitably involved discussions about the role of race, misdiagnosis, and government conspiracy theories. At the same time, no one suggested that it was all a mistake—all misdiagnosis and conspiracy. There are many people like Violet, and it is clear that something psychiatric is deeply wrong.

African-Caribbeans constitute about 1 percent of the population in England.[9] Yet they are overrepresented in prisons and secure psychiatric wards.[10] They are more likely to be diagnosed with schizophrenia than their white British counterparts. Once in the mental health-care system, African-Caribbean patients are more likely to be forcibly treated, and their treatments are more likely to rely on psychotropic drugs than on psychotherapy.[11] They are also perceived as more violent and potentially dangerous than white patients with schizophrenia. There have been high-profile cases of British African-Caribbean patients' deaths in psychiatric hospitals.[12] The elevated rates of schizophrenia diagnosis among British African-Caribbeans has fueled anti-immigration sentiments and reinforced a stereotypical image of blacks, particularly young black males, as violent and pathological.[13]

Yet while Violet challenged the diagnosis of schizophrenia and questioned the effect of medications on the course of her illness, she also acknowledged that she was ill. She described the illness through a complicated tale of loss, abuse, and exclusion that she recounted to me over the course of a year.

Violet's story begins with the typical Caribbean immigration. Her dad was the first in the family to migrate from Jamaica to England. Then her mom joined him, leaving behind their five daughters. At that time, Violet was only eight years old. Gradually, her parents sent for the youngest, and then the two older sisters, within two years of their departure to England. Violet was one of last two daughters to migrate and join the rest of the family, which now included her three youngest siblings, who had been born in England. By the time she left Jamaica for England, Violet was seventeen. She had been separated from her parents for nearly a decade.

Left behind in Jamaica, Violet moved from house to house, living with relatives and family friends. It was not easy:

> I experienced a lot of horrible, horrible things. . . . When we [were] staying with my sister's godmother, she really turned nasty. We were quite young and we had to cook our own food. We had to wash our own clothes before we go to school. We used to wash and hang them on the fence, and when we come home from school in the evening, if it rained, they were still there, wet. We had to cook outside with fire stone and when it's wet, you can imagine trying to get firewood to cook. My sister used to cry and look up in the sky, because my mum went in the aircraft. Then, my aunt, she did not even want us to go and get dinner. She would say to her daughter the dinner was ready. Take dad's dinner in, my uncle dinner in, and then sort of call you when she feels like it.

As a young child she lived first with her sister's godmother, who neglected her and left her to cook her own food and wash her own clothes. Then she moved with her uncle and, as Violet described it, "the nightmare continued":

> We left that house and went to live with my other sister and the nightmare started all over again. My sister's boyfriend at the time always came in our bed to molest us and everything . . . I did not tell my parents when I came here. I told my sisters . . . I don't think they fully did believe until about two years ago. I told this lady and then a month after, she rang me and said guess what? "I heard he's gone to prison for raping a nine-year-old baby, a little girl." I rang my sister and said you believe me now? A lot of things happened. I know that they contributed to the illness. You try to put it behind you and move on, but things didn't. . . . And the last straw now, as I said the job, when I did find an office job that I liked, the girls were the last straw. It was awful. The only thing I said to my sister, I blame you because, although you knew how bad it was when you came like she didn't say to the parents how bad it was. She forgot.

She was again mistreated, excluded from family activities and denied food.

Violet was excited to move to England. She thought it would be a new beginning, away from her history of pain. She once joked about telling her sisters at the airport that she was leaving Jamaica and would not look back.

At first things were fine. She reunited with her family, finished her studies, got involved in a relationship, and had her daughter. However, shortly after the birth of her daughter, she was abandoned once again, this time by her daughter's father. In hindsight, Violet admitted that during her twenties, she was under considerable stress and may have exhibited some signs of emotional health problems. With the support of her family, she was able to cope, to manage her day-to-day activities and raise her daughter, at least for a while.

Violet experienced her first major psychotic breakdown and was diagnosed with schizophrenia in her mid-twenties. At that time she was working as a secretary in a London firm, with other young Caribbeans. She felt that she was a talented, hard worker. Her supervisors praised her, she said. But she also drew the jealousy and hostility of her coworkers, who, she said, excluded her by giving her the "silent treatment." It is always hard to interpret someone's account of falling ill with schizophrenia, because their reports of ill treatment may simply be the expression of paranoia. But it is clear that she thought the job was stressful.

With the support of her family, Violet recovered from that first episode, and for several years she held multiple part-time jobs, providing for herself and her daughter. But after each subsequent episode, often precipitated by a major stressor, it became increasingly difficult to recover. With every psychotic hospitalization, she spent more time in the hospital than during the previous one—taking weeks, then months, to recover. Occasionally her symptoms flared and she needed to stay home from work. Over time, it became harder for her to maintain a permanent position and to find employment.

In her late forties, when I met her, finding a job had become difficult for Violet. Although she had several years of work experience and was skilled at computers, she had struggled to find work, even as a cashier at the local supermarket. She had completed several of the special trainings for clients with mental illness, but to no avail. She said she was willing to do anything, just to keep her out of her apartment and give her a sense of purpose. But she was a middle-aged black woman, and she carried a label of schizophrenia that she believed she must disclose to potential employers. Violet felt that the odds were stacked against her. Indeed, the unemployment rate for people with schizophrenia in England is excessively high, over 80 percent.[14] Moreover, as an African-Caribbean, she belonged to an ethnic group that has one of the highest rates of unemployment in the United Kingdom. After a string of rejections and disappointments, she had lost all hope of finding a job.

Violet took pride in being a self-reliant, independent woman. Work gave her purpose, kept her busy, and gave her a sense of accomplishment. But when she looked back at her life, she only saw failed opportunities and losses. She spoke mournfully about watching women with their "smart" outfits in the morning, rushing to work. Now, she had nowhere to go. She wanted to buy a house, like many women of her generation, and have disposable income to take regular trips to the Caribbean. With years of crippling psychiatric symptoms and unemployment, she relied on the government to meet her basic needs for food, housing, health care, and support of her daughter. Instead of being a contributing member of society, Violet saw herself as a liability, a dependent on government aid and, eventually, on her daughter.

Violet grappled with these losses in her life and with self-expectations. She was reminded every day of her unfulfilled dreams by watching her daughter, a mirror of her younger self, getting ready in the morning to go to the university, with her future ahead of her. She said to me, with envy and sadness in her eyes, "This used to be me once." At times of great pain like this, a loss of touch with reality seemed almost desirable. She thought that the disconnect she felt in active episodes of illness provided some comfort and escape from the realities of her life. During periods of mental clarity, Violet was painfully aware of her truncated life. She spent her days looking out her window, watching the crowd of men and women in their business clothes going to work, living dreams she had abandoned.

Without a job to go to in the morning, Violet's primary day-to-day challenge was boredom. Her daughter was a busy college student; soon she would leave the nest and become independent of her mother. Violet spent her day in idleness, walking, window-shopping on the main streets, or at home watching soap operas. After a while, these routines lost their appeal. She lived in what sociologists call a "service ghetto," an urban area packed with institutions that cater to those struggling with mental illness. So she had access to day care centers, community programs, soup kitchens, and the like. While these institutions are lifelines for people like Violet, they were also constant reminders of her disability and her shrinking social network. She didn't want to admit that she was one of those people who can't function independently, who drool or talk to voices no one else can see, outcasts from society. She wanted to branch out, to make friends with "normal" individuals, not just those who struggled with a mental health problem. But she couldn't. Healthy African-Caribbean British wanted nothing to do with her—let alone Britons of other racial and ethnic backgrounds.

And being African-Caribbean made thing worse. Like everyone, Violet would have liked to have a social network of friends, to have work, and to find love again. However, finding a suitable partner is a challenge for black women in England, even for those who are not ill. Violet was acutely aware of the difficulty. She often talked about black women in England and the fact that most of them are single mothers. Indeed, it has become a major social crisis in the Caribbean community:

> I was listening to the news going back a couple months ago. They said nine out of ten black men go out with white women. The black women don't have any fellows around because the black men are going out with the white women these days. That I don't like. Not many are going out with black women; they don't got anybody. A lot of them are having children with black women and then going off with white women and look after them and their children better than their black children. . . . They are not doing enough to take care of their black family. Even all the football players on the telly are with white women. When you go out it's all you see. With the schoolchildren they are only interested in the white girls, not the black girls. They aren't looking at them no matter how pretty they are.

She was sad about her fractious, fragmented community, and she was sad that so many men abandoned it and made finding companionship difficult for black women. She too was a single mother, left by her black partner to raise their child alone. Her sense of the state of the community seeped into her understanding of her psychosis and into her symptoms. One day, when she was in the midst of a florid psychotic episode, she walked up to a white woman with a mixed-race child at a local bus stop and unburdened her intense feelings about mixed-race children. That woman cursed her and chased her away. Looking back, Violet thought she was lucky she escaped unharmed.

It is not uncommon that people with schizophrenia become more isolated over time. Violet carried on her body the signs of being treated with high doses of powerful antipsychotics. She looked bloated (antipsychotics, particularly the new-generation ones, sometimes lead to substantial weight gain). Her face and fingers were swollen. Her hair had thinned dramatically; she had bald spots and wore an ill-chosen wig that made her look ten years older. Being heavier, she walked more slowly. Violet felt that she didn't need to tell people she was mentally ill, because her body announced it. And of course, when her symptoms flared, she behaved in ways that were "not herself." She fought with strangers, neighbors, and friends. Even when well, she was afraid of traveling alone, of taking public transportation to the city. She described this sense of not being herself:

I'm not the same person as the girl who used to do things. I give up. I give up feeling. It's easier, you know? I wake up in the mornings and I used to enjoy my coffee. That used to wake me up. I drink it now just for drinking's sake. It's not nice. I don't know what it is. I used to wake up at quarter of seven, seven o'clock and have my coffee and sit with it and go for the walks. Even that, I find difficult—to get up, to dress myself and to go for the walk. My niece said to me, "Oh, you don't phone any more. You used to wake us up in the morning." I don't phone anybody . . . I'm not in the mood. I just sit there. . . . It's my niece's birthday on Friday. I have to force myself to go down and get her a card. So when I leave here that's where I'm going and try to do a bit of shopping. I do the shopping but I wait until almost the food is empty and then I'll go. And then when I go I'll buy a few things that will last. I won't pop back in the week. I can't be bothered. . . . I don't know how to change it. The medication as I said, at first I said to the doctor you are giving me too much because of the way I feel. I get a lot more than I used to get before. . . . I don't know what it is, but I'm not the same person.

When I spoke with her, Violet lived in a neighborhood that was mostly white. She complained about feeling invisible and isolated. She believed that she would not have felt that way in Jamaica, where she grew up:

Your neighbors, they live so close, you see how the houses are [semi-attached], but people keep to themselves. It's not like back home [Jamaica], you know everyone from here to back to Timbuktu. Even when I went home back, in May last year, I miss, like getting up in the morning, saying good morning to people. If you say good morning to a complete stranger down the road [here] they think probably you're mad or something. You know what I mean? Back home, you say good morning, they answer. You may get a reaction and you have a little chat, and it is friendlier. . . . I miss that. I even go so far to say to my cousin if I had a husband, like say most people you know, then I probably would want to go back home. One of the ladies who was in the hospital with me, I saw her about two weeks ago and she said she was going back to Grenada. She was going back. Her flight was the very night. I say to her, "Lucky you!"

Here Violet reports what seems to be a highly subjective experience of isolation in her neighborhood that she thinks has made her illness worse. Yet social epidemiologists have demonstrated that as ethnic density decreases—as a neighborhood "whitens"—the risk for schizophrenia among dark-skinned inhabitants will rise.[15] African-Caribbeans and Africans living in South

London have a greater incidence of schizophrenia in neighborhoods where their neighbors are white rather than black.

Violet often wondered whether she would have fallen ill with schizophrenia if she had stayed in Jamaica. She told me that she would like to return to the Caribbean, but her physical and mental health conditions required constant and high levels of care that are costly and almost inaccessible in Jamaica. And her daughter and her siblings, who were her primary caretakers, lived in London. As her daughter was becoming more independent and making plans to move out of their shared apartment, Violet was left to worry about what would happen to her. She was terrified that her siblings might make plans to relocate overseas. She was fearful that her already isolated life might become even more desolate.

As I was getting ready to wrap up my fieldwork, Violet learned that her only friend had committed suicide. She, too, had schizophrenia. Of all persons with serious mental illness, those diagnosed with schizophrenia are at the greatest risk of completing suicide. On average, schizophrenia reduces life expectancy by up to fifteen years or more as a result of suicide, comorbid medical conditions, and substance abuse.[16]

Yet Violet was one of the few fortunate ones. Most African-Caribbeans in London, especially those with mental illness, live alone, have no social support, and spend most of their time revolving in and out of psychiatric hospitals. Many end up living in halfway houses or in homes away from their loved ones. Violet was fortunate to have had the support of her family, who helped her function independently for as long as she did, who took care of her and ensured that she was not lost, helpless on the streets. Her family support was her lifeline.

She told me that she would not commit suicide herself. She viewed suicide as the easy way out and as something that black people simply do not do. "[We] bear it [the illness], knowing that some days are better than others." This statement provided a margin of hope that Violet would be able to find ways to cope and fashion a meaningful life within her black African-Caribbean identity, even if it remained fragile and riddled with racism and social inequality.

Voices That Are More Benign

The Experience of Auditory Hallucinations in Chennai

T. M. LUHRMANN AND R. PADMAVATI

Persons with schizophrenia and other serious psychotic disorders often experience a wide range of auditory events. We call them "voices," but in fact, people also hear scratching, buzzing, and bangs. They hear voices inside their heads and voices that seem to come from outside, from the world. Sometimes the voices are clear, sometimes indistinct. Sometimes they make kind and even admiring remarks ("You're the one. You're the one I came for"). Sometimes they are horribly mean. Sometimes they command, and sometimes they comment. Existing studies suggest that these voices are more benign for people with schizophrenia in India than they are for many patients in the United States, and that those in India are more likely to experience their voices as people they know or as gods. That may make it easier to live with them. Padma introduced Sita to Tanya in Chennai in 2012.

———————

Even now, ten years later, Padma (R. Padmavati) could remember vividly the first time she met Sita.[1] One of her friends, an obstetrician, wanted her to see this woman who had come out of an operation behaving very oddly. The woman had been admitted for abdominal surgery soon after her second pregnancy. Padma could no longer remember what the surgery was for—maybe a cholecystectomy, maybe an appendectomy. She did know that the surgery had nothing to do with psychiatry, which is Padma's profession. When Padma arrived in the obstetrics ward she found Sita, this ordinary-looking, middle-class woman, shrieking and shouting at the top of her voice, her face distorted by rage, arguing with all these people who were trying to care for her. Sita talked and talked and talked, but she didn't want to talk to Padma and she certainly didn't want to take any of the medication Padma offered her. Eventually she did calm down somewhat. Then she agreed to swallow some of the pills, and soon the illness seemed to clear. "She settled down beautifully," Padma recalled. Sita went home and began caring for her new baby, and returned to her duties in the big extended family in which she lived.

Back then, if you watched carefully, you could tell that Sita was hearing voices. She would hear God speak to her, or a family member, even sometimes a family member who had already died. There were times when things got bad and her parents brought her in to see Padma again. Padma would adjust her medications, talk to her a little, and send her home to her husband, with whom she still lived. Sometimes there were more dramatic episodes. Once the phone rang in the middle of the night. Picking it up, Padma heard Sita's husband say stiffly, "She's not slept the entire night," and then he handed Sita the phone. "There was a very ghostly scream," Padma recalled. "Her voice sounded absolutely—well, it was a completely changed tone of voice. And she was shouting and screaming at three in the morning." And then the husband took the phone back and Padma told him to give her extra medication. They came in for a follow-up visit and everything went back to normal.

Padma remembered three or four crisis calls like that, but not more, over the ten years since she had met Sita for the first time. She was clear that Sita met criteria for schizophrenia. She knew her well at this point and thought that her symptoms still ranked as severe: "In terms of psychopathology, I would rate her as severe. Her functioning, her disability, is mild to moderate. But her PANSS rating [an interview instrument used internationally to evaluate the severity of hallucinations and delusions]—I mean, her PANSS rating would be quite severe."

And yet Sita had never been hospitalized for schizophrenia. She had pretty much always been able to care for her children, to see that they got to school and to keep track of their performance, to cook and serve dinner and otherwise fulfill her responsibilities as wife and mother in her middle-class home. She had a servant who helped her take care of their portion of the large house her husband's family had built many years ago (some of the house was sold to another family at one point, when finances were tight), but she did a good deal of the work herself. She was involved with the arts and drew and painted— quite well, Padma said. She had given up a full-time job when she fell ill, but that was also when she brought home a second child. These days she even had a job that she liked, as an insurance salesperson. "She's pretty good," Padma said. "Of course, she didn't succeed in selling me any. But I have no head for that anyway. My husband buys our insurance."

Sita is a good example of the South Asian puzzle of schizophrenia. From the perspective of the severity of her "positive" symptoms, she was really sick. (Positive symptoms are those, like hearing voices, that are effectively "added to" someone's life, as opposed to the "negative" symptoms, like flat affect, that are more like subtractions.) She did not have a mild case of schizophrenia. But she managed remarkably well in her day-to-day world. We know that among those with schizophrenia, there is a higher proportion of people like Sita in India—and quite possibly more in non-Western countries in general—than there are in the United States and the West. There are more people who seem to recover spontaneously, and more people who never quite recover but seem to hold down jobs and care for their families effectively. The cause of this more benign course and outcome seems to be within the "black box" of culture rather than in what one might call the inherent structure of the "disease."[2] What cultural features can we see in Sita's life story that may have contributed to her better outcome?

Part of the story probably has to do with her parents and the sheer amount of care they provided. Sita's parents did not presume, as American culture allows American parents to presume, that a child is independent at the age of eighteen. In the United States, federal and state disability programs structure their support with the expectation that the parents of disabled adults are not responsible for their care. India has no such social safety net. Parents not only remain caretakers of disabled children, but (if the child is married) they become, in effect, guarantors of the marriage.

Sita's in-laws, on the other hand, never entirely reconciled themselves to her condition. Padma remembered calling them individually—Sita's mother-in-law, her sisters-in-law, and so on—when things were bad and Sita raged and cried for reasons they could not understand. Padma called them to explain her illness, to tell them how to handle her and to reassure them that her worst symptoms would abate. While her in-laws did come to understand her condition as a psychiatric problem, Padma felt that Sita's husband always seemed more annoyed than empathic. "I always felt he never listened to her. He never bothered to understand." And why should he? Theirs was not a love match, but an arrangement between families. Sita's husband didn't sign up for a wife who shrieked and shouted in an irrational fugue. But he never divorced her. He never interfered with her case. And he never abandoned her. He kept his side of the bargain.

Sita's parents made sure that she kept hers. At least, they did everything they could to get her the care they thought she needed to be a good wife. It was her parents who took charge when she needed help. They would pick her up at her house and take her to the doctor. They sat in on her appointments with Padma and made sure she followed Padma's instructions. They filled her prescriptions and monitored whether she was taking the pills. "The moment the husband calls," Padma recalled, "they are there at her place. They are very supportive. In fact, her father had a falling out with one of Sita's sisters. That sister is now in the United States. She felt he was too involved." Padma herself had recently told Sita's father to allow Sita's husband to take more responsibility for her care, and not simply to take over when Sita got worse.

This level of family involvement is not remarkable in India. The hospital where Padma works, the Schizophrenia Research Institute, sends outreach teams into the rural areas. I (Tanya) traveled with the team one afternoon in late October. That day the van visited two rural villages, places so far from the city that it would take a day or more by bus to reach the clinic. In each village a small crowd waited for the van in the village *panchayat*, the equivalent of a U.S. town hall. In these monthly visits, the clinicians will see fifty patients or more in a few hours, the line snaking forward every five minutes or so. And for any one patient, there is a parent or sibling, someone who comes with the client, sits in on the interview, discusses the symptoms, and handles the medication. In many Indian psychiatric hospitals, it is required that a family member actually reside with the admitted patient. The anthropologist Michael Nunley writes about how startled he was by the warm conversational chaos he found after hours in Indian psychiatric hospitals, at least compared to the more antiseptic atmosphere of a San Francisco hospital, as family members chatted with each other while settling in for the evening.[3] In these hospitals, woefully understaffed by U.S. standards, family carry out much of the nursing care: they watch over the patients, pay attention to whether the patient actually takes the medication, and by necessity decide what kind of further medical care will be given, because they are the ones who must take time off from work in the fields to deliver it. Family involvement is a necessity in a society with fewer than five thousand psychiatrists for over a billion people with no social security, no disability, and no welfare.[4] It is not clear that this is good for the family. But it may make things easier for the patient. Part of the story of Sita's success may be the careful, consistent involvement of people whom she knows and who know her.

Another part of the story may have to do with the way they understand her illness. I sat with Sita and her father one afternoon to talk about her experience. Neither of them used the word *schizophrenia*, even though it was a term Padma had used in conversation with them to name Sita's illness. Another afternoon, I visited Sita at home and met her husband. He referred to her "problem" and her "shouting" but never used a diagnostic label. In fact, *schizophrenia* is not a word Padma uses often with her patients. At the Schizophrenia Research Institute, Padma will see eight to ten patients an hour. There is little time to explain a diagnosis. But even with her private patients like Sita, Padma doesn't talk much about diagnoses. Psychiatrists in India simply don't emphasize diagnosis the way that psychiatrists in the United States do, and patients neither demand a diagnosis nor treat diagnosis as important. Talking to me, Sita referred to her "turmoils," to her "shouting," to getting "agitated." She spoke about her "disturbances" and about her "psychological problem." At one point her father turned the conversation to my research. He wanted to know what I thought about Sita's condition. He called it "this kind of thing." When Sita set out to describe how helpful Padma had been, she did not talk about medication or treatment plans or counseling, all of which Padma had provided. Instead she explained that Padma had given her *tulsi* leaves to improve her circulation.[5] When I asked what the most important thing Padma had done to help her was, Sita beamed and said "Confidence!" Her father added, "I am not worried about the medicines inside. The confidence she is getting is good. She is okay. She can do things."

Sita herself attributed her problems to the stress of being a bride and marrying into a family, being "a person who comes to the line late in the family." She described in some detail how tough it was for her when she married into her husband's large joint family. Her elder sister-in-law's husband was ill with heart problems and in and out of the hospital. He would die within the next few years. Sita found herself responsible for her sister-in-law's two children as well as her own new baby, and the home was in chaos. She shook her head, remembering: "I couldn't take it." But she quickly said that Indian marriages were hard on all brides. They move into a new family, with its own ways of doing things, its own patterns, and they know no one. "What happens? Bridegroom, he does not change the place. Right from the start he is in the same place. Only the bride comes inside."

Sita was right about this, of course: it is famously stressful for young Indian brides when they marry and enter a new family. The new bride does not know the intricacies of the way her new family communicates with each other. She has no history of the way small disagreements trouble the relationship, and thus no sense of how to soothe them. Her mother-in-law may see the new bride as a threat to her own relationship with her son, and she may seek to ensure that her son remains more loyal to his mother than to his wife. And the new bride often enters her new family on the bottom rung of its domestic hierarchy. In the years before she has her own children, she may be treated almost as a servant.

Sita defined her own goal in terms not uncommon to South Asians but also not unrelated to her illness: she only wanted good relationships with people. And she thought that her "struggle," as she put it, was one she would win.

> I want good relationship with everybody. That's my point. It's going on, on, on. The struggle is there, you know. Always. But we need to win the struggle. That's the thing. Now that I am having the confidence and a way to get out of the problem, I am able to win it.

For her, here, the "struggle" seemed to mean everything that was rough in life, with her illness almost the least part. This is not the way that Americans think about schizophrenia. Americans are more likely to imagine it as a chronic illness of permanent impairment or, as some American clients put it, "a diagnosis of death." That difference may also have helped Sita cope with her illness.

There was something else. Sita seemed to experience schizophrenia differently, not just because she had more family support or because she imagined her illness with a more positive course and outcome, but because the actual experience of the most distinctive symptom of schizophrenia was different for her.[6]

Most people who meet criteria for schizophrenia report that they hear voices. Sometimes these are actual auditory experiences. People hear what appears to be a human voice. Sometimes it is close at hand, sometimes far away. Sometimes there is one clear, distinctive voice, sometimes two or three, sometimes many. Sometimes they carry on a conversation with each other, commenting on what the person does or thinks. "Look at her. She's getting dressed." A voice can leap from person to person, often identifiable (people say) as a single voice but taking different timbres as it moves from one body to another, coming from and moving among people who are actually present. Sometimes there is no clear voice at all, but a constant murmuring, or sounds that seem to reform into muttered voices, like noise from a passing car that resolves into a verbal patter. Sometimes the voices seem more quasi-auditory; sometimes they seem entirely interior and thought-like, but the person is very clear that the "voice" is not their own. At the beginning of someone's illness, the person often does not recognize that the voices are not real in the world and cannot be heard by everyone. And very often, what the voices say is crude and awful. In the West, at least, the voices that psychotic patients hear are usually both mean and violent. They are often described as the most distressing symptom of schizophrenia: indeed, the voices associated with schizophrenia are often simply called "distressing voices."

For example, Carolina, a sixty-year-old American woman with schizophrenia whom I interviewed in California, heard voices pretty constantly. Sometimes the voices were inside her head, sometimes outside; she was very clear that the inside voice was not a thought because it did not feel like her. She explained that the voices said "That I'm not good for nothing, that I am a bad person, that I don't know nothing, I don't know how to speak English very well, that I'm totally nothing good." They treated her "really bad." The voices told her what to do, although often she didn't do what they commanded. They said to fight, to not talk to people, to be mean. They could keep her awake at night. About three-quarters of the time, she heard them talking to each other about her. One of the voices belonged to a man that she once knew, but not the others. She was very clear that she didn't have a relationship with them. They were not friends. They were just there. She told them to stop, but they didn't stop. In my experience, this is a relatively common account of the way people in the United States with schizophrenia understand their voices.

But Sita seemed to interpret her auditory hallucinations somewhat differently, and that difference seemed to have an impact on what she heard the voices say.

I met Sita in the autumn of 2012, in a lovely old hotel near the heart of the noisy disarray that is urban Chennai. Even at a distance you could tell that she was anxious as she waited in the lobby. Her father sat by her side, a quiet and gentle man. She had come to talk to me about her voices. She knew that talking about these voices was the point of the meeting: Padma had called her and asked her if she would be willing to participate in an interview about her voice-hearing experience. Padma was there to introduce Sita to me before returning to the conference on schizophrenia taking place in the hotel. So it was striking that Sita began the interview by announcing that God was wonderful and took care of her. "We totally believe in this one thing. Let me tell you one thing. We totally believe in God. Wherever we are, whether I am with you or with anybody or all alone, God is there with me." And her father confirmed this, with a mild joke: "He does care about our recording" (the digital recorder was running). Then he turned to her and added, "You're going to be taken care of by someone else."

Sita and her father then went on to characterize God as a kind of force you could invoke. "Everything," she said, "is directed by some extra forces, in everyone's life, in your life or mine." And then they agreed that Sita had more access to those forces than her father did. She put it this way: "I can't explain myself. God is there with me. I say God is sitting in front of me. But you can't see that, unless you get the same frequency I have." Here her father interjected, "I want to describe [this aspect] to you. She has been saying that she hears the various vibrations, since she is talking to God and other things which I might not have experienced." Sita reiterated the point: "Not my father is experiencing this thing. But I am experiencing it. I get the vibrations. I get the frequency."

So right away in their initial encounter with an American stranger, who was sent to them by Sita's psychiatrist and came to talk about Sita's psychotic voices, Sita and her father redefined those voices. Her main phenomena, they suggested, were not auditory voices but emanations and vibrations—and, as such, they were instances of the divine stuff that exudes from God. She said that vibrations were "emerging from all the cosmic energies." They went on to expound this through the idea of *darshan*. The statue of a god, or idol, was mere wood or stone, they said. It was human-made. But when you stood before this wooden statue and prayed, sometimes something happened. Sita's father explained:

> We go to temple, see the deity there. When we pray for him, we find some kind of sparkling come from his eyes to us. His eyes to us. It is only an idol, decorated with various things. When you look at him and pray something, we feel innerly that we are blessed with his sight. That is Indian darshan.

It is not a standard experience of darshan that a worshipper hears vibrations with their ears, as actual sounds. But in describing Sita's auditory hallucinations as experiences of darshan, Sita's father was framing them for her as appropriate religious experiences.

Again, the auditory phenomena of psychosis are varied among individuals. From Western patients we know that people report, at the very least, the following:

Clear, identifiable, unembodied external voice(s), sometimes talking to each other

A voice—identified as a voice—"jumping" from person to person

Real people heard to say words different from the ones they spoke

Whispering and indistinct muttering

Ambiguous sounds (like passing cars, or noise in the next room, or a radiator) that resolve into voices

Internal, "not me" voices

Good voices ("You're the one I came for")

Bad voices ("You smell")

Neutral voices ("The radio is on")

Commands ("Don't touch that")

Scratching sounds, like a field of rats

Pops and bangs and whistles[7]

Sita could well have been reporting that her auditory experiences were primarily of a non-voice character.

As the interview unfolded, however, it became increasingly clear that she did not just hear "vibrations." She said, in an aside as the conversation about darshan continued, that "he or she will talk in some language to me." But it was as if she did not want to acknowledge that she heard voices. She switched immediately to talking about her family: how her two boys were doing, one studying engineering in his second year at university, the other still in high school, studying for his exams. And then she shifted into an account of the family drama that she held responsible for her illness—"that turmoil, I couldn't take it." She seemed to associate "voices" with something going wrong—but not "vibrations."

When I asked her when she had heard voices for the first time, she said, "Oh. Voices? When I was doing this puja for God." Sita was scrupulous, perhaps almost obsessively detailed, in her attention to her family and her religion, and disruptions to this attention seemed to bother her intensely. It was, after all, domestic upheaval that had led to her first breakdown. Here she said that it was in her attempt to do things perfectly in the temple during a time of family confusion that she heard voices speak to her for the first time. "I take everything very deeply. Deeply. Very, very seriously. Whatever is assigned to me is assigned by God, and I have to do it perfectly." Her association of obsessiveness with voice-hearing is not unique; some scientists are even tempted to describe schizophrenia as a kind of obsessive-compulsive disorder in which people think negative thoughts, like the repetitive skip of a scratched vinyl record, and attribute the thoughts to an external source because they can't bear to acknowledge them.[8] For Sita, the voices first came in the temple, and then all the time: "Wherever I go." She began to hear people talk to her directly, people that other people could not hear, and then she heard those people talk to her through another person's (real) body. God, too, would come and speak to her through other bodies.

But the voices weren't always God's. "First, initially, I didn't know whether it was God's voice or some other bad omen's voice." She knew it was not always God because she didn't like what it said. "It was the same voice, but after going there or after following the voices, I mean the instructions or whatever it is, only all that well I knew that no, this is not God's voice. After I was doing that activity, I have been put into so much turmoil." To be sure, the instructions did not seem very harsh. "Go to the temple. Go get that *kum-kum* and keep it on your husband's forehead and your child's forehead." (Kum-kum is a powder used to make a mark on someone's forehead, often as a sign of religious devotion or marital status.) But the voices did make her paranoid, she said. She was pregnant at the time, and a voice would say, "That person is going to take away your child." Sita felt scared when the voices said things like that. But the voices never told her to harm herself, nor to harm others, and in many respects she still felt as if she were the one in control. "I was very logical in my arguments towards the voices. Very, very logical in my way." She could talk to them and she could argue with them.

And then Sita seemed to backtrack. She insisted that many—most—of the voices were good.[9] She said that she heard her kin speaking with her, advising her, telling her what to do in daily tasks. She said that she heard her father back in the beginning, and she still heard him, even when he was not there. His voice was soothing, and his advice was good. "When I become agitated, or when I become angry or something like that, my father's voice will come, 'Sita no, that is not the way.'" She heard her mother and sisters and even her sisters-in-law, although the sister-in-laws "will be agitating me." But not always. "The same voices will come near me and say, 'No, Sita, that is enough for today.'" Her father's voice was always good. When she said that, her father joked that she said this only because he was sitting there, but it was also Padma's impression that when Sita heard her father's disembodied voice, it was a positive experience.

And then, in the midst of this discussion of the kind, soothing voices, as Sita was emphasizing how positive her voices were, my cell phone rang. Except that it wasn't really a ring—more like a loud, strong vibration from the depths of my bag. This threw Sita utterly. Her father told her that the cell phone sound was real and that she had not in fact heard vibrations. But she stopped in her conversational tracks. "I am totally disturbed," she said. "I am not able to talk further." She made as if to leave.

Hoping to distract her, I persuaded her to stay long enough to listen to fifty seconds of a digital track made by a psychologist who meets criteria for schizophrenia herself, to illustrate the experience of hearing distressing voices.[10] It contains whispering and muffled noises. At different points you hear (positive) voices saying, "You're the one. You're the one I came for." But most of these voices are negative: "You smell." "Look, look at their eyes. Their eyes say that you are disgusting." And there are commands—some gentle, some clearly not: "Don't touch that!"

Sita listened to the track with an intense, arrested expression on her face. She said that she had experienced voices and sounds like those depicted. And now she began to talk openly about some of those voices as being bad. "I used to shout . . . the voices I hear [now] are soothing, okay. But sometimes, I have seen [my father] as a bad person who is entering inside." She went on:

> I don't know what or who is there. Someone is coming and disturbing. Maybe it is my own imagination. I don't know. There can be only two answers for this. One is, my own imagination going on. But should be either true?. . . I should be intelligent enough to find out, because it is going to spoil my life. [And yet] so far it has really brought me up the positive side.

As Sita continued to speak, it was clear that she regularly heard a wide range of auditory phenomena. Good voices. Bad voices. Sensory experiences in all five senses, both good and bad. But these days, she said, when the bad voices came, "Krishna comes and tells me, 'That's enough.' He asks me to fight against this." Now, she was calm as she spoke. She decided to continue the conversation with me. And at this point she launched into an account of her relationship with

Krishna—how she truly relied upon him—how she trusted him and how he was going to save her. "I believe that Krishna is going to come and take me away from here. He'll come in person and take me. That's my expectation to the last."

Sita had many forms of Krishna at home. She had a statue that she dressed with her jewels and saris. She had danced with him and sung with him. "When she's alone," her father commented, "she used to dance and sing and dance." She said that Krishna was her lover and that he was with her always. "He is sitting beside me and just hugging me." She saw him when she closed her eyes, either as a small blue child, playing the flute, or as a handsome young man, with Radha or Rukhmani. She heard Krishna's singing in her ears sometimes.

As the conversation moved forward, I asked her if her husband knew about the voices. In answer, she said, "They [the voices] are my support." In fact, she described her voices as her community:

> I have two or three thoughts and two or three, multiple thoughts in my thing. You know that one is my family. The next circle is my society. The next circle is the whole world, something like that. You know you can group it. Say first your point. That's my family. Then after that, it comes through Chennai, then Tamil Nadu, then India. See, something—the whole world—in fact, I will hear voices, foreign voices also from someone somewhere, U.S. or U.K. or whatever it is. Some people have talked with me, something like that.
>
> Like, how you are talking, like that, American English or like Chennai people talks or low-class Tamil. So all kinds of voices mixed together. But when it comes to my family, the voices, what happens is, when that circle is there, that circle just depends is there. It depends on the circle of disturbance. The circle of disturbance is different. That's what I'll tell you.
>
> When it comes to the whole world, it becomes world peace, something like that.

Even from Sita's perspective, this largest aural community was not entirely positive. There was a circle of disturbance. And yet Sita envisioned this world of voices as protective, and she described her social world as located within it. "I have a circle around me. When someone is entering my circle I know. Some god enters, I don't say anything. When some bad enters, I shout. That's why these people say I am so noisy."

Over the years, Sita seemed to have improved. She seemed to respond to her voices less intensely than she once had. "Initially, when I heard a voice or something, I used to react for the voice. Immediately, I used to go to the temple. But nowadays, you know, the temple? What is the use of going to the temple?"

Sita was still ill. An American psychiatrist might have called her "floridly psychotic"—someone for whom the hallucinations of the illness were still vibrant. It was not as if these hallucinations no longer led her astray. Only three years earlier she had heard the *kanchi* of Kanchipuram—the head priest of the temple for which the area is renowned—calling her, and she walked out of the house to follow him without telling anyone. She was absent for an entire day, with just enough money at the end of it to call her worried father so that he could come and pick her up. Many of her religious idioms veered away from traditional Hinduism, even in its myriad forms. Whenever Sita grew more religious, her family grew concerned. They saw her intense religiosity as a problem and as a precursor to trouble.

Even so, she had never been hospitalized, she cared for her family, she worked, and she and her family were clear that over time, things had gotten better.

Beyond the warm support of her family and the absence of any framing of her struggle as chronic incapacity, Sita seemed to have contributed to her own good outcome in the way she imagined and interacted with her unusual auditory experience—with what, for lack of a better term, we are calling her "voices." Her reaction to the digital representation of auditory hallucinations and her subsequent discussion of her own phenomena suggested that the actual auditory experiences were not so different from those experienced by Americans with schizophrenia. Yet she seemed to pay selective attention to these experiences, and it may well be that her selective attention had altered at least the felt phenomenology of these experiences.

One could summarize the principles of Sita's selective attention as follows:

1. She identified some voices and phenomena which resulted from her schizophrenia as culturally normal. She did not regard them as symptoms of an illness.

2. She named some of these voices and gave them some degree of personhood (and godhood).

3. She imagined an "inner circle" of her mind and included the good voices within it. She identified these voices as part of her social world.

4. She argued and interacted with her voices.

5. She ignored or minimized her most negative experiences. She didn't like talking about them and she directed her attention elsewhere.

We know that as people age and improve, the intensity of their voices seems to lessen. The voices feel farther away and less commanding. In addition, new therapeutic approaches (largely based in the United Kingdom and in Europe) suggest that both the content and the frequency of voice-hearing can be affected by attention. Some of these approaches use cognitive-behavioral psychology techniques to alter the way people attend to their voices and to lessen their emotional reaction to them. Some emphasize interpreting the meaning of the voices. A new computer-based avatar therapy has demonstrated that giving people a sense of control over the voices may dramatically reduce both their frequency and their harshness.[11] The "Hearing Voices Movement," a new grass-roots practice, teaches people to name, respect, and negotiate with their voices; practitioners have found that this diminishes the volume of the voices and improves their content.[12] Sita's interactions with her voices followed these new therapeutic guidelines, not because she was taught to do so, but simply because of the way her culturally shaped expectations invited her to interact with these odd perceptual events.

I visited Sita again when I was last in India, in her house on an old and gracious street, wide enough for trees to form a canopy over the road. Her husband joined us for tea. He was under no illusions that Sita was completely well. He spread his hands as he talked about her problem and her shouting. He beseeched me to find a way to make the problem go away. But he also held up his hands with pride. She had been a good mother, he said. She cared for the house. She made sure the boys went to school. The boys did well.

Before I left, Sita pushed on me a book she had gotten at Sholingur, a hill temple associated with the relief of mental illness and evil spirits. Sita would not say precisely why she liked to go to Sholingur, but she went every year, she said, even though it was several hours away. She would stay and worship. She wanted me to go with her. She thought I would like to see the god, and worship him.

Demonic Voices

One Man's Experience of God, Witches, and Psychosis in Accra, Ghana

DAMIEN DRONEY

In Ghana, many people accept that humans are able to hurt each other by super-natural means, and that human malevolence is the ultimate cause of death and illness—the reason that someone falls ill with malaria, say, at a particular time and in a particular way. This "idiom of distress," to use Mark Nichter's phrase, is so common in thinking about schizophrenia that in the Accra General Psychiatric Hospital, far more patients use the term "spiritual attack" to describe psychosis than "schizophrenia." They often interpret the negative auditory hallucinations associated with schizophrenia as the voices of witches or demons. They also often hear God, who tells them to ignore the demonic voices. It is easy to see that a positive super-naturalist experience of voices might be helpful for someone who struggles with schizophrenia. But can it be helpful to experience negative auditory hallucinations as demonic—to give them perhaps more power and authority than they might have if they were imagined only as "symptoms"? That is the puzzle set for us by Charles, a twenty-four-year-old Ga man in Accra, whom Damien met in the summer of 2011.

Charles remembered clearly the first time he had heard a voice that he thought was the voice of a witch. One evening after dusk, he noticed that the lights in the neighbor's house were flickering on and off. Turning to find the source of the disturbance, he saw his female neighbor standing with her back toward him, apparently controlling the lights without touching the switch. When she turned to meet his stare, Charles was terrified, gripped by fear so deep it was apparent even when he spoke of it with me four years later. Some days after this experience, he was sitting in his home when the neighbor's voice rang out, though she was not in the room. "She told me to kill myself." Since that time, Charles has heard her voice almost constantly.

This woman was a tenant renting a room in Charles's father's compound house. She was about ten years older than Charles. He said that he would greet her, the way one greets a neighbor, but he never spent any time with her. Around this time, his mother died. "She fell sick. She had a lump in the breast and instead of my father encouraging her to do operation, so that the sickness will go, my father was slow. Because of that, this thing burst. The lump burst in the body. She became very weak and she died." His mother had been a devout Christian and had prayed often. But then she was gone, and the protection of her prayers was gone too. The tenant had fallen in love with Charles (as he understood it), but Charles did not love her, and she was angry. "This girl, she says she loves me and I don't love her. That's why she has been haunting me." But it was because he saw her flickering the lights with her ill-gotten supernatural powers that she attacked. "When I saw her, she turned and saw me. She tells me that I will die. I know her voice." She was afraid he would reveal to others that she was a witch. And so she set out to destroy him. "Witches stand on one thing. To destroy you."

She attacked him by pouring a supernatural powder on his head. At times he could smell it. Witches hate the smell of the powder, Charles told me, and the tenant witch did this in order to persuade other witches to join in the assault. When the powder was on his head, Charles could hear all the witches screaming at the same time—a terrible sound. Sometimes they all spoke to him.

> They started communicating with me spiritually. I hear their voices competing. They ask me, "What am I doing?" The girl will say, "Kill this girl. Kill this girl. Kill this girl," so they will be asking me, "Why am I doing this?" I used to tell them—I tell them it isn't me. The girl was broadcasting me. Spiritually the girl blocks my thoughts. She blocks my thoughts for the other witches not to hear what I'm thinking. She's using my voice in the spiritual world, in the spiritual realm, to say bad things about me.

She did other things too. She made him ejaculate against his will. "She ejaculates my penis and she talks to me, have I seen what she has done to me?" She disguised her voice as his, and told his cousins lies about how he had slept with his sister. Then he could hear his cousins as well, and he realized that they were witches too. Charles loved his cousins and was unsure what to do with this revelation. "It really troubles me."

Charles had other disturbing encounters with the supernatural. Witches can become demonic birds, he said, and when he worked as a security guard at a European woman's house, he became convinced that a bird in a nearby tree was actually a witch in animal form. His response to this event led his boss to fire him. On another occasion, Charles saw the dwarfs of Ghanaian lore broadcast live on television. When I suggested that this may have been a locally produced work of fiction with dwarfs and other supernatural characters, he insisted that it was a live broadcast of current happenings.

But the tenant witch was the most troubling. Charles heard her voice from morning until night, telling him to kill himself or threatening to destroy his life. "She is following me everywhere I go." He heard her even when he left home and, most troubling to him, she even spoke to him when he was in church, which he had thought was his most effective refuge from the attacks. As these attacks appeared to escalate, Charles consulted a pastor, who confirmed he was bewitched. The pastor encouraged Charles toward action, telling him not to fear witches but rather to be bold and confront them.

So he did. Charles confronted the tenant and told her to stop attacking him. This is when his father decided to hospitalize him for the first time. Charles thought his hospitalization was absurd: "I was going to church when my father brought me. When he brought me, I was even laughing at him. Because there is nothing wrong with me. This simple mistake—that's why I've been here."

I first met Charles, a twenty-four-year-old Ga man from the Labadi neighborhood of Ghana's capital, at the Accra General Psychiatric Hospital. The nice clothes that Charles liked to wear had been replaced by the shabby donations he shared in common with the other patients. Even so, he carried his tall, broad-shouldered frame with a certain unassailable dignity and poise. I thought him to be an intelligent, soft-spoken, and serious young man attempting to maintain his composure under difficult circumstances. The intake narrative described him as calm, articulate, and neatly groomed and dressed. He seemed to be middle class. He said he had attended a well-regarded secondary school in the area, where he got along with schoolmates. He was not a troublemaker. "We don't involve ourselves in trouble," he said of himself and his brothers. It was clearly something of a shock to find himself hospitalized.

The hospital was a ramshackle, maze-like, colonial-era building—now over one hundred years old—spread out over a large property. There was a courtyard in the middle of the dilapidated buildings with peeling paint and torn mosquito nets. That summer the wards were badly overcrowded. By the next summer the census would drop sharply (the director had finally persuaded the city to make some administrative changes), but at the time I met Charles, there were many more patients on the units than there were beds. In the afternoons the patients lay among the trees of the courtyard, played cards while sitting at tables, or shuffled around partially clothed. Some had refused clothes altogether, and others spent their days in conversation with their voices. Charles had been admitted to the cannabis-induced-psychosis unit, although he did not smoke, he said. Epidemiological research has shown that cannabis increases the risk of psychosis and schizophrenia, but in Ghana this relationship is often treated as absolute. Many instances of mental illness are assumed to result from substance use.[1] Many patients on the ward hovered between a diagnosis of cannabis-induced psychosis and schizophrenia, the latter replacing the former on the third or fourth admission.[2] The staff referred to the patients who had been diagnosed with schizophrenia as "the schizos."

This is where Charles spent his time playing cards with other patients, reading Christian literature, and preaching. When I first met him, he was on his third admission to the hospital and had been there for three months. "It's very sad for me to end up in the mental hospital. It is very sad." He hated it. He thought the food was bad and complained that the staff put little care into the cooking "because they think we are mad." He said that the staff still complained about how expensive it was to feed the patients, and that they would sometimes beat the patients with sticks, even compelling them to clean up for them. He did not like living with the patients. "The people around me are not clean; they are sick and all these things. In the midst of all these people who are not clean, how can you eat?"[3] He thought that *they* really were sick.

Actually, Charles thought that some patients were sick, while others had succumbed to spiritual attack. He said that you could tell the difference between someone who was mad and someone who was bewitched by whether they used cannabis or had a family history of mental illness. "When you are attacked spiritually it's when you don't smoke, you don't drink, don't involve yourself in drugs, and it is not in your family, that means that you are being attacked spiritually. But when it is in your family or you smoke or drink, that's when I call it—it's a mental disease." Charles said he worked hard to control

FIGURE 6. A sign and a waiting area at Accra General Psychiatric Hospital, which had over nine hundred inpatients during the period when Charles was admitted. (*Photos: T. M. Luhrmann*)

his behavior, making an effort to not use his mouth when he responded to the voices. "I don't behave strangely in here." However, he said that other patients did not have his self-control. "There is someone here who has been hearing the voices. When you finish talking to me, I'll call him so you can talk to him. He talks to them with his mouth. We tell him to stop." Those people were controlled by the voices. Not Charles. "Some people, their voices control them. But thank God, this voice it doesn't control me."

Ultimately, he explained, the important difference between spiritual attack and being mad was that those who were attacked either died or improved.

> It [spiritual attack and being mad] appears the same. It has the same features. But when they pray and they see no improvement, you come to the conclusion that it's because of the person smoking and drinking. But if they recover that's when you know that it's a spiritual thing. The mad do not get better. The bewitched can be healed.

Witchcraft beliefs are common in Ghana, and indeed throughout much of sub-Saharan Africa. If anything, talk about supernatural causation is more salient now than ever before as economies falter, income inequality becomes stark, and the youths see ever more clearly both the promise of modernity and the difficulty of fulfilling those promises for themselves.[4]

These ideas may ultimately be responsible for the new charismatic churches that in recent years have emerged in Accra. They are the big congregations in raw new buildings, with live Internet streaming and websites and CDs for sale so that you can listen to the sermons again and again. The sociologist Paul Gifford describes them: "Everyone is aware of charismatic prayer centers, their all-night services ('All Nights'), their crusades, conventions and Bible schools, their new buildings (or the schools, cinema and halls they rent), their car-bumper stickers and banners, and particularly the posters that everywhere announce an enormous range of forthcoming activities."[5] Such churches imagine a God who loves them more than he judges them, a God who is present there in the service and who sends them supernatural power that courses through their bodies and attacks the evils that beset them. The ideas here were nurtured by the American teachings of Kenneth Hagin and Oral Roberts, which were widely read in Ghana in the 1980s, but the churches were created by Africans, and they are popular in Accra because they speak to the realities faced by their urban, Ghanaian congregations. A leading Ghanaian scholar of these churches, Kwabena Asamoah-Gyadu, argues that their appeal is so deep precisely because, unlike the mainstream churches, they focus explicitly on the invisible realm of benevolent and malevolent power one finds in traditional African religion.[6] They affirm not only the reality of God but also of these other demonic supernatural entities, and offer specific responses to them and ways to stop their malevolence."[7]

Charles had joined one of these churches. He might well have interpreted his auditory hallucinations as being caused by witchcraft without participating in such a church, but as it was, his pastor was very clear that a witch's curse was to blame for his symptoms. The pastor even persuaded his more skeptical father that the voices were actually demonic (witches are a type of demon in the charismatic theology) and that Charles should be prayed over at length. The first time Charles was hospitalized, his father seemed to have agreed that he would be released to a pastor. "When someone has placed a curse on you," Charles said, "you need a pastor to pray over you to break that curse for you."

These ideas gave Charles a rich theology with which to make sense of his experience. He described the immaterial parts of himself in terms of two components, the spirit and the soul: "The spirit is made up of the mind, the heart. The soul contains the mind, the heart and the inner mind."[8] Sometimes his explanations took on the quality of formal religious doctrine rather than an intuitive understanding, and he became confused when describing differences between the spirit and the soul. "I've forgotten. The soul contains three things. The heart, the mind—I've forgotten." But that there was a difference between spirit and soul was clear to him, and important, because the difference explained why God's supernatural power could defeat another supernatural power—and yet, it remained true that the demons could potentially destroy Charles himself.

Witches did what they did by leaving their bodies:

When they go to sleep their soul—they relax the body, and the soul comes out from them. They go to meetings, they go on meetings. They will meet and discuss—if they want to kill someone they will discuss another person and they will find a way to kill that person. So when they sleep they—they will—when they sleep their soul comes out of them and they will meet, spiritually.

But Charles's spiritual self remained safe from attack when protected by prayer. "She can't attack my soul," he told me. When I asked why, he explained, "Because of the prayer. She has attempted to kill me several times but she couldn't kill me. You can see that because God's hand is upon me." He seemed to believe that his spirit belonged to God and that this protected his soul.

"Your spirit is a gift from God. It's what keeps you alive." But he also believed that his spirit could weaken and allow the witches to break through. "When you have weakness in spirit, they [witches] can attack your soul." I asked, "But because you are following God then it's strong?" Charles confirmed that this was the case.

Charles believed that spiritual weakness in his family was partly responsible for his misfortune: "My mother was very powerful in spirit. She used to pray a lot. So after my mother died is when [the witch] had a chance to communicate with me." The spiritual strength that Christianity provides to the faithful could protect him from the force of evil when his mother was actively praying. However, no one else in his family had the same protectively strong spirituality (and he was concerned that they didn't attend church as often as he would like).

Charles said that local gods and spirits also had the power to put voices in people's heads.[9] I asked him to enumerate all the beings that had the power to speak to people in their minds. He told me about witches, local gods, other supernatural beings—he called them spirits and sometimes ghosts—and ancestors. (These are supernatural beings identified in the Ga religion.) According to him, witches inflict harm on others out of the bilious feelings of their own spoiled souls. They become witches from early exposure to other witches, though he thought that they could acquire new methods of doing harm from the forest dwarfs with whom they conversed. It was when witches' souls left their bodies at night that they convened to plot their next attacks.

People would get involved with local gods and spirits because they offered gifts to humans in exchange for sacrifices. At first, this could help the person who sacrificed to them. "It helps at times." But then their demands would escalate until they asked for something that you could not provide—like a human life. In this way, they deceived people into following them:

> If you are offering a sacrifice at the time you come they will demand something from you, which you are not able to answer. At times they will demand even your children's lives. They will demand a human being. If you're not able to . . . give the spirit or god a human being, they will destroy your life. Yeah, they will cause madness in your family.

Illness could be caused by gods or spirits but could not be cured by them. Many Ghanaians I spoke to agreed that if several members of one family suffered from madness, it was likely that a local god had cursed the lineage.

Ancestors might similarly offer help, for a time, in exchange for sacrifices. However, they too would escalate their demands until they led the supplicant into doing evil. As with the local gods, if someone were to stop serving the ancestors, they would grow angry and inflict illness. "They will also destroy."

Charles distinguished the power of the local gods and ancestors from that of witches: "The witch will be communicating with you, telling you about your house affairs, but the god will control you, seeking to destroy life." The form of control the gods exerted over victims could include possessing their bodies. Sometimes they commanded their victims to harm themselves.[10] Charles described to me one psychiatric patient who had attempted to set the hospital on fire and returned home badly burned. Charles said that a local god had overtaken the patient and caused him to burn himself. That a mere witch had caused Charles's penis to ejaculate—that she took control of his body—he took as a sign that the tenant was a very powerful witch indeed.

It is not uncommon for contemporary Ghanaians, even Christian ones, to search out priests of the traditional religion in times of trouble, but Charles found this concept outrageous. M. J. Field's classic ethnography *Search for Security: An Ethno-Psychiatric Study of Rural Ghana* described the way individuals who were suffering what appeared to be full-blown psychotic episodes with hallucinations, delusions, and disorganized behavior would come to the local shrine she was studying, all of them convinced that they were suffering from witchcraft. Field found that they sometimes improved rapidly. Epidemiological comparisons between Western and non-Western settings (including a site in Nigeria) have found that acute psychosis that does not resolve into schizophrenia is more common outside of the West.[11] Field was astonished by the relief some patients got from their symptoms once they had grasped that the presiding deity would help them.[12]

However, when I asked Charles whether he had ever sought advice from a shrine or traditional priest, he laughed. Then he explained patiently, "Their ways are not the ways of God. They're actually worshipping Satan. You can't follow these people because their ways are not the ways of God." For most Ghanaian Christians (and particularly for those who attend the new charismatic churches), ancestors, lineage gods, and other spirits belong to the same dark world as witches and can never heal. The anthropologist Birgit Meyer points out that Christian missionaries in what is now Ghana "translated" Christian conceptions of the devil into the terms of traditional African religions, so that local deities became manifestations of evil.[13] I asked Charles what could be done for a person who was made ill by their ancestors, and Charles quickly responded that only the church could help, and the only cure was to pray for deliverance. For Charles, spiritually caused disorders were of demonic origin and required Christian healing.[14]

There is an obvious cost to someone like Charles when he understands his experience as demonic. As Charles heard voices, he heard evil beings, and so far, his prayers and those of his pastors had not conquered them. He now knew that his world was full of demons. "Witches are always all around. So through this I have come to know there are a lot of witches in our area. And they are haunting me."

Yet there may be advantages this understanding as well. Charles certainly lived in a world shot through with the supernatural, and it was one in which not only demonic but divine beings had more presence in humans' daily lives than in many other faiths. The new charismatic churches and the Pentecostal churches from which they emerged invite the worshipper to experience God directly—through dreams, visions, and His voice. And God was very real for Charles. He told me about a powerful dream of Jesus opening his hands to him:

> It was when I was in darkness [asleep] and he showed up with his hands open before me. They say when he does that, that means a sign of peace, and, actually, it also happened in Argentina. There was a war between Argentina and Chile, and when they were going to fight, Jesus showed up with his hands open, and they stopped the war.

This brought Charles peace, and it reinforced his long-standing commitment to become a pastor. "I saw that God was very close to me." (It was unclear whether this event predated his affliction.)

Charles's Christian practices provided resources that he described as protective and healing. When the voices became unbearable, Charles read scripture. He said that it helped his mind focus, and it was especially effective, he said, because it was holy and therefore offered protection against witchcraft. (Some American subjects who have unwanted auditory hallucinations find that speaking aloud will dampen their intensity.)

Moreover, Charles heard God speak audibly. When he read scripture, he explained, he sometimes heard the voice of the Holy Spirit saying the words to him. God spoke to him outside of the scripture reading, too, a voice he heard as the voice of a white man (Jesus is usually portrayed as white in African churches). At other times, Charles heard the Holy Spirit reassuring him, telling him not to worry. "I hear the Holy Spirit saying, 'Don't worry, it's part of life. Sometimes God tests us.' I hear scripture, the Holy Spirit speaking in the Bible, the things I read in the Bible—but to me." Charles estimated that this occurred about once every three days.

Charles certainly didn't feel that hearing God's voice was in any way pathological or related to his affliction. This voice was calming and beneficent. It offered both comfort and protection. It also felt and sounded quite different from the voice of the witch. Charles described it as "smooth" and "peaceful." God's voice "rushes through my ears like the wind." It was not disturbing like the tenant witch's voice. Hearing God's voice was "a wonderful thing" that helped guide his decisions. "When he speaks it's like a calm word that that's his—like I'm gonna do something, God tells you 'don't do this, do this one.' That's the voice of God." This helped him "discipline" his mind so that he would not "act in an irrational way." He was similarly comforted when, soon after her death, he was visited by his mother's ghost. He said that she spoke to him in a voice he could hear, and then she gave him a hug.

Finally, understanding his experience as caused by witchcraft normalized that experience for him. Charles's social world recognized the reality of witchcraft. Most Ghanaian Christians consider spiritual attack a real event. Religious leaders, friends, family, and even medical professionals could potentially recognize that a spiritual attack could produce the sorts of experiences that Charles described. When I met him, Charles had been ill for many years, and to most observers he probably seemed simply ill. He was not (yet) one of those who had recovered. But it was realistic for Charles to understand himself as bewitched. It gave him hope that he would recover. To see himself as bewitched might even underscore his commitment to his Christian faith. The devil is drawn to those of deeper faith. "I think I'm called into ministry. Maybe because of this, that's why I am going through these problems."

And to be bewitched is more respectable than being crazy. Charles returned to this point again and again as we talked. When you are crazy, he said, "people don't respect you." His father, Charles said, would respect him more if he believed that he was suffering from witchcraft and not from a mental illness. He'd learned not to talk out loud to the witches around his father because when he did that, his father thought that he was mad.

But this spiritual conviction also meant that he thought his medication did him no good. He believed that the antipsychotic medicines did nothing aside from their annoying side effects. His problem was a spiritual one, and therefore some tablets could be of no help. He told me that the first two times that he was in the hospital he regularly pretended to swallow his pills and later threw them away. However, the nurses now realized this and had begun to check his mouth to be sure that he had swallowed them. "In the beginning," he admitted to me, "I don't take the medicine because I know it was a spiritual thing. But, because I'm here I have to take it. If you don't take it they will bother you. And they don't believe what I say." During our first conversation, Charles displayed no side effects of medication, but when I visited the hospital a second time he appeared to suffer from a dry mouth.

I asked Charles how he knew that he was being attacked by witches and was not suffering from mental illness. He explained that he recognized the witch's voice so clearly that he knew it could not be coming from his mind. He furthermore believed that the experiences of smelling the powder and his penis ejaculating were uncharacteristic of mental illness and clear signs of spiritual attack. In addition, he recognized that this voice operated as a witch does. She picked one trivial issue and pursued it relentlessly with the aim of destroying his life: "Witches, that's how they are," he explained to me. "They'll stand on one problem because they want to destroy your life. They want me to start speaking with my lips; they will destroy my life because I know they are witches. That's why they are asking me these questions." He further explained, "They say witches, when you see that she is a witch, she will follow you everywhere she goes until she ends your life or she spoils you before she will leave you. So that's why she is following me everywhere I go." He thought there were other patients in the hospital incorrectly diagnosed and similarly under attack by witches.

Yet witchcraft and mental illness were not entirely mutually exclusive for Charles. He thought that one could lead to the other. He pointed out a patient who was speaking to himself and gesturing in the air. That person, he said, had succumbed to witchcraft and become insane. Charles explained that this man did not pray and was not as spiritually strong as he was and was therefore unable to protect himself from attack: "He's not strong in spirit, that's why he's talking back to them. That's why he's talking back to the voice. If he was strong in spirit he can control himself. Because he's doing—he will not be allowed to go home, because they will think he's mad." Charles also communicated with the voices, but he did so only with his mind, which the witch could understand. He said that if he started to speak aloud to the voice he would be defeated. He therefore believed witchcraft and mental illness to be potentially intertwined. Witchcraft could drive one mad. But he knew that it had not driven him mad yet.

Several months after our initial meeting, I met Charles in the part of Accra where we both lived. He looked much better in new, clean clothing but had the same broad smile. With pride, he played me a recording of a new song that he said he had written: "California Girl." Charles introduced me to his father, uncles, and friends and then we left to go to Labadi Beach. It was Republic Day and the beach would be crowded. When I asked Charles about the voices he heard, he was quick to dismiss the subject, telling me that the witch was finally leaving him alone. This was to be a normal day, without any discussion of his experiences. As we walked along the busy street, someone called out to him from a car. "Ei!" she exclaimed. "From Accra mental!" After asking about Charles's health, the woman told him that she was happy to see him doing well and wished him good luck. After she left, Charles gave me a sheepish look and explained that she had been a psychiatric nurse at the hospital.

I learned that Charles no longer told others about how he was being attacked by witches. It was only later that he spoke again about his spiritual attacks, which he now said had grown more pervasive. He seemed to have accepted that his family now believed he was ill. As he did in the hospital, he pretended to take his medicine by hiding the pill under his tongue. Still, his family usually respected him and, with some exceptions, they did not mention in his hearing that he was ill. He appreciated the love and respect with which his family treated him even though they did not believe him. According to Charles, other patients at the psychiatric hospital were treated much worse by their families. He explained that "They treat me very well but others say that . . . people tell them that they are mentally sick. Even if they are right people say that they are mentally ill." "So they won't take them seriously?" I asked. "Yes. But me, when I go to the house everybody respects me."

Still, this respectful silence regarding his illness meant that Charles had no one to talk to about his experiences. He held steadfast to his interpretation of his experiences as witchcraft attacks, even though he had stopped trying to convince others of this reality. After an interview, he told me how relieved he was to talk to someone about what he was going through who would simply listen and not judge him. No one else understood what it might be like to hear these voices, and he felt encouraged after sharing his techniques for coping with them. He said that he had even stopped telling pastors about the witch, so that he was quite alone in his spiritual fight. Charles was still focused on not being driven mad by his experiences, and on not behaving irrationally, and this focus seemed to help him control his behavior (he still never spoke aloud to the voices, for example). However, it was a lonely road for him. His affliction had become a secret struggle with unseen demons that he fought alone.

Madness Experienced as Faith

Temple Healing in North India

ANUBHA SOOD

Spirit possession is what anthropologists call a common "idiom of distress" in India. That is, anthropologists have observed that spirit possession is a way of behaving that signals emotional distress. Both the person possessed and the people around her (usually, those thought to be vulnerable to spirit possession are women) recognize that the person possessed is suffering and needs intervention. But spirit possession is not a physical illness, like tuberculosis, where a complete cure is desired. Sometimes, those who recover are understood to retain a relationship with the divinity, and the divinity can be understood to change its personality so that the person possessed becomes more like a prophet—even while she remains someone who needs special care. Spirit possession may participate in the construction of a valued social identity in which voices and visions are signs of the divine and not solely associated with a permanent, crippling illness. Anubha met Sunita in the temple town of Balaji, Mehndipur, where Sunita had lived for more than fifteen years.

The Balaji temple in Mehndipur, Rajasthan, is a popular healing center for people suffering from problems that might be considered psychiatric by clinicians but that are attributed to possession by spirits here.[1] The temple is dedicated to the infant form of the god Hanuman (child = *ba'l*; hence the name Ba'laji), known among Hindus as a divine healer and as *sankat-mochan*—"one who liberates from distress or danger." Hanuman is depicted in Hindu texts and mythology as having special powers to navigate the worlds of the divine and the demonic with equal ease.[2] Besides Balaji, the presiding deity of the temple, two other Gods, Bhairav and Pretraj, are also worshipped in the temple for their influence over wayward spirits believed to trouble the human world. In addition to these primary gods, a number of spirits, for instance, are believed to reside in the temple and assist in the healing process. These spirits, according to the temple myth, were once malevolent, like the ones that afflict people visiting the temple, but were eventually "corrected" and recruited by Balaji to assist in protecting the afflicted. Also, on the hills (pahari) surrounding the valley of Mehndipur, smaller temples dedicated to other major Hindu gods and goddesses were established over the years and are now frequented by devotees coming to the Balaji temple. Finally, Ganesh Puri, the now deceased head priest of the temple, is also worshipped as a deity in Mehndipur for his extraordinary healing powers in his lifetime and beyond. Babaji ("father" or "father-figure"), as Ganesh Puri was affectionately known, was a charismatic healer, and many believe that the healing fame of Balaji derives, in large part, from his life's work and legacy. After his death, a small shrine was set up in his memory on a piece of land close to the main temple. Called the "Samadhi" (i.e., resting place of a great soul), the space has since served as a major site of healing in the temple because it is believed that Babaji's healing powers are still incarnate there.

Even though a range of impediments and adversity in life may be ascribed to spirit affliction and treated in Balaji, people seeking healing in the temple do so primarily for problems that are behavioral, emotional, and/or relational in nature—ailments to which no clearly evident physical cause can be assigned or those that are untreatable in any other way. Generally speaking, Hindus (usually, less elite Hindus) think of spirit affliction as a probable cause of distress, for which they seek healing if someone behaves in a socially inappropriate or destructive manner, experiences serious strife in their relationships and social life, or suffers from disturbing thoughts and unexplainable fears. Often such problems are accompanied by headaches, vague bodily pains, fatigue, sleep disturbances, and complaints of an overall subjective sense of ill-being that seems unexplainable in medical terms.[3]

In Balaji such a constellation of symptoms is called bhut-pret ki bimari ("spirit illness"; bhut-pret = spirits, bimari = illness). Anthropologist Mark Nichter calls such patterns of identifiable psychosocial complaints "idioms of distress": a recognized expression of distress which encompasses vulnerability, apprehension, inadequacy, dissatisfaction, suppressed anger, and other anxiety states.[4] The idiom of distress is understood to be a legitimate reason to demand intervention and healing. And because the spirit is understood to be supernatural, when spirit possession is a socially recognized condition, people who hear voices and see visions can be identified as possessed by spirits. Those around them might eventually decide that they are not possessed, that they are mad. But the individual who hears voices may still cling to that identification and to the view that they are not mad but, rather, gifted.[5]

In local parlance, the most commonly used term for spirit illness is *sankat*—meaning "trouble" or "affliction" in Hindi, the word is used in Balaji both as a synonym for spirit illness, and also to refer to the afflicting spirit.[6] Those who come to the temple to seek healing are known as *sankat-walas*—"those afflicted with the spirit." A sankat-wala usually stays in the temple for the duration of the treatment, which may last up to a year or more. In other instances, the sankat-wala may travel back and forth between Balaji and home frequently and continue to do so for years. While at the temple, the sankat-wala will become possessed, often dramatically—beating her head against the wall, rolling on the ground, moaning, crying, and sometimes singing. During these times, one can interact with the possessing spirit who speaks through her—talking, commanding, and negotiating. Sometimes the afflicted person simply recovers and leaves, never to return. More often, possession is an ongoing process in which the person who has been possessed slowly learns to gain control over the possession, changing her relationship to the possessing spirit. Sometimes the spirit too reforms its character.

The temple receives hundreds of visitors every day from all over northern and central India. Most come for no more than a few days for *darshan*, the "viewing" of the sacred image of Balaji to seek his protection and blessings. In Hindu ritual tradition, viewing the sacred image confers the blessing of the deity to the devotee. In Hindu understanding, the deity is present in the image—darshan is not a symbolic act of seeing the significance of the image, but literally being in the sacred presence.[7] Darshan, thus, is an immediate and personal connection between the deity and the devotee. A renowned, powerful image bestows even the place where it is present with an auspicious power. For visitors to Balaji, simply being present in the place where the powerful image of Balaji resides and seeing the image are understood as healing. But many others who visit for the explicit purpose of being cured of their sankat end up staying in the town for weeks, months, and even years. Most of them are women, as are most who visit the site for shorter stays. My research in the temple was with the set of long-staying female sankat-walas, of which Sunita was one.

I was sitting in the Samadhi grounds one winter afternoon in 2009 when Sunita approached me. She wore a faded, mismatched *salwar-kameez* that was too big on her thin frame. Her slippers, also large on her feet, dangled as she walked. From afar, Sunita seemed to be one of the destitute people abandoned by families in Balaji's refuge that one occasionally met at the outskirts of town. As she drew close, however, I saw that her hair was oiled and neatly tied in a braid. Her clothes were spotlessly clean. She was wearing a *bindi* (a mark on the forehead that signifies devotion), and a cloth bag hung from her shoulder. She must have been in her late thirties, or perhaps a little older. Except for her raggedy attire, Sunita looked nice. Without greeting or an introduction, she pulled out a piece of paper from her bag and offered it for me to see. The typing on the paper looked like a bank receipt, but the fading ink was difficult to decipher. It was an old piece of paper, torn on the edges and yellowed with time. It had Sunita's name, the word for "guardian" with the name of a certain Mr. Aggarwal underneath it, a date from the year 1998, and an amount of "Rs. 1500" handwritten on it. Sunita told me that the receipt was from a local bank across the street.

The rest of Sunita's story was difficult to follow. Initially, I could only gather bits of it. She mentioned money in the bank, an uncle who had deposited it there, and a train she had to take that left from Balaji only once a week. She hopped from one topic to another and got lost in following tangents of conversation, which she interspersed at times with entirely random, unrelated thoughts and sentences. An observer with a psychiatric lens would call her "disorganized," a clinical term that refers to someone's difficulty in maintaining an orderly flow of thought and language. Yet Sunita could still communicate what she needed to, albeit with time. After an hour of questioning and listening to her, I understood that she needed my help in retrieving some money she had in a local bank. The money had been deposited in Sunita's name by an uncle who had visited her in Balaji regularly until some years ago. He had stopped visiting now, and without him to sign as her guardian for the bank account, Sunita could not claim the money.

Sunita told me that she had been observing me in the Samadhi grounds for many days and had decided to approach me for help only after Babaji had given *aagya* ("permission"). It sounded really peculiar the way Sunita put it, as if Babaji (the deceased head priest of the temple whose idol stood in these grounds) had *actually* conversed with her. When I asked her more, it became clear that this was, in fact, exactly what she meant. She took out some notebooks from her bag and showed me how she had been writing what Babaji narrated to her. She told me that she had hundreds of such notebooks filled with Babaji's dictates. I glanced through one of the notebooks to see that it consisted of a beautifully handwritten narrative and many figures and diagrams of human hands and geometric shapes. Sunita lent the notebook to me to read later. I also learned that she wished to buy a train ticket and gifts with the money in her bank account, in order to visit her daughter, who lived with Sunita's mother in the small city of Bilaspur in central India. She told me that the city was in the state of Madhya Pradesh. But Madhya Pradesh had split into two states in 2000, and Bilaspur was now located in the state of Chhatisgarh. That Sunita didn't know of this critical change suggested that she had not been in touch with her family in at least a decade.

In return for my help, Sunita promised to give me "knowledge about me" (*aapke bare mein gyaan de sakti hun*). When I asked her what that meant, she told me that she had a magical ability to know people for who they *really* are. She had been honing this special skill under Babaji's apprenticeship for many years.

I was intrigued. I knew that Babaji had been a much revered priest in Balaji in his lifetime, acclaimed as having great powers to heal people suffering from spirit afflictions. In fact, many women claim to have a direct communicative relationship with Babaji and other deities in the temple. The Samadhi, a fenced compound with a marble statue of Babaji sitting in deep meditation, has become a holy place of worship, and many spirit-afflicted women spend hours praying and practicing trance in front of Babaji's image. The possibility of such an intimate, interactive relationship is considered an important aspect of the magical powers of the site. Sunita's claim that she was acting according to Babaji's aagya was quite ordinary in this context. What was unusual about what Sunita told me, though, was the way Babaji spoke. Many devotees in Balaji often speak of "feeling," "sensing," or "knowing" God's direction. They do not say that they audibly hear God's voice. Sunita could hear Babaji speak with her ears, and she recorded what he said in writing *as he spoke*.

Sunita was convinced that her notebooks were treasures of important knowledge and of immense value to temple authorities. She wanted to offer them to the temple officials because they contained—as she understood it—a

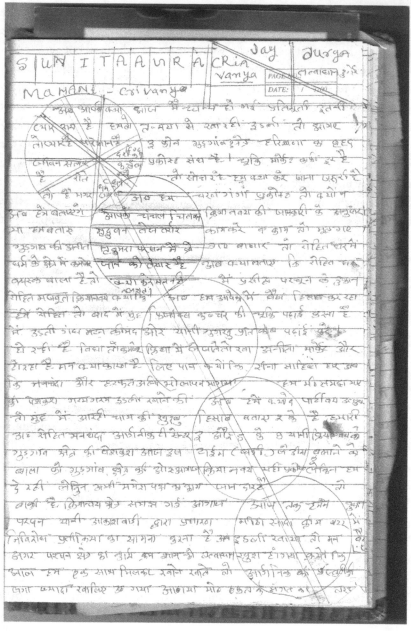

FIGURE 7. A page from one of Sunita's notebooks.

wealth of knowledge about happenings in the temple town and healing from spirit affliction. She hoped that the temple officials might even give her some money in return for the notebooks. She asked me if I could speak with them on her behalf. Reluctantly and ambivalently, I agreed that I would accompany her to meet someone that she considered appropriate. So she gave me the notebook to read over.

I spent the evening with that notebook. It began with Sunita's name on the front page and a dedication to "Shriya Agarwal," which I gathered was her daughter, and an address in Bilaspur below it. Sunita had titled her narrative "The story of my past life" (*mere punrjanm ki kahani*). The language of the narrative was literary and graceful. The story was told in the third person. It started by introducing a newly married young woman and her dreams of having a good life with her husband. She is filled with hope and romantic thoughts when she gets married. She moves away from the comforts and security of her natal home to her husband's house. But those dreams are soon shattered when her husband and in-laws turn out to be cruel and give her a very difficult time. They demand dowry and beat her. The woman begins experiencing a great deal of mental anguish. As time passes, she feels increasingly distressed and fearful. She begins to hear and see spirits residing behind the walls of her husband's house (*deewaron ke peechhe bhooton ka vaas tha*). She gives birth to a child, but the husband does not let her live with her baby girl. From there on, the story became a deeply reflective and poignant narrative of the hardships in a woman's life. It spoke about the victimhood and injustices that women experience in male-dominated society. Sunita wrote about how this particular woman in her story has continued to fight for her existence despite the tragedies in her life and has continued to place hope in God. The narrative read like it had been written for an audience. I suspected that the story was Sunita's own, and as I learned more about her life in subsequent weeks, I knew that it was. But Sunita did not claim the story to be hers in the entire time that we knew each other. She insisted that it was a text dictated word-for-word by Babaji.

About halfway through the notebook, however, the narrative became less and less coherent. Sunita had drawn a lot of diagrams with straight lines, geometrical figures, and tracings of hands on subsequent pages, and cramped sentences in between the shapes and lines. There were a lot of religious references, devotional hymns, and sacred Sanskrit verses strewn in with unconnected sentences. Soon the sentences became incomprehensible, only a string of gibberish words. In subsequent weeks, Sunita showed me many of her other notebooks and they had a similar pattern. They began with a dedication to her daughter Shriya and continued with a biographical narrative. At times the narrative went on for many pages and at other times it ended abruptly after a few, or it began somewhere in the middle and led into collections of unrelated words, drawings, and religious content. Sometimes certain sentences in between the lines and figures contained information about the lives of persons that Sunita might have known or believed she knew. At other times, it spoke about events in the temple town. But none of these themes were coherent or complete stories. And yet, despite the chaos that followed the narrative in each of the notebooks, they were still strangely meaningful. In reading them, I felt like I had experienced a piece of Sunita's difficult and distorted world. I thought that the notebooks might be her way of communicating with her absent daughter.

Sunita had lived in Balaji for fifteen years and knew a lot about places and people there. She liked to brag about her knowledge of all the streets and alleys in town, especially to someone like me who didn't know much past the temple and the market leading up to the Samadhi. In ensuing days, Sunita took me to a number of small tea shops and temples in Balaji that I had not known about. But she never took me to the bank that she had spoken about in our first meeting. One day, I asked her about it. Then she took me past the town crossing, into the Balaji temple, and up a series of stairs and alleys to an office area where employees of the temple management worked—another place I had not known existed. We wandered around in a room full of heaps of paper and people working at desks, looking for someone Sunita said could deal with her "case." But she soon explained that this person wasn't to be found and we would have to go again another day when he was available. So instead, we sat down to have tea and snacks at a local restaurant. When I asked her who she had been looking for, Sunita told me that he was someone Babaji had told her about. She did not know his name, she said, but she would recognize him if she saw him. Claiming this kind of special knowledge was something she did repeatedly. She had been calling me "Kusum" instead of my name. I had tried correcting her a few times about my real name, but she insisted that my *real* name was Kusum. That's what Babaji had told her.

In interactions with Sunita I felt like I had landed in an alternate world where, as Sunita said, "nothing is how it seems." Our conversations were peculiar, directed by Sunita, who connected apparently random topics and followed thoughts that I wasn't privy to. I could see that she had the symptoms a psychiatrist would classify as psychosis. Her drift from a shared reality was apparent in her disorganized speech, delusional thinking, and what appeared to be auditory hallucinations that she interpreted as communication from Babaji. What was so striking about Sunita, however, was that she had found ways to manage her symptoms within the social logic of the temple. She was able to understand her hallucinations within a worldview in which communicating with God is common. What a psychiatrist would call her delusions—"Do you think you are a very special person, with special abilities?" is one of the diagnostic questions used to assess psychosis—she could experience as legitimate in the magic-infused world of Balaji. Moreover, Sunita had a real social place at the temple. People recognized her, spoke to her, and behaved as if she belonged.

When I met her, Sunita had lived in a small room in one of the oldest *dharmshalas* (philanthropic guesthouses) in Balaji for over a decade. She told me that the owner of the guesthouse occasionally threatened to evict her but had let her stay in the little room this long for a paltry Rs. 20 a month (less than half a dollar). She earned occasional money from working in the many restaurants that lined the street leading up to the temple and served the huge influx of visitors year round. She used this money to pay the rent, buy food, and buy stationery for her writing. Some of Sunita's other needs, like clothes and other living essentials, were met by the charitable activities that took place regularly in the temple community. Even so, Sunita never had much money to get by. Employment was choppy. There were many days when she didn't have enough to eat.

Still, Sunita belonged in Balaji's peculiar milieu. She spent most of her days in the Samadhi grounds, sitting with a notebook and pen in front of Babaji's statue. As a result, she really did know a great deal about attendees to the temple, simply from observing them in the Samadhi grounds. She also claimed that Babaji told her about the specific visitors coming to the temple and about "the world as it really is." She offered this knowledge to those interested in learning about their present and future in exchange for small sums of money. There again, she was not out of place. Balaji is filled with healers, fortune-tellers, mind readers, astrologers, and the like, people with various sorts of magical and divine capacities who do good business catering to distraught visitors who seek to alleviate their suffering in Balaji. Sunita could present herself to visitors in the temple as someone with similar abilities and try to earn a living from it. She saw herself as using her magical abilities in the "service of humankind" (*janhit aur seva*).

In fact, she was not that successful in attracting clients. Many people were initially interested in her services, but she came across as too eccentric for most people over time. It probably didn't help that she frequently disappeared from the scene for many days at a stretch. On these days, Sunita told me, Babaji prohibited her from leaving her room and dictated to her continuously. Sunita wrote compulsively and at length on such days of "revelation." She told me that on days when Babaji revealed such knowledge, she forgot to drink, eat, or sleep and spent all of her time writing in her room. And yet she could understand her work as legitimate, generative, and important.

As I pieced Sunita's life story together from our many conversations, I inferred that she had started showing signs of what might be considered a psychotic illness when she was fifteen years old or so. Sunita herself did not have a coherent narrative of her unusual experiences. In speaking about the voices she heard from her early days, she neither acknowledged nor denied that they might have been pathological. She told me that she had been preparing for her board exams in high school when she first began to experience that "the world is not really how it seems." When she told me that she started hearing voices of people telling her that the world is not real, voices that Sunita could describe only vaguely to me, it seemed clear that these were not real people. She told me that this had not been a pleasant time. She had been scared and upset by many of these voices, since "she did not know better" (gyan nahi tha). The voices were mean. They tormented her.

From what Sunita told me, it seemed that she had been admitted to a number of hospitals for psychiatric treatment many times in her early life. She told me that she had visited the state psychiatric institutions in Agra, Gwalior, and Ranchi, three popular mental health facilities that were rather far from her hometown of Bilaspur.[8] It is not unusual for many people with psychiatric illnesses in India to travel far to seek psychiatric care. For Sunita, however, traveling far to three *different* facilities could only mean that her condition had been difficult to treat and that she had been admitted to these hospitals for psychiatric treatment for weeks or even months.

It was at such points in Sunita's narrative that I wondered whether she might, *on purpose*, not speak of her problems in illness terms. If she had been admitted to psychiatric institutions and spent long periods in treatment there, would she not surely know that she had a diagnosable mental illness? At such times, I struggled with understanding what it meant for Sunita to have insight into her condition and whether that would make any difference to how she understood her life in the temple. I sensed that she knew she was different and, in some senses, limited in her interactions with and understanding of the world around her. But I could also see that Sunita made sense of her different self by claiming special abilities of "knowing" more than what the others did.

It also seemed that Sunita's family had been involved in her treatment. Her father, who she said was a teacher, seemed to have been particularly attentive. Sunita spoke very fondly of him. She told me that her father had always encouraged her to do well in school. Indeed, she had earned a master's degree in Hindi literature. That explained her beautiful writing style. But then, when she married, her condition appeared to have worsened. From what she said, it seemed that she may even have fallen ill only after the marriage. In her journals, she wrote about feeling scared all the time after her marriage. Maybe the marriage further precipitated Sunita's condition and triggered her husband's negative reaction to her; maybe she fell ill as a result of her in-laws' ill-treatment of her. In either case, her husband abandoned her and their daughter not long after the marriage, and Sunita returned to her aging parents.

It seemed that it was her parents who left her in Balaji, maybe hoping that she would get better under Balaji's care or simply because they could no longer care for her themselves. Sunita came to the temple with her father and then stayed on. She told me that even though her father had said she could return home any time she wished, she never went back. Later she learned that her father had passed away, from the uncle who used to visit and give her money for sustenance. But the uncle had not visited in some years.

Now I understood why Sunita was unable to claim her money from the bank. In the bank's records, Sunita was probably a "person of unsound mind," an expression in the Indian legal system denoting persons with psychiatric disabilities.[9] People with psychiatric conditions are considered incapable of self-agency and denied an array of civil and political rights, including, as in Sunita's case, independently operating a bank account. That was why she had a guardian on a bank account that was in her name and could not withdraw the money in his absence. I continued to follow Sunita's lead in trying to procure the money from the bank until I realized that, for her, the *idea* of having that money was likely more important than actually acting on her plans of visiting her family if she got it. I learned that she had saved some money and even booked train travel to go home a few times in the past but had never actually left. She had traveled outside Balaji, though, as far as Delhi, accompanied by a group of visitors, to seek clients for her special abilities to "reveal" the present and foresee the future. But I learned from other women that she had never acted on her wish to go back to Bilaspur to her daughter and family.

These days, Sunita is well integrated into the life of the temple. She makes friends easily, and many women who are regular attendees to the temple know her and chat with her on a regular basis. They seem to realize that Sunita is different, yet they consider her as similar to them, as another woman who has sought refuge in Balaji's care. Moreover, while she still hears what we can call auditory hallucinations, these voices are no longer the hostile, distressing voices she seems to have heard when her illness first began. She hears Babaji, whom she knows as a benevolent healer and who chose her to be his vehicle. She is proud of her divine calling and she is confident that she fulfills it well.

Sunita's story is eerily similar to another well-known case of a woman with serious psychotic disorder, described by anthropologist João Biehl. Caterina was born into an intact family in São Paulo, Brazil. Like Sunita, she was once married and had children but became seriously impaired by psychotic illness. Like Sunita, she wrote long, intricate, and at times lyrical texts. And like Sunita, she was essentially abandoned by her family. But unlike Sunita, Caterina did not find herself in a social setting where she could persuade herself that she had useful work for which she was paid. Sunita's living conditions—poor as they may have been—gave her dignity. That is not the only difference between Caterina and Sunita. Caterina was born poor. She did not have the education Sunita did. Her family seems to have been less involved at the beginning. Nonetheless, Caterina, too, sought to persuade herself that she had a legitimate social role as a writer of texts. But she lived in a social world in which it would have been that much harder to persuade herself that she was right.

Faith Interpreted as Madness

Religion, Poverty, and Psychiatry in the Life of a Romanian Woman

JACK R. FRIEDMAN

The Romanian Orthodox Church was once the primary source of care for those who lived with serious mental illness in Romania. Its centrality to the care of madness eroded first with the rise of scientific psychiatric asylums in the late nineteenth and early twentieth centuries, and then by the total repression of the Church's role in caring for the suffering under the Communist Party after World War II. Prior to this, the Church had a large role in the care of the sick and sheltered them from poor treatment at the hands of family and others, even while it regarded those who fell ill as profoundly touched by Original Sin. When psychiatry became the dominant means to treat the mentally ill, beginning in the first quarter of the twentieth century, its reputation was marred because it was used as a tool of political oppression.[1] Since the end of state socialism in 1989, the psychiatric profession has sought to raise its standards of practice to those of the West. It does so within the context of a new religious reawakening. Jack met Alexandra in Romania while doing fieldwork in several psychiatric hospitals across the country. Her story illuminates the way fledgling religious movements (here, evangelical Protestantism) may collide with established religious sensibilities and biomedical protocols for treating schizophrenia.

I met Alexandra[2] in 2005, when she was an inpatient at a large psychiatric hospital in the northeast of Romania. Unlike many of the sad, disorganized patients who wandered the grounds of the hospital, Alexandra presented herself as a person of good cheer—hopeful, and with a spiritual message—despite the fact that she clearly struggled with her own suffering, brought on by her psychotic symptoms, her social isolation, and the poverty in which she lived. Yet her attending psychiatrist had told me that Alexandra was a "difficult person" for him to empathize with. It was not the psychotic behavior that she presented—paranoid fantasies and hallucinations—but aspects of her social world that made the psychiatrist uneasy. In particular, he found it hard to deal with her unusual (for Romania) religiosity.

Alexandra was a member of an evangelical Protestant church that had been brought to her tiny agricultural village by American missionaries in the early 1990s. She spoke openly of her faith and tried to articulate her spiritual message as often as she could. Her demonstrative religiosity and her claim that she had a personal relationship with God made her doctor uneasy. Alexandra's most frequent visitors during her time in the hospital were not members of her family, but members of her church. "They are nice people," the psychiatrist said, "but, they are strange—like a cult. They bring her food and clothing and they pray with her [publicly, in the open hospital bay wards]. They are strange."

Alexandra clearly met criteria for schizophrenia—she had delusions, and she experienced auditory and visual hallucinations. She experienced delusions of reference when watching television; she thought that the voice on the screen spoke specifically only to her. But it seemed to me that what bothered her psychiatrist were characteristics that, to the American anthropologist, were quite normal—her relative articulateness about God and her general ability to keep a smile on her face, which again she attributed to God. She was poor, bordering on abject poverty, but she always maintained her clothing and kept her appearance tidy. To the anthropologist, if this tidiness was the result of her religious optimism and sense of what God wanted for her, it was a healthy consequence of faith. But to her Romanian psychiatrist, both her incessant talk of her faith and her participation in prayer with members of her church during their visits to the hospital were more like symptoms. With bafflement he said to me, "She talks about God and Jesus all of the time!"—as if it would make intuitive sense to me that her experience of the supernatural world was evidence of some deeper feature of her pathology.

Yet the psychiatrist identified himself not as an atheist or nonbeliever, but as Romanian Eastern Orthodox. As is common among the professional and upwardly mobile classes in contemporary Romania, his faith seemed to be only occasionally relevant in his life: on high holidays, on the saint's days for which close loved ones were named, around rituals like the placement of a cross on the roof of a new house, or in the cycle of ritualized remembrances of the dead.[3] It seemed to aggravate him all the more that Alexandra did not contain her faith to these circumscribed religious spheres of practice. God and her faith were with her always; God was always loving her, always with her best interests at heart. She took everything the psychiatrist did as proof of God's care for her. When she told him that she had no money and, thus, it was "God's will" that made his help possible for her, that "God had brought him to her," he seemed to be completely flabbergasted. When he retold this story to me, he said, "It wasn't God, it was my duty! She was sick and I helped her. But she kept insisting that it was God who made it all possible. I was just doing my job because she was sick!" When we spoke, it was hard for him to articulate just *why* he was so uneasy about Alexandra's religious talk and faith. But it seemed pretty clear that he could not avoid thinking that her religion was part of her "bizarre delusions" and, as such, a part of the symptom cluster that composed her schizophrenia.

THE PROBLEM OF SPIRITUALITY AND PSYCHOSIS

It is not always easy to distinguish between things of the spirit and those of the injured psyche. Many who struggle with psychosis report what are called, in the psychiatric literature, "religious delusions." They report that they hear angels and demons, that they see God or perhaps that they are God—or maybe Satan. Those claims often occupy their whole attention and grip them with conviction. Often it is clear that such people are ill, because what they say is so far afield from the expectations of those around them and they hold on to their views with a perverse and desperate tenacity. In one famous example, clinicians in Ypsilanti, Michigan, arranged for three men, all diagnosed with schizophrenia and all claiming to be Christ, to be admitted to the same unit.[4] The clinicians hoped that constant confrontation with evidently absurd claims (they could not all be Christ) would shift the claims of each, and the rigid delusional structure each had built would begin to be more responsive to the world. For the most part, nothing changed. Each simply ignored the others, although one did change his name to "Dung," a cryptic assertion that his godliness was hidden beneath his human filth.

Sometimes it is more complicated. There are hard cases like that of Joan of Arc, who clearly heard audible voices that instructed her about what to do. One could see her conviction that she was to save her native France as a delusion—a fixed, false belief that she had been sent to lead the king's army to victory. Yet she persuaded the king, and she did lead the army to victory, at least a temporary one. She does not seem to have had the cognitive confusion that characterizes so many who struggle with schizophrenia—and that forms part of the formal criteria for the illness.

Alexandra's deeply experiential religiosity and its role in her life and illness will be familiar to those who are familiar with evangelical and charismatic religious movements. When this highly experiential Christianity is removed from its usual contexts it can seem odd, or even pathological, to those who are unfamiliar with its commitment to integrating spiritual experience into mundane aspects of everyday life. The evangelical experience often centers on a first-person experience of divinity and cultivates heightened attention to interpreting God's presence within the flow of sense perceptions and everyday events. In the context of Romanian Orthodoxy, these modes of experiencing and interacting with the divine are profoundly unfamiliar and can seem bizarre. And Alexandra's psychiatrist worried that her newfound religiosity had more to do with her vulnerability to delusion than with healthy membership in a like-minded community of faithful Christians—although he had difficulty articulating these concerns.

ALEXANDRA'S EARLY ILLNESS EXPERIENCES

Alexandra was in her mid-thirties when I met her. She had, at that point, been hospitalized for over seven months with a diagnosis of paranoid schizophrenia at a major psychiatric teaching hospital on the rural edges of a city in Romania's primarily agricultural northeast.[5] This was her third hospitalization, although it seemed from her life story as though her symptoms of mental distress had rarely abated over the decade and a half that was the focus of her narrative. Her first hospitalization took place in 1992. She was then in her early twenties, a period when she had left her natal village to work at a textile plant. She had begun to avoid others. She seems to have been depressed. Eventually she simply stopped speaking, which led her to the attention of others and, ultimately, to hospital care. This was also the beginning of the severe, chronic insomnia that she would suffer most of her adult life. During that hospitalization, she received a diagnosis of "neurasthenia with obsessive phobias." She had a clear causal explanation for her troubles: too much "stress" (stresul) at her job. She said that the stress led her to have trouble concentrating, and that this made her depressed and unwilling to talk to other people. She described herself as being "inadaptable" to the work that she needed to do: "'*inadapt-abilitate' sau nu știu cum îi zice, nu am putut să mă adaptez la condițiile colectivului*"—"'inadaptability' or, I don't know how to put it, but that I couldn't adapt myself to the conditions of the collective." She implied that her problem with being "inadaptable" stemmed partially from her illness but also related to the shock of having moved from her tiny agricultural village to the city to work in the textile factory. Eventually she lost that job, but she did find other employment, including working several years as a shop assistant in a store that sold school supplies. At the time I spoke with her, she had been unemployed for the past four years, a fact that caused her great distress and shame.

The year 1994 was an important one for Alexandra. Having left the city where she worked in the textile factory, she moved back to her natal village and resumed living with her parents on her family's small plot. During that time, Alexandra became involved with a man in the village who was "a few years older" than she. Soon she was pregnant. They were not married, and Alexandra described him as brutal and "uncivilized." She described her relationship with him as characterized by psychological manipulation. He had made her feel like she was his "concubine" more than his partner. It seemed unlikely that they would get married, and given the judgmental nature of the small village, Alexandra said that she faced the shame (*mi-e rușine*) of having a child out of wedlock, with few financial resources.

At the same time that she struggled with this situation, Alexandra met several Western missionaries and fellow congregants who had started an evangelical Protestant church in a neighboring city. Alexandra had been raised, nominally, in the Romanian Orthodox Church, and her mother was still an active member of the local church. However, Alexandra had felt increasingly distant from the Orthodox Church. She talked about having become disillusioned by what she saw as the corruption and greed of the Orthodox village priest. She said that he took money from the congregants and, instead of giving back to the poor, put the money "in his pockets." She was outraged at the fees that he charged for presiding over a funeral (her father having died a few years before our interviews), and she compared him to the Pharisees.[6] The evangelical church, on the other hand, supported her during this time of crisis with donations of food, clothing, and, occasionally, money.[7] Regardless of the assistance that Alexandra received, though, she said that she faced criticism and suspicion from her own family and the broader village community for her

FIGURE 8. The causal relationships between mental illness, poverty, and institutionalization are complex. After the closing of the mines in the Jiu Valley of Romania, many who had formerly depended on mining became impoverished, like this woman. For some, such as Alexandra, locally described as "social cases," institutionalization may be more compassionate than the alternatives. (*Photo: Aron Süveg*)

rejection of Romanian Orthodoxy and her embrace of the new evangelical community, as well as for her out-of-wedlock pregnancy.

It was here, at the intersection of her first psychiatric hospitalization, her increasingly tenuous situation with employment and income, her troubled romantic relationship, her pregnancy, and her newfound faith, that there was a turning point in her life. When Alexandra learned that she was pregnant, she faced a major crisis: whether to terminate the pregnancy or to proceed with it, knowing that the father would not provide the right kind of support for her and for their child, that she would face shame and scorn from her community, and that she would have to raise her child at the same time that she was struggling with mental illness and chronic poverty. She went to the Orthodox priest for guidance, but he didn't help. Moreover, she said, he didn't keep her confession in confidence. Soon the whole village knew of her pregnancy.

At this point she also spoke to one of the women from the evangelical church about her pregnancy. The woman showed deep compassion for Alexandra's struggles. She prayed with her and helped her decide against terminating the pregnancy (at the time I first met Alexandra, her son was ten years old). Alexandra soon joined this church.

EXPERIENCES OF PSYCHOSIS

In 1999 Alexandra was hospitalized for the second time. From her perspective this was a more severe crisis. She also seems to have had clear symptoms of psychosis. It was during this hospitalization that she received a diagnosis of paranoid schizophrenia. She was hospitalized for several months and then discharged back to live with her mother on their small farm with a prescription for an antipsychotic medication (haloperidol).

She seemed to have many of the classic symptoms of schizophrenia. Since the late 1990s, she had heard voices and seen things that others could not see. She felt that she would be responsible for an upcoming global Armageddon.[8] Before the 1999 hospitalization, she had grown increasingly concerned about a total solar eclipse that would pass over Romania on August 11, 1999. The eclipse had been highly publicized in Romania and had even been used as part of a Europe-wide Romanian tourism campaign (involving a vampire and a tourist). It had also been depicted on a one-time-only printing of the widely circulated 2000 lei paper currency. Alexandra had increasingly come to believe—and had been told by the voices that she heard—that her guilt would throw the planets out of alignment and *"că o să produc un nou genocid"*—she would produce a new genocide in the world. The voices said that she was like the loathed Elena Ceaușescu—the wife of former dictator Nicolae Ceaușescu who was executed with her husband during the Romanian Revolution that overthrew Communist

Party control on Christmas Day, 1989. The president and various popular personalities spoke to Alexandra from the television. At night, when she could not sleep, she would see the shadows of demons surrounding her bed. She described the floating head of Jesus Christ rising to speak to her, accusing her of hubris, asking her: "So, are you Jesus Christ, to be crucified for the sins of all mankind? Do you take yourself for all of that?" Figures emerged out of the shadows—figures of men—who threatened to take her son from her. They accused her of murdering four children. Sometimes what she heard would take on physical form as well; she described "seeing sounds at maximum volume coming from the walls" or "hearing the shadows" that she saw.

She described, with great emotion, the sadness she felt about the years of social isolation that had started with her problems with alogia (impoverished speech—a slow, awkward use of language common among those with schizophrenia) in the early 1990s but had continued afterward when she remained at home rather than facing shame—regarding her mental illness, her poverty, the situation around the birth of her son—outside among the villagers. Her home became, for her, a place of nightmares and isolation.

> Whenever I have been at my home [...] I think that, in a way, I translate my illness [cred că, într-un fel îmi traduc boala] ... how can I say it, I think that it shames me to say, but I think that [my home life] has contributed to [my illness]; that, and hormones, because I haven't had any stable relationships for such a long time.[9]

Home, as she described it, was a place of constant threat and humiliation. At any time, the shadows and demons could return to her. At the same time, her aged mother constantly nagged her about her inability to get a job, to work in the fields, to take care of her son.[10] Home was also profoundly boring to her—a place where all she could do to keep herself occupied was clean and watch television (and the latter activity was now lost to her because it had often fed into her psychosis). Together, these things seemed to undermine the idea that "home" could be a safe space for her.

Home was also a life of grinding poverty and tenuous, near-subsistence farming on her mother's small plot of land. She still referred to the community as "Colectiva" (The Collective), a term associated with the state socialist period, when agricultural land was primarily owned by the state. Describing the hardships she and her family faced, she noted:

> They worked from morning until night. In the winter they would earn three lei [...]. And, probably, they accepted that because they didn't have any other

way to feed themselves . . . we really didn't have any way to eat. There were days when we didn't know what we could eat. Only borscht with beans or borscht with potatoes, that was all there was on the menu. We three [Alexandra, her mother, and her son] live off of my mother's one million lei [monthly pension—less than $35 U.S. at the time]. That's how it is. And, since November [2004], when I returned here [to the hospital] it has been very difficult.[11]

She described a particular event in November 2004 when her son began to ask her why they never had a Christmas tree during the holidays. Alexandra said that she felt deep shame and didn't know how to respond. The cost of her medications alone could be as high as 500,000 lei—half of the household's income from her mother's pension. She couldn't imagine how they could afford a Christmas tree. But, she said, she felt such shame at her son's question— "Mama, why don't I have a Christmas tree when everyone else has one?"—that she bought a tree nonetheless. The dire financial situation got worse and the family was even forced to eat some of the chickens that they normally raised for egg production. "After that," she noted,

> I no longer had an appetite, I didn't eat. The treatment [medication], I took, but, I started to hide my face, I could no longer talk, I could no longer communicate with others, so I returned again to the hospital, and, since then, they have changed my treatment five times. After the fifth treatment, as you can see, I can speak a bit better. But, when it comes to politics, I won't have anything to do with it. So, you understand, when I am having my illness, I can no longer tolerate television.[12]

There was little doubt that Alexandra suffered from schizophrenia and that her poverty exacerbated her troubles. Nonetheless, the Romanian Orthodox church, the evangelical church, and her psychiatrist each understood her illness differently.

THE COMPLICATIONS OF FAITH

The hospital in which Alexandra was a patient was built on the grounds of a Romanian Orthodox church that could trace its origins back to the sixteenth century. Until the rise of modern scientific health care for the mentally ill began at the end of the nineteenth century, most of Romania's "mad" who were not cared for within the home found themselves in isolated monasteries. Although the Church was, ultimately, supplanted by scientific medical care in Romania, given the isolated nature of many remote Romanian villages and the traditional role of village priests as care providers for people who suffered from pathologies of conscience or consciousness, it remained common for families to bring their emotionally disturbed loved ones to the local church or monastery before taking them to a distant psychiatric hospital.

Resting next to the curving, tree-lined gravel road that ran up the hill from the highway to the buildings of the hospital, the small church was only a few dozen meters away from one of the patient wards. I spoke to the priest—dressed in his black cassock, a tall, powerfully built man with the traditional long, bushy beard—as we shared a glass of homemade wine under the shade of the small complex that functioned as his living quarters. The psychiatrists with whom I interacted daily at the hospital were generally dismissive of the priest's role in the care of the patients, characterizing him as a strange relic. In one case, a psychiatrist explicitly suggested that the priest's "religious explanations" could confuse a patient and make it more difficult for the hospital staff to convince the patient of the need to follow a particular treatment regimen. In our conversation, the priest, as if responding to this unspoken criticism, volunteered that he felt that the role of the church must remain "secondary" to the role of science in the treatment of mental illness. At the same time, he emphasized that the suffering that mental illness brings often leads to spiritual questions among the patients in the hospital. His role was to help them understand the spiritual components of their experiences—to minister to their souls while the psychiatrists cared for their brains.

And yet the priest could not restrain himself from casting mental illness in moral and theological terms.[13] As we walked through the church and he showed me the renovations that were taking place, he said to me that, though there was a scientific explanation for mental illness, the Orthodox Church believed that "rationality was the greatest gift given to Man by God" and that "to lose one's rationality was the greatest sin."[14] This sense of a relationship between madness and moral failure is still deeply embedded in Romanian Orthodoxy.

Perhaps this sense of inherent sinfulness pushed Alexandra away from Orthodoxy. Orthodox interpretations of her illness would cast her moral failings—having a child out of wedlock and considering terminating her pregnancy—as the sins that caused her illness. In contrast, her evangelical brethren emphasized God's love for her and, indeed, provided Alexandra with love and support. What she said, however, was that the priests refused to help her understand her experiences. She told me that she had been "visited" by both divine and demonic spirits since her first hospitalization. But when she talked to her village Orthodox priest about her experiences, he had insisted that she and her mother make "donations" to the priest to say prayers for her. She saw the request for money as corruption.

More offensive was his refusal to say whether she, a lay believer, could ever know whether her experiences were true communications with the divine. In Romanian Orthodoxy, priests place a great deal of emphasis on charismatic intuition for their interpretations of the mystical and the divine.[15] That is, they feel that their intuitions are given directly by God. Laypersons are assumed to be without access to this form of intuition. Only priests can be true interpreters of divine messages and symbols. Both the daily practice of Orthodox confession and the extraordinary experience of the divine reflect the fundamental mystery that cloaks the divine. In essence, this meant that Alexandra would have to find answers through a clergy that she did not trust and that she felt was only in it "for the money."

The reluctance of the priest to engage Alexandra in discussion of her communications from God and demonic spirits may be read as emerging from caution. The Romanian Church was recovering from the "Tanacu Scandal." In 2005, Irina Cornici, a woman diagnosed with paranoid schizophrenia, had died as the result of an exorcism that failed to remove offending demons from her body. The international media were focused on excoriating Romanian Orthodoxy for its mistreatment of a vulnerable, psychiatrically ill woman. In the wake of this scandal, it may be that the Orthodox priest whom Alexandra consulted, and who she believes failed her, deliberately withdrew from engaging with her about her experience of God and demons, preferring to defer such discussions of supernatural occurrences (with someone diagnosed similarly to Ms. Cornici) to her psychiatrist. But Alexandra came away from the encounter with a sense that there was no spiritual or emotional support for her—only a self-interested demand for money.

On the other hand, her evangelical *frații* ("brothers," as she referred to them) emphasized the possibilities of direct engagement with the divine—of a personal relationship with God. In Alexandra's eyes, this was a community of believers who were there to help her, rather than (as she characterized the Orthodox priest) simply being concerned with what they could take from her. She said that when she met with her fellow Evangelical church members, they would sit in a circle and sing and talk. Nobody sought to dominate her, and they helped her with her problems and helped her make sense of her experiences. They told her that she must pray and that they would pray with her—and that while she was absent from them, in the hospital, they would pray for her. When she went to them and told them about the voices and the visions—the demonic shadows, the floating heads—they explained them to her. They told her that she was being tested. They visited her in the hospital and helped support her son while she was hospitalized.[16] Alexandra told her psychiatrist that she had learned to speak with God through her participation in this church.

Meanwhile, when her psychiatrist spoke to me about her case, he said that he found this "relationship with God" to be a troubling aspect of her illness. He even called the group to which she belonged a "cult." To him, the idea of having a personal relationship with God was a profoundly foreign and awkward idea. That view was consistent with his Romanian Orthodox faith, which treats the divine as unknowable, mysterious, and reached only through the clergy. I had a sense that for him, when one overarching ideology (Communism) had been wiped away, another, more secular one (Biomedicine) had replaced it, precisely at the moment when Romania needed to commit itself to modern, rational, scientific ways of approaching its problems. So he framed spiritual epistemologies as markers of pathology and ignorance.

The story of Alexandra's schizophrenia is not, however, the story of the secularization of mental illness and psychiatry in Romania. In fact, psychiatry and lay perceptions of mental illness were almost entirely "secularized" during the nearly fifty years of Communist Party rule in Romania, during which religious life was publicly repressed—and privately pushed into the most secret realms of the lives of those who dared to maintain their faith. Similarly, during my fieldwork during the postsocialist period—whether among cosmopolitan urbanites or provincial rural folk—most people were generally aware of the categories of medical psychiatry. Many of the rural patients in my research were people with long psychiatric histories, some dating from the 1970s or '80s, and they expressed a general familiarity with the medical categories of psychiatry, even if they did not fully understand some of the subtleties associated with diagnosis and treatment.

But Alexandra's story does speak to a growing trend in Romania: some people are returning to religious traditions (e.g., those of Romanian Orthodoxy) that were repressed under Communism, while others seek out new meaning-systems through recently imported Protestant churches or, as one sees among more urbane, cosmopolitan youths, Eastern religious traditions (e.g., Buddhism). The upheaval, the constant change and crisis, that has marked out the years since 1989 in Romania has, for many, resulted in a search for meaning and solace in the spiritual—in new and old religions and new communities of faith. What Alexandra's story reveals, then, is the emergence of a spirituality so different from the country's traditional one that a skeptical, middle-class physician could interpret its theology, when expressed by someone with psychotic illness, as an expression of her madness.

CONCLUSION

What might seem to be religious intolerance—or, at the least, inflexibility—on the part of Alexandra's psychiatrist should be read cautiously. From his professional training and practice, he could hardly be unaware (at least intuitively) that individuals who hold elaborate religious delusions are more likely to have poorer treatment outcomes than those who have delusions of a nonreligious nature, and that certain religious beliefs feed into cycles of despair, guilt, and blame.[17] Couple a well-founded cautiousness toward encouraging religiosity in persons with severe mental illness, in general, with the foreignness of the experiential practices that Alexandra was participating in—seeking the supernatural presence of God in mundane events of everyday life—and you can see why he might be hesitant about her faith. Her practices might seem to give weight and authority to what he took to be psychotic hallucinations. It is not surprising that Alexandra's psychiatrist was worried that her newfound religious practices might exacerbate her illness, or that the strangeness of her new beliefs might indicate psychopathology.

In any case, Alexandra's life outside of the hospital had been difficult. She and her mother barely managed to feed themselves. She was scorned in her tiny village for having a child out of wedlock. For the doctor to release Alexandra from the hospital would have been to subject her again to the suffocating gossip and slights from others in her village, which would only feed her vulnerability to paranoia and social isolation. It is no wonder he preferred to err on this side of shielding her from a judgmental social milieu, and from economic circumstances in which she could barely meet her basic needs for food and shelter. As a "social case"—an individual who is institutionalized because they are too poor to maintain even a subsistence lifestyle in the neoliberal Romanian state—he allowed her to take advantage of the institution as a place of rest, food, adequate medical care, and protection.[18] While perhaps she did not unequivocally need to be institutionalized to manage her mental illness, he erred on the side of keeping her safe, warm, and adequately fed in the state-sponsored hospital.

On the other hand, I didn't think that Irina Cornici's case could really be compared to Alexandra's involvement with evangelical practices. While Alexandra had learned from her evangelical brethren that Jesus deeply and always loved her, and that, as a sign of this love, her fellows in faith would care for and love her, Irina was forced to "confess" to her possession by a demon. Irina was a victim not only of physical, sexual, and psychological violence, but of the "absence of love" during her childhood spent at a state orphanage, and she was actually crucified by a priest in an attempt to rid her of a demon "both aggressive and self-destructive." She did not experience this exorcism as help-ful—and then she was stuck with believing that she had a demon inside her that was trying to kill her. Her medical record stated, "Since awakening this inner demon, all of her thoughts and sentiments became profoundly nega-tive."[19] The medical record captured this involvement with the demon as she pled to her psychiatrist: "Don't leave me! I'm possessed by a demon! I'm in Hell!" Here, it is indeed possible to believe that her Orthodox priest's acknowl-edgment of the demon's reality, and the punitive measures he took to rid her of it, might have interacted negatively with the auditory hallucinations she experienced as a result of her schizophrenia.

By contrast, the evangelical church encouraged Alexandra's communication with the positive supernatural: God and Jesus at their most loving and accept-ing. And Alexandra's involvement had a positive effect on her—it lifted her mood, encouraged her to talk of God's love, and gave her pride in her appear-ance and the spiritual message she delivered to others. Her involvement with the church seemed to provide Alexandra with a narrative and an experience that stood apart from her experiences of paranoia. While mindful of her psychiatrist's hesitance, I wonder if Alexandra's spiritual life contributed to her well-being and her ability to cope with her symptoms.

The Culture of the Institutional Circuit in the United States

T. M. LUHRMANN

To many people in our society who struggle with schizophrenia, we deliver care that is disgraceful. This is not, it should be said, the care that our health system in some sense "intends" to deliver. An analysis of care-as-usual for persons with schizophrenia concluded that "the rates at which patients' treatment conformed to the [National Institute of Mental Health] recommendations were modest at best, generally below fifty percent."[1] Instead, care-as-usual has become a circuit of prison, shelter, hospital, and transitional housing that is notable mostly for the degree to which people opt out of services. Tanya met Zaney in Chicago, in what people who staff these neighborhood services call a "drop-in center."

———

Zaney—that is the name she gave me—was a white woman in her middle forties.[2] She was well-spoken, clean, and neatly dressed. This is notable because about half of every month, she slept on the El, Chicago's elevated train. It is neither safe nor easy to fall asleep on the train, but it is warm. She had come to Chicago from Wisconsin in her late twenties when she began to be taunted by an angry but nonexistent crowd. They shoved her on the street, they shouted "slut" and "whore" at her, and they banged on the walls when she tried to sleep. When she arrived in Chicago, the police picked her up and brought her to a hospital where she stayed for a few days, undoubtedly diagnosed with schizophrenia. She got a referral to a caseworker in a community mental health center, and she kept the appointment. The caseworker got her housing and, eventually, a regular social security check, about

$579 a month. Both the housing and the check were available to her because of her psychiatric diagnosis. Zaney stayed in the housing for about eight years, and then she lost it, either because she left or because she was evicted. Then she stayed in shelters for several years. She said that she was doing a routine chore at the shelter when someone rudely told her that she wasn't doing it well, and of course, she said, she stuck up for herself and they threw her out. The shelter director remembered that Zaney left the shelter of her own accord.

Zaney desperately wanted not to be homeless. When I met her, she was staying two weeks a month at a fleabag hotel, for about $160 a week, but she couldn't afford more than that. She came into the drop-in center every day with the classified ads, looking for apartments and work. She had been told repeatedly that she could get housing again if she were willing to see a psychiatrist. I'd heard the staff tell her this myself. Anyway, as far as I could tell, everyone in the drop-in center knew how you could get housed. Most women were homeless when they showed up there, and they talked about housing volubly and frequently. They would tick off the ways to get housed on their fingers: you had to be "crazy" or "addicted" or you had to have a job. "I ain't crazy and I don't got a job," one woman announced to me. "So I'm working on being addicted." What she meant by this was that she was beginning to go to the meetings with caseworkers and to Alcoholics Anonymous–like group meetings, which agencies usually required clients to attend for weeks before giving them an apartment of their own, usually a studio with a small refrigerator, a hotplate, and a bathroom, one of many off a long corridor.

By far the largest amount of subsidized housing is reserved for people who are diagnosable with serious psychotic illnesses, like schizophrenia or bipolar disorder. Even most of the housing associated by the women with addiction in fact depends on what psychiatrists call "dual diagnosis," which means that someone is diagnosable not only with substance abuse but also with another serious psychiatric disorder. Depression and other psychiatric illnesses like post-traumatic stress disorder can, of course, be crippling, and occasionally someone would obtain disability-related social security on the basis of those diagnoses—but it seemed to be rare, at least among the women who frequented the neighborhood. Typically, most psychiatric disability-related subsidies, including housing, seemed to depend upon a psychiatric diagnosis of psychotic disorder. And that was where Zaney balked. She was very clear that she was not "crazy," as she put it. I used to suggest to her that she just lie, that she "pretend" to hear voices, just to get a safer place to sleep. She always shook her head. "I'm not that kind of person," she said.

In 1955, there were 339 psychiatric beds for every 100,000 Americans, and half of them held people diagnosed with schizophrenia, for months or years at a time, in institutions that became kin and community for those they held.[3] When President Kennedy proclaimed the Community Mental Health Act in 1963—following the 1954 release of chlorpromazine, the first medication to treat psychotic symptoms successfully—the idea was to release patients from stagnation on the back wards of state psychiatric hospitals into the loving care of their community. We coined the word "deinstitutionalization" to celebrate their liberation from the supposedly Goffmanesque settings that forced patients' minds into institutional straitjackets.[4] It was a time when people were more likely to believe that a psychiatric diagnosis was some kind of arrogant "Establishment" mistake. Peter Shaffer had a Broadway hit with *Equus*, a play about a young boy who stabbed horses in the eye but—this was the play's point—was really a misunderstood, sensitive soul.

Fifty years later, we have what we might as well call "reinstitutionalization." By the mid-1990s, there were only twenty-two psychiatric beds for every 100,000 Americans, and about half the patients stayed in them for five days or less. (Now there are fewer than fifteen beds per 100,000.)[5] People who, in earlier decades, would have passed their lives in the back wards of cavernous state hospitals often spend their days in neighborhoods that sociologists call "service ghettos."[6] I met Zaney in a two- or three-block area in Chicago that probably had the densest concentration of persons with serious psychotic disorder in the entire state of Illinois, outside of the jails and prisons.[7] Within and around these blocks there were medical clinics, psychiatric clinics, housing services, social services, soup kitchens, drop-in centers, and agencies funded variously by the city, the state, the federal government, different religious groups, and a grab bag of charities. There were overnight shelters for single men, single women, women with infants, and families. There were halfway houses with trained staff who stayed overnight, and rambling, single-room-occupancy buildings with many tenants and little oversight. There were so-called nursing homes and cheap hotels and the closest the city comes to flophouses. And still, with all these services and thousands of subsidized beds, many people with psychotic disorder subsisted on the margins of the neighborhood, sleeping in the park or in the shelter, eating at the soup kitchens, coming in periodically for medical care, and getting raped and beaten in the alleys.

By now we know that homelessness is commonplace in the lives of people with serious psychotic disorders. That is, not only is it the case that many of those who remain homeless for months and years are psychotic; it is also true that many of those who are psychotic end up becoming homeless. This is a shocking claim. But it is what the data tell us. In 1998, *The American Journal of Psychiatry (AJP)* published research that tracked patients after they first made contact at one of ten (out of twelve) Long Island, New York, hospitals. In this study, one in six patients diagnosed with schizophrenia either had been homeless or would become homeless in the following two years.[8] In 2005, *AJP* published a study analyzing the records of all patients treated in the primary hospital cluster in San Diego, California. One in five clients diagnosed with schizophrenia was homeless at the time of contact.[9] Both studies—by the nature of their measurements and methods—undoubtedly underestimated the risk of periodic homelessness for those with schizophrenia or some other psychotic disorder. The New York study only looked at the first years of illness, usually the period before the patient's exhausted family reaches the limits of its tolerance and throws the patient out. The San Diego study was a snapshot of one moment in a patient's life across a single year, and even then it excluded two thousand people with that diagnosis in locked psychiatric facilities or in jails. Meanwhile, these days, we are as likely to jail as to hospitalize those who, because of their illness, disturb the public peace. At any one time in this country, there are more than three times as many people with serious mental illness behind bars as there are in hospitals.[10]

How did that happen? How did it come to pass, in one of the richest nations in the world, that we care for our sickest, neediest citizens on the street? The most important reason for the failure of the community mental health movement was that the money to support it never materialized. Kennedy's Act had guaranteed federal funding to the states for the first eight years, after which the states were meant to take on the costs of nonhospital care—subsidized housing, often with staff oversight.[11] For the most part, the states underfunded the programs. Subsidized housing—often described variously as "halfway houses" or "supported housing"—is far cheaper than inpatient hospitalization, but it costs real money, even in the bad part of town. From the beginning, in the 1960s and '70s, there wasn't enough housing. When the real estate boom

FIGURE 9. In the streets of Chicago, there are many people with serious psychotic disorders. Here, a woman with psychosis has run into the street and stands screaming at a car. (*Photo: T. M. Luhrmann*)

of the '80s led many landlords to convert their rental units into condos, the supply of cheap urban housing dwindled further. These days, the mental health system—at best a patchwork of different institutions—is seriously strapped for cash. In Chicago, experts estimated that there were fewer than a tenth as many beds as were needed in the city's supported housing.[12]

But there is another, more complicated reason why the community-health-care system fails, at least the community-mental-health system as we have created it in the aftermath of underfunding, in poor neighborhoods studded with services and supported housing. Many of the people who should be using the system often reject the help that it offers. Many people with schizophrenia end up on the street even when supported housing is available. In Chicago, the wait for non-disability-related low-income housing is currently seven years. I know people who have been told that if they were willing to see a psychiatrist, they could get *in two weeks* housing as good as any they could get with a "Section 8" voucher. Yet many who are eligible repeatedly refuse such housing, which in many cases is offered by decent, caring people. And they refuse many other offers—of medication or counseling or employment—not always consistently and not unambivalently but often, and for years at a time. People like Zaney wander in nomadic squalor between the homeless shelter, supported housing, inpatient hospitalization, and jail, a grim social cycle the anthropologist Kim Hopper calls "the institutional circuit."[13] Perhaps they do get housed—but then they become too disorganized to pay the rent, or they violate the curfew or end up in a fight. Eventually they land back on the street, evicted or by choice, living in the homeless shelter, ties broken with their families, hospitalized or jailed when their behavior gets out of hand, occasionally getting housed, then leaving or losing housing, and returning to the street again. The question is why.

To begin answering that question, I settled in to the drop-in center. It was a large, cheerfully painted room in an old hotel that had been built around World War I with hopes of glamour but now was home to an array of struggling social services. The psychiatric service on the third floor had changed its name three times in as many years, as one organization after another took it over in the wan hope that they would avoid a loss. The drop-in center teetered on insolvency, edging along quarter-to-quarter on an unpredictable combination of donations and grants. It had been founded, in the first flush of feminist enthusiasm, as a haven for women down on their luck. In those early days it was open from morning until night. Now they could only afford the staff for four hours on weekday afternoons. Anyone was welcome, as long as they were female. Most of the women who came in were homeless, at least when they first arrived. You could get a hot meal most days, wash your clothes, take a shower, talk to staff about where to get help in the neighborhood. I'd go there in the early afternoon and sit down at one of the tables scattered across the room and strike up a conversation with the other people at the table. Sometimes a woman would glare at me, or brusquely tell me to mind my own business and to go away. But gradually people got used to me. At first, the women knew immediately that I wasn't one of them. After a while, though, I seemed to pick up something of the aura of the place, and newcomers sometimes assumed that I was homeless too. I began to spend time in the shelters, meeting the women I saw at the drop-in center, watching television, passing time. I struck up relationships with staff at different agencies and sat over chicken soup with them in the local diner. Most days I spent some time with Zaney.

  If you listened to the clinicians and to other staff, you would conclude that someone like Zaney refused to see a psychiatrist because her illness corrupted her ability to think, her capacity to have what psychiatrists call "insight." That's certainly the inference you would draw if you were the psychiatrist in a room with her, fifteen minutes for the appointment, taking in her unkempt hair and the discreet but telltale plastic bags she carried. Some of what Zaney said about housing seemed pretty irrational, like her complaint that one landlord had evicted her because he didn't like her birthdate. But most people aren't psychotic all the time, in all dimensions of their lives. Much of the time Zaney was as coherent as I am.

In fact, had she not been competent in some basic ways, she wouldn't have survived. It takes moxie to make it on the street. Zaney found herself homeless because she had no one who would give her shelter and no money with which to buy it. Someone—maybe a police officer, maybe staff in a hospital's emergency room, maybe the person spooning food in the soup kitchen (the details were lost in her fog)—had handed her a list of shelters, maybe called ahead to secure a place, and maybe even given her a bus pass to get there. She made her way on the bus alone, transferring from one line to another, dragging her stuff, numb with the newness. She arrived and stood on line. People are always standing in long, resigned lines on the street, waiting for doors to open. I used to find that moment when the shelter opened unbearable, squeezing in at the main door with a sudden press of women, women with bulky bags, women who hadn't showered—not many, but one was enough—women who were angry or boisterous or glazed with dull, dissociated stares.

Once you get a bed in a shelter, you need a nose for whom to trust, whom to avoid. When the doors open, everyone must be registered, new people are interviewed, people are rolling out mattresses and finding blankets, sheets, and towels and lining up for showers. People are bumping into each other, looking for space, arranging their stuff. There's often a blowup, someone enraged that there's no space or no appointment, or at some accidental insult. The staff shout her down or throw her out, sometimes with the help of the police. There's a lot of warmth, too, sometimes. I liked hanging out in a corner, hugging the women I knew, joking with the staff. The staff know this world well; they've often climbed out of it themselves. But the mental illness makes them uneasy. Once I was in the back office of a shelter that did not, in theory, have anything to do with mental illness. The staff person, whom I will call Jean, was on the phone about a woman who had been diagnosed with schizophrenia and should have been getting disability but wouldn't sign her form because she'd changed her name when she got married and now she hated the guy. Jean was shouting into the phone, which was making this strange, loud buzzing sound, and then a woman (one of many who had knocked on the door by this point) put her head in and explained that she really needed help because people were trying to electrocute her with the fire alarm, and that "we" wanted to talk to you—and Jean said, "Who is the we?" And the woman said, "Never mind that, the mafia is the one that started it," and she went on to say that Jean needed to call the police and see how they rigged the place and she was going to have to get the fire department over and then the police because they were pumping electricity through the system against good people like her who were government people. Jean said, "Okay, I'll see what I can do," but the woman continued as if she had not spoken. Eventually Jean pushed her out the door, because someone else had come in, a woman who was not only psychotic but deaf and mute, who was upset because her locker didn't shut properly. Then the woman who wouldn't sign for her disability, who had a fibroid tumor which made her look pregnant, came in for a bus pass. When Jean finally came back after getting her the bus pass, I said, "This is really the way we treat serious mental illness in our society, isn't it?" "Yes," she said, and then sighed. "And you know, I am not trained for that."

Time behaves oddly in a shelter. There are stretched-out patches of boredom, no way to get comfortable because everything's a little damp and a little dirty and there's no place to sit that's yours. But time also has the compressed, intense quality of the unpredictable. The shock of arrival never fades. Getting used to a shelter is not like coming into a new school, sorting out the jocks and the nerds, and finding your niche. There are always new women, some newly released from prison or the psychiatric ward. Even the ones you know can explode, sometimes fueled by crack or psychosis, sometimes just from stress and noise. Even late in the evening, after the lights are out, it is not quiet. People turn and stretch in unfamiliar beds, lying next to people they don't know, tense about having cash or medication or even just their shampoo filched, clutching their most precious stuff under the pillow. People get up to pee during the night and trip over other people's bags, reaching out to grab something to steady themselves. People talk and mutter loudly. One of the most startling features of shelter life is how god-awful difficult it is to sleep through the night. Most of the people you see on the street are exhausted.

And then they have to be alert enough to find their way to soup kitchens and figure out where the social service agencies are and stand on line with people who are high or psychotic, who they worry might harass them. They have to figure out where people deal and where they turn tricks and where to walk if they don't want to do either. In the neighborhood around the shelters, I would see men standing in small, predatory groups on the corners, sometimes calling out to women as they skirted paths around them. Most of the women spoke casually of men beating girlfriends and men raping women. Stories circulated about women who had been found dead in an alley. I never discovered whether the stories were true, but it was obvious that the women who told them were nervous. I was walking down the street with a woman once when she saw a guy she knew a few yards ahead. She saw that he had a beer, which I hadn't noticed, and she grabbed my shoulder and pulled me across the street as if we were going somewhere else. By this point he was calling to her, saying hi, and she waved back cheerfully. Then she turned her face to me and lowered her voice: "I really don't like to be with him when he's drinking. Let's go this way."

To survive, someone like Zaney needs to learn all this fast. She doesn't have anyone to explain the cues or to protect her if she flubs. She has no friends, or at least she doesn't regard the people she talks with (like me) as friends. There are many reasons that few people develop friendships in a shelter. No one wants to be there. People in shelters say scathing, contemptuous things about each other and about people like themselves. They sweep their arms out at the room and denounce the women sitting in it. "You can't get away from the homeless here," a woman spat at me one afternoon. "You just can't get rid of them. You just trip over them when you walk out the door here." Zaney needed institutions because they offered free food and shelter. By contrast, peers were a threat. Once I asked Zaney to draw her social world, with her social relationships. She drew herself under a tree in the park. She drew the Buddhist temple where she sometimes went, and she drew the Department of Human Services. She didn't draw anything else. That's why, she said, it was important to be tough. "It's like they say about men going to jail, even if they're innocent, they gotta fight, and if they don't stand up for themselves, the other guys will take advantage and get even rowdier and you can get hurt, so it's better to try to stand up for yourself." She called the other people on the street "cowboys."

I could see that people on the street acted tough to each other. When I was with a woman in the park, and men from the neighborhood approached, she seemed to grow larger and belligerent, as if she were arching her back and stiffening her fur. "They don't mess with me," she would say when they left. In the face of uncertain danger from other human beings, people learn fast to

Page 9
PART TWO (one buspass, meal coupon, etc)

Now I'd like you to draw a map of your social world now—a map of your important social relationships, including God, if you like. You can also draw a map of your social world when your life was at its best, but do include a map of how you experience it right now.

FIGURE 10. Zaney was asked to draw her social world. She responded by drawing only herself, sleeping under a tree, and some of the institutions on which she depended.

signal to strangers that the strangers should let them be. They signal threat. They raise their voices, plant their feet, and throw their shoulders back. Zaney seemed to have learned to threaten people who, willfully or not, intruded into what she defined as hers. She'd sit peaceably in the drop-in center, and something ordinary would happen—she was shoved in line, commented on as she walked by, elbowed aside in the bathroom. She'd flare, raising her voice, throwing her shoulders back and her chest forward, acting fierce to get the offender to back down.

After a while, after I'd been in the neighborhood long enough that people were sometimes confused about whether I was homeless, it dawned on me that refusing housing was the same kind of signal. I realized that Zaney and the other women shared a culture in which the refusal to accept housing was a meaningful social signal, rather than just another symptom of psychosis, and that its meaning was tied up with the toughness it took to survive, and with what it meant—given the toughness—to be "crazy." On the street, people used the word "crazy" differently from the way I'd heard the term used by other psychiatric clients, even those struggling with schizophrenia and psychosis. Among people who were middle-class and ill, I'd heard the word "crazy" used with an ironic, grudging familiarity. "Yeah, that's when I was crazy," someone would say, telling a joke about how he had thought he'd walk from San Diego to New York and gave up when he got to the top of his first big hill a few blocks away. Politically active psychiatric clients—sometimes called "consumers" or, more angrily, "psychiatric survivors"—use the word "crazy" in a defiant way. They make political buttons with the word. They adopt it and reclaim it, using it to mean an identity rejected for the wrong reasons and an assertion that they are now going to set it right. The self-mocking edge runs throughout the psychiatric consumer literature. One of the main magazines, sadly no longer published, was called simply *Dendron* as if the reader were an aberrant neuron.

But nobody called themselves "crazy" in this neighborhood. I'd rarely seen a word used with such contempt. That caught my attention, my anthropological ear. And when I began to ask women what people mean by it, they were remarkably consistent. They would point to a woman who was flagrantly ill and talking to herself—at a shelter or a drop-in center, there was almost always at least one such woman present—and they'd say something derisive. "She's crazy, she don't need no friends."

That didn't tell me what the word meant; it told me who best represented the word, what you might call its "prototype." To figure out its meaning, I did what anthropologists do, which is to listen to many women use the word spontaneously and from that to infer its meaning. One strand of meaning was clearly being "weak." One woman made that clear, talking about the way her husband's suicide had caught her by surprise. "I didn't think anything was wrong with his head because he was a strong man. I just thought he was this strong man, that that wouldn't ever happen to him, you know, he would never be crazy, he would never be actually crazy because he was a strong-minded person, strong-minded man, strong, so it wouldn't happen to him. But I was wrong, because it did." Another strand was a kind of permanence, something that—as one woman said—"would never be fixed." Being crazy "is something you absolutely cannot control. And a lot of them don't even take medication. They have retardation and there's nothing you can do about it. Alcoholism you can do something about. You can stop drinking. Smoking, you can stop smoking. You can do those things and thereby reverse your situation, but someone who appears mentally ill can't do that." In fact, the women repeatedly spoke about mental illness as a kind of retardation. As one woman put it, "Half of these people [are] slow up here, you know what I'm saying, half of them got a little problem. They don't think that well." And yet another strain was the idea that the street would drive you crazy, and that if you weren't careful, you might be next. "She's been on the street too long," women would say about someone else, twirling their fingers or rolling their eyes to show that the person they were talking about was "crazy." Or "some people can't handle the pressure. . . . They break and become mentally ill."

The structure of this "cultural model," the phrase anthropologists sometimes use for these more-or-less shared cognitive schemas, seemed to be that flagrant psychosis arises when a woman is not strong enough to cope with the difficulties of homelessness; that the condition is permanent; and that only those who give up the struggle to get out become flagrantly ill. Being "crazy" is thus a stand-in for the worst thing that the street can do to you, which is to render you unfit for human contact. To be "crazy" is to be isolated, vulnerable, disliked, unreachable—what you fear may happen to you if you stay out there on the street too long. To be on the street is to face a continual sense of failure; to be crazy is a direct representation of what that can do to your mind. "To be mentally ill and homeless," another woman said to me one afternoon, shaking her head, "you really can't get much worse off than that."

On the street you can feel the toxic mixture of rage, despair, and terror in which the fear that you'll never get out could grip you at the throat. Sleeping in a shelter is about looking into the eyes of someone mad in the next bed and fearing that if you weren't careful enough, if you didn't watch out, you too could slide into that strange and eerie world forever and be caught. You can feel the simmering violence in a shelter, the distrust, the bracing against someone's hostile outburst. You can feel the hypervigilance, the scanning for trouble, the incipient anger at people who steal and shout, the exhaustion, the dull rage and despair at life itself. You see people who have lost it and you fear that you, too, live on a knife edge, clinging to reality. Psychosis is so close on the street. The women talked about it like something so primal you can smell

CULTURE OF THE INSTITUTIONAL CIRCUIT   +   165

it. "They down and out and you don't want to be like that. You go in there [the shelter] and right away you feel the aroma."

Sometimes, people who weren't psychotic tried to act that way in self-protection. "Act crazy, they'll leave you alone," one woman shrugged. But for those who fear they might be psychotic, those who smell the weakness in their own skin, the emotion is very different. Psychosis is a continuum. Not everyone who hears caustic, demeaning voices ends up as a gibbering idiot. But some do. And that endpoint is grim. You cannot know what it feels like to be a woman incapable of normal human communication, but what you can see is that she is despised. The most flagrantly psychotic women—the ones who are visibly talking to people no one else can see, who gesture to the empty air—are the most disliked women in the shelter. They are the ones who don't get the social cues, who talk volubly in the middle of the night, who don't respond in a way that makes sense. They are also the most vulnerable to violence. Once I arrived in the drop-in center to discover that a group of women had been standing on the street corner, pointing and jeering at a woman who was visibly mad. Sociological data tell us that such people are more likely to be beaten up than to be a danger to others, but you don't need those statistics to see that the street is more dangerous for the women who are most dramatically ill.[14] It is blatant.

Zaney knew she was different. She knew that other people didn't hear the crowd that taunted her from the streets outside the drop-in center, even though she sometimes heard them as audibly as she heard me speak when we sat together over sudoku in the drop-in center. She knew that when she saw her son in the shelter, when he tormented her by showing up by her bedside and slipping away suddenly, so fast she did not see him go, that he may not have really been there, even though she saw him as opaque and as dimensional as her pillow. She was afraid that she might be going crazy. Yet she was also afraid that her son might be there and in trouble, and if she didn't search for him he would be kidnapped and die, and she was afraid that if she didn't pay attention to the voices that threatened her, they would lead her into an alley and kill her. This is the terrible dilemma of madness, that if you ignore the phenomena—if you tell yourself that the voices and the visions are twisted figments of your imagination—and you are wrong, the cost is so very high, because the voices promise you your own destruction. Those are the grounds, after all, on which Pascal became a Christian, or at least so he recorded—that if he believed and he was wrong, he risked being a fool, but if he did not believe and he was wrong, he risked eternal damnation. He chose belief. We live, all of us, in the gray zone of interpretation, judging what in our world is truly real.

That dilemma is more precarious, and disbelief perhaps more risky, on the street than in the middle-class, housed world because it is interlaced with the rage, humiliation, and fear of everyday life on the street. Most people with psychosis go through many years of doubting even the most definitely made diagnosis. To accept the diagnosis, they must be able to see themselves as having symptoms—being able to identify their nagging worry that the house is bugged as meaning something quite different than what their mind insists. But when Zaney walks down the street, she does see people massing, watching her, probably engaged in criminal activity. Women do get raped on her block. People do taunt her. I've seen them do it. The danger the voices warn her of is real. And she knows that she is not like the wretched women who are flagrantly psychotic in the drop-in center and on the street corner, completely out of touch with the everyday world, easy victims of theft and assault. She knows she's not as badly off as that. They are crazy. She is strong. And so she neither wants nor—she thinks—needs the psychiatric care that other people offer her. She cannot allow herself to be that kind of person.

And so she says no to offers of help.

Return to Baseline

A Woman with Acute-Onset, Non-affective Remitting Psychosis in Thailand

JULIA CASSANITI

Psychiatrists and psychologists in the United States often think of schizophrenia as a lifelong illness with a downward, debilitating course. They have come to recognize that more people do better in the long term than this stereotype suggests. For most people in America who can be diagnosed with schizophrenia, the so-called positive symptoms of hallucinations and delusions often diminish around the age of forty or fifty. Still, few people during the first few decades of the illness are thought to have periods in which they seem completely free of symptoms.

In other parts of the world, most notably Southeast Asia, there are patterns of schizophrenia-like illness that take a different form. Intense periods of active psychosis (delusions and hallucinations) are followed by periods in which the sufferer seems completely free of all symptoms of mental illness. In these lucid periods, persons are able to work, parent, and participate in social life the same as any other healthy member of their culture. Sometimes the person seems dramatically, flagrantly psychotic and seems to meet all the criteria for schizophrenia—and then the illness simply clears up and goes away. Poi, a young, urban Thai woman Julia has known for more than ten years, appeared to suffer from this form of schizophrenia, called "non-affective acute remitting psychosis" (NARP) in the scientific literature.

When I get sick the world just kind of fades around me. It's like I'm on an island in the middle of the ocean. I can't get off the island. I'm not tired. I'll want to eat but I can't: the spirits show me the noodles I try to eat, but when I look the noodles are flesh, baby flesh. Sometimes there's blood everywhere. Sometimes it's funny; sometimes I don't feel scared. It's like a story is going on, like a novel. Like I have to go to a casting to be a movie star, and there are many characters in my story. My friends come and talks to me, like that, it's like a real situation. It's so funny and I laugh.

This is the way Poi, a young Thai woman, described her subjective world during her many psychotic episodes. In these episodes there is a lot going on in her mind. She meets "people" (spirits), has conversations, has experiences that are usually scary but sometimes funny. She has a rich inner life.

But on the outside during an episode, Poi is mostly silent, with flattened affect and few words. After a burst of paranoid suspicion, she becomes mostly unresponsive to the people around her. The episodes have usually occurred at Anusawari Monument, the main bus terminal in downtown Bangkok, where she has ridden on her motorbike, from her house two hours away, in a kind of dissociative fugue. She typically spends a few days to a few weeks at the bus station, dirty and homeless, eating little and barely sleeping. "The spirits, they'll push my face, push it to the floor" and she falls down; later there will be scars on her forehead from her falls in the crowds of the terminal. People may ask her if she's okay, but mostly they just leave her alone. Somehow, through the intervention of a police officer or through the efforts of her parents, she is eventually reconnected with her family. Her father then takes her to the Bangkok Chulalongkorn Psychiatric Hospital, where she is tied to the bed and injected with antipsychotic medications until she is well, about two weeks later. She then leaves the hospital, goes home, seems to recover completely, and begins again to seek cures for her illness and find a job. About four or five months later, she has another episode, and the cycle repeats.

I have known Poi for over ten years. I have watched her cycle through this pattern of psychosis and recovery as she tries, in her periods of clarity, to learn what is wrong with her and to put an end to it. While her symptoms have changed over time, along with her feelings about them, her debilitating illness continues today. Does she have schizophrenia? She doesn't know. Poi, and others in Thailand like her, live largely without a diagnosis: she has, no doubt, been diagnosed during her many short stays at the hospital, but she and her family are unaware of what such a diagnosis might be and are uninterested in finding out.

In fact, Poi meets most or all of the criteria for schizophrenia outlined in our psychiatric nosology. She has striking "positive" symptoms—hallucinations and delusions—and "negative" symptoms—flattened affect, impoverished speech. When she is ill, her cognitive capacity is clearly diminished. She has significant problems in living. Yet the form of her psychosis seems oddly unlike chronic schizophrenia, because her episodes clear up and go away. She may indeed have episodes that have lasted a month or more; she may have had signs of the disorder that one could pick out for longer periods of time. She may technically meet the classic psychiatric criteria for schizophrenia. But her episodes are often short, as short as a week; and between episodes, she returns to baseline, more or less. Poi's experience of acute onset, brief duration, and full inter-episode recovery seems to be a more common form of psychosis in Southeast Asia than in Europe and the United States.

This periodic pattern is not unknown in Western settings. The more we know about schizophrenia, the more heterogeneous its patterns of course and outcome appear to be. Yet epidemiological work has found that this pattern of intense, acute illness with what seem to be periods of nearly complete remission are, indeed, more common outside of the West.[1] In the World Health Organization studies comparing the outcome of schizophrenia in developing and developed countries, the pattern was twice as common among women as among men, and ten times as common in developing countries as it was in developed countries. These variations are poorly understood. We don't know whether NARP is a truly distinct subtype of schizophrenia, nor whether it ultimately resolves more completely. But anthropological work, particularly in Indonesia, supports the observation that this pattern of psychosis is more common outside of Euro-America.[2]

About eleven out of a thousand people suffer from some kind of psychosis in Thailand, and an estimated 8.8 per thousand fall within the criteria for schizophrenia. This rate places Thailand in the highest decile of global prevalence figures.[3] And yet, according to recent epidemiological data, 95 percent of people with schizophrenia are living in the community, without regular hospital contact.[4] These patients are very sick when they are sick, and yet they may be less disabled than many Americans who have been given the same diagnostic label.[5] If they do have the same disease, they have learned to handle it more effectively. Watching Poi over a decade, I have seen ways in which she has learned to interpret and reinterpret her symptoms. She seems to have some degree of control over them. She may be able to teach us something that we can teach others.

Poi comes from a Catholic, Chinese–Thai working-class family near Bangkok. Before the onset of her illness she had worked as an arts and education teacher and had married a young man, a paraplegic fellow artist, with whom she had a child. When I first met her in 2001, she was twenty-eight years old. She and her two-year-old daughter were living at an artists' community outside of Bangkok while she was in the process of divorcing her husband. We became friends right away. She was sweet and smart and creative. She told me that she was able to sometimes feel other people's "energy" or "auras." That seemed a little strange, but in the context of the hippie, New Age environment in which she was living, I thought she was just being "cool." Normal. Within a year, however, her experiences took a decided turn for the bizarre. Poi knew this. Later, she told me that the "aura" stage and what happened next were worlds apart. "[The auras, that] was people energy," she told me. "The sickness is Satan energy."

"The first time I experienced the spirit illness," Poi told me, using her own term for her sickness, "I was so, so scared. The energy was so strong." She said that it felt like she was turning into the devil, literally. "My nails got longer, and I had a tail. I felt my face and my body; it felt like I was Satan. I thought, 'I have to kill myself, to become like Jesus.' So I took a knife and cut myself, on my throat." She still has the scar today.

That episode, Poi said, was the scariest and most intense feeling she has ever experienced. Yet a week later—one week after slicing into her throat—she was fine again. She got treatment both at the hospital and at a Buddhist temple, and then she continued her everyday life. She said that about five months later she got sick again—and five months after that, and five months after that. More than ten years later, the cycle of episodes still continues.

Between her episodes she seemed wholly clear. She appeared to have completely remitted, with a full return to baseline. In between episodes, neither I nor any of her family, friends, or acquaintances could tell that there was anything unusual about her. Her intellectual, emotional, social, and bodily behaviors were all normal, and she was fully functional, traveling and working and taking care of her daughter. Each time we met, we sat down together to talk about how she was doing. As I took notes, she would tell me about her latest encounter with psychosis. She told me the stories because I was a friend, but also because she felt that, with my access to the clinical world of the United States, I might be able to help her somehow.

At this point, an American psychiatrist might interject that the very fact of Poi's return-to-baseline indicated that she suffered from bipolar disorder, an illness in which the patient oscillates between highs and lows that are fun-

FIGURE 11. A spirit house of the kind commonly found in forests and in front of houses throughout Thailand. Poi reported that as she drove past hundreds of these each day on her way home, she had to deal with the spirits she encountered at each of them. *(Photo: Julia Cassaniti)*

damentally "affective"—disturbances of mood, rather than of cognition. When someone with bipolar disorder becomes manic, they can appear much like someone with schizophrenia. Yet the characteristic presentation of the bipolar high involves feeling "high"—excited, energized, ebullient. The manic person has no need to sleep. She talks intensely, quickly, as if creativity were overflowing from mind to world. Poi's episodes never had these features; rather, they were typical of schizophrenia. She slowed down. Her thinking muddied. She developed elaborate ideas about people who wanted to hurt her. She wanted to hurt them in return. She found herself in a horrifying phastasmagoria.

"About a month ago," she recounted in 2008, "I'd finally gotten that job at the Waldorf," a position at an elementary school in Bangkok she had wanted for years. As usual, she was fine; no one would have been able to pick her out as "different." She continued:

> I'd just begun there, finally, when I got sick. It was awful. When the sickness came I started writing on my colleagues' office doors. I wrote in big letters crazy things: "You're dying" and "You're dead" and "There's blood everywhere." I ran away from there, I went to the Anusawari Monument. I saw things. I would see them for real, not just in my mind's eye but it's like it's real. People were bleeding everywhere around me. The spirits would come and try to throw me into a well, it was so scary. I was lost there for two weeks, in the spirit world. It's not like human energy, the spirit energy is just . . . like energy all around. It's like television but it's so real, not like dreaming, not like sleeping. They're just like people, but I know they're not human.

Another time, she had been at home when the sickness came on:

> I was lying in bed, and I felt pain in my body. I really wanted to vomit, and I did. They, the spirits, they said they wanted to make me feel the blood come out of my body. I smelled a strange smell, and the Satan energy came. It tried to bite me on the arm and I was hurt, like a dog had bit me. The Satan energy came and said my dad wanted to rape me—it's not true, but it felt real then, because I was in the spiritual sickness world. That time, I drove my motorbike sixty kilometers to Bangkok, but I still smelled the smell, like something rotten.

I visited Poi while she was living in an apartment in a squalid section of Bangkok, sharing a room with her male friend Thom and working as a teacher in a nearby elementary school. I had just flown in from the United States and was on my way up to Chiang Mai, but I stopped in to stay with Poi a few days. She was doing well, enjoying her new job. A few weeks later she called. She was at her parents' house, and she was recovering from another bout of illness. "It was so bad," she told me. "Everything had been fine, but then I lost it, I got sick again." She had begun having sex with Thom a few weeks earlier, and soon after that she noticed he was making international phone calls. She called a number he had used and found Thom's European male lover on the end of the line. She became upset with Thom, she became suspicious of him, and then she got sick.

Most of the time, however, real-world stress did not seem to have played an important part in triggering her episodes. "I can't think of anything that brought it on," she told me, responding to my questions and thinking back to her early childhood and to her life situation just before she got sick. "I think

I'm normal. Just normal compared to everyone." She could come up with only two problem areas in her life worth mentioning, but she minimized the impact of them on her life as not "very deep." Poi was sent to boarding school when she was only three years old, and stayed for eight years. She described that time as lonely, as "the first problem," but it was not, she admitted, an unusual one for someone of her socioeconomic background. The second "problem area" was her marriage. She had been in love with a man who decided to become an ordained monk, and instead of leaving the monkhood after a short stay, as most men in Thailand do before marriage, the man decided to stay ordained for life, and Poi lost him. Later she met another man, who did become her husband. She became pregnant, and married him "out of pity." She told me that they had "problems," but again, "nothing really serious." It was on meeting this man, though, that she first noticed something happening that was more than a little unusual, which alerted her that something might be wrong. "When I met him, I felt a sense of déjà vu. It was that feeling that made me sleep with him and get pregnant. At the time I didn't think much of it. But it was then that the sickness came on, and so yeah, that experience changed my life." She continued, "It was Satan's plan."

Often her stories of the onset of an episode involved some mention of sex. I asked her if she thought the sickness was about sex, but she said no. "But," she told me, "the Satan energy is always about sex." Poi's illness seemed, in part, to be about trust, and her uncertainty about others' intentions. Sometimes she encountered God in her strange, sick state and found his presence soothing: "Once I smoked, and God touched me; I could feel his energy and I know it's good, sweet." But even in those instances she was uncertain: "Once I asked God, 'Will I ever get better or not?' and I heard the voice, it said 'You will get better' but I didn't know. I don't know if it's God or not. Maybe it's Satan saying this, playing tricks on me."

This element of distrust was often present in the initial stages of her illness, although usually the paranoia was delusional. Within a few days, Poi would shift from seeming fine to suspecting those around her—everyone from her parents to her friends. Then, a few days later, she would completely lose touch with reality. Our good friend Aeh once ran into her in the beginning of an episode, at a mall on the edge of Bangkok. "She wouldn't trust me," he told me later, describing how he tried to bring her to a mall security guard to help call her parents. And indeed she had called me to warn me about Aeh the next day. "Don't trust him," she told me. "I saw him but I ran away." She told me sometimes that she distrusted her parents, who did all they could to help her; in her clear states she was extremely grateful to them, and when she told me she felt suspicious of them, I knew that soon I would not be hearing from her for a few weeks.

I saw the early stages of an episode firsthand once, when Poi came to Chiang Mai to visit me and to seek out a religious specialist she had heard about. The first few days of her visit were fine, and when I later asked the people who had met her then, they remembered her as a completely normal and sweet young woman. About a week into her trip, Poi and I went to a vegetarian restaurant for lunch. The restaurant was connected to a large compound dedicated to Guan Im, the popular Chinese goddess of compassion. Women in white were walking around the temple grounds of the compound, and chickens were passing through the chair legs of the restaurant. We were in the middle of our bowls of noodles when Poi looked up at me and whispered, wide-eyed, "Julia, let's go. We've got to get out of here. There are spirits here, bad spirits." When I looked at her, I saw that her eyes had changed. They had taken on a kind of wild, glossy look, as if she were looking at something that I couldn't see. We went back to my house and sat on the balcony. I felt nervous. She looked at me, and I could tell she was a little distrustful of me. "Why did we go to that place?" she asked. She didn't say anything outright, but I could tell she was wary of me, as if wondering whether I was really her friend at all. It was as if she were asking "Are you really on my side?" It was my worst fear about our friendship: that she would feel that she couldn't count on me, and even think I was trying to harm her. She left the next morning.

When I next heard from Poi a month later, in a phone call from Bangkok, she told me about her latest bout of sickness. She had wandered away from home and met a family of spirits, who talked to her and told her "bad things." She became lost in their world. I had gotten used to these periods in our friendship—she would disappear, and I would later hear about the events of the episode and the following "incarceration" at the psychiatric hospital. But that was the first time I had encountered the beginning of an episode. The change in her appearance and behavior was striking. Within a few weeks she went from a completely normal person to someone with severe psychiatric symptoms. And then, just as soon, she was back.

Poi was desperate to end her sickness. The episodes themselves were not always scary, but they usually terrified her. She hated the hospitals she ended up in and the medicines she was put on. And it was almost impossible for her to hold a job with this kind of sickness, even with its full remission between episodes. Poi couldn't tell employers about her condition, because, she said, "It's hard enough to find a job just as a regular person in Thailand." Given the almost immediate onset of an episode and the disturbing behavior that came with it, not to mention disappearing for weeks at a time until she got better, no employer would consider hiring Poi back after seeing her become sick. "But I need to work," she said. "I have to take care of my daughter." And her daughter was turning into a charming and effervescent young girl. Since her divorce in 2003, Poi had lived at home with her parents, a quiet and concerned older couple with whom I kept in touch over the years. They took care of Poi when she got sick, and helped in raising their grandchild. For work Poi practiced private tutoring for local children in a variety of subjects, including music, art, and English. With this arrangement she was able to (barely) create a semblance of a stable life. When she got sick, she only lost the clients she was working with at the time, and could pick up the work with new people when it was over.

Yet Poi didn't think that she had a mental illness. She thought she had spiritual problems. She didn't think that anything the doctors did actually helped. After her first episode, when she cut her throat with a knife, her family took her to the Chulalongkorn University Hospital in downtown Bangkok. From there they went to Srithanya, the local psychiatric hospital. "It's horrible there," Poi said. "It's a really bad hospital. They tie you down. There are people everywhere. If someone has to go to the bathroom the nurses say 'just go where you are' so there are people shitting in the room, all over. It's like a crazy, horrible place."

"What do the psychiatrists at the hospital say is wrong with you?" I asked. "What do they say when you tell them your symptoms?"

Poi laughed. "Oh, I never tell my story to the doctor." She explained: "When you're in the hospital you need to know what to do to make them release you. Because it's a bad place. So you have to be a nice person and just smile, and don't tell them anything."

When I pushed her to recall some psychiatric explanation, she told me that the psychiatrists said that there was something wrong with her brain. That it couldn't work in harmony. When I pushed her to try to remember some diagnosis, she told me that she didn't know. Then she said that the diagnosis just wasn't important. "At the hospital they talk to you just one minute and then they order the medicine. They don't listen to your story, they don't have time. I don't believe in the hospital. How can they heal with medicine? The idea that they give you medicine and the problem is gone is impossible. When you have a mental sickness it's from a problem you have to deal with yourself. The medicine can't get you better."

Over the years I have known her, Poi has been given a barrage of antipsychotic medicines, including clozapine, perphenazine, and a variety of tranquilizers. The medicine was injected into her in the hospital, while she was tied down, and then given in prescription form when she left the hospital. But, Poi said,

> The medicine never helps. I'll still get sick again. Because the energy still comes as usual. The medicine doesn't help get rid of the things I see or the sounds I hear. The last time I got sick was about one month and two weeks ago. Before that I had been taking the medicine for two months. When I got sick again, of course, I stopped taking the medicine. After I got better I took the medicine again, but my pastor said to stop it. I told the pastor I promised my dad I would keep taking it, but she said the medicine isn't good, that my dad isn't in the spiritual world so he doesn't know. In the spiritual world we need to rely on God, not on medicine.

"What medicine are you taking now?" I asked her once. To find out, she rummaged through some things on her desk to find the pills. The label was blank.

What did help, she said, was religious intervention. In addition to this largely involuntary and (from her perspective) largely futile engagement with the biomedical psychiatric world, Poi also actively pursued a variety of spiritual treatments. These ranged from retreats at Buddhist temples to visits to Christian churches throughout Thailand—places that, for the most part, boast a tradition of spiritual specialists and exorcists that, while popular and relatively mainstream, are at odds with more "orthodox" traditions of Buddhism and Christianity in the country.

After being released from the psychiatric hospital following her first episode, Poi went to see a Buddhist monk about what had happened and to take the *nam mon*, the holy water thought by Thai Buddhists to cure illness. She stayed at the temple for a month, and later returned for a month at a time about three years in a row. "At that place," she told me,

> there was one woman who dressed in the monk's color of robes, but she was a woman, and she said she is the Buddha and she's the Buddha that came to this world again. At the temple I have to chant many words that I don't understand, and they say "if you chant a thousand times you will know what will happen to

you" and I did that. They know a lot about religion. It was them who told me it was the Satan energy. They told the disciple of that temple that it's not a real god, but why Jesus died on the cross, he did many things; they have a lot of knowledge about many religions and they accept many things about Satan energy.

Poi learned a lot at the temple, but she decided that the place was not for her. "I didn't like the temple," she told me, "because they're so dry. They're just chanting, there's no love, no Jesus. I have to just chant by myself there, it's just lonely." It was at the psychiatric hospital that she met a girl who told her about the therapeutic power of the Bible:

> She said Jesus could help me, and I'm Catholic so I believed her. So I went to church, and they tried to help me, tried to pray for me. At that first church they had a set plan, with seven steps to freedom, and they asked me a lot of questions about my life, about what happened in my life from when I was a baby to when I grew up. They asked me if I suffered from anything, if I was angry any time, asked about my boyfriend, about everyone I've slept with. They wanted to know why the Satan energy came into my life.

But this, too, failed. She became sick again and again and again, even after returning to the church.

Yet Poi was convinced that her problem was spiritual, not psychiatric. She thought that the illness was the work of Satan—that it was within the spiritual realm of a battle between the goodness of Jesus, on one hand, and the evil of Satan on the other, which had become for her the meaningful discourse and explanatory model of distress. She believed the spiritual "specialists" she continued to see regularly, often traveling far to visit famous exorcists and specialists, even after many failed recovery attempts at such places. But she didn't agree with every pronouncement of Satan's intentions that she heard from these specialists. At one spiritual-healing retreat center, the pastor talked about her friend Thom. "Remember Thom?" she asked me recently. "The pastor says it's black magic from Thom that's hurting me. It's not about Thom being gay or not, it's about his spirit. The pastor said Thom has a disgusting spirit. That he slept with many men, and I don't know how to say it, but I feel it. . . . I don't know, I don't think it's that, exactly."

It seemed to me that Poi's insistence that her illness involved spirits had helped her, slowly, to improve. For she did improve during the time I was in contact with her. For about the first six years, I couldn't make out any change in her pattern of illness. She appeared completely sane when she was well, and was disconnected from reality for a week or more about every four or five months when she was sick. Gradually, though, I started to notice something new, both when she was well and from her stories of sickness. Her periods of full-blown illness were becoming less marked by a total separation from reality, showing what seemed like an improvement. At the same time, her periods of remittance were becoming less lucid. The hallucinatory, delusional world of her sickness had begun to enter into her regular life. In the past she had always described the spirits as part of a separate world, with the real world "fading" into the background. Now, however, she could begin to interact with them in her own plane of existence, and this meant holding a certain degree of control over her sickness.

The more flagrant symptoms of psychosis often (though not always) improve when someone reaches their forties and fifties, and Poi was close to forty when I noticed a change; her involvement with the spirits may have been a consequence of an improved condition, rather than its cause. But whether cause or effect, Poi's engagement with the spirits allowed her to see herself as part of a great battle, and not as a person with a broken brain. It allowed her to feel like she could do something. It helped her to feel that she was in control.

"A few days ago," she told me in 2010, as we were sitting in a storefront in Bangkok, drinking tea and talking normally, without feeling an episode coming on at all, "I passed the house of a family who had been killed. That night the family came from the house, and I went to that house in my vision. They tried to take me into their house. It was so real. I felt like I was in the house. I tried to pray and they released me, and they faded away." This ability to "make" the spirits fade away was new; I had never heard her engage with the spirits in that way, acting within the hallucination to do something to put an end to it.

Poi has also recently been able to interact with the spirits in a way that she feels can help others. She told me she had recently gone to the house of a student, where she encountered the spirits in the house at the red Chinese altar that every Chinese Buddhist in Thailand keeps in their home.

> The owner of the house is a friend of the family, and he asked me to talk to the spirit there at the altar. So I did, I talked to the spirit, and the spirit said many things, like what kind of food the spirits there like, how the people should offer the food. . . . The spirit said "talk to the owner of the house, tell him about one man who works for him, he's dangerous." And the next day I found out the man had just gotten out of prison and tried to take six thousand baht from the owner, but I had warned the owner.

These days she also has a different attitude about her illness. When I last spoke to her, in the summer of 2014, she showed me the perphenazine pills she had been prescribed. She still was not taking the pills, but instead of appearing anxious about them, she seemed confidently indifferent. Instead of the desperation in her voice when she spoke about trying to find a cure, she said that she had come to terms with her illness. "I've accepted it but," she told me, "I hope that every year I will get better. Because I can't believe that when I'm sixty or seventy years old I'll still be sick like this." According to her parents, herself, and my own observations, Poi has improved slowly but steadily over the years. There may yet be a day when her suffering becomes more ordinary—rather than extraordinary—and integrated into her daily life and into the realms of meaning she shares with others in her social world.

A Fragile Recovery in the United States

NEELY A. L. MYERS

Neely met Meg in 2006 while conducting ethnographic research in a public mental-health-treatment setting in an urban area of the United States. She wanted to understand how participating in mental health services shaped the everyday lives of the people who used them. The institution where she conducted research, here called the "Center," is widely considered to offer some of the most effective and innovative psychosocial rehabilitation treatment services available in the country. Its aim is to help those who use its mental health services (who call themselves "members") to recover meaningful lives. She found herself documenting instead the challenges that confront those who struggle with mental illness in the United States. Meg did better than most. But her story also shows the challenges created by the expectations of independence in our society and by the rules that guard against exploiting the offer of help.

————————

I have a younger brother who has had many different psychiatric diagnoses over the years. He has lived in a state institution most of his life. The question that drives me to engage in research with people experiencing psychotic disorders such as schizophrenia is very personal: What might I learn from those who have managed this often devastating illness about how to help my brother?

To understand more about recovery, I spent several days each week (including most weekends) at the Center in 2005–06. About two-thirds of its members had been diagnosed with schizophrenia at some point in their lives. I spent my time there talking to people, attending the classes they attended,

FIGURE 12. A member drew this cartoon of the Center.

and playing the games they played. I watched them surf the web on old desk-top computers and watch television in the living room, and I made art with them in the art room. I ate with them. Sometimes we took "field trips" to local parks, or to McDonald's or Starbuck's, and even to some mental-health advo-cacy events. During the fifteen months I spent at the Center, Meg was one of the few recovery "success stories" I encountered. Her story gives me hope, but it also illustrates how the odds in this country are stacked against people trying to live with schizophrenia.

I first noticed Meg one stormy afternoon as I settled into the lopsided circle of orange plastic seats at a therapy group I regularly attended called "Makin' It." Lightning streaked across a large windowpane behind her, accen-tuating the slightness of her frame. In this group, we were supposed to talk about what members were doing to "make it" in the community—how they were succeeding, and how they could learn from each other what it took to function effectively in the so-called normal world. As we settled in, Meg swiped at tears dripping from her jaw with the frayed edge of a gray Yale sweatshirt. I assumed she had gotten it from the free-clothes closet in the basement of the Center, which is where most members found their clothes.

Joel, the group leader, reminded everyone that there was a visiting anthro-pologist in the room (me) and asked if that was okay. Everyone nodded in agreement, and then he turned to Meg. "Are you okay, Meg? Do you want to share with the group?"

She groaned. "I am going to be evicted this weekend, and I have no way to pay for a U-Haul or storage or movers." As thunder shook the room, many of us jumped. "I am going to lose everything!"

The group nodded sympathetically. Rain spattered the window.

I was there to participate in people's lives, but anthropologists take different views of what participant observation entails. They draw the line in different places. I found myself moved by a strong impulse to do something, not just to watch her suffer.

After the group, I talked to some staff who regretted that they could not help Meg; they were obligated to maintain professional boundaries. I thought about it, and a day or two later, I told Meg that I could help her with her eviction. Offering my resources to Meg, I felt, was the right thing to do and would let her know that I wanted to be her friend. To my relief, she was delighted.

A few days later, in between more rain showers, Meg and I transferred her things to my car. As it happened, she lived only a few blocks from me. Her sixth-floor studio apartment overlooked the river. She had typical college-student furniture: a futon, a coffee table, a TV, and a long, narrow kitchen with dishes, pots and pans, a microwave, and a toaster.

"Wow," I said. "This is pretty nice. Not sure I could afford it." I was curious—the place was nice. I couldn't have afforded it on my graduate-student stipend.

"This is a rent-controlled building," she explained softly. "I have lived here ten years. And I have—well, I had—savings from when I worked." It turned out that she had worked as an executive secretary for the vice president of a corporation for five years, before things fell apart in her mid- to late twenties. She was older than I thought.

Meg had not packed. She did not have boxes. So, first, we asked for free boxes from the liquor store. They had holes in the sides for handles, but they were better than nothing. As we were finishing, I spotted a diploma on the wall. From Yale. I pictured her graduation under a blue New England sky with balloons, fanfare, and well-wishing. I carefully wrapped her degree in a towel and placed it in a battered whiskey carton. As I closed the lid, I felt a bit dizzy with fear. Her Yale diploma made her seem suddenly more like me. Would my diploma ever be packed away as I prepared to be evicted?

"Meg, where are we going?" I asked, sealing the box to keep out the rain.

"I am hoping we can take them to my new emergency housing shelter." Meg had been very private about her destination when we had arranged a time to meet. I was shocked to hear that we were going to a shelter.

"Don't you have a mom or something?" I blurted out in surprise.

She stared past me. "My mother has a very small studio apartment, and she has no space for me. Not even to sleep."

"Sure, okay," I said gently. I felt ashamed of my presumptions.

Months later, when she trusted me more, Meg told me that she also had an older brother, a child psychiatrist who lived in the suburbs. His young daughters, her nieces, were a great joy for her. He must not know her troubles, she insisted, or he would not let her visit her nieces. And so, after she lost her place, she met his family at the zoo or the American Girl store downtown. She planned days in advance to book the laundry room and shower at the Center so that she could freshly launder her best clothes and bathe before they met.

But the morning we moved her things, she only told me that she was going into a temporary shelter. It was one of those perfect spring mornings with puffy clouds, a bright sky, and crisp, refreshing air. I felt like I could have been Meg's mother, dropping her off at her college dorm. I imagined unloading her boxes, unpacking her new room, adding a few pleasant touches, and heading off to walk on the river or have a picnic in the park. As she climbed into my car, I asked about the futon, the table, the chairs, and the coffee table. She spoke softly: "They will probably be out on the street later, after the eviction, if you want them." We grew so quiet that I rolled down the windows to let in the wind.

I would come to know Meg better in the next months. Slowly she revealed pieces of her story. Her father, her hero, had shot himself in the head after a messy divorce. Afterward, Meg experienced a severe depression followed by what she called a "nervous breakdown." She began to hear her dead father, and to see him. She did not go into details about these experiences, which left her agitated and unable to concentrate. In fact, she never said anything about hearing dead people again. But at the time, Meg had found it impossible to manage her job as an executive administrative assistant. She couldn't concentrate, lost her interest in working, and started to miss work. She was fired. She took a break, trying to regroup, and lived off of her savings.

After that, it was difficult to find someone to hire her. People wanted to know what she had been doing during the six-month blank spot on her résumé, and that blank spot became a gap of years. The Americans with Disabilities

Act is supposed to protect people with psychiatric disabilities from job discrimination, but if you disclose having a psychiatric disability before being hired, members told me, people just don't hire you. And if you don't disclose, gaps in your work history remain unexplained. Research has found that 86 percent of people with psychiatric disabilities didn't know how to secure special accommodations using this law.[1]

After several humiliating job interviews, during which she reluctantly admitted her father's suicide and her subsequent breakdown and was not hired, Meg decided to use her savings and apply for Social Security disability benefits. She told me that this would be for the best. "Then I don't have to relive this experience every time I go for an interview—and still not get hired," she insisted. "Explaining myself in job interviews is so painful. I worry it might drive me into another breakdown. And I am not even sure I can work. It might be too stressful."

In fact, many of the members I met described the reentry work opportunities available to them after a mental health crisis, regardless of their education and skill set, as the "three C's—a cashier, a custodian, or a customer service representative." The night shift was a common starting position. For many, managing symptoms and the demands of a night shift, or a job in a fast-paced customer-service setting, was a challenge. And most could not rely on a parent or sibling for financial help.

To help keep people from abject poverty, there is a federally funded system that provides a small stipend (Social Security "disability" income) as well as some form of health insurance for people deemed unable to work. To get such a stipend, Meg had to be assessed as "psychiatrically disabled" by both a psychiatrist and a judge. Lawmakers have defined the category of "psychiatric disability" to describe anyone whose "mental illness significantly interferes with the performance of major life activities, such as learning, thinking, communicating, and sleeping, among others."[2] Meg set out to get the stipend, she told me, because her nervous breakdown had left her unable to work. She needed money to live, and she needed health insurance to afford the medications she needed to remain stable.

Woven into the social safety net of this psychiatric disability income and the insurance it provides is a powerful value system. According to American notions of social worth, adults should naturally seek to be rational, autonomous, and hard-working, to establish themselves as valued adults who are welcome in the mainstream community. Those who are unable to do so are thought of as in need of financial assistance. Unless they are independently wealthy, people often do need financial assistance to survive.

But the process of being assigned a financial stipend for a psychiatric disability tends to strip people of their sense of social worth and erode their sense of self.[3] It is challenging not to be able to meet the cultural expectations of gainful employment. Without work, people perceive themselves to be less valued by others in mainstream society. This is often described as alienating and painful.[4] It seems to signal the permanent loss of a promising future.

Many want the disability status (so that they will have a stipend and medical insurance to pay for expensive psychiatric medications) yet deny the symptoms that would gain them a diagnosis. Even when people are willing to admit such symptoms to a psychiatrist, the judge may not approve the psychiatric disability stipend. Judges familiar with the system are sometimes loath to grant disability, for the data suggest that those who are given the stipends rarely return to work.[5] It is not uncommon for people to try two, three, or more times to get disability status before they succeed. The process is cumbersome. The lines are long. The forms are confusing. Scheduling a hearing with a judge takes months. If your claim is denied, at least in the state where Meg lived, it can take another year to appeal the judge's decision.

The judge assigned to Meg's case did not initially grant her psychiatric disability. She told me that this was because she had a Yale degree and spotless work history and because he thought she was only depressed—a condition from which we assume people can recover. "Pull yourself up by your boot straps," the judge had told her. Meg appealed her case and did not apply for more jobs. By the time we met, her savings were gone.

So here we were: driver and passenger, housed and homeless. I double parked in front of a tall, cream brick building downtown. Shoddily dressed people smoked out front, hunching to keep their cigarettes dry as a light drizzle began.

To get her things safely inside, Meg guarded the elevator as I ran back and forth to the car, unlocking and relocking between trips. We piled the elevator with liquor boxes of books and records, a record player, and trash bags stuffed with clothes. They were now all of Meg's worldly possessions. Then we rode up to the sixteenth floor. The elevator opened to reveal a windowless foyer with a small desk, a fake tree, and two locked, alarm-rigged doors with secured glass windows on either side. I hesitated. This looked so much like . . . jail.

When Meg introduced herself, the woman behind the desk scowled. "You're late. Check-in was at ten. It's quarter past. And this is not a dorm, honey. You only get one suitcase."

My heart sank. Meg glanced back at the packed elevator with a sob.

"It's okay," I assured her. And then she hugged me, which surprised me greatly. She had been very aloof, but her veneer had dissolved. She needed that hug.

"Miss, she needs to pick one suitcase and you need to go. She is late for intake, and you are holding up the elevator!"

"Okay, Meg, I am going to take this stuff home and I will store it in an empty storage unit in the basement of my building." It was a hasty decision, but I thought I could find an unused storage unit and hoped the superintendent would not notice. "I will give you keys when you get out. Please do not worry. Your things will be there for you in sixty days, okay?"

Meg calmed down, dug out her primary suitcase, and offered to help me put her things back in my car, but the woman interrupted us. Meg could not leave. Now that Meg was inside, she had to remain there without visitors for two weeks before she could leave again, or she forfeited her spot. I gave her one last hug.

Everything seemed much heavier on the way back. When I got home, my husband helped me find and clean an empty storage space. It was just a concrete cell, but it could be locked. I took the whiskey box with her diploma in it and carefully placed it on top. If the basement flooded, at least her diploma wouldn't be ruined. We scrawled our apartment number and my maiden name on the outside of the unit to make it look like the others, and then shut Meg's belongings inside with a padlock.

When her sixty days at the transitional housing program ended, I met her to give her the key. She still had neither a disability income nor the prospect of a job. She had food stamps, soup kitchens, and a very tiny public-assistance stipend of about $25 per week. This is not unusual for those who enter into the temporary shelter system with psychiatric needs. Many people with serious psychotic disorders, with and without benefits, shuffle from one shelter to another, sometimes getting kicked out and landing on the street, sometimes getting supported housing, sometimes ending up in jail or a hospital bed. This is the long, slow, seminomadic life, struggling to live on "next to nothing," that anthropologist Kim Hopper has called the "institutional circuit."[6]

When her sixty days at the temporary shelter were over, Meg was sent to a homeless shelter in the basement of a Unitarian Church. "That is like the Ritz of the shelters," another member reassured me one afternoon as I fretted about Meg. "If you can get in there, you don't want to leave. As for the other shelters, well, mostly I'd rather be in jail . . . at least there's a guard."

I flinched. "Sorry, just being honest," he said. Ralph was also homeless and waiting to receive government disability benefits. He knew all about the shelters. In fact, he had stayed at the shelter Meg was now in, but he too had to leave when he reached the limit.

When Meg returned to the Center, she told me that the Unitarian Shelter carefully screened people before letting them stay. It was in no way like having her own place—Meg still slept, ate, and showered with others and had to leave from 7 A.M. to 7 P.M.—but it was clean and safe. Meg could store her belongings there during the day and sleep in the same bed each night.

In mid-July, Meg read in a local paper that a college friend was having a free art show across the city. "I haven't talked to her in years, but I would love to see her," she told me wistfully. The problem? The show started at 5:30 P.M., and it was at least a forty-five-minute bus ride each way. She had saved bus vouchers for the trip (the Center gave transport vouchers to people to get home, which they often saved), but the shelter staff would not let her in after seven, so she would need to leave the show by six. Meg begged; they said no. Rules were rules.

She went anyway, carefully staying only half an hour. She said that she never managed to talk to her friend. She knew she had to make it back on time. When she stepped outside of the art gallery, her heart sank. It was pouring rain. The streets were flooded and the buses were slow. She arrived at the shelter ten minutes late, and they would not let her in. Meg lost her bed. According to the rules, they could not reconsider her situation for six months. If you break the rules, they told her, you face the consequences.

Across the city, I was watching children whoop and swim in the flooded streets, looking out from a friend's window in the bright gleam of a fading summer day. The city's storm drains had backed up. Perched on my friend's balcony, I laughed at the scene. Half a mile away, Meg was wading toward a police station, with her suitcase on her head to keep it above the flooded streets. The white cotton dress she wore for the art show was soaked in foul, gritty water. When she finally arrived at the station, an officer told her that the shelters were full. More people want beds on a night with standing water in the streets.

Because she had Medicaid, the police offered to get her to a suburb, where there were beds. She could ride back the next day on public transportation. When they climbed into the car around 11 P.M., Meg immediately fell asleep.

When she awakened, she told me, she found herself at a nursing home in another state. She refused to stay. "First of all, I was in the wrong state. And they hold you for at least twenty-eight days when they admit you and you can't leave until they say so after that, and of course they want to keep you because they're collecting money from the government for housing you," Meg fumed later as we sorted donated clothes in the Center's basement. "It could have started my Social Security application over if it looked like I had switched states. A nightmare."

The police who had brought her there told her that she was in a different precinct now, so it was up to the local police to help her, and they left. Meg left, too. She found an all-night McDonald's and enough change to buy a cup of coffee.

As dawn approached, the McDonald's employees asked her to leave for loitering. She stayed nearby anyway, sitting on a curb in the morning fog. "At least," she sighed, "the rain had finally stopped." When the sun came up, Meg called her mom to pick her up.

When Meg arrived back in the city, her mom let her stay with her for a few days, but then she had to go back out on her own. She found a shelter that would take her, but she needed to get in line every day. She did so nearly every day for the next several months. The shelter wasn't particularly nice. She had bedbugs and lice. She had dark circles under her eyes and grimy, messy clothes. She carried only a few items—a change of clothes and toiletries. She used a rolling briefcase instead of a suitcase or backpack, so that she would look, she told me, like a businesswoman to passersby. Good idea, I thought—except for your torn T-shirts, ragged tennis shoes, and matted hair.

The rest of her items stayed in my storage unit, and I gave her a key. I spotted her going into and out of the storage area at odd hours. But I didn't invite her into my apartment. When I had invited two other people from the Center over earlier in the year, one of them had become paranoid (or that's how she explained it in a later apology) and claimed I was coercing them to talk to me by inviting them over for tea. After that, my research oversight board told me not to invite people to my home.

When the temperature fell in the autumn, I wondered if she slept in the storage unit. It was dark, cold, moldy, and infested with moths, mice, roaches, and silverfish. There was no running water or toilet. Still, it was relatively safe, peaceful, and quiet. The shelter where she had been staying was hard to get to, and the lines were long for everything—showers, meals, getting in, getting a bed. And the living was hard—drug addicts, prostitutes, felons, thieves. And her things were, after all, in the unit.

Early one morning, my husband went to fetch forgotten late-night laundry from the building's shared laundry room and spotted Meg sleeping there in the warm, sweet air. "I could not wake her," he said pensively. "She looked too peaceful." I had not thought of how the storage key could also open the laundry unit and the entry doors to the rest of the building, but I also could not bring myself to tell her to leave.

Not long afterward, I moved out. The superintendent approached Meg within days after I left, she told me later. He was polite but firm. Her things had to be out in twenty-four hours or he would call the police and report her for trespassing. Somehow Meg located $40 for a monthly storage unit a few miles away and stole a grocery cart to push her belongings there.

This time, Meg kept her papers with her in the briefcase. She feared something would happen to them in the storage unit. We looked through them one afternoon at the Center. She handled each paper as gently as a snakeskin. Creative-writing essays and poetry from college, letters from old friends bundled with string, and of course her college diploma.

One afternoon I found her at the Center in a bedraggled heap, curled up on a couch in the TV room. Workmen had caught her up on the Center's roof in the early-morning hours. In the hubbub, someone stole her suitcase. The suitcase really had nothing of monetary value, which only added to Meg's despair. I imagined someone crouched in an alley, tossing her papers into urine-soaked slush puddles, her Yale diploma crumpled next to a dumpster, its silver seal glinting in the sun.

Yet Meg somehow managed. She found another shelter. She registered, for free, for voice and guitar classes at a city music college, which she enjoyed immensely. These free classes fill up very quickly, and to register, she joined a long nighttime line of other people. "It's funny," she said. "The registration night was amazing because I am in a community of people all happy to be there out on the street. I am out there most nights, but they don't know that, and for them it's a fun occasion. They bring chairs and sleeping bags, coolers, you know. . . ."

That next fall, we rehearsed for a few months for a donor performance to raise funds for the Center. The afternoon of the dress rehearsal, Meg and I

FIGURE 13. The lives of those on the street and in the institutional circuit are hemmed in by rules, some of which are posted on this window and doors. *(Photos: T. M. Luhrmann)*

drove to pick up McDonald's for everyone's lunch. "Neely," she exclaimed, "I have some wonderful news!"

Ideas raced through my mind. A new job? A new partner? "Well, what is it?"

"I'm schizoaffective!" Meg proclaimed joyously.

I could only stammer in response.

"It's wonderful!" Meg gushed on. "Before, I was trying to get disability benefits with a depression diagnosis, but that is almost impossible anymore. With schizoaffective disorder, though, the judge can't say no!" She was radiant, jubilant, happier than I had ever seen her. She said she had received a letter from a psychiatrist certifying her as schizoaffective, which she would be able to use in court to justify her disability stipend. "Schizoaffective" describes someone who meets criteria for schizophrenia but is also fairly consistently depressed. At the time, my brother had the same diagnosis. Her announcement made me feel very uneasy as I thought about what this condition had meant for him.

It was never clear to me what Meg said to this psychiatrist in order to establish her disability. I knew things were not okay for her. Meg often thought that people were talking about her and following her. She had tried to have someone arrested who was "following her" when that person claimed they were not. At the Center, she accused other members of stealing from her and harassing her. She complained that the doctor said she had paranoid delusions and asserted that she did not agree.

It's not unusual for people to struggle with accepting what a doctor says about them and even to find it intolerable, especially when the doctor is interpreting the deeply personal experience of psychosis for them.[7] In the United States, the diagnosis of schizophrenia is often imagined to be a kind of death sentence.

What had allowed her to accept a diagnosis now? Over 85 percent of the people using the Center meet criteria for a diagnosis of schizophrenia. Maybe all the time she had spent there made it seem almost normal to her. When I had set out to fit in among the members to the best of my ability, I decided not to look at people's clinical records, so I can't confirm her previous diagnosis. Maybe she had always had this diagnosis, but had never talked about it before.

In any case, it was clear to me that in our own relationship, and likely in her relationship with clinicians, she initially resisted describing any symptoms other than those associated with depression, even though she knew that those other symptoms, like hearing voices or paranoid delusions, would help her obtain a stipend. While severe depression and other disorders qualify one for disability status, caseworkers and members often claimed that applications for disability were more likely to be granted to someone with psychosis. Now Meg seemed to be happy because she accepted a diagnosis that she thought would help her obtain disability status.

This whole situation worried me deeply. Disability stipends are better than public assistance, but they also leave a person living below the federal poverty level and include disincentives to work. I had seen many clients fall into the cyclical trap of the institutional circuit, scraping by on their small stipends, depending on food pantries and soup kitchens, accidentally violating the tough rules of cheap, supported housing environments as easily as Meg had violated the rules of the Unitarian Shelter, and ending up back on the street again.

I did not want this for Meg.

But as far as I could tell, things went well for her, at least in the next year or two. Her life improved. She got her disability stipend. Her mother let her move in with her, since she could help pay the mortgage. Next, Meg developed a life plan that motivated her. First, she would buy a guitar, and then save a down payment for her own place and find a good roommate. She envisioned playing music and singing, an occupation by which she hoped to ultimately make a living. She continued taking music lessons to work toward this goal. At Christmastime, Meg took me out for Thai food in the restaurant in her mom's building. She looked vibrant. She insisted on paying the tab. Meg had gone from being a homeless person who needed me to being a friend. A little money had made a huge difference.

A few months later, after I had moved away, Meg sent me a large box of goodies. Enclosed was a beautiful card. She wanted to thank me, she said, for all I had done. She had acquired an affordable apartment and a nice roommate, and was still taking free music classes. When I emailed to thank her, she told me that she had even had a chance to travel to the Superbowl with her mom and was elated.

The next time I was in the city, I drove by the return address from her card. The building, in a quiet, working-class neighborhood, was charming. It was a far cry from some of the homeless shelters Meg had lived in before. I parked on the quiet street and asked my passenger to wait. It was late and I didn't want to wake anyone, but there was her last name on the buzzer, next to number 305. As I climbed back into the car, I noticed a light in a third-floor window with white, lacy curtains. And then, almost as in a dream, I heard the faint strum of guitar strings. Sweet Meg finally had a place of her own.

Advocates define "recovery" as

> a process, a way of life, an attitude, and a way of approaching the day's challenges. . . . The need is to meet the challenge of the disability and to reestablish a new and valued sense of integrity and purpose within and beyond the limits of the disability; the aspiration is to live, work, and love in a community in which one makes a significant contribution.[8]

Meg seemed to have a life she considered worth living.

What enabled Meg to reach this point when so many others do not? This is a hard question for me to answer. I spent two years watching most everyone who attended the Center fail, and I've seen many other people fail since then. But I've seen others fair well, with some strong resources in place.

Part of what helped Meg, I believe, was that she persistently protected her sense of self. She believed that she was a strong woman with a lot to offer. No doubt this was formed in part by her pre-illness successes: a college degree from a prestigious university, a reasonably well-paying job she held for five years. She seemed to have had a stable middle-class upbringing, at least until her father's suicide, and her mother and brother lived middle-class lives. Her ability to draw upon a sense of herself as more than a patient—more than a member—and the social know-how she had developed before her illness allowed her to go out in the community and join music classes, attend art shows, and look for other free community events, which connected her to nonpatients. Many people with schizophrenia who use public mental-health care, by contrast, lose their sense of belonging in the mainstream community. The more isolated they become through participation in the mental health system, the more they lose practice in everyday chit-chat; with little to talk about, people forget how to have a "normal" conversation. Instead they talk to anyone about medications, symptoms, and other sad things. Outsiders shy away from these conversations.

Meg also benefited, very likely, from her complete absence of interest in street drugs and alcohol as a form of self-medication or an opportunity to "belong" with a group of users. Maybe she had used substances before, but in our time together, she told me that she absolutely did not. Many, many people living on the streets turn to drugs and alcohol for solace from symptoms and overdo it, especially in acute phases of the illness. Street drugs are a way to fit in when you are acting odd; psychiatric drugs are not. Estimates suggest that around half of people with schizophrenia in the public mental-health system are dually diagnosed, which means they have a history of substance abuse and a mental illness.[9] When I met her, Meg didn't even smoke cigarettes. Many women in the system also report using prostitution to make extra money, and they end up using drugs and alcohol to manage the often traumatic fallout of these choices. From what I could tell, Meg never participated in this "street" lifestyle. Also, Meg had never been (to the best of my knowledge) beaten or raped while living in the shelters or on the streets, something that many people with serious mental illness experience.

Meg's access to safe spaces, such as the comparatively safe emergency-housing program and the Unitarian Shelter, was due, at least in part, to her having the aptitude and means to find out about these opportunities and complete the paperwork correctly. She even managed to stay in a cheap hostel for international guests for a few days by pretending she was from another country and had lost her passport. And she located that free music school, and had the wherewithal to wait in line through the night for a slot.

Meg was smart, and she was lucky—she had no overt cognitive issues or negative symptoms. She described some problems that kept her from working well, like having paranoid thoughts about her coworkers, but overall she seemed very present and able to relate. When I interacted with her, she didn't seem odd, emotionally flat or inappropriate, or socially unresponsive in the way I had come to expect of many individuals at the Center who were diagnosed with schizophrenia. The cognitive impairments and the so-called negative symptoms of schizophrenia turn out to be the symptoms that are most costly for people; they are more strongly associated with inabilities to work and to live independently than the obvious, florid symptoms of hallucinations or delusions.[10]

Finally, Meg worked hard to maintain a good relationship with her family. She went to great lengths to impress her brother and remain a good aunt. This gave her another positive social role beyond her illness. Also, her mother helped her, and let her stay with her for a while. Several of the Center's clients that I met had little or no connection to their families, either because of their own struggles with drugs and alcohol or because they had broken their relationships with parents who they claimed had physically or sexually abused them.

I may have contributed, as well, to helping Meg recover. I did buy her a guitar. An anonymous donor gave me some money to buy Christmas presents for Center clients, and Meg helped me coordinate choosing, buying, and distributing the gifts. I asked her what she wanted. She said a guitar, and I gave it to her.

I hope she is still in the apartment. I have not been able to contact her. Her recovery was something like what I had wanted for my brother, but she helped me understand—at a time when he, too, was homeless and struggling—just how difficult recovery can be.

Conclusion

JOCELYN MARROW AND T. M. LUHRMANN

Schizophrenia is the story of the way that poverty, violence, and being on the wrong side of power drive us mad.[1] The madness only emerges from a body vulnerable to experience it, from genes and pathways we do not yet entirely understand. Of course, people whose bodies are more vulnerable are more likely to fall ill, and those with highly vulnerable bodies may fall ill in the midst of love and care. But schizophrenia is not a genetic lightning bolt. People who are humiliated and abused and bullied are more likely to fall ill with schizophrenia. People who are born poor or live poor are more likely to develop schizophrenia. People with dark skins are more likely to fall ill in white-skinned neighborhoods, probably (scientists think) because they feel their lesser social status more keenly. People who live in urban areas are more likely to fall ill with the condition, perhaps because they are more likely to feel socially threatened.[2] These are epidemiological findings about specific social circumstances. They suggest that when life beats people up, they are at more risk of developing psychosis. As our ethnography demonstrates, the conditions that challenge people—the ways in which the beating-up happens—shift from social setting to social setting. What the different conditions share is the experience of social defeat.

Social defeat is a common term in animal studies used to describe the physical defeat of one animal by another. When a male rat (the intruder) is placed in the cage of another male rat (the resident), the resident typically attacks the intruder and forces him to display submissive behavior. The defeat increases dopaminergic activity in the rat's mesolimbic dopamine pathway, the pathway thought to be associated with psychosis and with the delusions and hallucinations that form the core of the dramatic positive symptoms associated with schizophrenia.[3] Long-term isolation increases the effect; return to the original group mitigates it.[4] The psychiatric epidemiologist Jean-Paul Selten wondered whether chronic social defeat in humans might lead to the sensitization of their mesolimbic dopamine system, and so activate an individual's underlying genetic vulnerability to schizophrenia. When he looked epidemiologically at the increased risk for schizophrenia among the poor, the urban, the immigrants, he thought he was seeing the response to a chronic, long-term experience of social defeat in this more medical sense.[5]

We propose here an anthropological theory of social defeat that develops Selten's hypothesis and generalizes the animal model. This theory proposes that the experience of defeat in a social context is felt, in the body that is vulnerable to psychosis, so profoundly that it can make the body ill with serious psychotic disorder. Social defeat is not the same phenomenon as symbolic violence or structural violence. Violence may lead to defeat, but violence is a means. Defeat is an outcome. And social defeat is not symbolic but actual, felt in the body, experienced in our very cells and tissues. This is consonant with the more general observation in medicine that social status protects the body and social stress makes the body more vulnerable—as found in the new social epidemiology and health disparities research.[6] These are what Paul Farmer called the "biological reflections of social fault lines"[7]—the bodily consequences of the ways that human societies order their status hierarchies and, in general, organize their lives.

It is striking that before social epidemiology demonstrated the impact of social loss and humiliation on serious psychotic disorder, anthropologists had argued that something like the bodily experience of social defeat explained why some societies had higher-than-average rates of schizophrenia. They saw a daily, constant grind of humiliation and rejection that—they thought—made people ill. Nancy Scheper-Hughes, for example, went to rural western Ireland in the mid-1970s to make social sense of one of the highest hospitalization rates for schizophrenia in the world.[8] She found a demoralized, economically depressed society collapsing under the weight of lonely, isolated single men, men consistently rejected by women and relentlessly teased and scapegoated by parents living in increasingly poor villages. These parents were desperate to have them stay on in their homes, look after them into old age, and manage their economically inconsequential plots as the more capable sons and daughters fled across the ocean. Rural Ireland, she wrote, was "a broken culture."[9]

Scheper-Hughes's book came out in 1979, just before *DSM-III* appeared to usher in the biomedical revolution in psychiatry. As the years went by, many reading the book assumed that while her account of Ireland was accurate, the epidemiology she had relied upon was flawed, that she had brilliantly depicted a declining society, but not a schizophrenogenic one. Even she began to doubt the accuracy of her figures and their implications. In a later edition, she talks of misdiagnosis but points to rising rates of suicide and depression. "Something was gravely amiss."[10] But her original interpretation may have been correct. What she saw was a social world in which people were consistently made to feel small and ineffective by others—by parents, siblings, leaders, popular opinions, doctors, even by Irish people living in other countries who (in the new economy of the era) would no longer eat Irish food. She showed that those who were most belittled and socially insecure were more likely to develop schizophrenia—men isolated on family farms, rebuffed by women and teased by peers, left behind as others emigrated in search of a better life.

Previous ethnographers have also shown that once someone slides into psychosis—at least in the United States—their daily experience is one of repeated social failure. This is most striking on the street. Kim Hopper, Alex Cohen, Anne Lovell, and Robert Desjarlais all describe the experience of homelessness in terms of an assault on dignity and self-worth, the scorn of passersby, the sense that one is "cattle."[11] "You get no respect," people say. That is the assault of stigma: the public image of the homeless as waste product, as deviant, as disease—corrosive perceptions by others that eat at the soul.[12] The actual life of a homeless person on the street, Hopper writes, is marked by "the ever-present sense of trespass and threat of discovery that one learns to live with; the acute feeling of exposure and vulnerability that only fatigue dispels; the chronic, low-level fear."[13] One of Desjarlais's subjects explained: "A part of you dies on the street. Your spirit dies. You lose the wanting to live inside, the wanting to talk with someone. That part dies too. Once you're outside, you can't come back inside. . . . The street is tough."[14]

Sue Estroff's classic study demonstrated that just being labeled with a diagnosis of schizophrenia in the United States leads people to feel defeated. She found that (housed) clients strongly marked the distinction between the "crazies" and the "normals," and that to be "crazy" meant to be inept and abnormal.[15] At the same time, the marked distinction meant that people who found themselves "crazy" repeatedly recreated the conditions of their own social exclusion. From her perspective, clients "seemed perpetually engaged in wandering multiple mazes, passing by the right exits, and pursuing dead-ends or short circuits back to the beginning."[16] These are social interactions, consistently repeated, in which people feel that they have failed and in which they have, in fact, been socially subordinate.

This is not what Bourdieu describes as "symbolic violence." The power of his intervention lay in his identification of ordinary social interaction as implicitly violent when it enacted a relationship of domination and subordination that people took to be part of the natural order of things. That, at least, was the way he introduced the concept in *Outline of a Theory of Practice:*

> The system [of exchange between master and *khammes,* a permanently indebted worker] contains only two ways (and they prove in the end to be just one way) of getting and keeping a lasting hold over someone: gifts or debts, the overtly economic obligations of debt, or the "moral" or "affective" relationship created and maintained by exchange, in short, overt (physical or economic) violence, or symbolic violence—*censored, euphemized,* i.e. unrecognizable, socially recognized violence.[17]

The khammes stays in the relationship with the master in part because of his debt, but also in part because of his sense of loyalty, honor, moral obligation, and so forth, created by the master's apparent warmth and generosity. The khammes knows and does not know that these acts that maintain the symmetrical relationship are violent. He cannot recognize them as such and maintain his loyalty. "Domination . . . cannot take place overtly and must be disguised under the veil of enchanted relationships."[18] The violence is both more and less hidden than in a modern economy with the law, and law enforcement, behind it.

> Because the pre-capitalist economy cannot count on the implacable, hidden violence of objective mechanisms, it resorts *simultaneously* to forms of domination which may strike the modern observer as more brutal, more primitive, more barbarous, or at the same time, as gentler, more humane, more respectful of persons.[19]

This is the semi-recognized violence of credit, loyalty, gratitude, piety, and so forth, a violence enacted on people with their complicity. It is not the condition of those on the street who visibly and vocally hate the circumstances that landed them there.

"Structural violence" describes what Paul Farmer calls the insidious discrimination that keeps poor people poor, the conditions that force people to lead miserable and precarious lives. Gender, race, and class are axes of oppression, but structural violence includes all the conditions that produce the discrimination that, in turn, leads to extreme suffering. Farmer uses the term to capture

> a broad rubric that includes a host of offensives against human dignity: extreme and relative poverty, social inequalities ranging from racism to gender inequality, and the more spectacular forms of violence that are uncontestably human rights abuses.[20]

Structural violence is a term with a wide brushstroke—it includes all those social interactions that assault human dignity, although Farmer pays more attention to the extremes than to the everyday (as, for example, Erving Goffman did), and although he focuses his attention on grinding poverty.

Social suffering is a related term, largely introduced by Arthur Kleinman, Veena Das, and Margaret Lock to describe the way social life allows people to inflict horrors on each other.[21] Social suffering "brings into a single space an assemblage of human problems that have their origins and consequences in the devastating injuries that social force can inflict on human experience."[22] This is suffering that arises from what people do to each other—the trauma inflicted by poverty, war, conflict, and cold bureaucracy. These anthropologists reached out for the term because they wanted to sidestep the analytic categories more usual to social science and to focus attention on suffering in itself. "From these perspectives—these perspectives of anthropology, social history, literary criticism, religious studies and social medicine—the standard dichotomies are in fact barriers to understanding how the forms of social suffering can be at the same time collective and individual, how the modes of experiencing pain and trauma can be both local and global."[23] Their idea was to enable people to see the pain that was there, yet often invisible and incomprehensible—the pain that people often ignored.

Social defeat may follow from structural violence or symbolic violence or social suffering, but defeat is the state that results from the violence and the creation of the suffering. In defeat, you have lost the status war. You have accepted your subordinate role. You lie there beaten, in a ditch. That is why the resistance to being "crazy" of the women at the drop-in center where Tanya met Zaney (case 10) was so moving: they were insisting, in the face of all the evidence, that they would not be defeated, though in many ways they acknowledged that they had been. So much of what we attend to as observers of humans is ideas: negative beliefs about how others see one (stigma), negative beliefs about one's class or kind (stereotypes). The concept of social defeat draws our attention to our physical response to these social interactions. It tells us that social experience gets under our skin and can make us ill.

Our theory about the relationship of social defeat to psychosis makes the following claims:

I. Social defeat has effects on the body and brain and increases the risk of psychosis.

    a. Along with biological vulnerabilities (genetics, neuronal decay) and psychosocial vulnerabilities (difficulties due to abuse or abandonment during childhood, for example), the lived social environment is a risk factor for psychosis.

    b. Specifically, experiencing a social environment in which one repeatedly loses in social encounters increases the risk of developing a psychotic disorder.

    c. Social environments rich in opportunities for repeated "one down" interactions are frequently those in which the vulnerable individual is stigmatized or otherwise disempowered due to poverty, immigrant status, or skin color. Urban environments increase opportunities for social defeat relative to rural environments.

    d. Some opportunities for social defeat vary between social worlds. All social worlds have stressful transitions, but when and how such transitions occur, and what resources are available to manage them, may vary. For example, people work and marry in all social worlds, but what it means to work or to marry—and what it means not to work or not to marry—will also vary.

II. The effects of social defeat on people with psychosis makes their psychosis worse.

    a. All people with psychotic disorder struggle with their symptoms, but the social meaning of those symptoms, the meaning of an explicit diagnosis, and whether these meanings lead to "one down" interactions, depend on the social world.

    b. Among those with incipient or developed psychosis, opportunities for social defeat are more abundant in the developed world than in developing parts of the world.

c. As a result, symptoms of psychotic disorder are often better tolerated outside the developed world, and psychotic disorder may have a
less severe course and outcome in the developing world.

We believe that our case studies, in the context of epidemiological research,
have illustrated this last point (c). They show us that once someone falls ill,
for all the pain in madness everywhere, there seem to be more opportunities
for social defeat for a person with madness in the West. Madness is hard,
anywhere. But the conditions for corrosive social failure within care-as-usual
in the United States, and in the West more widely, may be more numerous
and are probably more harsh. Outside of the West, there are more ways in
which madness can be understood, more ways of interpreting symptoms; and,
on average, homelessness is not inevitably part of the lives of people with serious psychotic disorder. People are not channeled so relentlessly into social
encounters in which they repeatedly experience themselves to fail. Our case
studies show that the life of someone with serious psychotic disorder in the
United States is likely more rife with social defeat compared with such a
person in Chennai, for example. That may help explain why schizophrenia
becomes more benign in India and elsewhere, but more difficult in the United
States.

Our case studies also suggest that the social patterning of increased risk
of schizophrenia for some social worlds and better outcomes for others can
be explained by differing exposures to social defeat. Social defeat seems to
affect when people fall ill. In India, young women face the greatest threat of
constantly repeated social failure at marriage, as they enter into a new and
usually critical family as its lowest-status member, often married to a husband
they barely know. British African-Caribbeans are more at risk when they come
to a white land of privilege, where they feel alien and where they are exposed
to a racism that marks them as low status. Our older clinical inclination would
have been to see the social distress as a consequence of a psychotic break, not
a cause. Our ethnographic case studies, with the new social epidemiology,
suggest that defeating social experience may also play a role.

We can lay out these observations by examining the ways in which our case
studies illustrate the four domains Byron Good has identified as the social conditions that affect psychotic disorder: how severe madness is understood, whether
the mad person can work, whether and how their family is involved, and the
general social conditions in which the mad person lives.[24] To this we will add a

fifth: the experience of the symptoms themselves. In the following discussion, the case numbers correspond to the chapter in which the case study appears.

HOW MADNESS IS UNDERSTOOD

Our case studies illustrate that in the United States and the United Kingdom, people with schizophrenia have fewer options for their personally felt sense of identity than they would in India, Ghana, or Thailand. The diagnostic label of schizophrenia becomes central to who one is in the world, while it also asserts that one is not fully human. John Hood's (case 1) deliberately absurd way of introducing himself—"My name is John Hood, and I have a diseased brain"— captures the sharp awareness of diagnostic labels among Americans who struggle with madness. It captures, too, the sense that the label violates the fundamental capacity to be human. For John, to think of his thoughts, feelings, and beliefs as disordered, as sick, marked him as not fully alive—and his perceptions, intentions, and decisions thus became mere error, neuronal misfirings, to be corrected with powerful drugs. He managed that unbearable awareness by joking, and by describing himself as "a complicated truth": simultaneously shaman, schizophrenic, wizard, master therapist, dependent, and client, not human in the ordinary way. It was an awkward fix, and he knew it.

The problem is that the medical model of schizophrenia treats symptoms as a disease process apart from the self, the way persons with diabetes might consider the illness as distinct from who they are. Patients who have been treated and taught about their illness learn that their vivid experiences are false and meaningless—they are hallucinations, delusions. When Peter Kinderman and his team spoke with inpatients at a U.K. hospital who were actively suffering psychotic symptoms, they found that while in the throes of the positive symptoms of delusions and hallucinations, the patients did not think of the psychotic process as separate from other aspects of their lives.[25] Later, as they became less ill, they described what they had done, believed, and thought during a period of active psychosis as belonging to a self—not just a disease process—that had been dysfunctional and inadequate.[26]

In other words, patients with serious psychotic symptoms in remission did not narrate their remission as a positive step toward a meaningful, productive, or fulfilling life. They narrated it as a loss of self and a loss of the future. These were the *successfully* treated patients, people who had appropriate insight regarding their illness, and who had received treatment and become educated in the medical model of schizophrenic illness. But they took the labels of their condition as signs of their lesser humanity. They felt defeated.

Such was the demoralizing cycle of Violet's life (case 5). This African-Caribbean British woman had been thoroughly educated in the medical model over the twenty years she had lived with her symptoms in London. She was a small woman, barely five feet in height, but when ill she would walk nonchalantly through her rough, gang-infested neighborhood barefooted, provoking fights. She felt tough and strong doing that. When she took the antipsychotic medications that suppressed delusions and hallucinations, she said she'd "made a fool out of" herself. She was a "liability to society"—unable to work, her dreams abandoned. She said that the good thing about becoming actively psychotic was that at least when she lost touch with reality, she didn't feel so miserable about the way her life had turned out.

The experience was different, on balance, for our subjects in India. They knew they had trouble. They often felt despair. But while they may have been given a diagnosis, they often didn't use the diagnosis or even remember it, and their culture didn't invite them to treat that diagnosis as an identity. They didn't have a sense of "being" a disease. Most of them still held hope for the future.

In her ethnography of psychiatric care in northern India, Amy Sousa described this different approach to diagnosis in India as "diagnostic neutrality."[27] Psychiatrists practicing throughout India, particularly those working in settings that rely on public funding, have little time to spend with each patient and their family. Sometimes they see ten patients or more an hour.[28] Psychiatrists simply don't share facts about prognosis, course, or likely outcome. They don't foreground the patient's right to know. Indian families and patients often don't know that schizophrenia is a lifelong disorder that causes significant failure in social and occupational domains. And so they hope for more than a life of disability. They expect the patient to get better.

We saw this in Sita's story (case 6). Sita, her father, and her husband never used the word *schizophrenia*. They talked about Sita's "problem." They found the problem frustrating and wanted it to end, but they never described it as a permanent condition. Moreover, neither Sita's father nor her husband challenged her interpretation of her symptoms as a religious experience, at least within Tanya's hearing. (Her brother told Tanya in private that when she talked more about religion it was a sign that she was getting more ill.) Her father actively supported her religious interpretations.

In Ghana, where there were very few psychiatrists for a country of twenty-six million in 2013, it is also rare for patients diagnosed with schizophrenia to know their diagnostic label.[29] Charles did (case 7). But he identified as someone who was bewitched, and witchcraft was powerful enough within his social world that he could feel it to be a more legitimate interpretation than schizophrenia. Witchcraft explained his experience to him. He and his father disagreed about this, but witchcraft remained plausible to Charles. Moreover, he knew that his father would judge his sanity on the basis of his behavior—not his voices. As long as he didn't behave as mad, he wouldn't be judged mad. By the time of his second interview in 2013, he'd managed to pull that off for a year, even though the voices were getting worse.

This is not to advocate the deliberate withholding of information from patients and family members. But these case studies should urge us to think about what a society might look like in which persons suffering psychosis could make use of psychiatric treatment yet not define themselves by their diagnoses and not imagine themselves as possessing a permanently defective self.

WHETHER THE MAD CAN WORK

Our case studies also clearly demonstrate that it's more difficult for someone with serious psychotic disorder in the United States and the United Kingdom to work in a way they regard as meaningful and productive. In the United States, our social safety net also creates a culture of chronicity. In order to receive modest monetary support from the government, one must testify that one cannot work currently and does not expect to become able to work in the future. A doctor must certify that it is his or her opinion that the individual has a severe mental illness that causes impairment to the extent of being unfit for employment. As Sue Estroff explains so succinctly, clients are acutely aware that the U.S. cultural model of disability payments means that "their *disabilities* function as do others' *abilities*, that their *incompetence* reaps for them what others' *competence* earns."[30] The clients in her study felt inferior to the service professionals yet actively looked down on other clients, whom they perceived as ineffectual, powerless, and as lacking dependability—because those clients did not work, and subsisted on disability.[31]

Care providers in Europe and North America are sharply aware of the structural inequality between providers and clients and have worked with a grass-roots consumer movement to create an alternative approach. The Recovery Movement, now found in many treatment settings, attempts to empower clients by diminishing professionals' power to make and enforce financial, treatment, and personal decisions for them, even when ill persons' own choices may appear bizarre and even destructive. Standard programs of care in the 1990s provided almost daily contact with clients, making sure they took their medications, limiting how much of their disability check they could use at any one time, and monitoring personal hygiene, drug and alcohol use, and the safety and cleanliness of their living space.[32] The Recovery Movement emerged in reaction to this apparently coercive model of treatment.[33] It set out to replace a "culture of chronicity" with a culture of hope.[34]

Yet these new programs have succeeded in restoring to clients the dignity that Americans associate with independence—financial and otherwise—only marginally better than older ones. When Neely Myers set out to document an award-winning Chicago psychosocial rehabilitation organization's struggle to implement the Recovery model of mental health care in the mid-2000s, she found that it was nearly impossible to translate broad ideals of recovery into concrete practices that worked. For example, caseworkers at the organization knew from experience that if certain clients were given access to their entire disability check at the beginning of the month, it would be spent within the first few days on illegal goods and services. So they held on to the check.[35] And in the end, the scarcity of necessities (like housing) for persons with psychiatric disabilities, and the need for those resources to be distributed fairly, meant that a basic structural inequality between professionals and consumers remained. Few clients actually held jobs. Myers found that clients were often hesitant to hold a job outside the Center because of the daunting nature of the task. Jack Friedman also found, in his research on the Recovery Movement in the United States, that sometimes the stress involved in going to a job, paying rent, keeping food on the table, and maintaining relationships with others could overwhelm clients.[36] It was when John Hood (case 1) started working that his apparent recovery fell to pieces.

There are some Recovery success stories. Meg (case 12), the young Chicago woman who was diagnosed with schizoaffective disorder and who received Social Security benefits after a miserable period of homelessness, was doing well at the time Myers ended her research contact with her. Some of Meg's success may have had to do with her success before her illness. She had been able to complete college, at Yale. She had held a job for five years. Meg became a success because she accepted a diagnosis, acquired a disability stipend, and was able to look for and find an affordable apartment. She seemed happy, yet she didn't envision her recovery as involving paid employment in the near future.

Outside of these Western settings, the inability to fulfill one's roles—particularly those related to work—stands out as the central "symptom" of psychosis recognized by patients and family members alike. Lay diagnosis and treatment of severe mental illness in India seems to be driven by its "nuisance value," and not by the delusions and hallucinations we often think of as central indicators.[37] Families identify madness by its disruption to household routines, to the successful accomplishment of work in home, field, and school, and to the harmonious maintenance of family relationships.

In these settings, "work" does not necessarily imply the salaried compensation it does for someone like Meg. For women in nonelite Indian communities, work is understood as the ability to accomplish a myriad of household tasks, such as fetching water, grinding grain, cutting vegetables, washing vessels, dusting and sweeping, and responsibly minding children. In India, only 20 percent of the entire population is estimated to be involved in wage or salaried labor, with 32 percent engaged in casual labor and 49 percent "self-employed"—mostly on family farms.[38] Salaried labor—work at an office, construction site, or large retailer—is not usual or expected. It certainly isn't the mark of productive personhood that such work is for women in highly industrialized countries, such as Violet (case 5), who sat by her apartment window, wistful and envious, watching women in her neighborhood travel to and from work.

For the Chaturvedi family (case 2), the important difference between their two daughters, Veena and Anisha, was that Anisha was a productive family member—able to cook and clean along with her sister-in-law—while Veena was completely unresponsive to any family demands that were placed upon her. The difference between the two sisters was not that Veena had catatonic schizophrenia whereas Anisha suffered a subtype of schizophrenia (paranoid) in which personality and social functioning remains more intact. Rather, it was that the Chaturvedis understood Anisha as a competent homemaker whose odd ideas and ways of expressing herself could be tolerated.

Likewise, Madhu (case 4)—the once homeless, mentally ill woman Giulia Mazza met at the Banyan in Chennai—evaluated her difficulties in terms of her inability to do housework. Despite being medicated, Madhu had continued to experience delusions and hallucinations. However, her primary concern was not her voices: it was that she was not completing her housework in accordance with expectations. "Crazy" for Madhu and her family meant, as Madhu explained, that "I sit there . . . they [conjugal family members] told me, 'She is not working in the house'... I am just lazily... lazy, lazy girl." By the time that Giulia met her, she could work again. Even though she still heard voices, she understood herself to be well. The Banyan has found that they can often persuade families to accept such women back, as long as they can carry out household work. And Poi (case 11) and Sunita (case 8) worked. What they considered work—shamanism in Poi's case, spirit possession in Sunita's—may not have been entirely persuasive to the others around them, but their religious traditions modeled an active involvement with unseen spirits in a way that allowed them to interpret themselves as working.

HOW THE FAMILIES ARE INVOLVED

Our case studies illustrate that families in India, Ghana, and Thailand often offer support; and they grimly represent the almost complete absence of family help for our U.S. cases. Neely Myers describes Meg (case 12) as having had good family support, but her occasional visits to her mom and brother were less helpful than, say, Sita's parents' efforts (case 6) were for her. One consequence of the social safety net in many Western settings is that families can become uninvolved in the care for those who struggle with serious psychotic disorder. In these settings, adults are expected to be independent, and families expect children to leave. So the afflicted child often leaves home—either evicted by scared and frustrated parents or by choice—and eventually enters the institutional circuit and mental health services. To be clear, these American families are often pressed into doing a great deal of work—finding housing, intervening with the police, subsidizing rent and care. And yet the person who is ill still often lives within a shared culture (the culture of the street, the culture of chronicity) of symptoms, unemployment, and profoundly negative identity. Few people with serious psychotic disorder want to affiliate with others like themselves.[39] And as Janis Jenkins and Elizabeth Carpenter-Song point out in their study of persons living with psychosis in the midwestern United States, people afflicted with chronic psychotic illnesses are highly sensitized to the "look" of a person who has chronic mental illness.[40] Violet (case 5) thought that her extra weight, bloat, and slow gait—the side effects of her medication—marked her as someone taking an antipsychotic and, hence, someone no normal person would want to know.

The lack of a social safety net in India, Ghana, and Thailand means that the family becomes, of necessity, the treatment setting. Living with family is expected throughout the life course of most (and certainly of nonelite) Indian adult children. Living separately from family is a hardship, not a mark of the achievement of independence. This can be an advantage for the person with psychosis. As a family, the Chaturvedis (case 2) were remarkably accepting of both of their daughters and their relative capabilities, and this supportive environment may have contributed to lower stress levels for Anisha, which, in turn, may well have kept her symptoms in abatement.[41]

Anisha's story is not without pain. Her marriage was a failure. No doubt this was a great source of shame and regret for her and her family, as rejection by one's husband and his family is an insult to the bride and her kin. Rejected wives are stigmatized and often have difficulty remarrying. Yet she and her family imagined a future for her. Her roles as sister, daughter, aunt, and sister-in-law were important and valued. Despite the difficulties with arranging a second marriage for her, her family remained optimistic that she would be able to find a new, sympathetic husband one day.

Priyanka's illness (case 3) demonstrates how elastic the "sick" role can be for persons afflicted with schizophrenia in North India. Priyanka, like Anisha, had been diagnosed with paranoid schizophrenia. Her family had been told of her diagnosis, but it was fairly unimportant for the way they thought about who she was and how they should respond to her. Far more important were Priyanka's housework and her conformity to her role as a new, deferentially respectful bride. When her conjugal and natal family argued about her, they debated the degree to which Priyanka's role failure was due to illness or to whether she was lazy, insubordinate, and abusive.

Writing about physical and psychiatric stigma, Veena Das and Renu Addlakha coined the term "domestic citizenship" to describe settings (like India) where disability is managed, disciplined, contained, and treated within domestic space, rather than within civil society.[42] Domestic citizenship, they argue, creates flexibility in the way kin manage severe mental illness. It is why schizophrenia is defined by these Indian families through its impact on other household members, rather than as an intrapsychic phenomenon of hallucination and delusion. Priyanka's in-laws complained about Priyanka's gender-inappropriate behavior and her failure to contribute to household work; the extent to which Priyanka had control over her "symptoms" was of interest to them mostly insofar as what they believed those symptoms might indicate about her attitude toward her new family. Was Priyanka deliberately shirking her duties, expecting her mother-in-law to serve her? Or were these behaviors of no relevance to Priyanka's attitudes toward her new family because they were completely out of her control?

This is not to say that people with madness are always safe in families, or that families are always caring. In most of our case studies from India, with the exception of Sita, there hovered the specter of conjugal domestic violence and wife murder. It is difficult to separate out the impacts of failure as wife, psychosis, abandonment, and abusive husbands and in-laws. When is the fear that your husband's family will kill you realistic, and when is it paranoia? For both Priyanka and Anisha, the line between the two was murky. Sunita (case 8), the devotee of Balaji's temple in Mehndipur, Rajasthan, was beaten brutally by her husband when she fell ill. Madhu (case 4) was abandoned.

It is also true that families are not always safe from children with psychosis. To be clear: the risk of violence from people with schizophrenia is really quite low. The vast majority never commit violent acts. They are far more likely to be victims of violence than perpetrators.[43] But compared to the general population—according to U.S. and U.K. data—people with schizophrenia are more likely to commit violent crimes.[44] One of us remembers a caseworker on an outreach trip to a rural village in Tamil Nadu who shook her head after a consultation for a man who lived with his mother. "I am afraid he will kill her someday." John Hood (case 1) remembered standing on his staircase at his parents' home, shrieking as his terrified mother huddled at the foot of the stairs. It is not always easy for a family to have someone with psychosis in their midst. But as M.J. Field pointed out with regard to rural Ghana, it may be better for those with chronic psychosis to stay with people they know.[45]

THE GENERAL SOCIAL CONDITION

Our case studies illustrate the stark and appalling presence of homelessness in the lives of many with serious psychotic disorder. Homelessness is common, even normative, for persons in the United States who meet criteria for schizophrenia, and to be homeless or on the institutional circuit is to confront social defeat daily and in many dimensions.[46] The story of Zaney (case 10) makes that clear. The actual daily experience of living on the street (the messy world of the circuit between shelter, soup kitchen, sleeping out, and the social services that such women navigate) is one of constant vigilance against always simmering violence. Many on the street confront violence in both familiar and unfamiliar relationships. That simmering violence is considerably exacerbated by a quick readiness to fight, which Elijah Anderson called, in a different context, "the code of the street."[47] In social settings where police are unreliable and the law is weak, survival may depend upon an ability to overreact, to defend your turf so aggressively at the first hint of trouble that the trouble slinks away.

If the conflict were only between those on the street, one would assume that the people are as often victors as losers in these encounters. But those on the street spend their days moving between institutional settings in which they are supplicants to staff who set the rules and determine the outcome of any encounter. In each of these settings lie untold possibilities for unintended or intended insults. Over all of this hover the watchful eyes of the staff. If clients fight, even only with words, they are "barred"—dismissed and told not to return for a day, a week, a month—or forever if the infraction is severe.

The staff's goals are eminently laudable: to provide safety for clients within their doors. Yet those same rules humiliate the women they are set in place to protect. And there are countless small humiliations in a drop-in center. If someone doesn't return a coffee mug, no mugs are set out the next day. If the chairs are not all folded up and stored, no chairs can be used the next day. If people don't sign up for chores, the place closes early. When Meg (case 12) showed up to move in to the shelter with an elevator full of stuff, she was told she could bring in only one suitcase. Because she was late, she couldn't help her friend Neely get the rest back safely into the car. When she went to a friend's art show and the terrible weather caused her to come back after curfew, she lost her place.

All these rules serve a good. But they also repeatedly remind clients that this is not their home and that they don't decide what happens. These are constant small defeats. And they underscore the basic tension between the tight control the staff tries to maintain within the institution, the schoolmarm expectation of middle-class civility, and the in-your-face toughness people need to protect themselves in a world where the police are usually busy someplace else.

It may be because of these humiliations, large and small, that homelessness becomes such a corrosive, punitive identity. Whatever the cause, the identity is toxic. It is clear that women like Zaney hate the label, and that they associate homelessness with a profound sense of loss and failure. Partly it is the experience of homelessness that they hate. As one homeless woman said to Tanya, "Homelessness is hell. You ever wondered what hell is like? This is it." But partly it is the very idea of homelessness that evokes a crushing sense of failure. People depict people like themselves with sneering, venomous phrases. "You can't get away from the homeless [in this neighborhood]," one woman said. "You just can't get rid of them. You just trip over them when you walk out the door here."

Living on the street or in the institutional circuit may well kindle an incipient psychosis; no doubt these are terrible places for those who have fallen ill and are trying to recover. And these settings are less prevalent in India and elsewhere outside the West (the United States in particular). There are—as we have seen with Madhu (case 4)—homeless women with psychoses in India, enough for good Samaritans to have created an agency to assist them. There are homeless psychotic people on the streets of Accra. But there is no evidence that homelessness is near normative for persons with psychosis outside the West, and there is good evidence that at least intermittent homelessness is extremely common in the lives of those in the United States who struggle with psychotic disorder.

THE EXPERIENCE OF ILLNESS ITSELF

Finally, our case studies illustrate that auditory hallucinations in India and Ghana (at least) may be less caustic than in the United States. In our Indian cases, the hallucinated voices themselves seemed less corrosive. Luhrmann and her colleagues found that the voices of persons with serious psychotic disorder in Chennai and Accra were, on balance, more interactive and more positive than those of similar clients in San Mateo, California.[48] We see this also in our case studies. At least, the willingness to interpret as supernatural what the biomedical observer would call psychiatric symptoms seems to have allowed Sita (case 6) to shift the quality of those auditory experiences over time. Sunita (case 8), too, found that her voices became more benign over time. Persons with psychosis often experience a range of auditory and quasi-auditory events—kind voices, mean voices, commanding voices, murmuring voices. It is possible that different cultural invitations[49] shift the way someone pays attention to his or her auditory experiences, and that these shifts become habituated and orient the dominant content of the voice-hearing experience.

After her illness had begun, Sunita toured, involuntarily, the custodial psychiatric institutions of North India and found no help in managing the evil spirits she saw coming out from the walls of her dwelling. She was abandoned at Balaji, probably by her parents, although this was not clear. She later dedicated herself to conveying the deity's revelation, to which she believed she had special access. With that commitment, she said that she was not tormented by voices only she could hear and visions only she could see. Instead, she experienced voices and visions as a welcome blessing and mark of the deity's favor. Whereas once she had experienced malevolent ghosts and tormenting voices, now, with great pride, she saw, heard, and recorded the auspicious revelations of God.

Perhaps we might think of the curative potential of the Balaji temple in terms of the way it presents a model of interaction with voices and visions that no one else can hear or see. Balaji himself presides over a number of supernatural beings who had been persuaded (as devotees of the shrine might say) to desist from their evil ways through human worship and devotion and to become benevolent helpers of Balaji and his petitioners. According to vernacular Hindu and Islamic beliefs at healing shrines all over India, malevolent ghosts and troublesome spirits need to have some of their desires fulfilled, so that they become satisfied and will stop bothering humans, or even become a source of blessings and revelation. Meeting their needs involves eliciting their names and their desires, and then negotiating with them.[50] Indian shrines, *mazaars* (burial grounds of saints), and temples such as the Balaji provide cultural invitations to persons who experience hallucinations to work with those experiences in particular ways. Perhaps when those with psychosis interpret voices in this way, they expect the voices to become more benign, and so remember and attend to more benign auditory experiences (aging, too, may lessen the severity of psychotic symptoms).

The technique does not always work. Madhu (case 4) negotiated with the voices of spirits. She had learned that she could reason with, appease, and even flatter her spirits by engaging them. But she still didn't have significant control over the voices of the spirits, and they tormented her and distracted her from work.

Over the course of the years in which Julia Cassaniti observed her, Poi (case 11) also seemed to have improved. At first, she had experienced discrete periods of florid psychosis in which she lost touch with reality completely. She would drive frantically to Bangkok's main transportation hub, but people there appeared to her to be severely injured, grotesquely wounded and bleeding profusely. She didn't sleep, eat, or bathe during these periods. She rarely spoke. Once she slit her own throat.

But after ten years, Poi's episodes of psychosis had become milder. She had learned to exert some control over the spirits that appeared to torment her during periods of psychosis. Now she continued to interact with them during more lucid periods; she took this to be her religious role, because she had begun to consider herself a shaman—of sorts—conversing with household deities in order to ascertain their desires and learn of prescient knowledge they might have. She never accepted the medical model of schizophrenia; in fact, it seemed to Julia that she had perhaps never learned it, despite her many brief stays in hospitals. She had never thought of herself as a person who saw and heard things in error. Instead, even during lucid periods, she believed that she periodically had access to a world of spirits, and this had been progressively reinforced by priests and fellow parishioners in the Catholic churches in which she had participated since her childhood. Yet her spirits were Satanic, not godly. Hers was a heroic struggle against the powers of evil entities.

This leads us to an important question. What difference does religiosity make? It's a complicated issue. Charles (case 7) could avoid acknowledging that he had schizophrenia because he experienced what he called "witches." But that left him with being bewitched. While he may not have thought of the condition as permanent, the content of what the voices said may have been worse because he interpreted them as demons.

Mental-health-services research conducted in predominantly English-speaking countries (United States, United Kingdom, Canada, etc.) has found that the positive and negative impacts of religion and spirituality in the lives of persons with severe mental illness may be difficult to disentangle.[51] Religious practices may serve as coping behaviors, and religious experiences, beliefs, and social networks may lead to better mental-health outcomes.[52] On the other hand, there is evidence that religious delusions are associated with poorer treatment outcomes than delusions of a nonreligious nature. Some religious beliefs have a negative impact on coping with illness.[53] And yet the religious interpretation of psychotic symptoms seems to have been helpful for Sunita, Sita, and Poi, and possibly for John Hood as well.

At least one reason Poi's religious interpretation may have been helpful to her was that she had acquired supportive friends and associates through her quests for spiritual healing. That also appears to have been true for Alexandra (case 9). This poverty-stricken, mentally ill woman in Romania seemed to have benefited from her association with a close-knit, supportive evangelical church. Alexandra's decisions to embrace one religious group, the American Evangelical Church, and reject another, the Romanian Orthodox Church, had a lot to do with the support, nurturance, and positive coping each held out to

her. Moreover, her evangelical brethren helped her make sense of the disturbing voices and visions only she could see, in ways that she found helpful. They
explained that she was being tested by God and must meet the challenge that
he had set for her. Her son back in the village received material support from
this evangelical church while she was in the hospital. They were a bright
spot in an otherwise dismal social network of fellow psychiatric patients and
judgmental villagers who looked down on her because she had a child out of
wedlock and was unable to work.

These specific cases, nested within the data of the new social epidemiology,
strongly suggest that the question is not so much what India and other places
in the developing world are doing well, but what we in the United States are
doing poorly. The ways in which people with serious psychotic disorder
encounter care within the United States create for them one experience of
social defeat after another.

　　To be very clear, this is not a romantic interpretation in the vein of "Our
schizophrenia is their shamanism." People with serious psychotic disorder are
usually recognized to be severely ill no matter where they are. The care in
developing countries can be abysmal. People can indeed be chained to logs, as
Field reported from rural Ghana so many decades ago and as reporters find
today. Depression, drug abuse, and schizophrenia are predicted to be the three
leading causes of lost economic output around the world by 2030.[54] Nevertheless, the data suggest that the network of American cultural and institutional
practices around mental illness is far from ideal and is less effective, on average,
than less well-funded interventions elsewhere.

　　So what can we do about it?

PRAGMATIC LESSONS

What practical lessons have we learned here? What are the ethical and pragmatic conclusions we can draw about the care of persons with serious psychotic
disorder from these case studies about care abroad that might help us improve
care here in the United States?

　　The obstacles that stand in the way of improving the conditions of life for
someone with serious psychotic disorder in the United States—with the
expectation that improving those conditions would diminish the severity of
the illness—are formidable. We have a patchy, poorly funded mental health

system, and it is a political and economic challenge to provide safe housing and care in a social world in which we expect people to be independent from their families after early adulthood. There are many competing ideas about how best to provide care, and competing political views about how much care the state should provide or subsidize. One reason why a place like the neighborhood in Chicago where Zaney roamed the street has perhaps sixty agencies in an area of several square blocks is that there are so many different institutional visions of how best to help, and so many different interests at stake.

Our case studies from non-Western settings do, however, lend support to three interventions that are often perceived as radical, marginal, and (depending on the observer) hopelessly naive.

Housing First

Housing First is an alternative approach to the often highly regimented programs that are common in our cities today. Many of the existing standard programs demand first that the client receive an explicit diagnosis. The client must participate in a diagnostic interview and is sometimes given a sheet with the diagnosis, which the client must take to the program office prior to receiving housing. Housing is typically then contingent upon an agreement to stop using drugs and alcohol and to agree to psychiatric care. Housing First programs simply provide housing to those in need in a manner that downplays explicit diagnosis and minimizes coercion. This is not to say that diagnosis and psychiatric care are not relevant to these programs, but rather that the programs are structured in a way that allows clients not to submit to an explicit diagnostic interview and to make their own decisions about whether to take psychiatric medication. These programs also do not require sobriety before housing. This model flies in the face of many American instincts, including the patient's right to know and the resistance to "freeloading" on the system. The programs also depend on a stock of affordable housing and can be hamstrung by the many competing claims to the affordable housing that exists. But they maintain the sense of personal independence so highly valued by Americans. They also enact diagnostic neutrality, which seemed so helpful in our Indian case studies, and convey respect for the clients' capacity to make decisions about their own lives. Many smaller studies have supported this model.[55] A large, randomized trial recently found that when intervention followed this model, participants were more likely to remain housed compared with controls. They also showed significantly greater behavioral gains.[56]

Hearing Voices and Similar Meaning-Centered Approaches

A new consumer movement, the Hearing Voices Network, teaches people who hear voices to search for the meanings their voices hold for them and, often, to treat these voices as people. The Hearing Voices Network claims that it is possible to improve a person's relationship with their voices by teaching them to name, respect, and interact with the voices, and that doing so can make the voices less punitive and less mean—sometimes with the eventual result that the voices go away for good.[57] While there is no definitive outcome study at present, a series of initial analyses suggest that the method may be useful.[58] In fact, a range of newer therapeutic methods have emerged that may help people experience their voices differently (and less harshly).[59]

"Avatar" therapy asks patients to sit in front of a computer and select a face and vocal timbre to represent the most caustic voice they hear. The therapist speaks to the patient through the voice avatar in such a way that the patient experiences the voice as responding to what the patient says and gradually becoming kinder. The first published trial gave sixteen patients—all of whom had heard voices for years--six sessions of thirty minutes each. Most reported that their voice-hearing diminished, and three found that they stopped experiencing voices altogether.[60]

Cognitive behavioral therapy teaches people to engage with their voices differently—to listen to the voices, to consider whether the voices are accurate in what they say, and to respond based on that assessment. In this approach, the way clients understand and react to their voices takes center stage.[61] Yet another method is mindfulness.[62] Drawing upon contemplative traditions, patients who experience distressing voices are taught to alter their relationship with the voices through mindful awareness, acceptance, and compassion. Like the other approaches, this method does not challenge the existential basis of psychotic experiences, but focuses on learning to engage them. Finally, Acceptance and Commitment Therapy uses a related array of approaches.[63]

These approaches go against the grain of much American psychiatry. In the biomedical model, symptoms like voices are often understood to be irrational and, as such, are not encouraged or treated as significant. Yet this new orientation toward engaging directly with voices is now so dominant in the United Kingdom that the British Psychological Society recently published a manual on treating psychosis which argues that it is critical for people who hear voices to talk about them. Moreover, the manual states that it is not important for people to treat these experiences as symptoms of an illness. "It is vital that mental health workers are open to different ways of understanding experiences, and do not insist that people see their difficulties in terms of an illness. This simple change will have a profound and transformative effect on our mental health services."[64] The manual recommends Hearing Voices groups.

Our case studies support at least two dimensions of these approaches. First, they support the idea that insight—a scientifically accurate understanding of serious psychotic illness and its symptoms—may not be as helpful as a meaningful explanatory model. Many of our case-study subjects seemed to find it useful to interpret their voice-hearing experiences in ways that were culturally appropriate, but not scientifically accurate. Second, they support the observation that engaging with voices may make the voices more responsive. This was evident for several of our subjects.

Open Dialogue and Similar Active-Social-Support Programs

Open Dialogue is an approach particularly focused on those experiencing their first psychotic break. It is, on the surface, alarming to scientifically minded and biomedically oriented clinicians: the program presents itself as modeled on Mikhail Bakhtin's dialogic principles, and it speaks openly of "poetics" and "micropolitics." But the program might be described more concretely as an approach in which subjects in first-break psychosis and their network are plunged into active, ongoing dialogue with a treatment team that does not insist that the subject hold a scientifically accurate account of psychotic experience. Instead, the emphasis is on active social engagement, with choice-making participation in treatment planning on the part of the acutely ill subjects and their families—a far cry from forced medication and inpatient hospitalization in which the subject's wishes may be treated as symptoms of acute illness. "Open Dialogue allows every person to enter the conversation in his or her own way."[65] It does not so much put the treatment team in charge as it make the team available for the subject. It insists that no decision about care be made without the subject present. The approach shares similarities with the standard Recovery model and with elements of Hearing Voices groups, but it is more radical, more encompassing, and—crucially—more social. Initial outcome studies in western Lapland reported remarkable success: 35 percent of the Open Dialogue group required antipsychotics, compared to 100 percent of the control group; and at the two-year follow-up, 82 percent had no or only mild symptoms, compared to 50 percent of the control group.[66]

Parachute NYC represents an experimental adaptation of the Open Dialogue program, with the aim of providing better care and better health at lower costs for New York City residents. Implementation has been difficult, partly because of the more dispersed urban area in which treatment teams operate, partly because of the very different approach to care traditionally used in the city, partly because of the different pragmatic expectations of the Scandinavian team and the local Americans, and partly because of the substantially greater material need among New York City families than among their welfare-state Scandinavian counterparts.[67] Nevertheless, the strikingly more active engagement by families in our more successful case studies (e.g., cases 2, 3, and 6) suggests that an approach that involves active social involvement and minimizes a sense of defeat should be taken seriously.

In general, our case studies suggest the following practical points:

Minimize diagnosis talk and maximize diagnostic neutrality. It is clear that when people who meet criteria for schizophrenia understand themselves primarily as persons with schizophrenia, they imagine themselves as inherently incompetent and without the capacity to live a normal human life. Our ethnographic case studies suggest that avoiding labeling in treatment settings and in the social conditions of care may provide better care.

Focus on behavior rather than on intrapsychic phenomena. The voice-hearing experience in the United States is strikingly harsh, and this may be in part because such auditory experiences are taken as a sign that one is crazy. Perhaps as a result, people are more likely to hate their voices and to judge themselves as incompetent because of them. But of course what matters in human interaction is behavior, not inner experience. Our case studies suggest that in settings where people focus on the way someone behaves rather than on whether someone hears voices, the experience of the illness is more benign.

Enable work. The ability to be productive and effective is deeply tied to self-worth in all social worlds, although what it means to be productive and effective—to work—will shift. Our case studies suggest that enabling someone to work effectively is important, and that the American emphasis on work as a cash-generating job outside the home is unfortunate for people who meet criteria for schizophrenia. Our case studies (in particular, cases 2, 4, 6, and 8) suggest that to identify oneself as someone who can be productive and effective, rather than to identify oneself by a diagnosis, can be helpful.

Minimize social isolation and encourage family involvement. This is a complicated issue, because persons with serious psychotic disorder have difficulties with their families, often for good reasons. The behavior of persons with florid psychosis is often disruptive and difficult to live with. Nevertheless, our case studies and other ethnography and clinical research suggest that it is better for people with psychosis to be with those who know them and do not fear them without reason, and to be with people who can tolerate their periodically unpredictable behavior. The most obvious difference in the care of persons with serious psychotic disorder in India, compared to the United States, is that in India people stay with their family and their family remains involved with their care.

Provide safe and secure housing. The violence and uncertainty of life on the street is terrible for people with serious psychotic disorder. Yet the U.S. social safety net often leads people with serious psychotic disorder to the street. It does so, in part, because of the emphasis on diagnosis and the often rigid expectations around rule-following in our social services. Figuring out how to keep people with serious psychotic disorder off the streets and out of shelters is crucial.

Engage with voices. Our case studies support the use of new techniques that teach people who hear voices to interact with the voices in ways that help them feel more mastery and control over the voices. We need more research to understand which techniques are effective, and for which subjects. Nonetheless, our case studies suggest that persons who become able to interact constructively with their voices feel less at the mercy of those voices.

Practice compassion and respect for the experience of psychosis. Our case studies suggest that the awareness, acceptance, and compassion of important social others toward their friends', intimates', family members', and clients' experiences of psychosis are important. Note that we are advocating respect for the *experience of* psychosis in addition to respect for the *person with* psychosis. Voices and visions are real experiences. They deserve the same respect and consideration that we—as professionals, friends, family, and intimates—allow for emotional experiences like depression. It is worth observing that all the individuals from the developing world in our case studies lived in social milieus in which the experience of private voices and visions could—under the right circumstances—be credible and even respectable. Their experiences mattered socially.

What we know for sure is that social context matters for schizophrenia. In the wealthy, developed, postindustrial society of the United States and more broadly in the West, serious psychotic disorder is understood to be a disease—and little else. Sufferers are expected to understand their symptoms as perceptual error; they expect their disability to be lifelong; and their identity, as a result, is perniciously marred. The underfunded social safety net that cares for the ill also creates a culture of chronicity in which people often spend their lives in a circuit of jail, hospital, supported housing, and homelessness, and in which they acquire a label that simultaneously defines and defiles them. They are vulnerable in many different ways to the sense that they have been defeated at the hands of others. The experiences of persons with psychosis outside of wealthy, developed, postindustrial societies demonstrate that there are alternatives to these expectations, even while they seek psychiatric treatment. There are many options for conceptualizing the meanings of visions and voices that only the sufferer can hear, and many ways of belonging that can be negotiated within communities and families, and so there are alternative ways of understanding and managing the experience of psychosis. This is not to say that the alternatives always promote healing, or always dignify the person—far from it. But the evidence suggests that illness trajectory is more benign when a psychiatric model of schizophrenia is not all encompassing, and when sufferers are integrated into family and community, rather than sequestered in dismal environments among fellow sufferers. The evidence suggests that the way we treat the person may be as important as anything drugs do for that person's brain, and that social defeat can make vulnerable people ill and make their illness worse.

NOTES

FOREWORD

1. This quotation appears in Philip Thomas and Eleanor Longden, "Madness, Childhood Adversity and Narrative Psychiatry."

INTRODUCTION

1. This essay is based in part on Luhrmann, "Social Defeat," with permission from Springer Science and Business Media.

2. Shapin begins *The Scientific Revolution* with this: "There was no such thing as the Scientific Revolution, and this is a book about it."

3. Emil Kraepelin first identified schizophrenia as a distinct mental illness (called "dementia praecox") in the late nineteenth century, in his great classification scheme that many take to be the origin of modern psychiatry; the fifth edition of his *Psychiatrie* textbook (1896) was particularly important. Eugen Bleuler described the illness (more or less) as "schizophrenia" in 1911, in *Dementia Praecox*. The sizable genetics research on schizophrenia is well represented at one of the foremost Internet sites, schizophreniaforum.org. The anti-psychiatry movement has been active at least since the 1960s, when authors like Thomas Szasz (*The Myth of Mental Illness*, 1961) and R. D. Laing (*The Divided Self*, 1960) argued that the apparent symptoms of mental illness were best understood as expressions of nonpathological distress. A useful account of the arguments over whether schizophrenia is a real, recognizable, unitary, and stable object of inquiry can be found in Berrios, Luque, and Villagrán, "Schizophrenia: A Conceptual History," whose epigraph quotes Nolan Lewis: "When the story of dementia precox is written it will be the history of psychiatry." One of the most compelling accounts of living with schizophrenia can be found in Elyn Saks's memoir, *The Center Cannot Hold*. One of the most striking accounts of early psychosis is Aviv, "Madness."

4. These scholars have argued that while madness is found in the plays of Shakespeare and in the Bible, those mad characters don't seem to have the dull, flat expression and chronic course characteristic of schizophrenia. The interested reader should consult Irving Gottesman, *Schizophrenia Genesis*; and E. Fuller Torrey, *Schizophrenia and Civilization*. Others have argued against this interpretation (e.g., Jeste et al., "Eighteenth

Century"). Among them, Nigel Bark makes a compelling case that Henry VI of England fell ill with schizophrenia and that three decades of brutal war followed directly from it (Bark, "English History"). H. C. Erik Midelfort's A History of Madness points out that the question is almost impossible to answer. Some of those who argue for a more recent origin suggest that schizophrenia was caused by a virus (Torrey et al., "Toxoplasma"; Brown et al., "Toxoplasmosis") and that the domestication of cats in the tightly packed factory towns created by the industrial revolution gave rise to the illness. It is hard, however, to reconcile a recent, industrial cause of schizophrenia with the identification of the illness in rural, non-Western settings. Littlewood and Dein ("Christianity") suggest that schizophrenia was caused by Christianity, because the attention to the internal demanded by Christianity parallels the apparent externalization of inner experience associated with schizophrenia. And yet, again, it is hard to reconcile the only discontinuous origin point suggested for schizophrenia in the literature (the nineteenth century—the origin point Littlewood and Dein suggest) with the observation that Christianity has existed for two thousand years and dominated Europe for hundreds of years before the apparent emergence of schizophrenia.

5. This is the Research Domain Criteria (RDoC) approach, which focuses research on a matrix of neuroscientific and psychological features.

6. The U.S. rate is 8.5/1,000 (Buchanan and Carpenter, "Introduction and Overview,"1097). In fact, the rate varies far more around the globe than was once assumed (Brown, Bresnahan, and Susser, "Environmental Epidemiology," 1373; McGrath et al., "Concise Overview") but it hovers around that figure, although Saha et al. ("Prevalence") found a global prevalence of 4/1,000.

7. The term comes from Read, "The Bio-Bio-Bio Model."

8. The Broken Brain was published in 1985. It drew attention not only for its cogent prose but because its author, Nancy Andreasen, was a formidable scientist. She would go on to become editor of the American Journal of Psychiatry, the profession's flagship journal, and to receive the President's National Medal of Science. She also held a Ph.D. in English and had been appointed as an English professor as the University of Iowa. Her strong statement in favor of biomedicine was thus compelling.

9. Epigenetics is the study of the cellular and physiological phenotypic trait variations caused by environmental factors. Re-Visioning Psychiatry (edited by Kirmayer, Lemelson, and Cummings) offers an account that is both psychiatrically and anthropologically rich.

10. McGrath et al., "Concise Overview." Hopper et al., Recovery from Schizophrenia.

11. McGrath et al. (ibid.) provide a comprehensive analysis of 158 studies drawn from thirty-two countries. Also see Ethan Watters, Crazy Like Us.

12. Gilbert Herdt and Robert Stoller used this term somewhat differently (Herdt, "Clinical Ethnography").

13. Examples include Mary-Jo and Byron Good's work in Indonesia; Kim Hopper's work in New York City, with colleagues Lauren Cubellis; Paul Brodwin; Cristiana Giordano; Angela Garcia; Rebecca Seligman; Alex Hinton; Devon Hinton; Rebecca Lester; and others; and, of course, the authors of this volume.

14. Whitley, "Beyond Critique."

15. This tale of civilized moral degeneration had a complex relationship to representations of actual non-Europeans (see Pagden, *Natural Man*). Nevertheless, the idea that it was civilization that frayed the nerves was deeply resonant at the time.

16. "Everything degenerates in the hands of man" is the first line of *Emile*; Nordau's declamation appears in *Degeneration*, 537.

17. Lévi-Strauss, *Tristes Tropiques*, 382, 293; cf. Luhrmann, "Our Master."

18. Field, *Search for Security*, 13.

19. Admittedly, there are also undercurrents that lead colonizers to imagine Africans, in particular, as mad, and dangerously so. There are some remarkable anthropological and historical accounts of colonial psychiatry, among them Richard Keller's *Colonial Madness* (French North Africa), Jonathan Sadowsky's *Imperial Bedlam* (southwest Nigeria), and, of course, Megan Vaughan's *Curing Their Ills* (East and Central Africa). Johannes Fabian's *Out of Our Minds* describes the madness of the colonizers in their encounter with Africa.

20. Seligman, *Temperament*.

21. Field, *Search for Security*, 13.

22. These days, Christian prayer camps have become primary treatment centers for psychiatric illness in Ghana and many other sub-Saharan African countries. Not everyone taken to such camps is ill, but many people who are ill do seem to have been taken to the camps at some point.

23. A study published in 1969 found that American hospital staff were more likely to use the term *schizophrenia*, while British hospital staff were more likely to use the term *manic-depressive*; for the British, the term *schizophrenia* was already reserved for the very ill (Gurland et al., "Cross-National Study").

24. Field, *Search for Security*, 444–9.

25. Ibid., 86.

26. Ibid., 36.

27. "Literate Africans, perhaps educated in Mission schools, accustomed to attend church on Sundays, employed as clerks, teachers, storekeepers and in a hundred other detribalized jobs are frequently pictured by the European as being [in] conflict." This conflict was held to create "all sorts of mental troubles and neurosis." No such conflict, she said, existed. Their vulnerability came from the fact that they didn't have jobs (ibid., 52–3).

28. "Anyone who has attempted to compile a history of even one small town anywhere in Ghana knows that few towns and states did not begin as heterogeneous settlements of refugees, displaced persons, prisoners of war, slaves, traders, remnants of defeated armies. . . . West Africa has always been in a state of flux" (ibid., 49).

29. Marrow and Luhrmann ("Social Abandonment") argue over whether care-as-usual is worse for people with schizophrenia in urban India and the urban United States. Jocelyn was dismayed by some of the treatment she saw in Varanasi, with patients confined to back rooms by families humiliated by their presence; I saw women beaten and raped on the Chicago streets to which they were released in the name of freedom by deinstitutionalization.

30. Alexander Leighton, *My Name Is Legion*. The new study was *Psychiatric Disorder among the Yoruba*.

31. Leighton et al., *Psychiatric Disorder among the Yoruba*, 109.

32. Ibid., 126. Similar results were found in the next study of its kind, in India, this one not only a joint venture of Westerners and locals, but using instruments designed for the local setting. In *The Great Universe of Kota*, Carstairs and Kapur systematically surveyed three small communities on the Karnataka coast. They found that, on average, persons in these communities who were better educated and better off financially were less ill overall. However, out of more than 1,200 people, sixteen had psychoses, most of them men, and those with psychoses were more educated and more modernized (six of the seven males with psychosis were Brahmins). They also found that the community with the greatest social stress overall had the highest frequency of mental disorder in general.

33. Edgerton, "Conceptions of Psychosis."

34. This story is well told in Gilkeson, *Anthropologists and the Rediscovery of America, 1886–1965*; Stocking, *Malinowski, Rivers, Benedict, and Others*; and LeVine, *Culture, Behavior, and Personality*.

35. Benedict, "Anthropology and the Abnormal," 60.

36. Devereux, "Normal and Abnormal," 226.

37. Noll, "Shamanism and Schizophrenia."

38. Murphy ("Psychiatric Labeling") has some good ethnographic data about this point. Crocker's *Vital Souls* also illustrates the tight constraints within which the shaman must operate. He must have certain prescribed experiences—a stump must talk, he must have a certain kind of dream—but he must have them authentically, with enough personalization to persuade others that they are real. At the same time, he must report events that do not stray too far outside these expectations, or he will be thought mad.

39. This is a relatively new question in the current literature, raised both by the politics of labeling as discussed by the Hearing Voices movement (see Case 13) and by recent attention to the role of trauma in schizophrenia. Longden, Madill, and Waterman ("Lived Experience") found that voice-hearing was predicted by trauma and hence argued that voice-hearing is primarily a dissociative phenomenon.

40. Fromm-Reichmann, "Treatment," 164.

41. Ibid., 163–4; Hornstein, "Redeem," 133–5.

42. Tietze, "Mothers," 57, 61; Dolnick, "Madness on the Couch"; see also Lidz et al., "Environment"; Lidz et al., "Mothers of Schizophrenic Patients."

43. Neill, "Schizophrenogenic Mother"; Hale, "Rise and Crisis"; Scull's *Madness in Civilization* also provides an overview of the era, as does Staub's *Madness Is Civilization*.

44. Jackson, "Trauma," 184.

45. Stanton and Schwartz, "The Mental Hospital," 99.

46. Bateson et al., "Theory of Schizophrenia," 258.

47. Light, *Becoming Psychiatrists*, 7.

48. Quoted in Kandel, "Intellectual Framework," 458–9. The quoted piece was actually coauthored by M. Day for *The Harvard Guide to Modern Psychiatry*, published in 1978.

49. Luhrmann, *Two Minds*, 220

50. Gurland et al., "Cross-National Study."

51. Rosenhan, "On Being Sane." It's true that the admitting diagnosis in one of the twelve was not schizophrenia; but the patient nonetheless was discharged—as were all the others—with the diagnosis of "schizophrenia in remission."

52. American Psychiatric Association, *Diagnostic and Statistical Manual* (first edition), 31.

53. Kirk and Kutchins, *Selling*.

54. *American Psychiatric Association Diagnostic and Statistical Manual of Mental Disorders*, Second Edition, 33; *American Psychiatric Association Diagnostic and Statistical Manual of Mental Disorders*, Third Edition, 188–89.

55. Among the exemplary texts (and theorists) were *Being Mentally Ill* (Thomas Scheff, 1966), *Outsiders* (Howard Becker, 1963), and, of course, the work of Erving Goffman.

56. Murphy, "Labeling," 1027.

57. In *Kaplan and Sadock's Comprehensive Textbook of Psychiatry* (2000), Bustillo, Keith, and Lauriello ("Schizophrenia," 1210) remark soberly that "the pain and suffering inflicted on families during that [pre-biomedical] period of thought still resonates through the professional community. It was a time when families were accused of causing schizophrenia, excluded from the treatment process, and forced to pay the financial and psychological prices for both."

58. This conclusion was still supported by an authoritative guide to psychiatric knowledge, the 2000 edition of *Kaplan and Sadock's Comprehensive Textbook of Psychiatry* (Buchanan and Carpenter, "Schizophrenia," 1097) and in some recent literature (Dohrenwend et al., "Socioeconomic Status"). The classic sources for social drift theory are Faris and Dunham, *Mental Disorders in Urban Areas* (1939), and Clark, "The Relationship of Schizophrenia to Occupational Income and Occupational Prestige" (1948) and "Psychoses, Income, and Occupational Prestige" (1949). The initial study (Faris and Dunham, 1939) argued that the highest rates of first hospital admission for schizophrenia were in the central city areas of lowest socioeconomic status, rates going down as one retreated to the suburbs; Clark (1948, 1949) demonstrated that the highest rates of schizophrenia were among the lowest-status occupations, the rates decreasing as the occupational status rose. Faris and Dunham's finding about poverty and urbanicity was soon confirmed in many settings, including Providence, Peoria, Kansas City, St Louis, Milwaukee, Omaha, Worcester, Rochester, and Baltimore; this was summarized and reported in 1970 by Kohn, "Social Class and Schizophrenia." The finding was supported again in three famous studies, Hollingshead and Redlich, *Social Class and Mental Illness* (1958); Srole et al., *Mental Health in the Metropolis: The Midtown Manhattan Study* (1962); and Leighton, *My Name is Legion* (1959); and in Leighton et al., "Psychiatric Findings of the Stirling County Study" (1963). Despite the common emphasis on downward drift, some work took a different line. Kohn's 1973 review argued that while there was downward drift, poor families produced a proportionately larger number of people who developed schizophrenia.

59. Adebimpe, "Overview"; Mukherjee et al., "Misdiagnosis"; Neighbors et al., "Racial Factors"; Strakowski et al., "The Effects of Race on Diagnosis"; Strakowski et al., "The Effects of Race and Comorbidity"; Strakowski et al., "Racial Influence"; Trierweiler et al., "Clinical Attributions."

60. Neighbors et al., "Racial Factors."

61. See Good, "Culture" and "Context."

62. Srole et al., *Metropolis*, 290–1. To be fair, the main finding in the work is that lower socioeconomic status predicts lesser mental health and that mental health problems increase with age, both of which would be deemed correct today.

63. Singh-Manoux, Adler, and Marmot, "Subjective Social Status"; the story is, of course, complex (see www.macses.ucsf.edu/research/psychosocial/subjective.php, which describes the research that came out of the MacArthur network project on subjective social status, socioeconomic status and health; Adler and Stewart, "MacArthur Scale").

64. Braslow, "Manufacture."

65. Davidson et al., "Concerns," 641.

66. Hopper, "Rethinking Social Recovery." Other useful guides are Davidson et al., "Top Ten Concerns"; Davidson, Rakfeldt, and Strauss, *Roots of the Recovery Movement*; and Jacobson, *In Recovery*. All these authors have worked in the mental health system to promote recovery, and all of them report on the chastened effort to change the system to make Recovery work. Myers's *Recovery's Edge* offers an ethnographic account of one of the best examples of implementation. She points out that American expectations of self-sufficiency hinder the most successful implementation, because even the best program rarely returns people to the independence they feel that society expects from those without illness.

67. Brown, "Discharged" and "Expressed Emotion." See Jenkins and Karno, "Meaning of Expressed Emotion."

68. Hatfield, Spaniol, and Zipple ("Family Perspective") present families who have inferred from their clinicians that expressed emotion caused their family member to fall ill. By contrast, Jenkins and Karno ("Meaning of Expressed Emotion") summarize more recent research, which presumes that expressed emotion is a response to an ill relation.

69. Harrison et al., "Social Inequality."

70. Allardyce et al., "Comparison"; Pedersen and Mortensen, "Urbanicity"; Harrison et al., "Urban Place of Birth."

71. Halpern, "Minorities and Mental Health"; Boydell et al., "Ethnic Minorities in London."

72. Harrison et al., "A Prospective Study"; Wessely et al., "Schizophrenia and Afro-Caribbeans"; van Os et al., "Clarification"; Bhugra et al., "Incidence and Outcome"; King et al., "Incidence of Psychotic Illness"; McGrath et al., "Systematic Review." Craig Morgan, Kwame McKenzie, Paul Fearon, and others summarize this work in the excellent *Society and Psychosis*, as does Myers, "Update: Schizophrenia across Cultures."

73. Harrison et al., "Increased Incidence."

74. See the summary discussions in Kirkbride et al., "Psychoses, Ethnicity and Socio-economic Status"; and in Morgan, McKenzie, and Fearon, eds., *Society and Psychosis*. To be clear, this is not an entirely new hypothesis: in 1932, Ødegaard ("Emigration and Insanity") reported that Norwegian immigrants to the United States were twice as likely as the local nonimmigrant population to fall ill with schizophrenia.

75. See van Os, Kenis, and Rutten, "The Environment and Schizophrenia," and the discussion in Häfner, "The Concept of Schizophrenia." Also see, for specific populations, Hickling and Rodgers-Johnson, "Jamaica"; Mahy et al., "Barbados"; Bhugra et al., "Whites, African-Caribbeans and Asians"; Selten et al., "Immigrant Groups"; Selten et al., "Surinamese Immigrants."

76. Selten et al., "Surinamese Immigrants."

77. Cantor-Graae and Selten, "Schizophrenia and Migration."

78. Morgan, McKenzie, and Fearon, *Society and Psychosis*, 1.

79. Identified by Cantor-Graae, "Contribution of Social Factors"; also see Myers, "Update: Schizophrenia across Cultures."

80. See Jablensky and Sartorius, "What Did the WHO Studies Really Find?" The main findings were reported in Jablensky et al., "World Health Organization Ten-Country Study." The centers included Aarhus, Agra, Cali, Chandigarh, Dublin, Honolulu, Ibadan, Moscow, Nagasaki, Nottingham, Prague, and Rochester.

81. Harrison et al., "Recovery from Psychotic Illness."

82. Hopper et al., *Recovery from Schizophrenia*; "Harrison et al., "Social Inequality"; Craig et al., "Outcome."

83. Hopper, "Interrogating," 76.

84. Thara and Eaton, "Madras"; Thara, "Madras."

85. Hopper, Harrison, and Wanderling, "Course and Outcome," in Hopper et al., *Recovery from Schizophrenia*, 27.

86. Cohen et al. ("Questioning an Axiom") offer a recent analysis of outcome studies in twenty-three countries, including India, Indonesia, Nigeria, Brazil, and China. Those studies were quite heterogeneous, carried out by different scholars using different methods at different times. Even so, in general, course and outcome in India—and Indonesia—seemed more benign, although the authors assert that other sites reported poorer outcome. Jablensky and Sartorius ("Really Find," 254) point out that if these data had been analyzed as the WHO data were analyzed, "nearly all studies report extraordinarily high proportions of 'complete recovery,' 'no or minimal psychotic symptoms,' 'no impairment,'" and so forth.

87. Fortes and Mayer, "Social Change."

88. Waxler, "Traditional Societies." See also Warner, *Recovery from Schizophrenia*.

89. Susser and Wanderling, "Epidemiology."

90. Johns et al., "Hallucinatory Experiences"; Tien, "Distribution of Hallucinations"; Romme and Escher, "Hearing Voices"; Grimby, "Bereavement"; Slade and Bentall, *Sensory Deception*; McGrath et al., "Psychotic Experiences."

91. Hopper, "Interrogating," 74.

92. Hopper and Wanderling, "Revisiting."

93. Jenkins and Karno, "Meaning of Expressed Emotion." They actually use the phrase to refer to expressed emotion, but others have picked it up to describe culture. Or, as Jablensky and his coauthors put it ("World Health Organization Ten-Country Study"): "[A] strong case can be made for a real pervasive influence of a powerful factor which can be referred to as 'culture,'" 88–89.

94. Hopper, "Interrogating," 65.

95. Nunley, "Involvement of Families."

96. Chadda and Deb, "Indian Family Sytems," but see Padmavathi et al., "Prevalence." While usually taken to be a protective factor, joint families may present their own difficulties. This research group points out that many of those individuals left untreated—a full third of those surveyed—were located within joint and extended families.

97. Warner, *Recovery*.

98. Leff et al., "Relatives' Expressed Emotion."

99. Sousa, "Pragmatic Ethics."

100. Luhrmann et al., "Differences in Voice-Hearing."

101. Halliburton, "Finding a Fit"; Hopper et al., "To Have and to Hold."

102. Good, "Context."

CASE 1: "I'M SCHIZOPHRENIC!"

1. At the time, I was doing fieldwork for a book on psychiatry that would be published as *Of Two Minds*.

2. Some of the quotations have been shortened for conversational flow.

3. The quotation is actually from a different song, "Ballad of a Thin Man."

4. The Hindi verb "eat" is also used to describe taking pills, including antipsychotics. Jocelyn reports than Varanasi psychiatrists often told skeptical families that the patient needed to eat his antipsychotics to survive and be healthy—"just as he needs to eat his daily bread (*roz-roti*)."

5. For example, see Moran et al., "Benefits."

6. Brodwin, *Everyday Ethics*, 10.

CASE 2: DIAGNOSTIC NEUTRALITY

1. During my fieldwork, I often found myself in the awkward position of knowing a person's diagnosis when he or she didn't. Because I didn't want my research endeavors to interfere with or hinder the way in which mental illness was dealt with in this context, I didn't reveal the names of diagnoses to those who didn't know them otherwise.

2. Thara and Padmavati, "Disorder."

3. Corin, Thara, and Padmavati, "Staggering World."

4. *Kaplan and Sadock's Comprehensive Textbook of Psychiatry*, 7th ed. (Sadock and Sadock, eds., 2000); van Os, Kenis, and Rutten, "The Environment and Schizophrenia."

5. There are many different hypotheses for the decline of catatonic schizophrenia in developed nations. These include changes in diagnostic practices and previous

incidences of misdiagnosis; treatment changes since the 1930s that altered the presentation and outcome of the disorder; and changes in the nature and manifestations of schizophrenia itself over the past several decades. By contrast, catatonic schizophrenia's continued presence in developing nations suggests that environmental and public health factors may influence its development (for an overview of these hypotheses, see Caroff et al., eds., *Catatonia*). In *Psychiatry around the Globe*, psychiatrist Julian Leff argues that catatonic symptoms are somatic expressions of delusions that the patient could not otherwise express within the severe disciplinary environments of asylums in the nineteenth and early twentieth centuries. As patients became more able to verbally express emotions, the catatonic symptoms abated.

6. Taylor, "Clinical Examination."

7. That Veena and Anisha both suffered from serious mental illness suggests a possible genetic predisposition within the Chaturvedi family. Findings gathered from twin studies show that there is a 50 percent rate of discordance for developing schizophrenia among monozygotic twins. Given that monozygotic twins share the same genes, environmental factors presumably account for this discordance. If the environment is favorable, the course of schizophrenia may be prevented or ameliorated. Environmental risk factors are diverse and include exposure to viral infection, socioeconomic status, social isolation, and immigration, among many other things (Brown, Bresnahan, and Susser, "Schizophrenia: Environmental Epidemiology").

8. *Kaplan and Sadock's Comprehensive Textbook of Psychiatry*, 7th ed.; Deister and Marneros, "Subtype."

9. Jenkins and Carpenter-Song, "New Paradigm," 380.

CASE 3: VULNERABLE TRANSITIONS

1. See Henry, "Chant," 174.

2. Hopper, Wanderling, and Narayanan, "To Have and to Hold."

3. "Presenting problem" refers to the problem as it was presented by those who brought her in for treatment.

4. Addlakha, *Deconstructing*, 172, 248.

5. Carstairs and Kapur, *Kota*, 71.

6. American Psychiatric Association, *DSM-IV*, 273.

7. Corin et al., "Staggering World," 124.

8. Wilce, "Madness," 361; see also Halliburton, "Just Some Spirits," 119, for a discussion of the psychophysiology of spirit-possessed persons in South India.

9. Chakraborty, "Mental Health," 42–3.

10. Also note that many of the male respondents in the Chennai study of psychosis report the feeling of being under critical and hostile scrutiny at all times (Corin et al., "Staggering World," 118–9). Corin et al.'s essay does not refer specifically to whom they attribute this critical and hostile scrutiny.

11. Shweder, "Barbecue," 245.

12. See Narayan, "Singing from Separation," 28; and Raheja and Gold, "Listen to the Heron's Words," 128.

13. Derné, *Culture in Action*.

14. Bateson, *Steps to an Ecology of Mind*; Scheper-Hughes, *Saints, Scholars, and Schizophrenics*.

15. Nichter, "Social Relations"; Pyati, "Going the Cultural Distance."

16. Lamb, *White Saris*, and Mishra, *Devotional Poetics*.

17. Zimmermann, "Consumptive."

18. Gold, "Love's Cup"; Lutgendorf, "Monkey in the Middle"; Mishra, *Bollywood Cinema*; Upadhayaya, *Bhojpuri*; Zimmermann, "Consumptive," 187.

19. Orsini, "Introduction," 10.

20. Zimmermann, "Consumptive," 189, 185.

21. Marrow, "Family Values"; Zimmermann, "Consumptive."

CASE 5: RACISM AND IMMIGRATION

1. See Morgan et al., "Cumulative Social Disadvantage"; Fearon and Morgan, "Environmental Factors"; Harrison et al., "Increased Incidence" and "Prospective Study"; Bhugra, Mallett, and Leff, "Schizophrenia and African-Caribbeans"; Mahy et al., "Barbados"; Hutchinson et al.,"Morbid Risk"; Hickling and Rodgers-Johnson, "Jamaica"; McGovern and Cope, "Admission Rates"; Cole et al., "Pathways to Care."

2. On social defeat, see Selten and Cantor-Graae, "Social Defeat," and Luhrmann, "Chronicity."

3. Foner, "The Jamaicans"; Modood et al., *Minorities*.

4. Pilkington, *Disadvantage*; Berthoud and Beishon, "People"; Bhugra et al., "Incidence and Outcome"; Littlewood and Lipsedge, "Aliens and Alienists."

5. Mangalore et al., "Income-Related."

6. Faris and Dunham, *Urban Areas*; Jablensky, "Horizon."

7. Brown, Birley, and Wing, "Influence"; Bateson et al., "Theory of Schizophrenia"; Bateson, *Ecology of Mind*.

8. The two paragraphs of the quotation have been transposed.

9. See Office for National Statistics at www.statistics.gov.uk/default.asp.

10. Birchwood et al., "Relapse"; Bhui et al., "Brixton"; Coid et al., "Differences."

11. Sainsbury Centre for Mental Health, "Briefing"; Healthcare Commission, "Count Me In Census," 2006 (2005), 2008 (2007).

12. See Macpherson, "Report"; Norfolk, Suffolk and Cambridgeshire Strategic Health Authority (2003), "Independent Inquiry into the Death of David Bennett."

13. Moodley and Perkins, "Routes to Care"; Lewis, Croft-Jeffreys, and David, "Racist?"; Sainsbury Centre for Mental Health, 2002.

14. Wu et al., "Economic Burden."

15. Halpern and Nazroo, "Density"; Boydell et al., "Ethnic Minorities in London" and "South-East London."

16. Sullivan, "Genetics."

CASE 6: VOICES THAT ARE MORE BENIGN

1. Padma (R. Padmavati) and Tanya (T. M.) talked about this material and both worked on the draft, but in keeping with the style of this book, the following narrative is written in first person, from Tanya's point of view.

2. See Hopper et al., *Recovery*, and Jenkins and Karno, "Expressed Emotion."

3. Nunley, "Involvement of Families."

4. Royal College of Psychiatrists blog post, "One Psychiatrist per 200,000 People" (www.rcpsych.ac.uk/discoverpsychiatry/overseasblogs/india/onepsychiatristper200,000.aspx).

5. *Tulsi* is a local plant that is associated with well-being and to which many healing capacities are attributed.

6. For a formal comparison of the voice-hearing experiences in San Mateo, California; Accra, Ghana; and Chennai, India, see Luhrmann et al., "Differences in Voice-Hearing."

7. Tuttle describes these variations in "Hallucinations and Illusions," still one of the best phenomenological accounts of voice-hearing.

8. See Insel and Akiskal, "Obsessive-Compulsive."

9. This does appear to be more common among persons with schizophrenia in Chennai than among those in the United States. Luhrmann et al., "Differences in Voice-Hearing."

10. Pat Deegan's Hearing Voices training track (www.patdeegan.com/pat-deegan/training/hearing-voices-training).

11. Thomas et al. ("Auditory Hallucinations") summarize the current state of psychological treatment for voice-hearing.

12. The Hearing Voices movement was founded by Marius Romme and Sandra Escher. See intervoiceonline.org.

CASE 7: DEMONIC VOICES

1. The risk appears to be dose dependent: the more someone consumes, the greater the risk of developing schizophrenia. See Arendt et al., "Cannabis-Induced Psychosis"; Moore et al., "Cannabis Use"; Malchow et al., "Effects of Cannabis."

2. Many people in Accra Psychiatric Hospital eagerly told me that they had never smoked marijuana and therefore could not be insane.

3. This sentence has been mildly edited for ease of reading. The meaning remains intact.

4. See Comaroff and Comaroff, "Occult Economies."

5. Gifford, *New Christianity*, 23–4.

6. Birgit Meyer makes this argument in *Translating the Devil*; her observations about Ewe Pentecostalism ring true for the Accra charismatic churches.

7. Asamoah-Gyadu, *African Charismatics*.

8. "Spirit" and "soul" are the common English translations of the terms for the two-part immaterial components of the self in a number of Ghanaian languages; the Ga terms are *susuma* and *kla* (Field, *Religion and Medicine*). For similar discussions among Akan peoples, see Rattray, *Ashanti*; Field, *Search for Security*; Appiah-Kubi, *Cures*, 10; and Fortes, *Kinship*. For Ewe, see Greene, *Sacred Sites*, and Meyer, *Translating the Devil*.

9. For a description of how the gods were related to therapy in Charles's neighborhood of Labadi in the 1970s, see Mullings, *Therapy*, 67. The Ga pantheon incorporates gods from neighboring areas (Field, *Religion and Medicine*; Mullings, *Therapy*, 14).

10. Ga gods are understood to possess individuals, and sometimes to call them to be their interpreters, or *woyei* (Mullings, *Therapy*, 69–73; Field, *Search for Security*).

11. Nugent, Paksarian, and Mojtabai, "Uncertainties"; Susser and Wanderling, "Epidemiology."

12. Field, *Search for Security*, 201–3.

13. Meyer, *Translating the Devil*.

14. Mullings (*Therapy*, 130–60), like Meyer (*Translating the Devil*), says that Labadi Christians interpreted witchcraft to be of the devil, and witches were commonly blamed for spiritual illness.

CASE 8: MADNESS EXPERIENCED AS FAITH

1. It has been described by Ann Grodzins Gold (*Fruitful Journeys*) and by Sudhir Kakar (*Shamans, Mystics, and Doctors*). See also Satija et al., "Temple"; Pakaslahti, "Traditional Healers"; Dwyer, *Divine and Demonic*.

2. Lutgendorf, "Monkey in the Middle."

3. See also Dwyer, *Divine and Demonic*.

4. Nichter, "Idioms," 403.

5. Bourguignon's *Possession* provides a comprehensive overview of spirit possession. For a remarkable collection of case studies, see Crapanzano and Garrison, eds., *Spirit Possession*. Lewis's *Ecstatic Religion* is the classic argument that such practices allow those with lesser power to assert authority. In *Wombs and Alien Spirits*, Boddy describes the Zār spirit-possession cult in the Sudan; and in *The Devil in the Shape of a Woman*, Karlsen describes devil possession in colonial New England.

6. Pakaslahti, "Terminology."

7. Eck, *Darsan*, 7.

8. As a result of rules set out for the functioning of state mental hospitals under the Indian Mental Health Act of 1987, which discourages a stay in the hospital for more than three consecutive months, it is common practice for people with psychiatric illnesses to spend time incarcerated in a number of state psychiatric institutions over many years. Such persons are considered "revolving-door patients" and, more often than not, eventually end up adding to the large numbers of long-staying, chronically ill people in Indian state psychiatric facilities.

9. Dhanda, *Legal Order*.

CASE 9: FAITH INTERPRETED AS MADNESS

1. See Mueller, "Psychiatry under Tyranny."

2. All names have been changed to protect patient confidentiality. In addition, in order to protect other informants who assisted in this research, I have changed various details about the locations, dates, and so on.

3. For an interesting discussion of the challenges of comparing Eastern Orthodoxy with other forms of Christianity, see Tomka, "Sociology of Religion," and Hann and Goltz, "The Other Christianity?"

4. Rokeach, *Three Christs.*

5. The length of Alexandra's hospitalization is not unusual in Romania, a country where the mental health system has remained primarily "institutionalized." The length of her hospitalization, her poverty, and her lack of social support make her a good candidate for being seen as a "social case" (Friedman, "Social Case"). For an overview of the Romanian mental health system, see Friedman, "Mental Health Reform in Romania" and "Mapping the Terrain."

6. Some of Alexandra's severe criticism of the Romanian Orthodox Church might stem from, as Melissa Caldwell has suggested is the case in Russia, "holding Orthodox churches accountable in ways that observers do not for non-Orthodox congregations" ("Changing Ethics of Benevolence," 346).

7. See a similar discussion in Verdery, *The Political Lives of Dead Bodies.*

8. It is, perhaps, significant that the evangelical faith to which Alexandra belongs has a long-standing tradition (going back to the nineteenth century) of millennial beliefs and a richly developed eschatological quality to its theology.

9. Here, Alexandra is implying a link between her unhappiness, her illness, her social isolation, and her lack of sexual relationships (the reference to "hormones"). Alexandra suggested, throughout my time seeing her, that her lack of a romantic relationship and sexual life was one of the central concerns in her life that caused her great distress and sadness.

10. I was never able to meet or interview Alexandra's mother, so I can't confirm these stories, but it is possible that the course of her illness might have been affected by the "expressed emotions" found in her household.

11. Her reference to two different scales of currency in this fragment ("three lei" and "one million lei") meant that the referent for her story bridged both the state socialist period and the postsocialist period.

12. This final comment about politics reveals Alexandra's self-knowledge about the problems she has had with hallucinations and delusions about politics and politicians that have been projected to her from television.

13. For an interesting study of the role of morality in the treatment of illness in an Eastern Orthodox context in Russia, see Zigon, "HIV Is God's Blessing."

14. Larchet (*Mental Disorders and Spiritual Healing*), surveying Eastern Orthodox approaches to mental illness, notes that

Although, for the Fathers, one category of mental illness or form of insanity had a somatic etiology, and a second category a demonic one, the third category is of spiritual origin. While the first has (our fallen) nature for its cause and the second demons, the free will of an individual is responsible for the third, even if demonic activity and our free will sometimes share responsibility in the first two situations. (89)

For a more extreme example of the conflation of immorality and madness, see Chirilă, *Conceptul de Medicină*, 88–104. For a more measured dialogue between Church and physicians on these topics, see Chirban, ed., *Sickness or Sin?*

15. Forbess, "Spirit."

16. Her particular evangelical church, unlike some, does not promote suspicion of, or see a threat posed by, psychiatry.

17. Huguelet et al., "Spiritual Assessment"; Koenig, "Research on Religion."

18. Friedman, "Social Case."

19. Bran, *"Cartea Judecătorilor."*

CASE 10: THE CULTURE OF THE INSTITUTIONAL CIRCUIT

1. Lehman and Steinwachs, "Patterns."

2. This essay is closely related to my "Down and Out in Chicago," published in the 2010 issue of *Raritan*. It is used with permission from *Raritan*.

3. Talbott, *Death of the Asylum*; Frank and Glied, *Better but Not Well.*

4. In *Asylums*, Erving Goffman described psychiatric hospitals as "total institutions" that shaped not only what people did but what they thought.

5. Mechanic, McAlpine, and Olfson, "Patterns"; Lamb and Weinberger, "Shift of Psychiatric Care."

6. Dear and Wolch, *Landscapes of Despair.*

7. According to police and mental health professionals in the area.

8. Herman et al., "Homelessness."

9. Folsom et al., "Prevalence and Risk."

10. Torrey et al., "Jails and Prisons" and "Treatment of Persons."

11. Talbott, *Death of the Asylum.*

12. Mark Heyrman, personal communication, 2006.

13. Hopper et al., "Homelessness."

14. Teplin et al., "Crime Victimization."

CASE 11: RETURN TO BASELINE

1. Susser and Wanderling, "Epidemiology"; Alaghband-Rad et al., "Remitting Psychosis"; Arranz et al., "Predictors"; Mojtabai, Susser, and Bromet, "Clinical Characteristics."

2. Supporting work in Indonesia is described in Good and Subandi, "Psychosis in Javanese Culture."

3. Saha et al., "Systematic Review."

4. Phanthunane et al., "Schizophrenia in Thailand," 4.

5. Phanthunane et al. ("Schizophrenia in Thailand"), using standard measures, report a lesser disease burden than the global average.

CASE 12: A FRAGILE RECOVERY IN THE UNITED STATES

1. For more, see Granger, "Role of Psychiatric Rehabilitation Practitioners."
2. See https://cpr.bu.edu/resources/reasonable-accommodations/what-is-psychi-atric-disability-and-mental-illness.
3. For more, see Estroff et al., "Pathways."
4. For more, see Myers, *Recovery's Edge*.
5. For more, see Estroff et al., "Pathways," and Cook, "Employment Barriers."
6. Hopper et al., "Homelessness."
7. For two excellent first-person accounts, see Saks, *The Centre*, and Schiller and Bennett, *The Quiet Room*.
8. See Ridgway et al., *Pathways to Recovery*.
9. See Drake et al., "Implementing."
10. Milev et al., "Predictive Value."

CONCLUSION

1. Jocelyn Marrow and T. M. Luhrmann contributed equally to this essay. Portions of the chapter are drawn from Luhrmann, "Social Defeat," with permission from Springer Science and Business Media.
2. References to support these claims are provided in the richer discussion of the Introduction.
3. Tidey and Miczek, "Social Defeat."
4. Isovich et al., "Social Isolation."
5. Selten et al., "Update"; Selten and Cantor-Graae, "Social Defeat."
6. Goldstein and McEwen, "Allostasis"; McEwen and Lasley, "Allostatic Load." More generally, the Introduction discussed the work of Michael Marmot and Nancy Adler, which has demonstrated that both objective and subjective social status have powerful medical implications for the body.
7. Farmer, *Infections and Inequalities*, 5.
8. In 1955 the Republic of Ireland saw 10.82 psychiatric hospitalizations per thousand, compared to 5.65 in the United States and 5.88 in Canada. In 1965 the rates dropped somewhat, but the Republic of Ireland still remained the highest by some significant degree; half of these admissions were for schizophrenia (Scheper-Hughes, *Saints, Scholars, and Schizophrenics*, 137). More recent epidemiological work suggests that the rates are no longer different, as Scheper-Hughes acknowledges. Ireland has, of course, changed a good deal, and current epidemiological rates cannot disprove earlier ones, though of course they raise doubts. But the older Ireland was a markedly grimmer place.
9. Ibid., 61.

10. Ibid., 42.

11. Hopper, *Reckoning with Homelessness*; Desjarlais, *Shelter Blues*; Lovell, "The City Is My Mother"; Cohen, "Eventfulness."

12. Hopper, *Reckoning with Homelessness*, 63.

13. Ibid., 71.

14. Desjarlais, "Struggling Along," 122.

15. Estroff, *Making It Crazy*.

16. Ibid., 250.

17. Bourdieu, *Outline*, 191.

18. Ibid.

19. Ibid.

20. Farmer, *Pathologies*, 8.

21. Kleinman, Das, and Lock, *Social Suffering*.

22. Ibid., ix.

23. Ibid., x.

24. Good, "Context."

25. Kinderman et al., "Illness Beliefs."

26. Ibid., 1909.

27. Sousa, "Pragmatic Ethics, Sensible Care."

28. This is the pace of work described by R. Padmavati for public psychiatrists in Chennai.

29. Luhrmann et al., "Differences in Voice-Hearing."

30. Estroff, *Making It Crazy*, 119 (emphasis in original).

31. Ibid., 177–80; see also Jenkins and Carpenter-Song, "Stigma Despite Recovery."

32. Floersch, *Meds, Money, and Manners*.

33. Myers, "Culture, Stress, and Recovery," 503–4.

34. Ibid., 504; see also Luhrmann, *When God Talks Back*, 32–3; Braslow, "Manufacture."

35. Myers, "Culture, Stress, and Recovery," 511.

36. Friedman, "Inactivity," 4.

37. Carstairs and Kapur, *Kota*.

38. Ministry of Labour and Employment, Government of India, 2012; www.dnaindia .com/india/report-51-of-indian-workforce-self-employed-survey-1850820.

39. Estroff, *Making It Crazy*; Jenkins and Carpenter-Song, "Stigma despite Recovery."

40. Jenkins and Carpenter-Song, "Stigma Despite Recovery," 390, 392, 397.

41. However, it bears noting that many women who have been cast out of their conjugal homes by their husbands—mentally ill or not—are not accepted back among their natal kin. Thara et al., "Broken Marriages," parts I and II.

42. Das and Addlakha, "Disability."

43. Teplin, Abram, and McClelland, "Psychiatric Disorder."

44. Walsh, Buchanan, and Fahy, "Violence and Schizophrenia"; Swanson et al., "Violent Behavior."

45. Field, *Search for Security*.

46. The argument that homelessness is near normative is made in case 12 and in Luhrmann, "Chronicity." It rests not only on ethnographic interviewing, but on a series of papers, including Folsom et al., "Prevalence and Risk," and Herman et al., "Homelessness," which looked at an entire group of persons with schizophrenia and discovered rates of homelessness that, extended across the decades-long span of the illness, suggest that some period of homelessness is extremely common. See also Hopper et al., "Institutional Circuit."

47. Anderson, *Code of the Street*.

48. Luhrmann et al., "Differences in Voice-Hearing."

49. Cassaniti and Luhrmann, "Cultural Kindling."

50. See, for example, Bellamy's *The Powerful Ephemeral* for a detailed description of this process at the Husain Tekri Dargah of Rajasthan.

51. Huguelet and Koenig, *Religion and Spirituality*.

52. Mohr et al., "Integration"; Hawkins and Abrams, "Disappearing Acts"; Schwab and Petersen, "Religiousness."

53. Koenig, "Research on Religion"; Huguelet et al., "Religious Explanatory Models."

54. Bloom et al., *Global Economic Burden*.

55. Tsemberis, Gulcur, and Nakae, "Housing First"; Greenwood et al., "Decreasing Psychiatric Symptoms"; Larimer et al., "Health Care"; Padgett, "Choices" Padgett et al., "Housing First."

56. Aubry et al., "Housing First."

57. The Hearing Voices Network website is intervoiceonline.org.

58. Ruddle, Mason, and Wykes, "A Review"; Thomas et al., "Psychological Therapies"; Meddings et al., "Effective?"

59. Jenner, van der Willige, and Wiersma, "Cognitive Therapy"; Leff et al., "Avatar Therapy"; Khoury et al., "Mindfulness Interventions."

60. Leff et al., "Avatar Therapy."

61. Chadwick, Birchwood, and Trower, *Cognitive Therapy*.

62. Khoury et al., "Mindfulness Interventions."

63. Morris, Johns, and Oliver, *ACT and Mindfulness for Psychosis*.

64. British Psychological Society, *Understanding Psychosis and Schizophrenia*, 72.

65. Seikkula and Olson, "Open Dialogue," 410.

66. Ibid.; see also Seikkula et al., "Open Dialogue"; Gromer, "Need-Adapted"; Alanen, "More Humanistic"; Alanen et al., "Need-Adapted."

67. Pope, Cubellis, and Hopper, "Dirty Work."

BIBLIOGRAPHY

Addlakha, Renu. *Deconstructing Mental Illness: An Ethnography of Psychiatry, Women, and the Family*. New Delhi: Zubaan, an Imprint of Kali for Women, 2008.

Adebimpe, Victor R. "Overview: White Norms and Psychiatric Diagnosis of Black Patients." *American Journal of Psychiatry* 138 (1981): 279–85.

Adler, Nancy, and Judith Stewart. "The MacArthur Scale of Subjective Social Status." University of California San Francisco Research Network on SES and Health. Revised March 2007. Retrieved from www.macses.ucsf.edu/research/psychosocial /subjective.php.

Alaghband-Rad, Javad, Mehran Boroumand, Homayoun Amini, Vandad Sharifi, Abbas Omid, Rozita Davari-Ashtiani, Arshia Seddigh, Farzad Momeni, and Zahra Aminipour. "Non-affective Acute Remitting Psychosis: A Preliminary Report from Iran." *Acta Psychiatrica Scandinavica* 113 (2006): 96–101.

Alanen, Yrjö O. "Towards a More Humanistic Psychiatry: Development of Need-Adapted Treatment of Schizophrenia Group Psychoses." *Psychosis* (2009): 156–66.

Alanen, Yrjö O., Klaus Lehtinen, Viljo Räkköläinen, and Jukka Aaltonen. "Need-Adapted Treatment of New Schizophrenic Patients: Experiences and Results of the Turku Project." *Acta Psychiatrica Scandinavica* 83 (1991): 363–72.

Allardyce, Judith, Jane Boydell, Jim Van Os, Gary Morrison, David Castle, Robin Murray, and Robin McCreadie. "Comparison of the Incidence of Schizophrenia in Rural Dumfries and Galloway and Urban Camberwell." *British Journal of Psychiatry* 179 (2001): 335–9.

American Psychiatric Association. *Diagnostic and Statistical Manual of Mental Disorders*. Washington, DC: American Psychiatric Association, 1952.

American Psychiatric Association. *Diagnostic and Statistical Manual of Mental Disorders*, 2nd ed. Washington, DC: American Psychiatric Association, 1968.

American Psychiatric Association. *Diagnostic and Statistical Manual of Mental Disorders*, 3rd ed. Washington, DC: American Psychiatric Association, 1980.

American Psychiatric Association. *Diagnostic and Statistical Manual of Mental Disorders: DSM-IV*, 4th ed., rev. Washington, DC: American Psychiatric Association, 1994.

Anderson, Elijah. *The Code of the Street: Decency, Violence and the Moral Life of the Inner City.* New York: Norton, 1999.

Andreasen, Nancy C. *The Broken Brain: The Biological Revolution in Psychiatry.* New York: Harper and Row, 1985.

Appiah-Kubi, Kofi. *Man Cures, God Heals.* New York: Friendship Press, 1981.

Arendt, Mikkel, Raben Rosenberg, Leslie Foldager, Gurli Perto, and Povl Munk-Jørgensen. "Cannabis-Induced Psychosis and Subsequent Schizophrenia-Spectrum Disorders: Follow-Up Study of 535 Incident Cases." *British Journal of Psychiatry* 187 (2005): 510–5.

Arnold, Lesley M., Paul E. Keck Jr., Jacqueline Collins, Rodgers Wilson, David E. Fleck, Kimberly B. Corey, Jennifer Amicone, Victor R. Adebimpe, and Stephen M. Strakowski. "Ethnicity and First Rank Symptoms in Patients with Psychosis." *Schizophrenia Research* 67 (2004): 207–12.

Arranz, Belen, Luis San, Nicolas Ramírez, Rosa María Dueñas, Victor Perez, Jose Salavert, Iluminada Corripio, and Enrique Alvarez. "Clinical and Serotonergic Predictors of Non-Affective Acute Remitting Psychosis in Patients with a First-Episode Psychosis." *Acta Psychiatrica Scandinavica* 119 (2009): 71–7.

Asamoah-Gyadu, Kwabena. *African Charismatics: Current Developments within Independent Indigenous Pentecostalism in Ghana.* Leiden: Brill, 2004.

Aubry, Tim, Sam Tsemberis, Carol E. Adair, Scott Veldhuizen, David Streiner, Eric Latimer, Jitender Sareen, Michelle Patterson, Kathleen McGarvey, Brianna Kopp, Catharine Hume, and Paula Goering. "One-Year Outcomes of a Randomized Controlled Trial of Housing First with ACT in Five Canadian Cities." *Psychiatric Services* 66 (2015): 463–9.

Aviv, Rachel. "Which Way Madness Lies." *Harper's Magazine.* (2010): 35–46.

Bark, Nigel. "Did Schizophrenia Change the Course of English History? The Mental Illness of Henry VI." *Medical Hypotheses* 59 (2002): 416–21.

Barrett, Robert J. *The Psychiatric Team and the Social Definition of Schizophrenia: An Anthropological Study of Person and Illness.* Cambridge: Cambridge University Press, 1996.

Bateson, Gregory. *Steps to an Ecology of Mind.* Chicago: University of Chicago Press, 2000 [1972].

Bateson, Gregory, Don D. Jackson, Jay Haley, and John Weakland. "Toward a Theory of Schizophrenia." *Behavioral Science* 1 (1956): 251–64.

Becker, Howard. *Outsiders.* New York: Free Press, 1963.

Bellamy, Carla. *The Powerful Ephemeral: Everyday Healing in an Ambiguously Islamic Place.* Berkeley: University of California Press, 2011.

Benedict, Ruth. "Anthropology and the Abnormal." *Journal of General Psychology* 11 (1934): 59–80.

Bentall, Richard P., Charles Fernyhough, Anthony P. Morrison, Shôn Lewis, and Rhiannon Corcoran. "Prospects for a Cognitive-Developmental Account of Psychotic Experiences." *British Journal of Clinical Psychology* 46 (2007): 155–73.

Berrios, German E., Rogelio Luque, and Jose M. Villagrán. "Schizophrenia: A Conceptual History." *International Journal of Psychology and Psychological Therapy* 3 (2003): 111–40.

Berthoud, Richard, and Sharon Beishon. "People, Families and Households," in *Ethnic Minorities in Britain: Diversity and Disadvantage*, edited by Tariq Modood and Richard Berthoud, 18–59. London: Policy Studies Institute, 1997.

Bhugra, Dinesh. "Migration, Distress and Cultural Identity." *British Medical Bulletin* 69 (2004): 129–41.

Bhugra, Dinesh, Marcel Hilwig, Rosemary Mallett, Bryan Corridan, Julian Leff, John Neehall, and Sian Rudge. "Factors in the Onset of Schizophrenia: A Comparison between London and Trinidad Samples." *Acta Psychiatrica Scandinavica* 101 (2000): 135–41.

Bhugra, Dinesh, Julian Leff, Rosemarie Mallett, Geoff Der, Bryan Corridan, and Sian Rudge. "Incidence and Outcome of Schizophrenia in Whites, African-Caribbeans and Asians in London." *Psychological Medicine* 27 (1997): 791–8.

Bhugra, Dinesh, Rosemary Mallett, and Julian Leff. "Schizophrenia and African-Caribbeans: A Conceptual Model of Aetiology." *International Review of Psychiatry* 11 (1999): 145–52.

Bhui, Kamaldeep, Philip Brown, Tim Hardie, James P. Watson, and Janet Parrot. "African-Caribbean Men Admitted to Brixton Prison: Psychiatric and Forensic Characteristics and Outcome of Final Court Appearance." *British Journal of Psychiatry* 172 (1998): 337–44.

Birchwood, Max, Ray Cochrane, Fiona Macmillan, Sonja Copestake, Jo Kucharska, and Margaret Carriss. "The Influence of Ethnicity and Family Structure on Relapse in First-Episode Schizophrenia. A Comparison of Asian, Afro-Caribbean and White Patients." *British Journal of Psychiatry* 161 (1992): 783–90.

Bleuler, Eugen. *Dementia Praecox oder Gruppe der Schizophrenien*. Leipzig: Deuticke, 1911.

Bloom, D. E., E. T. Cafiero, E. Jané-Llopis, S. Abrahams-Gessel, L. R. Bloom, S. Fathima, A. B. Feigl, T. Gaziano, M. Mowafi, A. Pandya, and others. *The Global Economic Burden of Noncommunicable Diseases*. Geneva: World Economic Forum, 2011.

Boddy, Janice. *Wombs and Alien Spirits: Women, Men, and the Zār Cult in Northern Sudan*. Madison: University of Wisconsin Press, 1989.

Bourdieu, Pierre. *Outline of a Theory of Practice*. Cambridge: Cambridge University Press 1977.

Bourguignon, Erika. *Possession*. San Francisco: Chandler & Sharp, 1976.

Boydell, Jane, Jim van Os, Maria Lambri, David Castle, Judith Allardyce, Robin G. McCreadie, and Robin M. Murray. "Incidence of Schizophrenia in South-east London between 1965 and 1997." *British Journal of Psychiatry* 182 (2003): 45–9.

Boydell, Jane, Jim van Os, Kwame McKenzie, Judith Allardyce, R. Goel, Robin G. McCreadie, and Robin M. Murray. "Incidence of Schizophrenia in Ethnic Minorities in London: Ecological Study into Interactions with Environment." *British Medical Journal* 323 (2001): 1336–8.

Bran, Tatiana Niculescu. *Cartea Judecătorilor: Cazul Tanacu.* Bucharest: Humanitas, 2008.

Braslow, Joel Tupper. "The Manufacture of Recovery." *Annual Review of Clinical Psychology* 9 (2013): 781–809.

British Psychological Society. *Understanding Psychosis and Schizophrenia,* edited by Anne Cooke. London: British Psychological Society Division of Clinical Psychology, 2014.

Brodwin, Paul. *Everyday Ethics: Voices from the Frontline of Community Psychiatry.* Oakland: University of California Press, 2013.

Brown, Alan, Michaeline Bresnahan, and Ezra Susser. "Schizophrenia: Environmental Epidemiology," in *Kaplan and Sadock's Comprehensive Textbook of Psychiatry,* edited by Benjamin J. Sadock and Virginia Alcott Sadock, 1371–81. Philadelphia: Lippincott Williams & Wilkins, 2000.

Brown, Alan, Catherine A. Schaefer, Charles P. Quesenberry, Liyan Liu, Vicki P. Babulas, and Ezra S. Susser. "Maternal Exposure to Toxoplasmosis and Risk of Schizophrenia in Adult Offspring." *American Journal of Psychiatry* 162 (2005): 767–73.

Brown, George. "The Discovery of Expressed Emotion: Induction or Deduction?" in *Expressed Emotion in Families,* edited by J. Leff and C. Vaughn, 7–25. New York: Guilford, 1985.

Brown, George. "Experiences of Discharged Chronic Schizophrenic Mental Hospital Patients in Various Types of Living Groups." *Millbank Memorial Fund Quarterly* 27 (1959): 105–31.

Brown, George W., John L. T. Birley, and John K. Wing. "Influence of Family Life on the Course of Schizophrenia Disorders: A Replication." *British Journal of Psychiatry* 121 (1972): 241–58.

Buchanan, Robert, and William Carpenter. "Schizophrenia: Introduction and Overview," in *Kaplan and Sadock's Comprehensive Textbook of Psychiatry,* edited by Benjamin J. Sadock and Virginia Alcott Sadock, 1096–109. Philadelphia: Lippincott Williams & Wilkins, 2000.

Bustillo, Juan, Samuel Keith, and John Lauriello. "Schizophrenia: Psychosocial Treatment," in *Kaplan and Sadock's Comprehensive Textbook of Psychiatry,* edited by Benjamin J. Sadock and Virginia Alcott Sadock, 1210–7. Philadelphia: Lippincott Williams & Wilkins, 2000.

Caldwell, Melissa. "The Russian Orthodox Church, the Provision of Social Welfare, and Changing Ethics of Benevolence," in *Eastern Christians in Anthropological Perspective,* edited by Chris Hann and Hermann Goltz, 329–50. Berkeley: University of California Press, 2010.

Cantor-Graae, Elizabeth. "The Contribution of Social Factors to the Development of Schizophrenia: A Review of Recent Findings." *Canadian Journal of Psychiatry* 52 (2007): 277–86.

Cantor-Graae, Elizabeth, and Jean-Paul Selten. "Schizophrenia and Migration: A Meta–Analysis and Review." *American Journal of Psychiatry* 162 (2005): 12–24.

Caroff, Stanley N., Stephan C. Mann, Andrew Francis, and Gregory L. Fricchione, eds. *Catatonia: From Psychopathology to Neurobiology*. Arlington: American Psychiatric Publishing, 2004.

Carstairs, G. M., and R. L. Kapur. *The Great Universe of Kota: Stress, Change, and Mental Disorder in an Indian Village*. Berkeley: University of California Press, 1976.

Cassaniti, Julia L., and Tanya Marie Luhrmann. "The Cultural Kindling of Spiritual Experiences." *Current Anthropology* 55 (2014): S333–43.

Chadda, Rakesh and Koushik Sinha Deb. "Indian Family Systems, Collectivistic Society and Psychotherapy." *Indian Journal of Psychiatry* 55 (2013): 5299–5309.

Chadwick, Paul D., Max Birchwood, and Peter Trower. *Cognitive Therapy for Delusions, Voices and Paranoia*. Oxford: John Wiley & Sons, 1996.

Chakraborty, Ajita. "Mental Health of Indian Women: A Field Experience," in *Mental Health from a Gender Perspective*, edited by B. V. Davar, 34–60. New Delhi: Sage Publications India, 2001

Chirban, John. *Sickness or Sin? Spiritual Discernment and Differentiated Diagnosis*. Brookline: Holy Cross Orthodox Press, 2001.

Chirilă, Pavel. *Conceptul de Medicină Creștină*. Bucharest: Christiana, 2001.

Clark, Robert. "Psychoses, Income, and Occupational Prestige." *American Journal of Sociology* 54 (1949): 433–40.

Clark, Robert. "The Relationship of Schizophrenia to Occupational Income and Occupational Prestige." *American Sociological Review* 13 (1948): 325–30.

Cohen, Alex. "The Search for Meaning: Eventfulness in the Lives of Homeless Mentally Ill Persons in the Skid Row District of Los Angeles." *Culture, Medicine, and Psychiatry* 25 (2001): 277–96.

Cohen, Alex, Vikram Patel, Thara Rangaswamy, and Oye Gureje. "Questioning an Axiom: Better Prognosis for Schizophrenia in the Developing World?" *Schizophrenia Bulletin* 34 (2008): 229–44.

Coid, Jeremy, Nadji Kahtan, Simon Gault, and Brian Jarman. "Ethnic Differences in Admissions to Secure Forensic Psychiatry Services." *British Journal of Psychiatry* 177 (2000): 241–7.

Coid, Jeremy W., James B. Kirkbride, Dave Barker, Fiona Cowden, Rebekah Stamps, Min Yang, and Peter B. Jones. "Raised Incidence Rates of All Psychoses among Migrant Groups: Findings from the East London First Episode Psychosis Study." *Archives of General Psychiatry* 65 (2008): 1250–8.

Cole, Eleanor, Gerard Leavy, Michael King, Eric Johnson-Sabine, and Amanda Hoar. "Pathways to Care for Patients with a First Episode of Psychosis: A Comparison of Ethnic Groups." *British Journal of Psychiatry* 167 (1995): 770–6.

Cole, Jennifer. *Sex and Salvation: Imagining the Future in Madagascar*. Chicago: University of Chicago Press, 2010.

Comaroff, Jean, and John Comaroff. "Occult Economies and the Violence of Abstraction." *American Ethnologist* 26 (1999): 279–303.

Connor, Charlotte, and Max Birchwood. "Power and Perceived Expressed Emotion of Voices: Their Impact on Depression and Suicidal Thinking in Those Who Hear Voices." *Clinical Psychology and Psychotherapy* 20 (2013): 199–205.

Connor, Charlotte, and Max Birchwood. "Through the Looking Glass: Self-Reassuring Meta-cognitive Capacity and Its Relationship with the Thematic Content of Voices." *Frontiers of Human Neuroscience* 7 (2013): Article 213: 1–7.

Cook, Judith A. "Employment Barriers for Persons with Psychiatric Disabilities: A Report for the President's New Freedom Commission." *Psychiatric Services* 57 (2006): 1391–1405.

Corin, Ellen, Rangaswamy Thara, and Ramachandran Padmavati. "Living through a Staggering World: The Play of Signifiers in Early Psychosis in South India," in *Schizophrenia, Culture, and Subjectivity: The Edge of Experience*, edited by J. H. Jenkins and R. J. Barrett, 110–45. Cambridge: Cambridge University Press, 2004.

Craig, Thomas, Carole Siegel, Kim Hopper, Shang Lin, and Norman Sartorius. "Outcome in Schizophrenia and Related Disorders Compared between Developing and Developed Countries." *British Journal of Psychiatry* 170 (1997): 229–33.

Crapanzano, Vincent, and Vivian Garrison, eds. *Case Studies in Spirit Possession*. New York: Wiley, 1977.

Crocker, Jon Christopher. *Vital Souls: Bororo Cosmology, Natural Symbolism, and Shamanism*. Tucson: University of Arizona Press, 1985.

Das, Veena, and Renu Addlakha. "Disability and Domestic Citizenship: Voice, Gender, and the Making of the Subject." *Public Culture* 13 (2001): 511–31.

Davidson, Larry, Maria O'Connell, Janis Tondora, Thomas Styron, and Karen Kangas. "The Top Ten Concerns about Recovery Encountered in Mental Health System Transformation." *Psychiatric Services* 5 (2006): 640–5.

Davidson, Larry, Jaak Rakfeldt, and John Strauss. *The Roots of the Recovery Movement: Lessons Learned*. London: Wiley–Blackwell, 2011.

Dear, Michael, and Jennifer Wolch. *Landscapes of Despair*. Princeton: Princeton University Press, 2014 [1992].

Deister, Arno, and Andreas Marneros. "Prognostic Value of Initial Subtype in Schizophrenic Disorders." *Schizophrenia Research* 12 (1994): 145–57.

Dernè, Steve. *Culture in Action: Family Life, Emotion, and Male Dominance in Banaras, India*. Albany: State University of New York Press, 1995.

Desjarlais, Robert. *Shelter Blues: Sanity and Selfhood among the Homeless*. Philadelphia: University of Pennsylvania, 1997.

Desjarlais, Robert. "Struggling Along: The Possibilities for Experience among the Homeless." *American Anthropologist* 96 (1994): 886–901.

Devereux, George. "Normal and Abnormal," in *Cultural Psychiatry and Medical Anthropology: An Introduction and Reader*, edited by Roland Littlewood and Simon Dein. London: Athlone Press, 2000.

Dhanda, Amita. *Legal Order and Mental Disorder*. New Delhi: Sage, 2000.

Dohrenwend, Bruce, Itzhak Lehav, Patrick Shrout, Sharon Schwartz, Guedalia Naveh, Bruce Link, Andrew Skodol, and Ann Stueve. "Socioeconomic Status and Psychiatric Disorders: The Causation-Selection Issue." *Science* 255 (1992): 946–52.

Dolnick, Edward. *Madness on the Couch: Blaming the Victim in the Heyday of Psychoanalysis.* New York: Simon and Schuster, 1998.

Drake, Robert, Susan M. Essock, Andrew Shaner, Kate B. Carey, Kenneth Minkoff, Lenore Kola, David Lynde, Fred C. Osher, Robin E. Clark, and Lawrence Rickards. "Implementing Dual Diagnosis Services for Clients With Severe Mental Illness." *Psychiatric Services* (2001): 469–76.

Durkheim, Émile. *The Division of Labor in Society.* New York: Macmillan, 1933.

Durkheim, Émile. *Suicide: A Study In Sociology.* New York: Free Press, 1997.

Dwyer, Graham. *The Divine and the Demonic: Supernatural Affliction and Its Treatment in North India.* London: Routledge, 2003.

Eck, Diana. *Darsan.* New York: Columbia University Press, 1998.

Edgerton, Robert B. "Conceptions of Psychosis in Four East African Societies." *American Anthropologist* 68 (1966): 408–25.

Estroff, Sue E. *Making It Crazy: An Ethnography of Psychiatric Clients in an American Community.* Berkeley: University of California, 1981.

Estroff, Sue E., Donald L. Patrick, Catherine R. Zimmer, and William S. Lachicotte Jr. "Pathways to Disability Income among Persons with Severe, Persistent Psychiatric Disorders." *Milbank Quarterly* 74 (1997): 495–532.

Fabian, Johannes. *Out of Our Minds: Reason and Madness in the Exploration of Central Africa.* Berkeley: University of California Press, 2000.

Faris, Robert, and Warren Dunham. *Mental Disorders in Urban Areas.* Chicago: University of Chicago Press, 1939.

Farmer, Paul. *Infections and Inequalities: The Modern Plagues.* Berkeley: University of California Press, 1999.

Farmer, Paul. *Pathologies of Power.* 2005. Berkeley: University of California Press.

Fearon, Paul, and Craig Morgan. "Environmental Factors in Schizophrenia: The Role of Migrant Studies." *Schizophrenia Bulletin* 32 (2006): 405–8.

Field, Margaret Joyce. *Religion and Medicine of the Gā People.* New York: AMS Press, 1937.

Field, Margaret Joyce. *Search for Security: An Ethno-Psychiatric Study of Rural Ghana.* New York: Norton, 1960.

Floersch, Jerry. *Meds, Money, and Manners: The Case Management of Severe Mental Illness.* New York: Columbia University Press, 2002.

Folsom, David P., William Hawthorne, Laurie Lindamer, Todd Gilmer, Anne Bailey, Shahrokh Golshan, Piedad Garcia, Jürgen Unützer, Richard Hough, and Dilip V. Jeste. "Prevalence and Risk Factors for Homelessness and Utilization of Mental Health Services among 10,340 Patients with Serious Mental Illness in a Large Public Mental Health System." *American Journal of Psychiatry* 162 (2005): 370–6.

Foner, Nancy. "The Jamaicans: Cultural and Social Change among Migrant in Britain," in *Between Two Cultures: Migrant and Minorities in Britain,* edited by James L. Watson. Oxford: Basil Blackwell, 1977.

Forbess, Alice. "The Spirit and the Letter: Monastic Education in a Romanian Orthodox Convent," in *Eastern Christians in Anthropological Perspective,* edited by Chris Hann and Hermann Goltz, 131–54. Berkeley: University of California Press, 2010.

Fortes, Meyer. *Kinship and the Social Order: The Legacy of Lewis Henry Morgan.* New Brunswick: Aldine Transaction, 2006.

Fortes, Meyer, and Doris Y. Mayer. "Psychosis and Social Change among the Tallensi of Northern Ghana." *Cahiers d'études africaines* 6(21) (1966): 5–40.

Foucault, Michel. *Madness and Civilization: A History of Insanity in the Age of Reason.* New York: Vintage, 1988.

Frank, Richard G., and Sherry A. Glied. *Better but Not Well: Mental Health Policy in the United States since 1950.* Baltimore: Johns Hopkins University Press, 2006.

Friedman, Jack. "The Challenges Facing Mental Health Reform in Romania." *Eurohealth* 12 (2006): 36–9.

Friedman, Jack. "Mapping the Terrain of Mental Illness and Psychiatry: Anthropological Observations on Romania's Mental Health Reforms as It Enters the European Union." *Revista Româna de Psihiatrie* 9 (2007): 73–7.

Friedman, Jack. "The Social Case: Illness, Psychiatry, and Deinstitutionalization in Postsocialist Romania." *Medical Anthropology Quarterly* 24 (2009): 375–96.

Friedman, Jack. "Thoughts on Inactivity and an Ethnography of Nothing: Comparing Meanings of 'Inactivity' in Romanian and American Mental Health Care." *North American Dialogue* 15 (2012): 1–9.

Fromm-Reichmann, Frieda. "Notes on the Development of Treatment of Schizophrenics by Psychoanalytic Psychotherapy," in *Psychoanalysis and Psychotherapy,* edited by D. M. Bullard. Chicago: University of Chicago Press, 1952.

Gifford, Paul. *Ghana's New Christianity: Pentecostalism in a Globalizing African Economy.* Bloomington: Indiana University Press, 2004.

Gilkeson, John S. *Anthropologists and the Rediscovery of America, 1886–1965.* Cambridge: Cambridge University Press, 2010.

Goffman, Erving. *Asylums: Essays on the Social Situation of Mental Patients and Other Inmates.* New York: Anchor, 1961.

Goffman, Erving. *Stigma: Notes on the Management of a Spoiled Identity.* Englewood Cliffs: Prentice Hall, 1963.

Gold, Ann Grodzins. *Fruitful Journeys: The Ways of Rajasthani Pilgrims.* Prospect Heights: Waveland Press, 2000.

Gold, Ann Grodzins. "Love's Cup, Love's Thorn, Love's End: The Language of *Prem* in Ghatiyali," in *Love in South Asia: A Cultural History,* edited by Francesca Orsini, 303–30. Cambridge: Cambridge University Press, 2006.

Goldstein, David, and Bruce McEwen. "Allostasis, Homeostats, and the Nature of Stress." *Stress* 5 (2002): 55–8.

Good, Byron. "Culture, Diagnosis and Comorbidity." *Culture, Medicine, and Psychiatry* 16 (1992): 427–46.

Good, Byron. "Studying Mental Illness in Context: Local, Global or Universal?" *Ethos* 25 (1997): 230–48.

Good, Byron, and M. A. Subandi. "Experiences of Psychosis in Javanese Culture: Reflections on a Case of Acute, Recurrent Psychosis in Contemporary Yogyakarta, Indonesia," in *Schizophrenia, Culture, and Subjectivity: The Edge of Experience*, edited by Janis Hunter Jenkins and Robert John Barrett. Cambridge: Cambridge University Press, 2003.

Gottesman, Irving I. *Schizophrenia Genesis: The Origins of Madness*. New York: W.H. Freeman, 1991.

Government of India. "Second Annual Employment & Unemployment Survey 2011–2012." Chandigarh: Labour Bureau Ministry of Labour and Employment, 2012.

Granger, Barbara. "The Role of Psychiatric Rehabilitation Practitioners in Assisting People in Understanding How to Best Assert Their ADA Rights and Arrange Job Accommodations." *Psychiatric Rehabilitation Journal* 23 (2000): 215–23.

Greenberg, Joanne. *I Never Promised You a Rose Garden*. New York: Holt, Rinehart and Winston, 1964.

Greene, Sandra E. *Sacred Sites and the Colonial Encounter: A History of Meaning and Memory in Ghana*. Bloomington: University of Indiana Press, 2002.

Greenwood, Ronni, Nicole Schaefer-McDaniel, Gary Winkel, and Sam Tsemberis. "Decreasing Psychiatric Symptoms by Increasing Choice in Services for Adults with Histories of Homelessness." *American Journal of Community Psychology* 36 (2006): 223–38.

Grimby, Agneta. "Bereavement among Elderly People: Grief Reactions, Post-Bereavement Hallucinations and Quality of Life." *Acta Psychiatrica Scandinavica* 87 (1993): 72–80.

Gromer, Jill. "Need-Adapted and Open-Dialogue Treatments: Empirically Supported Psychosocial Interventions for Schizophrenia and Other Psychotic Disorders." *Ethical Human Psychology and Psychiatry* 14 (2012): 162–77.

Gurland, Barry, Joseph Fleiss, John Cooper, Robert Kendell, and Simon Robert. "Cross-National Study of Diagnosis of the Mental Disorders: Some Comparisons of Diagnostic Criteria from the First Investigation." *American Journal of Psychiatry* 125 (1969): 30–9.

Häfner, Heinz. "The Concept of Schizophrenia: From Unity to Diversity." *Advances in Psychiatry* 2014 (2014): article 929434.

Hale, Nathan. *The Rise and Crisis of Psychoanalysis in the United States: Freud and the Americans 1917–1985*. New York: Oxford University Press, 1995.

Halliburton, Murphy. "Finding a Fit: Psychiatric Pluralism in South India and Its Implications for WHO Studies of Mental Disorder." *Transcultural Psychiatry* 41 (2004): 80–98.

Halliburton, Murphy. "'Just Some Spirits': The Erosion of Spirit Possession and the Rise of 'Tension' in South India." *Medical Anthropology* 24 (2005):111–44.

Halpern, David. "Minorities and Mental Health." *Social Science and Medicine* 36 (1993): 597–607.

Halpern, David, and James Nazroo. "The Ethnic Density Effect: Results from a National Community Survey of England and Wales." *International Journal of Social Psychiatry* 46 (2000): 34–46.

Hann, Chris, and Hermann Goltz. "Introduction: The Other Christianity?" in *Eastern Christians in Anthropological Perspective*, edited by Chris Hann and Hermann Goltz, 1–29. Berkeley: University of California Press, 2010.

Harrison, Glynn, Dimitris Fouskakis, Finn Rasmussen, Per Tynelius, Adrien Sipos, and David Gunnell. "Association between Psychotic Disorder and Urban Place of Birth Is Not Mediated by Obstetric Complications or Childhood Socio-economic Position: A Cohort Study." *Psychological Medicine* 33 (2003): 723–31.

Harrison, Glynn, Cris Glazebrook, John Brewin, Roch Cantwell, Tim Dalkin, Richard Fox, Peter Jones, and Ian Medley. "Increased Incidence of Psychotic Disorders in Migrants from the Caribbean to the United Kingdom." *Psychological Medicine* 27 (1997): 799–806.

Harrison, Glynn, David Gunnell, Cris Glazebrook, Kevin Page, and Rosemary Kwiecinski. "Association between Schizophrenia and Social Inequality at Birth: Case-Control Study." *British Journal of Psychiatry* 179 (2001): 346–50.

Harrison, Glynn, Kim Hopper, Thomas Craig, Eugene Laska, Carol Siegel, Joe Wanderling, K. C. Dube, Kimon Ganev, Robert Giel, Wolfram an der Heiden, and others. "Recovery from Psychotic Illness: A 15- and 25-Year International Follow-up Study." *British Journal of Psychiatry* 178 (2001): 506–17.

Harrison, Glynn, David Owens, Anthony Holton, David Neilson, and Daphne Boot. "A Prospective Study of Severe Mental Disorder in Afro-Caribbean Patients." *Psychological Medicine* 18 (1988): 643–57.

Hatfield, Agnes B., Leroy Spaniol, and Anthony M. Zipple. "Expressed Emotion: A Family Perspective." *Schizophrenia Bulletin* 13 (1987): 221–6.

Hawkins, Robert Leibson, and Courtney Abrams. "Disappearing Acts: The Social Networks of Formerly Homeless Individuals with Co-occurring Disorders." *Social Science & Medicine* 65 (2007): 2031–42.

Healthcare Commission. "Count Me In Census 2005." London: HC, 2006. www .healthcarecommission.org.uk/_db/_documents/Count_Me_In_2006.pdf.

Healthcare Commission. "Count Me In Census 2007." London: HC, 2008. www .healthcarecommission.org.uk/_db/_documents/Count_me_in-2007.pdf.

Henry, Edward O. *Chant the Names of God: Music and Culture in Bhojpuri-Speaking India*. San Diego: San Diego State University, 1988.

Herdt, Gilbert. "Clinical Ethnography and Sexual Culture." *Annual Review of Sex Research* 10 (1999): 100–9.

Herman, Daniel B., Ezra S. Susser, Lina Jandorf, Janet Lavelle, and Evelyn J. Bromet. "Homelessness among Individuals with Psychotic Disorders Hospitalized for the First Time: Findings from the Suffolk County Mental Health Project." *American Journal of Psychiatry* 155 (1998): 109–13.

Hickling, Frederick W., and Pamela Rodgers-Johnson. "The Incidence of First Contact Schizophrenia in Jamaica." *British Journal of Psychiatry* 167 (1994): 193–6.

Hollingshead, August, and Frederick Redlich. *Social Class and Mental Illness*. New York: John Wiley & Sons, 1958.

Hopper, Kim. "Interrogating the Meaning of 'Culture' in the WHO International Studies of Schizophrenia," in *Schizophrenia, Culture, and Subjectivity,* edited by Janis Hunter Jenkins and Robert John Barrett, 62–87. Cambridge: Cambridge University Press, 2004.

Hopper, Kim. *Reckoning with Homelessness.* Ithaca: Cornell University Press, 2003.

Hopper, Kim. "Redistribution and Its Discontents: On the Prospects of Committed Work in Public Mental Health and Like Settings." *Human Organization* 65 (2006): 218–26.

Hopper, Kim. "Rethinking Social Recovery in Schizophrenia: What a Capabilities Approach Might Offer." *Social Science and Medicine* 65 (2007): 868–79.

Hopper, Kim, Glynn Harrison, Aleksandar Janca, and Norman Sartorius, eds. *Recovery from Schizophrenia: An International Perspective.* Oxford: Oxford University, 2007.

Hopper, Kim, John Jost, Terri Hay, Susan Welber, and Gary Haugland. "Homelessness, Severe Mental Illness, and the Institutional Circuit." *Psychiatric Services* 48 (1997): 659–64.

Hopper, Kim, and Joseph Wanderling. "Revisiting the Developed versus Developing Country Distinction in Course and Outcome in Schizophrenia: Results from ISoS, the WHO Collaborative Followup Project." *Schizophrenia Bulletin* 26 (2000): 835–46.

Hopper, Kim, Joseph Wanderling, and Prakash Narayanan. "To Have and to Hold: A Cross-Cultural Inquiry into Marital Prospects after Psychosis." *Global Public Health* 2 (2007): 257–80.

Hornstein, Gail. *To Redeem One Person Is to Redeem the World: The Life of Frieda Fromm Reichmann.* New York: Free Press, 2000.

Huguelet, Philippe, and Harold G. Koenig. *Religion and Spirituality in Psychiatry.* Cambridge: Cambridge University Press, 2009.

Huguelet, Philippe, Sylvia Mohr, Carine Betrisey, Laurence Borras, Christiane Gilliéron, Adham Mancini Marie, Isabelle Rieben, Nader Perroud, and Pierre-Yves Brandt. "A Randomized Trial of Spiritual Assessment of Outpatients with Schizophrenia: Patients' and Clinicians' Experience." *Psychiatric Services* 62 (2011): 79–86.

Huguelet, Philippe, Sylvia Mohr, Christiane Gilliéron, Pierre-Yves Brandt, and Laurence Borras. "Religious Explanatory Models in Patients with Psychosis: A Three-Year Follow-Up Study." *Psychopathology* 43 (2010): 230–9.

Hutchinson, Gerard, Noriyoshi Takei, Thomas A. Fahy, Dinesh Bhugra, Catherine Gilvarry, Paul Moran, Rosemarie Mallett, Pak Sham, Julian Leff, and Robin M. Murray. "Morbid Risk of Schizophrenia in First-Degree Relatives of White and African-Caribbean Patients with Psychosis." *British Journal of Psychiatry* 169 (1996): 776–80.

Insel, Thomas R., and Hagop Akiskal. "Obsessive-Compulsive Disorder with Psychotic Features: A Phenomenologic Analysis." *American Journal of Psychiatry* 143 (1986): 1527–33.

Isovich, Elenora, Mario Engelmann, Rainer Landgraf, and Eberhard Fuchs. "Social Isolation after a Single Defeat Reduces Striatal Dopamine Transporter Binding in Rats." *European Journal of Neuroscience* 13 (2001): 1254–6.

Iyer, Srividya N., Ramamurti Mangala, Rangaswamy Thara, and Ashok K. Malla. "Comparing Outcomes of First-Episode Psychosis in Canada and India." *Schizophrenia Research* 98 (2008): 83–4.

Iyer, Srividya N., Ramamurti Mangala, Rangaswamy Thara, and Ashok K. Malla. "Preliminary Findings from a Study of First-Episode Psychosis in Montreal, Canada and Chennai, India: Comparison of Outcomes." *Schizophrenia Research* 121 (2010): 227–33.

Jablensky, Assen. "The Epidemiological Horizon," in *Schizophrenia*, 2nd ed., edited by Stephen R. Hirsch and Daniel R. Weinberger, 203–31. Boston: Blackwell, 2003.

Jablensky, Assen, and Norman Sartorius. "What Did the WHO Studies Really Find?" *Schizophrenia Bulletin* 34 (2008): 253–5.

Jablensky, Assen, Norman Sartorius, Gunilla Ernberg, Martha Anker, Ailsa Korten, John E. Cooper, Robert Day, and Aksel Bertelsen. "Schizophrenia: Manifestations, Incidence and Course in Different Cultures: A World Health Organization Ten-Country Study." *Psychological Medicine* (1992): Monograph Supplement 20: 1–97.

Jackson, Don D. "A Note on the Importance of Trauma in the Genesis of Schizophrenia." *Psychiatry* 20 (1957): 181–4.

Jacobson, Nora. *In Recovery: The Making of Mental Health Policy.* Nashville: Vanderbilt University, 2004.

Jenkins, Janis H. *Extraordinary Conditions: Culture and Experience in Mental Health.* Oakland: University of California Press, 2015.

Jenkins, Janis H., and Robert J. Barrett. *Schizophrenia, Culture, and Subjectivity: The Edge of Experience.* New York: Cambridge University Press, 2004.

Jenkins, Janis H., and Elizabeth Carpenter-Song. "The New Paradigm of Recovery from Schizophrenia: Cultural Conundrums of Improvement without Cure." *Culture, Medicine, and Psychiatry* 29 (2005): 379–413.

Jenkins, Janis H., and Elizabeth A. Carpenter-Song. "Stigma Despite Recovery: Strategies for Living in the Aftermath of Psychosis." *Medical Anthropology Quarterly* 22 (2008): 381–409.

Jenkins, Janis H., and Martin Karno. "The Meaning of Expressed Emotion: Theoretical Issues Raised by Cross-Cultural Research." *American Journal of Psychiatry* 149 (1992): 9–21.

Jenner, Jack A., Gerard van de Willige, and Durk Wiersma. "Effectiveness of Cognitive Therapy with Coping Training for Persistent Auditory Hallucinations: A Retrospective Study of Attenders of a Psychiatric Out-Patient Department." *Acta Psychiatrica Scandinavica* 98 (1998): 384–9.

Jeste, Dilip V., Rebecca Del Carmen, James B. Lohr, and Richard Jed Watt. "Did Schizophrenia Exist before the Eighteenth Century?" *Comprehensive Psychiatry* 26 (1985): 493–503.

Johns, Louise, James Nazroo, Paul Bebbington, and Elizabeth Kuipers. "Occurrence of Hallucinatory Experiences in a Community Sample and Ethnic Variations." *British Journal of Psychiatry* 180 (2002): 174–8.

Kakar, Sudhir. *Shamans, Mystics, and Doctors: A Psychological Inquiry into India and Its Healing Traditions.* Chicago: University of Chicago Press, 1991.

Kandel, Eric. "A New Intellectual Framework for Psychiatry." *American Journal of Psychiatry* 155 (1998): 457–69.

Karlsen, Carol F. *The Devil in the Shape of a Woman: Witchcraft in Colonial New England.* New York: W.W. Norton, 1998.

Keller, Richard. *Colonial Madness: Psychiatry in French North Africa.* Chicago: University of Chicago Press, 2007.

Khoury, Bassam, Tania Lecomte, Brandon A. Gaudiano, and Karine Paquin. "Mindfulness Interventions for Psychosis: A Meta–Analysis." *Schizophrenia Research* 150 (2013): 176–84.

Kinderman, Peter, Erika Setzu, Fiona Lobban, and Peter Salmon. "Illness Beliefs in Schizophrenia." *Social Science & Medicine* 63 (2006): 1900–11.

King, Michael, Eleanor Coker, Gerard Leavey, Amanda Hoare, and Eric Johnson-Sabine. "Incidence of Psychotic Illness in London: Comparison of Ethnic Groups." *British Journal of Psychiatry* 309 (1994): 1115–9.

Kirk, Stuart, and Herb Kutchins. *The Selling of DSM.* New York: Aldine de Gruyter, 1992.

Kirkbride, James B., Dave Barker, Fiona Cowden, Rebekah Stamps, Min Yang, Peter B. Jones, and Jeremy Coid. "Psychoses, Ethnicity and Socio-Economic Status." *British Journal of Psychiatry* 193 (2008): 18–24.

Kirmayer, Laurence, Robert Lemelson, and Constance Cummings, eds. *Re–Visioning Psychiatry.* Cambridge: Cambridge University Press, 2015.

Kleinman, Arthur, Veena Das, and Margaret M. Lock, eds. *Social Suffering.* Berkeley: University of California Press, 1997.

Kleinman, Arthur, and Joan Kleinman. "Somatization: The Interconnections in Chinese Society among Culture, Depressive Experience, and the Meanings of Pain," in *Culture and Depression: Studies in the Anthropology and Cross-Cultural Psychiatry of Affect and Disorder*, edited by Arthur Kleinman and Byron Good. Berkeley: University of California Press, 1986.

Koenig, Harold G. "Research on Religion, Spirituality, and Mental Health: A Review." *Canadian Journal of Psychiatry* 54 (2009): 283–91.

Kohn, Melvin. "Social Class and Schizophrenia," in *Social Psychology and Mental Health*, edited by Henry Wechsler, Leonard Solomon, and Bernard Kramer, 113–27. New York: Holt, Rinehart and Winston, 1970.

Kohn, Melvin. "Social Class and Schizophrenia: A Critical Review and a Reformulation." *Schizophrenia Bulletin* 1 (1973): 60–79.

Kraepelin, Emil. *Lehrbuch der Psychiatrie*, 5th ed. Leipzig: Barth, 1896.

Laing, R. D. *The Divided Self.* London: Tavistock, 1960.

Lamb, H. Richard, and Linda E. Weinberger. "The Shift of Psychiatric Care from Hospitals to Jails and Prisons." *Journal of the American Academy of Psychiatry and the Law* 33 (2005): 529–34.

Lamb, Sarah. *White Saris and Sweet Mangoes: Aging, Gender, and Body in North India.* Berkeley: University of California Press, 2000.

Larchet, Jean-Claude. *Mental Disorders and Spiritual Healing: Teachings from the Christian East.* Hillsdale: Sophia Perennis, 2005.

Larimer, Mary E., Daniel K. Malone, Michelle D. Garner, David C. Atkins, Bonnie Burlingham, Heather S. Lonczak, Kenneth Tanzer, Joshua Ginzler, Seema L. Clifasefi, William G. Hobson, and G. Alan Marlatt. "Health Care and Public Service Use and Costs before and after Provision of Housing for Chronically Homeless Persons with Severe Alcohol Problems." *Journal of the American Medical Association* 301 (2009):1349–57.

Leff, Julian. *Psychiatry around the Globe: A Transcultural View.* New York: Marcel Dekker, 1981.

Leff, Julian, Narendra Wig, Abhishek Ghosh, H. Bedi, David K. Menon, Liz Kuipers, Ailsa Korton, Gunilla Ernberg, Robert Day, and Norman Sartorius. "Influence of Relatives' Expressed Emotion on the Course of Schizophrenia in Chandigarh." *British Journal of Psychiatry* 151 (1987): 166–73.

Leff, Julian, Geoffrey Williams, Mark Huckvale, Maurice Arbuthnot, and Alex P. Leff. "Avatar Therapy for Persecutory Auditory Hallucinations: What Is It and How Does It Work?" *Psychosis: Psychological, Social and Integrative Approaches* 6 (2014): 166–76.

Lehman, Anthony, and Donald Steinwachs. "Patterns of Usual Care for Schizophrenia." *Schizophrenia Bulletin* 24 (1998): 11–20.

Leighton, Alexander. *My Name Is Legion.* New York: Basic Books, 1959.

Leighton, Alexander, Adeoye Lambo, Charles Hughes, Dorothea Leighton, Jane Murphy, and David Macklin. *Psychiatric Disorder among the Yoruba.* Ithaca: Cornell University Press, 1963.

Leighton, Dorothea C., John S. Harding, David B. Macklin, Charles C. Hughes, and Alexander H. Leighton. "Psychiatric Findings of the Stirling County Study." *American Journal of Psychiatry* 119 (1963): 1021–6.

LeVine, Robert. *Culture, Behavior, and Personality: An Introduction to the Comparative Study of Psychosocial Adaptation.* New Brunswick: Aldine Transaction, 1982.

Lévi–Strauss, Claude. *Tristes Tropiques,* translated by John and Doreen Weightman. New York: Penguin, 1974.

Lewis, Glyn, Caroline Croft-Jeffreys, and Anthony David. "Are British Psychiatrists Racist?" *British Journal of Psychiatry* 157 (1990): 410–5.

Lewis, Ioan Myrddin. *Ecstatic Religion: A Study of Shamanism and Spirit Possession.* New York: Routledge, 1971.

Lewis, Nolan. *Research in Dementia Praecox.* New York: National Committee for Mental Hygiene, 1936.

Lidz, Theodore, Alice Cornelison, Stephen Fleck, and Dorothy Terry. "The Intrafamilial Environment of the Schizophrenic Patient: Marital Schism and Marital Skew." *American Journal of Psychiatry* 114 (1957): 241–8.

Lidz, Theodore, Alice R. Cornelison, Margaret T. Singer, Sarah Schafer, and Stephen Fleck. "The Mothers of Schizophrenic Patients," in *Schizophrenia and the Family,* edited by Theodore Lidz, Stephen Fleck, and Alice R. Cornelison. New York: International Universities Press, 1965.

Light, Donald. *Becoming Psychiatrists*. New York: Norton, 1980.

Littlewood, Roland, and Simon Dein. "Did Christianity Lead to Schizophrenia? Psychosis, Psychology, and Self Reference." *Transcultural Psychiatry* 50 (2013): 397–420.

Littlewood, Roland, and Maurice Lipsedge. *Aliens and Alienists: Ethnic Minorities and Psychiatry*, 3rd ed. London: Routledge, 1997.

Longden, Eleanor, Anna Madill, and Mitch G. Waterman. "Dissociation, Trauma, and the Role of Lived Experience: Toward a New Conceptualization of Voice Hearing." *Psychological Bulletin* 128 (2011): 28–76.

Lovell, Anne. "The City Is My Mother." *American Anthropologist* 99 (1997): 355–68.

Luhrmann, Tanya Marie. "Down and Out in Chicago." *Raritan* 29 (2010): 140–66.

Luhrmann, Tanya Marie. "Living with Voices: A New Way to Deal with Disturbing Voices Offers Hope for Those with Other Forms of Psychosis." *American Scholar* (Summer, 2012): 48–60.

Luhrmann, Tanya Marie. *Of Two Minds: An Anthropologist Looks at American Psychiatry*. New York: Knopf, 2000.

Luhrmann, Tanya Marie. "Our Master, Our Brother: Lévi-Strauss's Debt to Rousseau." *Cultural Anthropology* 5 (1990): 396–413.

Luhrmann, Tanya Marie. "Social Defeat and the Culture of Chronicity: Or, Why Schizophrenia Does So Well Over There and So Badly Here." *Culture, Medicine, and Psychiatry* 31 (2007): 135–72.

Luhrmann, Tanya Marie. "The Street Will Drive You Crazy: Why Homeless Psychotic Women in the Institutional Circuit in the United States Often Say No to Offers of Help." *American Journal of Psychiatry* 165 (2008): 15–20.

Luhrmann, Tanya Marie. *When God Talks Back: Understanding the American Evangelical Relationship with God*. New York: Knopf, 2012.

Luhrmann, Tanya Marie., Ramachandran Padmavati, Hema Tharoor, and Akwasi Osei. "Differences in Voice-Hearing Experiences of People with Psychosis in the U.S.A., India, and Ghana: Interview-Based Study." *British Journal of Psychiatry* 206 (2015): 41–4.

Lutgendorf, Philip. "Monkey in the Middle: The Status of Hanuman in Popular Hinduism." *Religion* 27 (1997): 311–32.

Macpherson, William. "The Stephen Lawrence Inquiry: Report of an Inquiry by Sir William Macpherson of Cluny." London: Stationery Office, 1999.

Mahy, George E., Rosemarie Mallett, Julian Leff, and Dinesh Bhugra. "First Contact Incidence Rates of Schizophrenia on Barbados." *British Journal of Psychiatry* 175 (1999): 28–33.

Malchow, Berend, Alkomiet Hasan, Thomas Schneider-Axmann, Alexander Jatzko, Oliver Gruber, Andrea Schmitt, Peter Falkai, and Thomas Wobrock. "Effects of Cannabis and Familial Loading on Subcortical Brain Volumes in First-Episode Schizophrenia." *European Archives of Psychiatry and Clinical Neuroscience* 263 (2013): S155–68.

Mangalore, Roshini, Martin Knapp, and Rachel Jenkins. "Income-Related Inequality in Mental Health in Britain: The Concentration Index Approach." *Psychological Medicine* 37 (2007): 1037–45.

Marmot, Michael. "Economic and Social Determinants of Disease." *Bulletin of the World Health Organization* 79 (2001): 988–9.

Marmot, Michael. "Inequalities in Health." *New England Journal of Medicine* 345 (2001): 134–6.

Marrow, Jocelyn. "Psychiatry, Modernity and Family Values: Clenched Teeth Illness in North India." Ph.D. dissertation, University of Chicago, 2008.

Marrow, Jocelyn, and Tanya Marie Luhrmann. "The Zone of Social Abandonment in Cultural Geography: On the Street in the United States, inside the Family in India." *Culture, Medicine, and Psychiatry* 36 (2012): 493–513.

McEwen, Bruce, and Elizabeth Lasley. "Allostatic Load: When Protection Gives Way to Damage." *Advances in Mind-Body Medicine* 19 (2003): 28–33.

McGovern, Donald, and Rosemarie Cope. "First Psychiatric Admission Rates of First and Second Generation Afro-Caribbeans." *Social Psychiatry* 22 (1987): 139–49.

McGrath, John, Sukanta Saha, Ali Al-Hamzawi, Jordi Alonso, Evelyn J. Bromet, Ronny Bruffaerts, José Miguel Caldas-de-Almeida, Wai Tat Chiu, Peter de Jonge, John Fayyad, and others. "Psychotic Experiences in the General Population: A Cross-National Analysis Based on 31 261 Respondents from 18 Countries." *JAMA Psychiatry* 72 (2015): 697–705.

McGrath, John, Sukanta Saha, David Chant, and Joy Welham. "Schizophrenia: A Concise Overview of Incidence, Prevalence, and Mortality." *Epidemiologic Reviews* 30 (2008): 67–76.

McGrath, John, Sukanta Saha, Joy Welham, Ossama El Saadi, Clare MacCauley, and David Chant. "A Systematic Review of the Incidence of Schizophrenia: The Distribution of Rates and the Influence of Sex, Urbanicity, Migrant Status and Methodology." *BMC Medicine* 2 (2004): 644–57.

Mechanic, David, Donna D. McAlpine, and Mark Olfson. "Changing Patterns of Psychiatric Inpatient Care in the United States, 1988–1994." *Archives of General Psychiatry* 55 (1998): 785–91.

Meddings, Sara, Linda Walley, Tracy Collins, Fay Tullett, Bruce McEwan, and Kate Owen. "Are Hearing Voices Groups Effective? A Preliminary Evaluation." Sussex: Sussex Partnership Trust, 2004. Unpublished manuscript. Retrieved from www.intervoiceonline.org/2678/support/groups/are-hearing-voices-groups-effective.html.

Metzl, Jonathan. *The Protest Psychosis: How Schizophrenia Became a Black Disease.* Boston: Beacon Press, 2009.

Meyer, Birgit. *Translating the Devil: Religion and Modernity among the Ewe of Ghana.* Edinburgh: University of Edinburgh Press, 1999.

Midelfort, H. C. Erik. *A History of Madness in Sixteenth Century Germany.* Stanford: Stanford University Press, 2000.

Milev, Peter, Beng-Choon Ho, Stephan Arndt, and Nancy C. Andreasen. "Predictive Value of Neurocognitive and Negative Symptoms on Functional Outcomes in

Schizophrenia: A Longitudinal First-Episode Study with 7-Year Follow-Up." *American Journal of Psychiatry* 162 (2005): 495–506.

Mishra, Vijay. *Bollywood Cinema: Temples of Desire*. New York: Taylor and Francis, 2002.

Mishra, Vijay. *Devotional Poetics and the Indian Sublime*. Albany: State University of New York Press, 1998.

Modood, Tariq, Richard Berthoud, Jane Lakey, Janes Nazroo, Patten Smith, Satnam Virdee, and Sharon Beishon. *Ethnic Minorities in Britain: Diversity and Disadvantage—The Fourth National Survey of Ethnic Minorities*. London: Policy Studies Institute, 1997.

Mohr, Sylvia, Pierre-Yves Brandt, Laurence Borras, Christiane Gillieron, and Philippe Huguelet. "Toward an Integration of Spirituality and Religiousness into the Psychosocial Dimension of Schizophrenia." *American Journal of Psychiatry* 163 (2006): 1952–9.

Mojtabai, Ramin, Ezra S. Susser, and Evelyn J. Bromet. "Clinical Characteristics, 4-Year Course, and DSM-IV Classification of Patients with Nonaffective Acute Remitting Psychosis." *American Journal of Psychiatry* 160 (2003): 2108–15.

Moodley, Parimala, and Rachel E. Perkins. "Routes to Psychiatric Inpatient Care in an Inner London Borough." *Social Psychiatry and Psychiatric Epidemiology* 26 (1991): 47–51.

Moore, Theresa, Stanley Zammit, Anne Lingford-Hughes, Thomas R. E. Barnes, Peter B. Jones, Margaret Burke, and Glyn Lewis. "Cannabis Use and Risk of Psychotic or Affective Mental Health Outcomes: A Systematic Review." *Lancet* 370 (2007): 319–28.

Moran, Galia S., Zlatka Russinova, Vasudha Gidugu, Jung Yeon Yim, and Catherine Sprague. "Benefits and Mechanisms of Recovery among Peer Providers with Psychiatric Illnesses." *Qualitative Health Research* 22 (2012): 304–19.

Morgan, Craig, J. Kirkbride, Gerard Hutchinson, Tom Craig, Kevin Morgan, Paola Dazzan, Jane Boydell, Gillian A. Doody, Peter B. Jones, Robin M. Murray, Julian Leff and Paul Fearon. "Cumulative Social Disadvantage, Ethnicity and First-Episode Psychosis: A Case-Control Study." *Psychological Medicine* 38 (2008): 1701–15.

Morgan, Craig, Kwame McKenzie, and Paul Fearon, eds. *Society and Psychosis*. Cambridge: Cambridge University Press, 2008.

Morris, Eric M. J., Louise C. Johns, and Joseph E. Oliver, eds. *Acceptance and Commitment Therapy and Mindfulness for Psychosis*. New York: Wiley, 2013.

Mueller, Gerard. "Psychiatry under Tyranny: A Report on the Political Abuse of Romanian Psychiatry." *Current Psychology* 12 (1993): 3–17.

Mukherjee, Sukdeb, Sashi Shukla, Joanne Woodle, Arnold Rosen, and Silvia Olarte. "Misdiagnosis of Schizophrenia in Bipolar Patients: A Multiethnic Comparison." *American Journal of Psychiatry* 140 (1983): 1571–4.

Mullings, Leah. *Therapy, Ideology, and Social Change: Mental Healing in Urban Ghana*. Berkeley: University of California Press, 1984.

Murphy, Jane. "Psychiatric Labeling in Cross-Cultural Perspective." *Science* 191 (1976): 1019–28.

Myers, Neely L. "Culture, Stress, and Recovery from Schizophrenia: Lessons from the Field for Global Mental Health." *Culture, Medicine, and Psychiatry* 34 (2010): 500–28.

Myers, Neely L. *Recovery's Edge: An Ethnography of Mental Health Care and Moral Agency.* Nashville: Vanderbilt University Press, 2015.

Myers, Neely L. "Update: Schizophrenia across Cultures." *Current Psychiatry Reports* 13 (2011): 305–11.

Narayan, Kirin. "Singing from Separation: Women's Voices in and about Kangra Folksongs," in *Songs, Stories, Lives: Gendered Dialogues and Cultural Critique,* edited by G. G. Raheja, 23–53. New Delhi: Raj Press (Kali for Women), 1997.

Neighbors, Harold, James Jackson, Linn Campbell, and Donald Williams. "The Influence of Racial Factors on Psychiatric Diagnosis: A Review and Suggestions for Research." *Community Mental Health Journal* 25 (1989): 301–11.

Neill, John. "Whatever Became of the Schizophrenogenic Mother?" *American Journal of Psychotherapy* 44 (1990): 499–505.

Nichter, Mark. "Idioms of Distress: Alternatives in the Expression of Psychosocial Distress: A Case Study from South India." *Culture, Medicine, and Psychiatry* 5 (1981): 379–408.

Nichter, Mark. "The Social Relations of Therapy Management," in *New Horizons in Medical Anthropology: Essays in Honour of Charles Leslie,* edited by M. Nichter and M. Lock, 81–110. London: Routledge, 2002.

Noll, Richard. "Shamanism and Schizophrenia: A State-Specific Approach to the 'Schizophrenia Metaphor' of Shamanic States." *American Ethnologist* 10 (1983): 443–59.

Nordau, Max. *Degeneration.* New York: D. Appleton, 1895.

Norfolk, Suffolk and Cambridgeshire Strategic Health Authority. "Independent Inquiry into the Death of David Bennett." Cambridge: NSCSHA, 2003.

Nugent, Kate L., Diana Paksarian, and Ramin Mojtabai. "Non-affective Acute Psychosis: Uncertainties on the Way to DSM-V and ICD-11." *Current Psychiatry Reports* 13 (2011): 203–10.

Nunley, Michael. "The Involvement of Families in Indian Psychiatry." *Culture, Medicine and Psychiatry* 22 (1988): 317–53.

Ødegaard, Ørnulv. "Emigration and Insanity: A Study of Mental Disease among the Norwegian Born Population of Minnesota." *Acta Psychiatrica et Neurologica* 7 (1932): Supplement 4.

Orsini, Francesca. "Introduction," in *In Love in South Asia: A Cultural History,* edited by Francesca Orsini, 1–39. Cambridge: Cambridge University Press, 2006.

Padgett, Deborah K. "Choices, Consequences and Context: Housing First and Its Critics. *European Journal of Homelessness* 7 (2013): 341–7.

Padgett, Deborah K., Victoria Stanhope, Ben F. Henwood, and Ana Stefancic. "Substance Use Outcomes among Homeless Clients with Serious Mental Illness: Comparing Housing First with Treatment First Programs." *Community Mental Health Journal* 47 (2011): 227–32.

Padmavathi, Ramachandra, Sadanand Rajkumar, Narendra Kumar, A. Manoharan, and Shantha Kamath. "Prevalence of Schizophrenia in an Urban Community in Madras." *Indian Journal of Psychiatry* 30 (1988): 233–9.

Pagden, Anthony. *The Fall of Natural Man: The American Indian and the Origins of Comparative Ethnology.* Cambridge: Cambridge University Press, 1986.

Pakaslahti, Antti. *Temples and Healers. Traditional Treatment of Psychiatric Patients in India* (Video). Book of Abstracts. X World Congress of Psychiatry, 1996.

Pakaslahti, Antti. "Terminology of Spirit Illness," in *Mathematics and Medicine in Sanskrit: Papers of the World Sanskrit Conference,* edited by Dominik Wujastyk. Delhi: Motital Banarsidass, 2009.

Pakaslahti, Antti. "Traditional Healers as Culturally Accepted/Sanctioned Mental Health Practitioners," in *Mental Disorders in Children and Adolescence: Need and Strategies for Intervention,* edited by Savita Malhorta, N. Gupta, and A. Malhorta. Delhi: CBS, 2005.

Pedersen, Carsten, and Preben Mortensen. "Evidence of a Dose–Response Relationship between Urbanicity during Upbringing and Schizophrenia Risk." *Archives of General Psychiatry* 58 (2001): 1039–46.

Phanthunane, Pudtan, Theo Vos, Harvey Whiteford, and Melanie Bertram. "Health Outcomes of Schizophrenia in Thailand: Health Care Provider and Patient Perspectives." *Asian Journal of Psychiatry* 3 (2010): 200–5.

Pilkington, Andrew. *Racial Disadvantage and Ethnic Diversity in Britain.* New York: Palgrave McMillan, 2003.

Pope, Leah, Lauren Cubellis, and Kim Hopper. "Signing on for Dirty Work: Taking Stock of a Public Psychiatry Project from the Inside." *Transcultural Psychiatry.* In press.

Pyati, Aarti. "Going the Cultural Distance: Worldview-Relevant Counseling at India's Premiere Psychiatric Institute." Ph.D. dissertation, University of Chicago, 2004.

Raheja, Gloria Godwin, and Ann Grodzins Gold. *Listen to the Heron's Words: Reimagining Gender and Kinship in North India.* Berkeley: University of California Press, 1994.

Rattray, Robert Sutherland. *Ashanti.* New York: Negro University Press, 1923.

Read, John. "The Bio-Bio-Bio Model of Madness." *Psychologist* 18 (2005): 596–7.

Ridgway, Priscilla, Diane McDiarmid, Lori Davidson, Julie Bayes, and Sarah Ratzlaff. *Pathways to Recovery: A Strengths Recovery Self–Help Workbook.* Lawrence: Univ. of Kansas School of Social Welfare, 2002.

Rokeach, Milton. *The Three Christs of Ypsilanti.* New York: New York Review Classics, 2011.

Romme, Marius, and Alexandre Escher. "Hearing Voices." *Schizophrenia Bulletin* 15 (1989): 209–216.

Rosenhan, David. "On Being Sane in Insane Places." *Science* 179 (1973): 250–8.

Rousseau, Jean–Jacques. *Emile,* translated by Allan Bloom. New York: Basic Books, 1979.

Ruddle, Anna, Oliver Mason, and Til Wykes. "A Review of Hearing Voices Groups: Evidence and Mechanisms of Change." *Clinical Psychology Review* 31 (2011): 757–66.

Sadock, Benjamin J., and Virginia A. Sadock, eds. *Kaplan and Sadock's Comprehensive Textbook of Psychiatry*, 7th ed. Philadelphia: Lippincott Williams & Wilkins, 2000.

Sadowsky, Jonathan. *Imperial Bedlam*. Berkeley: University of California Press, 1999.

Saha, Sukanta, David Chant, Joy Welham, and John McGrath. "A Systematic Review of the Prevalence of Schizophrenia." *PLoS Medicine* 2 (2005): 413–33.

Sainsbury Centre for Mental Health. "Briefing 17: An Executive Briefing on Breaking the Circles of Fear." London: SCMH, 2002.

Saks, Elyn. *The Center Cannot Hold: My Journey through Madness*. New York: Hyperion, 2007.

Satija, D. C., Deeksha Singh, S. S. Nathawat, and V. Sharma. "A Psychiatric Study of Patients Attending Mehandipur Bali Temple." *Indian Journal of Psychiatry* 23 (1981): 247–50.

Scheff, Thomas. *Being Mentally Ill*. Chicago: Aldine Transactions, 1966.

Scheper-Hughes, Nancy. *Saints, Scholars, and Schizophrenics: Mental Illness in Rural Ireland*. Berkeley: University of California Press, 2001 [1979].

Schiller, Lori, and Amanda Bennett. *The Quiet Room: A Journey Out of the Torment of Madness*. New York: Grand Central, 2008.

Schwab, Reinhold, and Kay Uwe Peterson. "Religiousness: Its Relation to Loneliness, Neuroticism and Subjective Well-Being." *Journal for the Scientific Study of Religion* 29 (1990): 335–45.

Scull, Andrew. *Madness in Civilization: A Cultural History of Insanity, from the Bible to Freud, from the Madhouse to Modern Medicine*. Princeton: Princeton University Press, 2015.

Seikkula, Jaakko, Birgitta Alakare, Jukka Aaltonen, Juha Holma, Anu Rasinkangas, and Ville Lehtinen. "Open Dialogue Approach: Treatment Principles and Preliminary Results of a Two-Year Follow-Up on First Episode Schizophrenia." *Ethical Human Sciences and Services* 5 (2003): 163–82.

Seikkula, Jaakko, and Mary E. Olson. "The Open Dialogue Approach to Acute Psychosis: Its Poetics and Micropolitics." *Family Process* 42 (2003): 403–18.

Seligman, Charles Gabriel. "Temperament, Conflict and Psychosis in a Stone Age Society." *British Journal of Medical Psychology* 9 (1929): 187–202.

Selten, Jean-Paul, and Elizabeth Cantor-Graae. "Social Defeat: Risk Factor for Schizophrenia?" *British Journal of Psychiatry* 187 (2005): 101–2.

Selten, Jean-Paul, Elizabeth Cantor-Graae, Joris Slaets, and René Kahn. "Ødegaard's Selection Hypothesis Revisited: Schizophrenia in Surinamese Immigrants to the Netherlands." *American Journal of Psychiatry* 159 (2002): 669–71.

Selten, Jean-Paul, Elsje van der Ven, Bart P. F. Rutten, and Elizabeth Cantor-Graae. "The Social Defeat Hypothesis of Schizophrenia: An Update." *Schizophrenia Bulletin* 39 (2013): 1180–6.

Selten, Jean-Paul, Natalie Veen, Wilma Feller, Jan Dirk Blom, Rene Kahn, Diede Schols, Wibo Camoenie, Johannes Oolders, Madeleine Van Der Velden, Hans W. Hoek, and others. "Incidence of Psychotic Disorders in Immigrant Groups to the Netherlands." *British Journal of Psychiatry* 178 (2001): 367–72.

Shapin, Steven. *The Scientific Revolution*. Chicago: University of Chicago Press, 1996.

Shweder, Richard A. *Why Do Men Barbecue? Recipes for Cultural Psychology*. Cambridge: Harvard University Press, 2003.

Singh-Manoux, Archana, Nancy E. Adler, and Michael G. Marmot. "Subjective Social Status: Its Determinants and Its Association with Measures of Ill-Health in the Whitehall II Study." *Social Science and Medicine* 56 (2003): 1321–33.

Singh-Manoux, Archana, Michael G. Marmot, and Nancy E. Adler. "Does Subjective Social Status Predict Health and Change in Health Status Better Than Objective Status?" *Psychosomatic Medicine* 67 (2005): 855–61.

Slade, Peter, and Richard Bentall. *Sensory Deception: A Scientific Analysis of Hallucination*. Baltimore: Johns Hopkins University Press, 1988.

Sousa, Amy. "Pragmatic Ethics, Sensible Care." Ph.D. dissertation, University of Chicago, 2011.

Srole, Leo, Thomas Langner, Stanley Michael, Marvin Opler, and Thomas Rennie. *Mental Health in the Metropolis: The Midtown Manhattan Study*. New York: McGraw Hill, 1962.

Stanton, Alfred H., and Morris S. Schwartz. *The Mental Hospital: A Study of Institutionalized Participation in Psychiatric Illness and Treatment*. New York: Basic Books, 1954.

Staub, Michael E. *Madness Is Civilization: When the Diagnosis Was Social, 1948–1980*. Chicago: University of Chicago Press, 2011.

Stocking, George W., Jr. *Malinowski, Rivers, Benedict, and Others: Essays on Culture and Personality*. Madison: University of Wisconsin Press, 1988.

Strakowski, Stephen, Heather Lonczak, Kenji Sax, Scott West, Abby Crist, Ramona Mehta, and Ole Thienhaus. "The Effects of Race on Diagnosis and Disposition from a Psychiatric Emergency Service." *Journal of Clinical Psychiatry* 56 (1995): 101–7.

Strakowski, Stephen, Susan McElroy, Paul Keck, and Scott West. "Racial Influence on Diagnosis in Psychotic Mania." *Journal of Affective Disorders* 39 (1996): 157–62.

Strakowski, Stephen, Richard Shelton, and Meridith Kolbrener. "The Effects of Race and Comorbidity on Clinical Diagnosis in Patients with Psychosis." *Journal of Clinical Psychiatry* 54 (1993): 96–102.

Sullivan, Patrick F. "The Genetics of Schizophrenia." *PLoS Medicine* 2 (2005): 212.

Susser, Ezra, and Joseph Wanderling. "Epidemiology of Nonaffective Acute Remitting Psychosis vs Schizophrenia: Sex and Sociocultural Setting." *Archives of General Psychiatry* 51 (1994): 294–301.

Swanson, Jeffrey W., Marvin S. Swartz, Richard A. Van Dorn, Eric B. Elbogen, H. Ryan Wagner, Robert A. Rosenheck, T. Scott Stroup, Joseph P. McEvoy, and Jeffrey A. Lieberman. "A National Study of Violent Behavior in People with Schizophrenia." *Archives of General Psychiatry* 63 (2006): 490–499.

Szasz, Thomas. *The Myth of Mental Illness*. New York: Harper and Row, 1961.

Talbott, John. *Death of the Asylum*. New York: Grune and Stratton, 1979.

Taylor, Michael A. "Clinical Examination," in *Catatonia: From Psychopathology to Neurobiology*, edited by Stanley N. Caroff, Stephan C. Mann, Andrew Francis, and

Gregory L. Fricchionne, 45–52. Washington, DC: American Psychiatric Publishing, 2004.

Teplin, Linda, Karen M. Abram, and Gary M. McClelland. "Does Psychiatric Disorder Predict Violent Crime among Released Jail Detainees? A Six-Year Longitudinal Study." *American Psychologist* 49 (1994): 335–42.

Teplin, Linda, Gary McClelland, Karen Abram, and Dana Weiner. "Crime Victimization in Adults with Severe Mental Illness." *Archives of General Psychiatry* 62 (2005): 911–21.

Thara, Rangaswamy. "Twenty-Year Course of Schizophrenia: The Madras Longitudinal Study." *Canadian Journal of Psychiatry* 49 (2004): 564–9.

Thara, Rangaswamy, and William Eaton. "Outcome of Schizophrenia: The Madras Longitudinal Study." *Australian and New Zealand Journal of Psychiatry* 30 (1996): 516–22.

Thara, Rangaswamy, Shanta Kamath, and Shuba Kumar. "Women with Schizophrenia and Broken Marriages—Doubly Disadvantaged? Part I: Patient Perspective." *International Journal of Social Psychiatry* 49 (2003): 225–32.

Thara, Rangaswamy, Shanta Kamath, and Shuba Kumar. "Women with Schizophrenia and Broken Marriages—Doubly Disadvantaged? Part II: Family Perspective." *International Journal of Social Psychiatry* 49 (2003): 233–40.

Thara, Rangaswamy, and Ramachandran Padmavati. "Psychotic Disorder and Bipolar Affective Disorder," in *Contemporary Topics in Women's Mental Health*, edited by Prabha S. Chandra, Helen Herrman, Jane Fisher, Marianne Kastrup, Unaiza Niaz, Marta B. Rondon, and Ahmed Okasha, 9–35. West Sussex: Wiley-Blackwell, 2009.

Thomas, Neil, Mark Hayward, Emmanuelle Peters, Mark van der Gaag, Richard P. Bentall, Jack Jenner, Clara Strauss, Iris E. Sommer, Louise C. Johns, Filippo Varese, and others. "Psychological Therapies for Auditory Hallucinations (Voices): Current Status and Key Directions for Future Research." *Schizophrenia Bulletin* 40 (Supplement 4) (2014): S202–12.

Thomas, Philip and Eleanor Longden. "Madness, Childhood Adversity and Narrative Psychiatry: Caring and the Moral Imagination." Medical Humanities 39 (2013): 119–125.

Tidey, Jennifer W., and Klaus A. Miczek. "Social Defeat Stress Selectively Alters Mesocorticolimbic Dopamine Release: An In Vivo Microdialysis Study." *Brain Research* 721 (1996): 140–9.

Tien, Allen Y. "Distribution of Hallucinations in the Population." *Social Psychiatry and Psychiatric Epidemiology* 26 (1991): 287–92.

Tietze, Trude. "A Study of Mothers of Schizophrenic Patients." *Psychiatry* 12 (1949): 55–65.

Tomka, Miklós. "Is Conventional Sociology of Religion Able to Deal with Differences between Eastern and Western European Developments?" *Social Compass* 53 (2006): 251–65.

Torrey, E. Fuller. *Schizophrenia and Civilization*. New York: Aronson, 1980.

Torrey, E. Fuller, John J. Bartko, Zhao-Rong Lun, and Robert H. Yolken. "Antibodies to *Toxoplasma gondii* in Patients with Schizophrenia: A Meta-analysis." *Schizophrenia Bulletin* 33 (2007): 729–36.

Torrey, E. Fuller, Aaron D. Kennard, Don Eslinger, Richard Lamb, and James Pavle. "More Mentally Ill Persons Are in Jails and Prisons Than Hospitals: A Survey of the States." *Treatment Advocacy Center Report* (May 2010). Retrieved from www .treatmentadvocacycenter.org/storage/documents/final_jails_v_hospitals_study. pdf.

Torrey, E. Fuller, Mary T. Zdanowicz, Aaron D. Kennard, Richard Lamb, Donald F. Eslinger, Michael C. Biasotti, and Doris A. Fuller. "The Treatment of Persons with Mental Illness in Prisons and Jails: A State Survey." *Treatment Advocacy Center Report* (April 8, 2014). Retrieved from www.tacreports.org/storage/documents /treatment-behind-bars/treatment-behind-bars-abridged.pdf.

Trierweiler, Steven J., Harold Neighbors, Cheryl Munday, Estina Thompson, Victoria Binion, and John Gomez. "Clinician Attributions Associated with the Diagnosis of Schizophrenia in African American and Non–African American Patients." *Journal of Consulting and Clinical Psychology* 68 (2000): 171–5.

Tsemberis, Sam, and Ronda F. Eisenberg. "Pathways to Housing: Supported Housing for Street-Dwelling Individuals with Psychiatric Disabilities." *Psychiatric Services* 51 (2000): 487–93.

Tsemberis, Sam, Leyla Gulcur, and Maria Nakae. "Housing First, Consumer Choice, and Harm Reduction for Homeless Individuals with a Dual Diagnosis." *American Journal of Public Health* 94 (2004): 651–6.

Tuttle, George T. "Hallucinations and Illusions." *American Journal of Psychiatry* 58 (1902): 443–67.

Upadhayaya, Krishnadev. *Bhojpuri Lok Geet*. Prayag: Hindi Sahitya Sammelan, 2000.

van Os, Jim, David Castle, Noriyoshi Takei, Geoffrey Der, and Robin Murray. "Psychotic Illness in Ethnic Minorities: Clarification from the 1991 Census." *Psychological Medicine* 26 (1996): 203–8.

van Os, Jim, Gunter Kenis, and Bart Rutten. "The Environment and Schizophrenia." *Nature* 468 (2010): 203–12.

Vaughan, Megan. *Curing Their Ills*. Stanford: Stanford University Press, 1991.

Verdery, Katherine. *The Political Lives of Dead Bodies*. New York: Columbia University Press, 2000.

Walsh, Elizabeth, Alec Buchanan, and Thomas Fahy. "Violence and Schizophrenia." *British Journal of Psychiatry* 180 (2002): 490–5.

Warner, Richard. *Recovery from Schizophrenia: Psychiatry and Political Economy*. New York: Brunner–Routledge, 1985.

Watters, Ethan. *Crazy Like Us*. New York: Free Press, 2010.

Waxler, Nancy E. "Is Mental Illness Cured in Traditional Societies? A Theoretical Analysis." *Culture, Medicine, and Psychiatry* 1 (1977): 233–53.

Wessely, Simon, David Castle, Geoffrey Der, and Robin Murray. "Schizophrenia and Afro-Caribbeans: A Case-Control Study." *British Journal of Psychiatry* 159 (1991): 795–801.

Whitley, Rob. "Beyond Critique: Rethinking Roles for the Anthropology of Mental Health." *Culture, Medicine, and Psychiatry* 38 (2014): 499–511.

WHO. "Mental Health Atlas 2011." World Health Organization, Department of Health and Substance Abuse, 2011.

Wilce, James M., Jr. "Madness, Fear, and Control in Bangladesh: Clashing Bodies of Power/Knowledge." *Medical Anthropology Quarterly* 18 (2004): 357–75.

Wu, Eric Q., Howard G. Birnbaum, Lizheng Shi, Daniel E. Ball, Ronald C. Kessler, Matthew Moulis, and Jyoti Aggarwal. "The Economic Burden of Schizophrenia in the United States in 2002." *Journal of Clinical Psychiatry* 66 (2005): 1122–9.

Zigon, Jarrett. *"HIV Is God's Blessing": Rehabilitating Morality in Neoliberal Russia.* Berkeley: University of California Press, 2010.

Zimmermann, Francis. "The Love-Lorn Consumptive: South Asian Ethnography and the Psychosomatic Paradigm," in *Anthropologies of Medicine,* edited by Beatrix Pfleiderer and Gilles Bibeau. Heidelberg: Vieweg, 1991.

CONTRIBUTORS

JULIA CASSANITI received her Ph.D. from the University of Chicago in 2009. She has been conducting research on the co-construction of mind and culture in Southeast Asia since 2002, with a focus on issues of affect, subjectivity, and mental health. Her book *Living Buddhism: Mind, Self, and Emotion in a Thai Community* (Cornell University Press, 2015) speaks to psychological engagements with Buddhist ideologies of change in a small Northern Thai community, and to the implications that these engagements have for global discourses of health and well-being. She is currently an assistant professor of medical and psychological anthropology at Washington State University.

DAMIEN DRONEY received his Ph.D. in anthropology from Stanford University in 2015. His dissertation research analyzes the science of herbal medicine in the West African nation of Ghana. More broadly, he studies the cultural politics of science, technology, and medicine from perspectives in the postcolonial world.

JOHANNE ELIACIN, Ph.D., HSPP, is a research scientist at the Center for Health Information and Communication, Richard L. Roudebush VA Medical Center. She is also a research scientist at the Regenstrief Institute and an assistant scientist in psychology at Indiana University–Purdue University, Indianapolis. She received a joint Ph.D. in clinical psychology and anthropology from the University of Chicago. She conducted ethnographic fieldwork in Haiti and in England, including two years of research on the "epidemic" of schizophrenia among British African-Caribbeans. Her current work examines mental-health communication among African-American veterans and disparities in health-services utilization among patients with brain injuries.

JACK R. FRIEDMAN received his Ph.D. in cultural anthropology from Duke University in 2003. He has conducted research in Romania since 1995, including fourteen months of research in psychiatric hospitals throughout the country. Since 2007, he has also conducted research on public mental health care in Southern California and on how primary care physicians provide mental health care to people lacking access to mental health care in rural Oklahoma. His current work explores mental-health indicators as a proxy for the human impacts of climate change and environmental decline. He is currently a research scientist at the University of Oklahoma.

TANYA MARIE LUHRMANN is the Watkins University Professor in the Stanford Anthropology Department. In general, her work focuses on the way that beings without material presence come to seem real to people, and the way that ideas about the mind affect mental experience. She was elected to the American Academy of Arts and Sciences in 2003 and received a John Guggenheim Fellowship award in 2007. She is the author of *Persuasions of the Witch's Craft, The Good Parsi, Of Two Minds,* and *When God Talks Back.* She has worked with people with psychosis for nearly twenty years.

JOCELYN MARROW is a cultural anthropologist who received her Ph.D. from the Department of Comparative Human Development at the University of Chicago in 2008. Her publications, and a book-length manuscript underway, draw upon more than twenty-four months of fieldwork in North India on psychiatric illness and healing. Recent ethnographic work focuses on the delivery of mental health services to U.S. populations, including veterans and the poor. She is currently a senior study director at Westat in Rockville, Maryland, specializing in qualitative methods and program evaluation to support federal and international government programs and health care industries.

GIULIA MAZZA is an anthropologist who uses a human-centered approach to help companies build better products, services, and brands. In her current practice, she combines design-thinking methods with experience drawn from undergraduate research on culture and psychology in South India and graduate research on the relationship between time, technology, and well-being in Bhutan. She earned an M.A. in cultural anthropology from Stanford University in 2014 and is currently a consultant in San Francisco.

NEELY A. L. MYERS, Ph.D., is an assistant professor of anthropology at Southern Methodist University. Her ethnographic research focuses on the everyday experience of serious emotional distress (especially trauma and psychosis) and mental health recovery, both in the United States (since 2003) and in Tanzania, especially among the Maasai (since 2013). An additional National Institute of Mental Health and Hogg Foundation–funded project on youth engagement in mental health services for early psychosis is currently underway. Her recent book is *Recovery's Edge: An Ethnography of Mental Health Care and Moral Agency* (Vanderbilt University Press, 2015).

R. PADMAVATI completed her postgraduate psychiatry degree at the University of Bombay and is now an "additional director" of the Schizophrenia Research Foundation (SCARF) in Chennai, India. She has been involved in several research areas, including epidemiological studies, drug trials, untreated schizophrenia, culture and psychoses, and metabolic disorders in mental illness. Her key interests have been in sociocultural aspects of mental illnesses. She is currently working on stigma in mental illness and on physical comorbidities in schizophrenia. She has produced a large number of publications in national and international peer-reviewed journals.

ANUBHA SOOD, Ph.D., is a postdoctoral fellow in anthropology at Southern Methodist University. Her research interests lie at the intersection of psychological and psychiatric anthropology, the anthropology of religion, and gender studies. She has worked extensively on gender and human rights concerns in state-run psychiatric facilities in India. Her most recent research project was a comparative study of women's therapeutic experiences with Western psychiatry and religious healing in North India. She is currently a researcher on a National Institute of Mental Health study on treatment decision-making among youth with first-episode psychoses in the American psychiatric system.

AMY JUNE SOUSA received her Ph.D. from the Department of Comparative Human Development at the University of Chicago in 2011. Amy conducted research in psychiatric hospitals, clinics, private homes, and communities in the North Indian state of Uttar Pradesh between 2006 and 2010. Her work focused on the ways culture and biomedical technologies intersect to shape the social and physical experience of serious mental illness. Amy continues her investigations into the intersection of culture and technology as a senior researcher at Microsoft, where her work informs the next generation of digital tools that are shaping how humans create and learn.

INDEX

Page numbers in italics refer to illustrations and tables. Page numbers in boldface refer to authors of chapters.

abandonment: and African-Caribbean British, 94; in Balaji Temple (India), 130, 138, 213; and Caterina (São Paulo, Brazil), 138; in Chennai (India), 72, 210–11; and Madhu (case 4), 73, 81, 211; and social defeat, 210–11, 213; and Sunita (case 8), 130, 138, 213; and Violet (case 5), 94

Acceptance and Commitment Therapy, 218

Accra (Ghana), 113–126, 205–6, 213; Labadi Beach, 125; Labadi neighborhood, 115, 234n9, 234n14

Accra General Psychiatric Hospital, 113, 115–16, 117, 118, 233n2

addictions, 51, 92, 154. See also substance use/abuse

Addlakha, Renu, 62, 210

Adler, Nancy, 237n6

affect, flattened, 2, 15, 101, 168, 194, 223n4

Africa/Africans, 7–8, 21, 22, 97–98, 225n19; and Hood, John (case 1), 39; sub-Saharan Africa, 118, 225n22; traditional religion of, 119, 121; West Africa, 16. See also names of African countries

African-Americans, 18

African-Caribbean British, 20, 86–98, 204–6, 208–9; negative stereotypes of, 92; and second/third generations, 88–89

age factors, 20, 112, 167, 178–79, 214, 228n62

Agra (India), 44, 136

agricultural labor, 22–25; in Ghana, 8; in India, 208; in Romania, 145–47

Ahmed, Kemal (case 2), 50–55

akathisia, 51–52

Alcoholics Anonymous, 154

alcohol use/alcoholism, 116, 118, 164, 193–94, 206–7, 217. See also substance use/abuse

Alexandra (case 9), 139–152, 215–16

alien invasions, 31

Allahabad (India), 59, 61, 64, 66

alogia, 146–47. See also speech, incoherent/impoverished

Alternatives, 27

American Journal of Psychiatry, 156, 224n8

American Psychiatric Association, 13

Americans with Disabilities Act, 183–84

ancestors: and Charles (case 7), 120–22; and Sita (case 6), 100

Anderson, Elijah, 212

Andreasen, Nancy, 2, 224n8

angels, 33, 141

animal studies, 197–98

Anisha (case 2), 43–50, 54, 208, 210–11, 231n7

"Anthropology and the Abnormal" (Benedict), 9

anti-anxiety medication, 52

anti-psychiatry movement, 13, 223n3, 227n51

antirabies medication, 54

Anusawari Monument (Bangkok), 168, 172

anxiety, 6, 10, 13; and African-Caribbean British, 89; in Balaji Temple (India), 128; and Priyanka (case 3), 58–59

Asamoah-Gyadu, Kwabena, 118–19

Ashanti country towns, 7, 22

Asia/Asians: East Asia/East Asians, 20; South Asia/South Asians, 20, 80, 101, 104; Southeast Asia, 167, 169. *See also names of Asian countries*

astral journeys, 33

asylums: and catatonic schizophrenia, 230n5; and Madhu (case 4), 75; in Romania, 139

auditory hallucinations, 15, 24; in Accra (Ghana), 113, 119, 213; and Alexandra (case 9), 140; and Anisha (case 2), 47; in Balaji Temple(India), 135, 138, 214; in Chennai (India), 104–7, 109, 111; and Cornici, Irina, 152; creaks, 30, 40; in India, 47; in Romania, 140, 152; scratching, buzzing, and bangs, 99, 107; and Sita (case 6), 104–7, 109, 111; and social defeat, 213–14; and Sunita (case 8), 135, 138, 214; in United States, 122. *See also* voices

"aura" stage, 170

authoritarian oppression, 36

autistic self-preoccupation, 10

Avatar therapy, computer-based, 112, 218

Ayodhya (charitable organization), 81

Ayurvedic, 69

Baba (Hindu temple priest), 77–78, 81, 84–85

Babaji (Ganesh Puri), 128, 130–31, 133–36, 138

Bakhtin, Mikhail, 219

Balaji (deity), 127–29, 214

Balaji Temple (India), 127–138, 132, 208–9, 211, 213–15

Banaras Hindu University, Department of Psychiatry, 58, 63, 67

Bangkok (Thailand), 167–179, 214

Bangladesh, 64

banks, 130, 134, 137

Banyan (nongovernmental organization), 71–74, 83–84, 208

banyan tree, 72

Bark, Nigel, 223n4

Barrett, Robert, 4

baseline functioning, return to, 4, 22–23, 169–170

Bateson, Gregory, 9, 11

bathing/showering, 28, 35, 44, 50, 73, 77, 158–59, 183, 187, 214

Beatles, 37, 39, 230n3

Becker, Howard, 227n54

begging, 73, 81–83

behaviors, 8–9; in Accra (Ghana), 116, 118, 123–26, 205; and African-Caribbean British, 92, 96–97; and Anisha (case 2), 49; in Balaji Temple (India), 128; and Charles (case 7), 116, 118, 123–26, 205; and the Colonel (case 2), 53; and *DSM-III*, 14–15; and Madhu (case 4), 84; in India, 49, 53, 56–57, 60–64, 67–70, 99, 210; and Poi (case 11), 170, 174–75; and pragmatic lessons, 217, 220–21; and Priyanka (case 3), 56–57, 60–64, 67–70, 210; and Sita (case 6), 99; and social defeat, 205, 210; in Thailand, 170, 174–75; and Veena (case 2), 49; and Violet (case 5), 92, 96–97

Being Mentally Ill (Scheff), 227n54

Benedict, Ruth, 9, 15

Bering Sea Island, 15–16

Beverly Hillbillies (television program), 35

Bhagavad Gita, 39–40

Bhairav (Deity), 128

Bible, 122–23, 177, 223n4

Biehl, João, 138

Bihar (India), 45, 64

Bilaspur (India), 131, 133, 136, 138

bindi, 130

biographical narratives: and Caterina (São Paulo, Brazil), 138; and Sunita (case 8), 131–36, 132

biomedical model/psychiatry, 10, 15–19, 224n8; "bio-bio-bio" model, 2–3, 224n7; "diseased brain," 34, 203–4; and Hood, John (case 1), 33–34, 203–4; moral stance of, 16; in India, 42–43, 54–55, 64, 71; and Poi (case 11), 176, 214; and pragmatic lessons, 218–19; and Priyanka (case 3), 64, 71; in Romania, 139, 147–48, 150; and social defeat, 199, 203–4, 213–14; in Thailand, 176, 214

bipolar disorder, 1, 17–18, 43, 154, 170–71

Black Africans, 20. *See also* African-Caribbean British

black magic, 64, 177

Black Power period, 18

Bleuler, Eugen, 1, 223n3

Bourdieu, Pierre, 200

Brahmins, 226n32

Braslow, Joel, 19

Brazil, 229n86

British Psychological Society, 218
Brodwin, Paul, 36–37
The Broken Brain: The Biological Revolution in Psychiatry (Andreasen), 2, 224n8
Buddhism, 150, 161, 170, 176–78

Caldwell, Melissa, 235n6
California Board of Mental Health, 27–28, 34–35
Canada, 215
cancer, 13, 114
cannabis, 116, 233n1
care-as-usual, 153, 202
Caribbean/Caribbeans, 94–96, 98. *See also* African-Caribbean British
Carpenter-Song, Elizabeth, 209
caseworkers, 3; and Hood, John (case 1), 40; and social defeat, 207, 211; in United States, 40, 153–54, 192, 207; and Zaney (case 10), 153
Cassaniti, Julia, 167–179, 214, 265
catalepsy, 49
catatonic schizophrenia, 48–49, 208, 230n5
Caterina (São Paulo, Brazil), 138
Catholics, 169, 177, 215
cats, 223n4
Ceaușescu, Elena, 145–46
Ceaușescu, Nicolae, 145
cell phones, 109
chai, 73, 84
Chakraborty, Ajita, 64
Chandigarh (India), 22
chapatis. *See* roti
charismatic churches, 118–123, 126, 142, 233n6
charities, 135, 143, 155, 158
Charles (case 7), 113–126, 206, 215
Chaturvedi family (case 2), 43–50, 54, 209, 208, 209–10, 231n7
Chennai (India), 22–23, 231n10; and Madhu (case 4), 77, 78, 82–83, 208, 211, 213–14; and Sita (case 6), 99–112, 205, 209–10, 213, 215; and social defeat, 203, 205, 208–11, 213–15, 238n28
Chhatisgarh (India), 131
Chiang Mai (Thailand), 172, 174
Chicago (Ill.), 153–166, 157, 225n29; and pragmatic lessons, 216–17; and social defeat, 201, 207, 211–12; Department of Human Services, 161
children: in Accra (Ghana), 120; and African-Caribbean British, 90, 94–96, 98; and

Alexandra (case 9), 143–47, 150–51, 215–16; in Chennai (India), 99–100, 103–4, 107–8, 112; and Madhu (case 4), 76, 79–80, 83; mixed-race children, 96; in North India, 49, 57, 131, 133–34, 137–38, 208; and Poi (case 11), 170, 175; in Romania, 143–47, 150–51, 215–16; and schizophrenogenic mothers, 10–11, 16; and Sita (case 6), 99–100, 103–4, 107–8, 112; and social defeat, 208–9, 211, 215–16; and Sunita (case 8), 131, 133–34, 137–38; in Thailand, 170, 175; in United States, 165, 209; and Violet (case 5), 90, 94–95, 98; and Zaney (case 10), 165
China/Chinese, 21, 169, 174, 178, 229n86
chlorpromazine, 155
Christianity, 223n4; in Accra (Ghana), 114–16, 118–123, 234n14; and Alexandra (case 9), 139–144; attention to internal, 223n4; and Charles (case 7), 114–16, 118–123; Mission schools in Ghana, 225n27; and Pascal, 165–66; and Poi (case 11), 176; prayer camps in Ghana, 225n22; in Romania, 139–144; in Thailand, 176. *See also* churches
Christmas, 145–46, 147, 192, 195
chronic mental illness, 7–8, 25, 223n4, 225n23; and African-Caribbean British, 90; "culture of chronicity," 206; and *DSM-III*, 15–18; and Indian Mental Health Act (1987), 234n8; and Madhu (case 4), 76; and Poi (case 11), 169; and pragmatic lessons, 222; and Recovery Movement, 19; and Sita (case 6), 111; and social defeat, 202, 206, 209, 211; in Thailand, 169; in United States, 104, 206, 209, 222; and Violet (case 5), 90
Chulalongkorn Psychiatric Hospital (Bangkok), 168, 175
churches: in Accra (Ghana), 115, 118–123, 126, 233n6; Catholic church, 169, 177, 215; charismatic churches, 118–123, 126, 142, 233n6; evangelical Protestantism, 139–140, 142–45, 147–150, 152, 215, 235n8, 235n16; Pentecostal churches, 122, 233n6; in Romania, 139–145, 147–150, 152, 215, 235n6, 235n8, 235n14, 235n16; Romanian Orthodox Church, 139–145, 147–150, 152, 215, 235n6, 235n14; in Thailand, 169, 176–77, 215; Unitarian Church, 187, 192, 194
cigarettes, 33, 51, 164, 185, 194

client counselors, 19. *See also* peer counselors
clinical ethnography, 4–5, 224n12
clinician bias, 18–20, 92
clinics. *See* hospitals/clinics, psychiatric
clozapine, 176
cognitive behavioral therapy, 112, 218
Cohen, Alex, 199
the Colonel (case 2), 53–55
colonial expansion, 5–6; colonial psychiatry, 225n19
Columbia University, 9
Communist Party, 139, 145–46, 150
Community Mental Health Act (1963), 155–56
community mental health system, 153, 155–57
compassion, 9, 69, 144, 145, 174, 218, 221
computers, 94, 112, 181, 218
confidence, 103–4
conjugal families. *See* in-laws
consumers, 27, 34–36, 39, 163, 207, 217
Corin, Ellen, 64, 231n10
Cornell University, 8
Cornici, Irina, 149, 152
counterculture, 29, 37
crack cocaine, 160
"crazy," 10; in Accra (Ghana), 123; and Anisha (case 2), 46; and Charles (case 7), 123; and Hood, John (case 1), 33, 35–36; and Madhu (case 4), 208; in North India, 46, 60; and pragmatic lessons, 220; and Priyanka (case 3), 60; and social defeat, 199–201, 208; in United States, 33, 35–36, 154, 163–66, 199–201, 220; and Zaney (case 10), 154, 163, 165–66, 201
crying: in Balaji Temple (India), 129; and Priyanka (case 3), 59–61, 68; and Sita (case 6), 101; and Violet (case 5), 90–91
culture, 3–4, 9, 16, 19–21, 23–25, 230n93; and African-Caribbean British, 89; "black box" of, 23, 101; in Chennai (India), 112, 213; cultural heretics, 33, 37; "cultural model," 164; and Hood, John (case 1), 33–34, 37; in Ireland, 199; and Meg (case 12), 185; in North India, 43, 54, 69, 71, 205; and pragmatic lessons, 219; and Priyanka (case 3), 69, 71; and Recovery Movement, 19; and Sita (case 6), 101, 111–12; and social defeat, 205–6, 209, 213–14; in Thailand, 167; in United States, 33–34, 37, 164, 185, 206, 209
curfews, 158, 187, 212
curses, 44, 80, 96, 119

dal, 75
darshan, 106–7, 129
Das, Veena, 201, 210
daughter-in-law murder, 45–46, 49–50, 66, 210–11
Davidson, Larry, 19
"Decade of the Brain" (NIMH), 2
Degeneration (Nordau), 5, 225n16
deinstitutionalization, 155, 225n29
deities. *See* God/Gods
Delhi (India), 44, 62, 137
delusions, 2, 3; and African-Caribbean British, 90, 204; and Alexandra (case 9), 140–42, 151, 235n12; and Anisha (case 2), 45–46, 49; in Balaji Temple (India), 135; and catatonic schizophrenia, 230n5; and *DSM-II*, 14; and *DSM-III*, 14–15; and Hood, John (case 1), 30–31; and Joan of Arc, 141–42; and Madhu (case 4), 77, 80, 84, 208; and Meg (case 12), 191–92; in North India, 45–46, 49, 63–64, 66, 135, 207, 210; paranoid delusions, 45–46, 49, 191–92; and Poi (case 11), 168, 173, 178; and Priyanka (case 3), 63–64, 66; "religious delusions," 141; in Romania, 140–42, 151, 235n12; and Sita (case 6), 100; and social defeat, 198, 204, 207–8, 210, 215; and Sunita (case 8), 135; in Thailand, 167–68, 173, 178; in United States, 167, 191–92, 194; and Violet (case 5), 90, 204
"dementia praecox," 223n3
demographics of schizophrenia, 2, 4, 21–22, 224n6; in England, 92, 94–95, 98; and gender, 4; in India, 102
demons/demonic voices: in Accra (Ghana), 113–15, 119, 122, 126, 215; and Alexandra (case 9), 141, 146, 148–150; and Charles (case 7), 113–15, 119, 122, 126, 215; and Cornici, Irina, 149, 152; in Romania, 141, 146, 148–150, 152, 235n14; and social defeat, 215
Dendron magazine, 163
depression, 1, 7, 19, 64; and African-Caribbean British, 91; and Alexandra (case 9), 142–43; in Ireland, 199; and Meg (case 12), 183, 185, 191–92; in North India, 43, 46, 59; and pragmatic lessons, 221–222; in Romania, 142–43; and social defeat, 216; in United States, 154, 183, 185, 191–92; and Violet (case 5), 91
Desjarlais, Robert, 199

developing countries, 21–24; and catatonic
    schizophrenia, 230n5; and NARP (non-
    affective remitting psychosis), 169; and
    social defeat, 216. *See also names of devel-
    oping countries*
Devereux, George, 9
diabetes, 204
diagnosis, 1, 3–4, 8–10, 17–18; in Accra
    (Ghana), 116, 124, 205; and African Amer-
    icans, 18; and African-Caribbean British,
    87, 91–92; and Ahmed, Kemal (case 2), 52;
    and Alexandra (case 9), 142, 149; and Ani-
    sha (case 2), 44, 47–50; and anti-psychia-
    try movement, 12–13, 227n51; and Charles
    (case 7), 116, 124, 205; in Chennai (India),
    103; and the Colonel (case 2), 53; "diagno-
    sis of death," 104; diagnostic criteria in
    DSM-III, 3, 13–15, 20, 21–22; "dual diag-
    nosis," 154; and Hood, John (case 1), 9, 27,
    33–35; in Ireland, 199; and Meg (case 12),
    191–92, 194, 207; misdiagnosis, 92, 199; in
    North India, 42–44, 47–50, 52–53,
    62–64, 71, 136, 205, 210, 230n1; and Poi
    (case 11), 168, 175; and pragmatic lessons,
    217, 220–21; and Priyanka (case 3), 63–64,
    71, 210; in Romania, 142, 149–150; and Sita
    (case 6), 103; and social defeat, 202–7, 210;
    and Sunita (case 8), 136; in Thailand, 168–
    69, 175; in United States, 103–4, 153–55,
    159, 166, 167, 169, 180, 185, 191–92, 194, 207,
    217, 221; and Veena (case 2), 44, 47–48,
    50; and Violet (case 5), 87, 91–92; and
    Zaney (case 10), 153–54. *See also* labels,
    diagnostic; *entries beginning with*
    diagnostic
diagnostic codes, 22, 43, 47, 52
diagnostic neutrality, 43, 53, 55, 205, 217, 220
disability programs, 207; and African-
    Caribbean British, 95; in Chennai (India),
    101–2; and social defeat, 206–7; in United
    States, 38–39, 153–54, 159–160, 187, 206–7.
    See also social security
discrimination, 20, 200–201; job discrimina-
    tion, 183–84; racial discrimination, 87–88,
    91. *See also* racism
"diseased brain," 34, 203–4
disorganized behavior, 15, 121, 130, 135
dissociation, 9–10, 168, 226n39
The Divided Self (Laing), 12
divorce, 24, 46, 61, 102, 170, 175, 183
domestic citizenship, 210

domestic violence, 45–46, 49, 62, 66, 133, 161,
    194, 210–11
DOSMeD, 21–22
double agent, 36–37
double binds, 11, 66, 89
downward drift, 227n58
dowry, 57, 59–60, 65–66, 79, 133
Droney, Damien, 113–126, 265
drop-in centers, 37, 153–55, 158, 163, 165–66,
    201, 212
drug use/abuse, 29, 38, 189, 193–94, 206–7,
    216–17. *See also* substance use/abuse
DSM (*Diagnostic and Statistical Manual of
    Mental Disorders*, 1952), 13
DSM-II (*Diagnostic and Statistical Manual of
    Mental Disorders*, second ed.), 13–14
DSM-III (*Diagnostic and Statistical Manual of
    Mental Disorders*, third ed.), 3, 13–17,
    20–22, 80, 199
Durkheim, Émile, 5–6, 8
dwarfs of Ghanaian lore, 115, 120
Dylan, Bob, 29

"eat," 34, 54, 230n4
economic conditions, 7, 225n27, 226n32; in
    Accra (Ghana), 118; and African-Caribbean
    British, 88, 95; and Alexandra (case 9),
    140–47, 151, 235n5; in Balaji Temple
    (India), 130–31, 133, 135, 137; economic
    social adversity in childhood, 21; in
    Ireland, 198; and Madhu (case 4), 74–76,
    79; and Meg (case 12), 182–89, 191–92; in
    Romania, 140–44, 144, 145–47, 151, 235n5;
    and Sita (case 6), 100; and social defeat,
    197, 216; and social drift theory, 17; and
    Sunita (case 8), 130–31, 133, 135, 137; in
    United States, 158–59, 182–89, 191–92; and
    Violet (case 5), 95; and Zaney (case 10),
    159. *See also* poverty
Edgerton, Robert, 8
education, 226n32; in Accra (Ghana), 115; and
    African-Caribbean British, 88, 93–95; and
    Charles (case 7), 115; and Hood, John (case
    1), 28–29; and Madhu (case 4), 74–77, 80;
    and Meg (case 12), 181–82, 185, 189, 192–93,
    207; and Poi (case 11), 173; and social
    defeat, 207; and Sunita (case 8), 136–37; in
    Thailand, 173; in United States, 28–29,
    181–82, 185, 189, 192–93, 207; and Violet
    (case 5), 93–95
Egba Yoruba, 16

ejaculation, 114, 121, 124

El (Chicago, Ill.), 153

El Cajon (Calif.), 39–40

electroconvulsive therapy, 44, 63, 67

Eliacin, Johanne, 4, 86–98, 265

Emile (Rousseau), 5, 225n16

engaged anthropology, 5

English language, 43, 46–47, 105; and Madhu (case 4), 73–75; and Sita (case 6), 110

environmental factors, 3, 224n9, 231n7

"Epidemiological Catchment Area Study" (1980s), 18

epigenetics, 3, 224n9

Equus (play), 155

Escher, Sandra, 233n12

Eskimos, Yupik-speaking, 15–16

Estroff, Sue, 199, 206

ethnic density, 20, 21

ethnography, 1, 3–4, 22–23, 24–25, 197; clinical ethnography, 4; and *DSM-III*, 15; and gender, 4; in London, 87; rich ethnography, 3

Europe, 5–6, 20, 112, 169, 206. *See also names of European countries*

evangelical Protestantism, 139–140, 142–45, 147–150, 152, 215, 235n8, 235n16

Everyday Ethics (Brodwin), 36–37

evictions, 38, 135, 154, 158–59, 182–83, 209

exclusion, social, 53; and African-Caribbean British, 91–94; and Violet (case 5), 91–94

exorcism/exorcists, 149, 152, 176–77

expressed emotion, 19–20, 228n68; and African-Caribbean British, 86–87, 89–90; and Alexandra (case 9), 235n10; community expressed emotion, 86–87, 89–90; in Romania, 235n10

faith. *See* religious practices

families, 8, 23–25, 225n29; in Accra (Ghana), 114–15, 119–120, 123, 125, 205, 209; and African-Caribbean British, 89–91, 93–94, 97–98; and Ahmed, Kemal (case 2), 50–52, 54–55; and Alexandra (case 9), 140, 143, 145–47, 151, 235n10; and Charles (case 7), 114–15, 119–120, 123, 125, 205; Chaturvedi family (case 2), 43–50, 54, 208, 209–10, 231n7; in Chennai (India), 100–105, 107–11, 209; and the Colonel (case 2), 53–54; dysfunctional, 19–20; and expressed emotion, 19–20, 228n68; extended families, 24, 54, 82, 89, 100, 230n96; family networks, 89; as guarantors

of daughter's marriage, 101; and Hood, John (case 1), 28–29, 31, 33–34, 211; in Ireland, 198–99; joint families, 24, 70, 103, 230n96; and Madhu (case 4), 73–77, 79–84, 208; and Meg (case 12), 183, 188, 192–94, 209; in North India, 42–55, 48, 56–65, 67, 69–70, 70, 131, 133, 137–38, 205, 208, 208, 209–10, 231n7, 238n41; nuclear families, 89; and Poi (case 11), 168, 170, 172–76, 178–79; and pragmatic lessons, 216, 219–222; and Priyanka (case 3), 56–65, 67, 69–70, 70, 210; in Romania, 139–140, 143, 145–48, 151, 235n10; schizophrenogenic, 10–11, 16, 19, 227n57; and Sita (case 6), 100–105, 107–11, 209; and social defeat, 203, 205–11, 213, 238n41; and Sunita (case 8), 131, 133, 137–38; in Thailand, 168, 170, 172–76, 178–79, 209; in United States, 28–29, 31, 33–34, 155–56, 158, 183–84, 188, 192–94, 209, 211, 216, 221; and Violet (case 5), 90–91, 93–94, 97–98. *See also* in-laws

Farmer, Paul, 198, 200–201

fears, 10, 12; and African-Caribbean British, 92; and Anisha (case 2), 46, 50; in Bangladesh, 64; and Meg (case 12), 182; and Poi (case 11), 174; and Priyanka (case 3), 58–60, 63, 66; supernatural fear, 64; in Thailand, 174; in United States, 164–66, 182; and Violet (case 5), 92

femininity, norms of, 62

feminism, 158

Field, M.J., 6–8, 22, 121, 211, 216, 225nn27–28

folklore, North Indian, 69

folk ontologies, Bangladeshi, 64

food pantries, 192

food stamps, 186

Fortes, Meyer, 22–23

Foucault, Michel, 13

fragmentation, social, 86–87, 89–90, 96

France, 141–42

Franklin, Benjamin, 5

Freud, Sigmund, 12, 33

Friedman, Jack, 139–152, 207, 265–66

Fromm-Reichmann, Frieda, 10

Gandhi, Sonia, 76

Ganesha (Deity), 84

Ga people, 113, 115, 120, 234nn8–10. *See also* Charles (case 7)

gauna, 58–60, 65

gays, 172, 177

gender, 4; gender inequality, 201; gender roles, 63, 210; and NARP (non-affective acute remitting psychosis), 169

genetics, 1–3, 16–17, 20, 223n3, 231n7; and African-Caribbean British, 87; gene-environment interactions, 230n93; and mesolimbic dopamine system, 198; and social defeat, 197–98, 202

Germany, 21

Ghana, 6–8, 22–23, 121, 225n22, 225nn27–28; Accra (Ghana), 113–126, 205–6, 209; and social defeat, 204, 205–6, 209, 216

ghosts, 64, 77, 120, 123, 213–14. *See also* spirits

Gifford, Paul, 118

God/Gods, 14; in Accra (Ghana), 113, 118–123, 234nn9–10; and Alexandra (case 9), 140–42, 148–152, 215; in Balaji Temple (India), 127–29, 131, 133, 135, 213; and Charles (case 7), 118–123, 234nn9–10; in Chennai (India), 99–100, 106–12; God's voice, 99, 108, 122–23, 131; Hindu gods/goddesses, 127–28; and Hood, John (case 1), 30, 39; lineage gods, 121; local gods, 120–21, 234nn9–10; and Madhu (case 4), 82, 84–85; and Poi (case 11), 173, 176, 214; in Romania, 140–42, 148–152, 215; and Sita (case 6), 100, 106–12; and social defeat, 213–15; and Sunita (case 8), 131, 133, 135, 214; in Thailand, 173, 176, 214; in United States, 30, 39. *See also names of Gods*

Godrej cupboard, 59–60, 65

Goffman, Erving, 27, 155, 201, 227n54, 236n4

Good, Byron, 24–25, 203

government conspiracy theories/spying, 31, 92

Grateful Dead, 37

The Great Universe of Kota (Carstairs and Kapur), 226n32

Guan Im (Deity), 174

guardians, 130, 137

guilt, 11, 17, 34, 36; and Alexandra (case 9), 145, 151; in Romania, 145, 151

guns, 60, 63, 66

Gwalior (India), 136

Hagin, Kenneth, 118

halfway houses, 98, 155–56

hallucinations, 1–2, 3, 8–9, 23–24; and African-Caribbean British, 204; and Alexandra (case 9), 140, 151, 235n12; in Balaji Temple (India), 135, 214; and *DSM-II*, 14; and *DSM-III*, 15; and Madhu (case 4), 84, 208;

and Meeta (case 2), 42; in North India, 63, 207, 210; and Poi (case 11), 168, 178; in Romania, 140, 151, 235n12; and Sita (case 6), 100, 111; and social defeat, 198, 204, 207–8, 210, 214; and Sunita (case 8), 135, 214; in Thailand, 167–68, 178; in United States, 167, 194; and Violet (case 5), 204. *See also* auditory hallucinations

haloperidol, 145

Hanuman: Hanuman temple (Allahabad, India), 64; infant form of, 127

health insurance, 12, 19, 184–85

Hearing Voices Network, 112, 218–19, 226n39, 233n12

Henry VI, King of England, 223n4

Hindi language/literature, 47, 129, 137, 214, 230n4

Hinduism, 111

Hispanics, 18

Holy Spirit, 122–23

homelessness: in Accra (Ghana), 213; in Chennai (India), 78, 82–83, 208, 213; and "code of the street," 211; and Hood, John (case 1), 29–30, 40; and Madhu (case 4), 72–74, 78, 80–83, 208; and Meg (case 12), 185–89, 192, 194–95, 207; and Poi (case 11), 168; and pragmatic lessons, 221–22; and social defeat, 203, 207, 211–13, 239n46; in Thailand, 168; in United States, 29–30, 40, 154, 156–59, 161–66, 185–89, 192, 194–95, 199, 207, 211–13, 221–22, 239n46; and Zaney (case 10), 154, 157, 159, 161–62

Hood, John (case 1), 9, 27–41, 32, 204, 207, 211, 215

Hopper, Kim, 19, 21–23, 158, 186, 199

hospitals/clinics, psychiatric, 8, 10–12, 20; in Accra (Ghana), 113, 115–19, 117, 121, 124–25, 233n2; and African-Caribbean British, 86–87, 89–92, 97–98; and Ahmed, Kemal (case 2), 50–53; and Alexandra (case 9), 140, 142, 144–45, 147–48, 150–52, 215, 235n5; and Anisha (case 2), 44, 47; and Charles (case 7), 115–19, 117, 121, 124–25; in Chennai (India), 100, 102–3, 111; and the Colonel (case 2), 53–54; high profile cases of deaths in, 92; and Hood, John (case 1), 28, 30, 35–40; and Indian Mental Health Act (1987), 234n8; in Ireland, 198, 237n8; and Madhu (case 4), 73; in North India, 42–44, 47, 48, 50–54, 56, 58–59, 62–63, 66–70, 136; and Poi (case 11), 168, 170,

hospitals/clinics, psychiatric (*continued*)
174–77, 214–15; and pragmatic lessons,
219, 222; and Priyanka (case 3), 56, 58–59,
62–63, 66–70; in Romania, 139–140, 142,
144–45, 147–48, 150–52, 215, 235n5; and
Sita (case 6), 100, 111; and social defeat,
204, 214–15; and Sunita (case 8), 136; in
Thailand, 168–170, 174–77, 214–15; tied to
bed in, 168, 175–76; in United States, 28,
30, 35–40, 153, 155–56, 158–160, 186, 222,
236n4; and Veena (case 2), 44, 49; and
Violet (case 5), 86–87, 90–91, 97–98; and
Zaney (case 10), 153, 159. *See also names of
hospitals/clinics*
hotels: in Chennai (India), 105–6; and Hood,
John (case 1), 29, 39–40; and Sita (case 6),
105–6; in United States, 29, 39–40, 154–
55, 158; and Zaney (case 10), 154
housework. *See* work
housing: affordable housing, 217; and African-
Caribbean British, 88, 95; and Hood, John
(case 1), 33, 37, 39; and Meg (case 12), 183,
185–86, 188, 192, 194–95, 207; and pragmatic lessons, 216–17, 221–22; and social
defeat, 207, 209, 217; subsidized housing,
154–58; supported housing, 39, 156–58,
186, 192, 222; in United States, 33, 37,
39, 153–59, 162–63, 183, 185–86, 188, 192,
194–95, 207, 209, 216–17, 222; and Violet
(case 5), 88, 95; and Zaney (case 10),
153–54, 157–59, 162–63. *See also* shelters
Housing First, 217
human rights abuses, 201
hygiene, personal, 62–63, 206. *See also*
bathing/showering

ICD (International Classification of Diseases), 22, 43, 47, 52; ICD-9, 22; ICD-10,
47
identities, cultural/social, 4; and African-
Caribbean British, 86–87, 89–90, 98, 203;
in Balaji Temple (India), 127; and Hood,
John (case 1), 9, 27–28, 34–35; in North
India, 43, 53, 55, 127, 205; and pragmatic
lessons, 220, 222; and social defeat, 203,
205–7, 209, 212; and Sunita (case 8), 127; in
United States, 9, 27–28, 34–35, 163, 203,
207, 209, 212; and Violet (case 5), 98
idiom of distress, 113, 127–29
immigrants/immigration, 4, 18, 20–21, 21,
229n74, 231n7; and African-Caribbean

British, 87, 89, 93–94; and Irish, 198–99;
and second generation, 20; and social
defeat, 197–98, 202; and Violet (case 5), 87,
93–94
independence: and African-Caribbean British, 95, 98; and Housing First, 217; and
Recovery Movement, 19, 228n66; and Sita
(case 6), 101; and social defeat, 209, 216–17;
in United States, 19–20, 180, 194, 209,
216–17, 228n66
India, 4, 21–24, 31, 225n29, 226n32, 229n86;
Balaji Temple (Mehndipur), 127–138, 132,
208–9, 211, 213–14; Chennai, 22–23, 77, 78,
82–83, 99–112, 205, 209–11, 213–14, 231n10;
North India, 42–55, 48, 56–71, 127–138,
205, 208–9, 210–11, 230n1; and pragmatic
lessons, 217, 221; schizophrenia's more
benign course in, 4, 23–24, 99, 101, 204,
213–14, 221; and social defeat, 203, 205,
207–14, 216
Indian Mental Health Act (1987), 234n8
Indonesia, 169, 229n86
industrial revolution, 5, 223n4
inequality, economic/social, 87–88, 98, 118,
201, 207
I Never Promised You a Rose Garden (Greenberg), 10
in-laws: and Anisha (case 2), 45–46, 49–50,
210; in Chennai (India), 100–101, 103–4,
108; and daughter-in-law murder, 45–46,
49–50, 66, 210–11; and Madhu (case 4), 73,
79–80, 208; in North India, 45–46,
49–50, 56–71, 210–11, 133, 137, 238n41; and
Priyanka (case 3), 56–71, 210; and Sita
(case 6), 100–101, 103–4, 108; and social
defeat, 208, 210–11, 238n41; and Sunita
(case 8), 133, 137
inner experience, 8, 13; externalization of,
223n4; and Madhu (case 4), 76; and
Poi (case 11), 168; and pragmatic lessons,
220
insomnia, 142
institutional circuit, 4, 158, 186, 190, 192, 209,
211–12, 222
institutionalization: and Alexandra (case 9),
151–52; and "deinstitutionalization," 155;
in North India, 49; and "reinstitutionalization," 155; in Romania, 144, 151–52; in
United States, 4, 155, 236n4; and Veena
(case 2), 49. *See also* hospitals/clinics,
psychiatric; prisons

"International Pilot Study of Schizophrenia" (IPSS), 22
Internet, 118
IPSS ("International Pilot Study of Schizophrenia"), 21
Ireland, 198–99, 237n8
Islamic beliefs, 214
isolation, social, 231n7; and African-Caribbean British, 90, 96–98; and Alexandra (case 9), 140, 142, 146, 151, 235n9; and Hood, John (case 1), 29; in North India, 58, 60–61; and pragmatic lessons, 220–21; and Priyanka (case 3), 58, 60–61; in Romania, 140, 142, 146, 151, 235n9; and social defeat, 198; in United States, 29, 164; and Violet (case 5), 90, 96–98
ISoS study, 21–23

jails. See prisons
Jamaica/Jamaicans, 86, 93–94, 97–98. See also African-Caribbean British
Jehovah's Witnesses, 37–38
Jenkins, Janis, 4, 23, 209
Jesus, 122–23, 140, 146, 152, 170, 177
Joan of Arc, 141–42
judges, U.S., 184–85, 191
Jungian psychology, 33

Kanchipuram, Kanchi of, 111
Kardiner, Abram, 9
Karnataka coast (India), 226n32
Karno, Martin, 23
Kennedy, John F., 155–56
khammes (permanently indebted worker), 200
Kinderman, Peter, 204
Kleinman, Arthur, 201
kohl, 44
Kolkata (India), 64
Kovalam (India), 73, 83–84
Kraepelin, Emil, 1, 17, 49, 223n3
Krishna (god), 109–10
kum-kum, 108

labeling theory, 15–16, 227n54
labels, diagnostic, 1, 13, 23–24, 226n39; and Hood, John (case 1), 27, 34–35, 203–4; in North India, 42–43, 46–48, 53; and pragmatic lessons, 220, 222; and social defeat, 203–5
Laing, R. D., 12, 223n3

Lambo, Adeoye, 8
Lapland, 219
Leff, Julian, 230n5
Leighton, Alexander, 8
Lévi-Strauss, Claude, 6
lightning-bolt model, 16–17, 197
Linton, Ralph, 9
literacy, 7, 225n27, 226n32
Lock, Margaret, 201
loitering, 188
London (Eng.), 20, 23; and African-Caribbean British, 86–98, 204; and Hood, John (case 1), 28–29, 31; North London, 86–87; South London, 97–98
loneliness, 29, 126, 173, 177
Long Island (N.Y.), 156
lorazepam, 47
love-as-suffering, 67–71
Lovell, Anne, 199
Lucknow (India), 42–55, 230n1
Luhrmann, T. M., 1–41, 99–112, 153–166, 197–222, 212–13, 225n29, 266; and Sita (case 6), 102–3, 105–12, 205, 233n1; and Zaney (case 10), 201

Madhu (case 4), 72–85, 78, 208, 211, 213–14, 214
Madhya Pradesh (India), 131
Madness and Civilization (Foucault), 13
manic-depressive, 171, 225n23
Marmot, Michael, 237n6
marriage, 8; and Anisha (case 2), 44–45, 49–50, 210; in Chennai (India), 100–104, 108, 110, 112; daughter's family as guarantor of, 101; and Madhu (case 4), 75–77, 79–81, 83; in North India, 44–45, 49–50, 56–71, 57, 133, 137–38, 210, 238n41; and Poi (case 11), 169–170, 173; and Priyanka (case 3), 56–71, 210; and Sita (case 6), 100–104, 108, 110, 112; and social defeat, 202–3, 210; and Sunita (case 8), 133, 137–38; in Thailand, 169–170, 173; in United States, 163
Marrow, Jocelyn, 56–71, 197–222, 225n29, 230n4, 266
Mass Mental (Massachusetts Mental Health Center), 12
maya, 69
Mayer, Doris, 22–23
mazaars, 214
Mazza, Giulia, 72–85, 208, 266
McDonald's, 24, 90, 181, 188, 191

Mead, Margaret, 9
media, British, 92
Medicaid, 188
medical model. *See* biomedical model/
   psychiatry
medication, antipsychotic, 2, 17, 22; in Accra
   (Ghana), 124–25; and African-Caribbean
   British, 90–92, 96–97, 205, 209; and
   Ahmed, Kemal (case 2), 51–52; and Alexandra (case 9), 145, 147; and Anisha (case
   2), 45, 47; and Charles (case 7), 124–25; in
   Chennai (India), 100, 102–3; and the Colonel (case 2), 53–54; concealing of, 54,
   124–25; to "eat," 34, 54, 230n4; and health
   insurance, 184–85; and Hood, John (case
   1), 30, 33–35, 37–38, 204, 230n4; and
   Madhu (case 4), 73, 208; and Meg (case
   12), 184–85; in North India, 43–45, 47, 49,
   51–55; and Poi (case 11), 168, 175–76, 179;
   and pragmatic lessons, 217, 219, 222;
   in Romania, 145, 147; side effects of, 49,
   51–52, 124, 209; and Sita (case 6), 100,
   102–3; and social defeat, 204, 206, 209;
   in Thailand, 168, 175–76, 179; in United
   States, 30, 33–35, 37–38, 155, 157, 160, 164,
   184–85, 193, 204, 217, 230n4; and Veena
   (case 2), 44, 49; and Violet (case 5),
   90–92, 96–97, 204, 209. *See also names
   of drugs*
Meeta (case 2), 42
Meeting Place (client-run drop-in center), 37
Meg (case 12), 180–195, 207–9, 212
Mehndipur (India), 127–138, 211
memory, 73–75
menopause, 8
mental health centers, 207; and African-Caribbean British, 95; and Madhu (case 4), 73;
   and Meg (case 12), 180–83, 188–89, 191, 193–
   95; and social defeat, 207; in United States,
   153, 180–83, *181*, 187–89, *190*, 191, 193–95, 207;
   and Violet (case 5), 95; and Zaney (case 10),
   153. *See also* drop-in centers
Mental Health Person of the Year (San Diego
   County), 27–28, 35, 38
The Mental Hospital (1954 study), 11
mesolimbic dopamine system, 197–98
metaphorical as communicative frame, 11
Metzl, Jonathan, 18
Meyer, Birgit, 121, 233n6
middle class: and African-Caribbean British,
   88; and Charles (case 7), 115; and Hood,

John (case 1), 33; and Madhu (case 4), 75;
   and Meg (case 12), 193, 212; in North India,
   50, 53–54, 61; in Romania, 151; and Sita
   (case 6), 100; in United States, 163, 166,
   193, 212. *See also* social class/status
Midelfort, H. C. Erik, 223n4
"Midtown Manhattan Study" (1962), 18,
   228n62
mindfulness, 218
missionaries, Christian, 121, 140, 143
modernization, 8–9, 226n32
Mooshika (rat), 84
moral degeneration, 5, 225nn15–16
multiple personality disorder, 15
Mumbai (India), 78, 81
murder. *See* daughter-in-law murder
Murphy, Jane, 15–16
music: and Hood, John (case 1), 29, 33, 35–37,
   39; and Meg (case 12), 189, 192–95
mutism, 44, 49
Myers, Neely, 180–195, 207, 209, 212, 266
The Myth of Mental Illness (Szasz), 12–13

Nambikwara, 6
nam mon (holy water), 176
NARP (non-affective acute remitting psychosis), 8, 23, 167, 169–170, 201
nash, 43
natal families. *See* families
National Alliance for the Mentally Ill, 27
National Medal of Science, 224n8
negative symptoms, 2, 101, 168, 194. *See also*
   affect, flattened; speech, incoherent/
   impoverished
nervous breakdowns, 183–84
Netherlands, 20
neurasthenia with obsessive phobias, 142
neuronal connections, decay of, 202, 204
neuroscientific markers, 1, 224n5
New Age environment, 170
New Guinea, 6
New York City, 220
Nichter, Mark, 113, 128
Nigeria, 8, 121, 229n86
NIMH (National Institute of Mental
   Health), 1–2, 153; "Decade of the Brain," 2
Noble Savage, 6
Noll, Richard, 9
Nordau, Max, 5, 225n16
North India, 42–55, *48*, 56–71, 230n1; Ahmed,
   Kemal (case 2), 50–55; Chaturvedi family

(case 2), 43–50, 54, 208, 209–11, 231n7; the
 Colonel (case 2), 53–55; Priyanka (case 3),
 56–71, 210–11; Sunita (case 8), 127, 130–38,
 132, 208–9, 211, 213–15; and social defeat,
 207–11, 213
Norway/Norwegians, 229n74
nosologies, psychiatric, 62–63, 69, 168
nuisance value, 62, 207
Nunley, Michael, 102
nursing homes, 155, 188

obsessive-compulsive disorder, 43, 108
"one down" interactions, 202
Open Dialogue, 219
optimism, 43, 52, 140, 210
Original Sin, 139
Outline of a Theory of Practice (Bourdieu), 200
outpatient medical records, 43, 46–47, 52–53
Outsiders (Becker), 227n54

Padmavati, R., 99–112, 238n28, 266; and Sita
 (case 6), 99–103, 105–6, 109, 233n1
panchayat, 73, 102
PANSS rating, 100
Parachute NYC, 220
paranoia: and African-Caribbean British, 94;
 and Alexandra (case 9), 140, 142, 145,
 151–52; and Anisha (case 2), 45–46, 49,
 208; in Chennai (India), 108; and the Colonel (case 2), 53–54; and Cornici, Irina,
 149; and Hood, John (case 1), 33; and Meg
 (case 12), 191–92, 194; in North India,
 45–46, 49, 53–54, 60, 63–64, 208, 211;
 paranoid delusions, 45–46, 49, 191; paranoid schizophrenia, 33, 49, 53, 63, 140,
 142, 145, 149, 151–52, 208, 210–11; and Poi
 (case 11), 168, 173; and Priyanka (case 3),
 60, 63–64, 210; in Romania, 140, 142, 145,
 149, 151–52; and Sita (case 6), 108; and
 social defeat, 208, 210–11; in Thailand, 168,
 173; in United States, 33, 188, 191–92, 194;
 and Violet (case 5), 94
paraplegics, 170
parathas, 54
Parkinsonism, 51
Pascal, 165–66
paternalism: in North India, 52–53; and
 Recovery Movement, 19
peer counselors: and Hood, John (case 1),
 35–38; and Recovery Movement, 19. See
 also client counselor

Pentecostal churches, 122; Ewe Pentecostalism,
 233n6
perphenazine, 176, 179
persecution, sense of, 58, 64
personal accountability, 19
pimozide, 47
playing cards, 39–40, 116
Poi (case 11), 167–179, 171, 209, 214–15
police: and African-Caribbean British, 86, 88,
 91–92; and Hood, John (case 1), 40; and
 Meg (case 12), 187–89, 212; police brutality,
 88; and Poi (case 11), 168; and social defeat,
 209, 211–12; in Thailand, 168; in United
 States, 40, 153, 159–160, 187–89, 209, 212,
 236n7; and Violet (case 5), 86, 91–92; and
 Zaney (case 10), 153, 159
politics, 76, 216
positive symptoms, 2–3, 80, 101, 167–68, 198,
 204. See also delusions; hallucinations
post-traumatic stress disorder, 15, 154
poverty, 7–8, 17–25, 227n58; and African-
 Caribbean British, 88; and Alexandra
 (case 9), 140, 142–47, 151, 215, 235n5; federal poverty level, 192; in Ireland, 198–99;
 and Meg (case 12), 192; in Romania, 140,
 142–47, 144, 151, 215, 235n5; and social
 defeat, 197–98, 200–202, 215; in United
 States, 184, 192
pragmatic lessons, 216–222; Acceptance and
 Commitment Therapy, 218; Avatar therapy, computer-based, 112, 218; cognitive
 behavioral therapy, 218; Hearing Voices
 Network, 112, 217–19, 226n39, 233n12;
 Housing First, 217; mindfulness, 218;
 Open Dialogue, 219; Parachute NYC,
 219–220
praying: in Accra (Ghana), 114, 118–120, 122,
 124; and Alexandra (case 9), 140, 145,
 149–150; and Charles (case 7), 114, 118–120,
 122, 124; and Chaturvedi family (case 2),
 44; in Chennai (India), 106; in North
 India, 44; and Poi (case 11), 177–78; in
 Romania, 140, 145, 149–150; and Sita (case
 6), 106; in Thailand, 177–78
pregnancies: and Alexandra (case 9), 143–45,
 148; in Chennai (India), 99, 108; and Poi
 (case 11), 173; in Romania, 143–45, 148; and
 Sita (case 6), 99, 108; in Thailand, 173. See
 also children
presenting problems, 62–63, 231n3
Pretraj (deity), 128

prisons: in England, 92; in Thailand, 178; in
    United States, 153, 155–56, 158, 160–61,
    186–87, 222
Priyanka (case 3), 56–71, 210–11
prodromal stage, 28
prophets, 127
prophylactics, 51–52
prostitution, 189, 194
The Protest Psychosis (Metzl), 18
psychiatric anthropologists, 3–5
psychiatric disability, 184–86
psychiatric survivors, 35, 163
psychiatrists, 2, 8, 12, 16–18, 24; and African-
    Caribbean British, 90–91; and Ahmed,
    Kemal (case 2), 50; and Alexandra (case
    9), 140–42, 147, 149–152; and Anisha (case
    2), 47, 50; in Chennai (India), 102–3, 106,
    238n28; and Cornici, Irina, 152; in Ghana,
    205; and Hood, John (case 1), 28, 30–31;
    and Meeta (case 2), 42; and Meg (case 12),
    184–85, 191; in North India, 42–44, 47, 50,
    59, 62, 65, ,m 135, 205; and Poi (case 11),
    175; and Priyanka (case 3), 59, 62, 65; in
    Romania, 140–42, 147–152; and Sita (case
    6), 102–3, 106; and social defeat, 205; and
    Sunita (case 8), 135; in Thailand, 175; in
    United States, 28, 30–31, 103, 111, 154,
    157–59, 167, 170, 184–85, 191; and Veena
    (case 2), 44; and Violet (case 5), 90–91;
    and Zaney (case 10), 154, 158–59. *See also*
    names of psychiatrists
psychoanalysis, 2, 9–13, 18, 33
psychosis, 2–4, 7–12, 14, 18–25; in Accra
    (Ghana), 113, 116, 213; and African-
    Caribbean British, 88, 90, 94, 96, 204–6;
    and Alexandra (case 9), 139–141, 145–46,
    151; and Anisha (case 2), 49; in Balaji Tem-
    ple (India), 134–36, 214; cannabis-induced,
    116, 233n1; and Caterina (São Paulo, Bra-
    zil), 138; in Chennai (India), 213; floridly
    psychotic, 18, 96, 111, 194, 214; and Hood,
    John (case 1), 28, 31, 33; and Madhu (case
    4), 74–76, 213; and Meg (case 12), 191–92;
    in North India, 49, 54, 56, 59, 62–64, 66,
    69, 134–36, 210, 214; and Poi (case 11),
    167–170, 178, 214; and pragmatic lessons,
    218–222; and Priyanka (case 3), 56, 59,
    62–64, 66, 69; in Romania, 139–141, 145–
    46, 151; and Sita (case 6), 99, 106–7, 111;
    and social defeat, 198, 202–7, 209–16; in
    South India, 64, 99, 106–7, 111, 231n10; and

Sunita (case 8), 134–36, 214; in Thailand,
    167–170, 178, 214; in United States, 28, 31,
    33, 154–56, 157, 159–160, 163–66, 180, 186,
    191–92, 199, 206, 211–13, 216, 218–19; and
    Violet (case 5), 90, 94, 96, 204–5; and
    Zaney (case 10), 159. *See also* bipolar disor-
    der; NARP; schizophrenia
public assistance, 33, 186, 192
Puerto Ricans, 18
pujas, 44, 107
Pune (India), 74, 77, 79–81, 83
Puri, Ganesh. *See* Babaji (Ganesh Puri)

race/ethnicity, 18–20; and African-Caribbean
    British, 94–96; and ethnic density, 20, *21,*
    97; and social defeat, 197, 201. *See also*
    racism
racism, 7–8, 18–20; and African-Caribbean
    British, 86–88, 90–92, 98, 203; and social
    defeat, 201, 203; and Violet (case 5), 87,
    90–92, 98
Radha, 110
Ranchi (India), 136
rape, 93, 156, 161, 166, 172, 194, 225n29
RDoC (Research Domain Criteria), 224n5
recordings, 31, 33, 36, 39; and Hood, John
    (case 1), 29–30; and Sita (case 6), 106,
    109, 111
recovery, 4, 19, 21–24; and Anisha (case 2),
    49–50; in Balaji Temple (India), 127, 129;
    and Charles (case 7), 123; and Hood, John
    (case 1), 35; and Madhu (case 4), 83–85;
    and Meg (case 12), 180–81, 193–95, 207; in
    North India, 49–50, 53, 127; and Poi (case
    11), 167–69, 177–79; and Sita (case 6), 101;
    and social defeat, 207, 212; and Sunita
    (case 8), 127; in Thailand, 167–69, 177–79;
    in United States, 180–81, 193–95, 207, 212;
    and Violet (case 5), 94
Recovery Movement, 19, 35, 207, 219, 228n66
reinstitutionalization, 155
relapses: and African-Caribbean British, 89;
    and expressed emotion, 19–20, 89; in
    North India, 59; and Priyanka
    (case 3), 59
religious practices, 24; in Accra (Ghana),
    114–16, 118–123, 215; and Alexandra (case
    9), 140–152, 235n6, 235n8, 235n16; in Balaji
    Temple (India), 133–34, 208–9, 215; and
    Charles (case 7), 114–16, 118–123, 215; dar-
    shan, 106–7, 129; and Hood, John (case 1),

31, 37–38; and Poi (case 11), 174, 176–77, 208–9, 214–15; in Romania, 139–152, 235n6, 235n8, 235n16; and Sita (case 6), 100, 106–12, 205, 215; and social defeat, 205, 208–9, 214–15; and Sunita (case 8), 133–34, 208–9, 215; in Thailand, 174, 176–77, 208–9, 214–15; and traditional religions, 119, 121. *See also* churches; God/Gods; temples; *names of religions*

remission, 21–23, 227n51; and NARP (non-affective remitting psychosis), 23, 170, 174–75, 177–79, 201; and Poi (case 11), 170, 174–75, 177–79; and social defeat, 204; in Thailand, 170, 174–75, 177–79

respect: in Accra (Ghana), 123, 125; in North India, 53, 62, 217; and pragmatic lessons, 221; and social defeat, 199, 217–18; in United States, 199, 217–18

restlessness, 51–52, 55

retardation, 164

rich ethnography, 3

rights of mental health patients, 27, 35, 205–6, 217

risk factors, 4, 7–8, 19–20, 21, 88–90, 231n7; and African-Caribbean British, 86–87; and social defeat, 198, 203

risperidone, 53

Roberts, Oral, 118

Romania, 139–152, *144*, 215–16, 235n11

Romanian Orthodox Church, 139–145, 147–150, 152, 215, 235n6, 235n14

Romanian Revolution, 145–46

Romme, Marius, 233n12

roti, 54, 67, 75

Rousseau, Jean-Jacques, 5, 225n16

Rukhmani, 110

rural areas: in Africa, 8–9; in Ghana, 6–8, 216; in Ireland, 198–99; in North India, 45, 56, 211; in Romania, 140, 142–43, 145–47, 150; in South India, 102

sacrifices, 120–21

salwar-kameez, 79, 130

Samadhi grounds (Balaji Temple), 128, 130–31, 134–35

San Diego (Calif.), 27–41, 156, 163

sankat mochan, 127

sankat-walas, 129–130

San Mateo (Calif.), 213

São Paulo (Brazil), 138

Sapir, Edward, 9

saris, 68, 75, 79, 110

Sasaram (India), 64

Satan, 121, 123, 141, 170, 172–73, 215; Satan energy, 170, 172–73, 177

Scandinavians, 219–220

Scheff, Thomas, 227n54

Scheper-Hughes, Nancy, 198–99, 237n8

schizoaffective disorder, 3, 62, 191, 207

schizophrenia, 1–4, 7–25; in Accra (Ghana), 113, 116, 205, 215; and African-Caribbean British, 86–92, 94, 96–98, 203; and Ahmed, Kemal (case 2), 51–52; and Alexandra (case 9), 140–42, 145–47, 150–52; and Anisha (case 2), 44, 46–49, 211; catatonic schizophrenia, 48–49, 208, 230n5; and Charles (case 7), 113, 116, 205, 215; in Chennai (India), 100–101, 103–6, 108–11, 233n9; chronic schizophrenia, 7–8, 15–19, 25, 169, 225n23; and the Colonel (case 2), 53–54; and Cornici, Irina, 149, 152; cultural studies of, 21–23; demographics of, 2, 4, 21–22, 92, 94–95, 98, 102, 169, 224n6; diagnostic codes for, 22, 43, 47, 52; and double bind, 11, 66; and *DSM-III*, 3, 13–17, 20–22, 80; and Hood, John (case 1), 27–28, 32, 33–35, 204; in Ireland, 198–99, 237n8; and lightning-bolt model, 16–17, 197; and Madhu (case 4), 73; and Meeta (case 2), 42; and Meg (case 12), 181, 191–94; more benign course in India, 4, 23–24, 99, 101, 203, 213–14, 221; negative symptoms of, 2, 101, 168, 194; in North India, 44, 46–49, 51–54, 56, 63, 205, 208, 210–11; paranoid schizophrenia, 33, 49, 53, 63, 140, 142, 145, 149, 151–52, 208, 210–11; positive symptoms of, 2–3, 80, 101, 167–68, 198, 204; and Poi (case 11), 168–171, 214; and pragmatic lessons, 220–22; and Priyanka (case 3), 56, 63, 210–11; and psychoanalysis, 9–12; risk factors for, 4, 7–8, 19–20, 21, 88–90, 198, 203, 231n7; in Romania, 140–42, 145–47, 149–152; and Sita (case 6), 100–101, 103–4, 108–11, 233n9; and social defeat, 25, 87, 90, 203–5, 208, 210–11, 214–16, 239n46; in Thailand, 167–171, 214; in United States, 104–5, 111, 153–57, 159, 163, 167, 180–81, 191–94, 199, 203–4, 211, 220, 233n9, 239n46; and Veena (case 2), 44, 46–49; and Violet (case 5), 86–87, 90–92, 94, 96–98; and Zaney (case 10), 153. *See also* NARP

Schizophrenia, Culture, and Subjectivity
(Jenkins and Barrett), 4
Schizophrenia Research Institute, 102–3
schizophrenogenic mothers/families, 10–11,
16–17, 19, 227n57
Science, 12, 15
The Scientific Revolution (Shapin), 223n2
Search for Security (Field), 7–8, 121, 225nn27–28
"Section 8" vouchers, 157
self-sufficiency, 19, 228n66
Seligman, C. G., 6
Selten, Jean-Paul, 198
Semrad, Elvin, 12
servants: and Madhu (case 4), 75, 77; and Sita
(case 6), 100, 104
service ghettos, 95, 155, 216–17
sexual abuse, 194
sexually active: and Alexandra (case 9), 143,
146, 235n9; and Madhu (case 4), 82–83;
and Poi (case 11), 173; and Priyanka (case
3), 59, 66; in Thailand, 173
Shaffer, Peter, 155
Shakespeare, William, 223n4
shamans/shamanism, 9–10, 16, 226n38; and
Hood, John (case 1), 31, 33, 35, 38, 204; and
Poi (case 11), 209, 214; and social defeat,
204, 208, 215, 216
shame: and African-Caribbean British,
89–90; and Alexandra (case 9), 143, 145–
47; and Anisha (case 2), 210; and Madhu
(case 4), 81; in Romania, 143, 145–47; and
social defeat, 210
Shapin, Steve, 1, 223n2
shelters: and Meg (case 12), 183, 185–89, 192,
194, 212; and pragmatic lessons, 221; and
social defeat, 211–12; temporary shelter
system, 185–87; in United States, 154–161,
163–65, 183, 185–89, 192, 194, 211–12, 221;
and Zaney (case 10), 154, 157, 159, 211
Shiva (deity), 84
Sholingur Temple, 112
shouting, 7–8; and Hood, John (case 1), 38;
and Sita (case 6), 99–100, 103, 109–10, 112;
and Violet (case 5), 90–91
shrines: in Balaji Temple (India), 128, 214; in
Ghana, 6–7, 121
sinfulness, 16; in Ghana, 7; in Romania, 139,
146, 148, 235n14
single mothers: and African-Caribbean British, 86, 96; and Alexandra (case 9), 143–
45, 151, 215–16; in Romania, 143–45, 151,

215–16; and social defeat, 215–16; and
Violet (case 5), 86, 96
Sita (case 6), 99–112, 205, 209–11, 213, 215
sleeping medicine, 52
slum dwellers, 72
smoking, 33, 51, 116, 118, 164, 173, 185, 194
"social cases," 144, 151, 235n5
social class/status, 17–21, 21, 24–25, 227n58,
228n62; in Accra (Ghana), 115; and
African-Caribbean British, 88, 203; and
Charles (case 7), 115; and Madhu (case 4),
74–76; and Meg (case 12), 192–93; in
North India, 50, 53, 61, 231n7; and Poi
(case 11), 169; in Romania, 140, 151; and
Sita (case 6), 100; and social defeat, 197–
98, 201, 203, 237n6; in Thailand, 169; in
United States, 163, 166, 192–93
social defeat, 25, 197–215; in Accra (Ghana),
205–6, 209, 213, 215; and African-Caribbean
British, 87, 90, 204–5, 208; in Chennai
(India), 203, 205, 208–11, 213–14; and experience of illness, 213–16; and families, 203,
205–11; in Ireland, 198–99; in North India,
205, 207–10; and pragmatic lessons, 220,
222; in Romania, 215–16; and social conditions, 211–13; in Thailand, 209, 214–15; and
understanding of madness, 203–5; in
United States, 199–200, 202–4, 206–9,
211–13, 215–16; and work, 202–3, 206–9
social drift theory, 17, 227n58
social epidemiology, 3, 18–19, 86, 97, 198, 203, 216
socialism, 139, 145–46, 150, 235n11
social security, 102, 153–54; and psychiatric
disability, 184–86, 188, 191–92, 207
social selection theory, 17, 227n58
social suffering, 201
social worlds, 2–6, 8–9, 18–21, 21, 25, 226n32;
in Accra (Ghana), 123, 205; and African-
Caribbean British, 86–91, 95–98; and
Alexandra (case 9), 140, 143–46, 144, 151,
215, 235n5; and Anisha (case 2), 49; in Balaji Temple (India), 128–29, 135, 138; and
Caterina (São Paulo, Brazil), 138; and
Charles (case 7), 123, 205; in Chennai
(India), 101, 110–11; and *DSM-III*, 15, 20;
and Hood, John (case 1), 27–28, 30, 33–34;
in Ireland, 198–99; and Madhu (case 4),
73, 80; and Meg (case 12), 181–85, 187, 189,
193–94; in North India, 43, 49, 55–56,
61, 64, 66, 135, 138; and Poi (case 11), 170,
173, 179, 215; and pragmatic lessons, 216,

219–222; and Priyanka (case 3), 56, 61, 64, 66; in Romania, 140, 143–46, *144*, 151, 215, 235n5; and Sita (case 6), 101, 110–11; social contract, 5; and social defeat, 198, 200–203, 205, 211–13, 215, 220; social networks, 215; social safety nets, 101, 184, 206, 209, 221–22; and structural violence, 200–201; and Sunita (case 8), 135, 138; and symbolic violence, 198, 200; in Thailand, 167, 170, 173, 179, 215; in United States, 27–28, 30, 33–34, 158–166, *162*, 181–85, 187, 189, 193–94, 209, 216, 221–22; and Violet (case 5), 86–87, 90–91, 95–98; and Zaney (case 10), 159, 161–63, *162*. *See also* entries beginning *with* social

Society and Psychosis, 20

solar eclipse, 145

somatoform disorders, 59

Sood, Anubha, 127–138, 267

souls, 9, 44, 64, 148; spirit/soul, 119–120, 234n8

soup kitchens, 95, 155–56, 159–160, 186, 192, 211

Sousa, Amy June, 42–55, 205, 267

speech, incoherent/impoverished, 2, 15; and Ahmed, Kemal (case 2), 51; and Alexandra (case 9), 142, 146–47; in Balaji Temple (India), 135; in North India, 44, 51, 63, 135; and Poi (case 11), 168–69; in Romania, 142, 146–47; and Sunita (case 8), 135; in Thailand, 168–69; and Veena (case 2), 44

spirit affliction/illness: in Balaji Temple (India), 128–29, 131, 133; and Poi (case 11), 170; and Sunita (case 8), 131, 133; in Thailand, 170

spirit houses (Thailand), *171*

spirit possession, 121, 127–29, 209, 234n10 (Ch7), 234n5(Ch8)

spirits, 9, 44, 64; in Accra (Ghana), 120–21; and Alexandra (case 9), 148–49; in Balaji Temple (India), 127–29, 213–14; in Chennai (India), 77, 112; and Madhu (case 4), 77–79, 214; and Poi (case 11), 167–68, *171*, 172, 174, 177–78, 214–15; in Romania, 148–49; and social defeat, 213–15; and Sunita (case 8), 133, 213–14; in Thailand, 167–68, 171, 172, 174, 177–78, 214–15

spirit/soul, 119–120, 234n8

spiritual attacks, 113, 116, 118, 123–26

Spitzer, Robert, 14

Sri Lanka, 23

Srithanya (psychiatric hospital), 175

Stanford University, 12

Starbuck's, 181

stereotypes, negative, 43, 69, 92, 167, 202

stigma, 24; and Hood, John (case 1), 34–35; in North India, 61, 67, 210; and Priyanka (case 3), 67, 210; and social defeat, 199, 202, 210

Stirling County study, 8

straddling irrational/rational, 36–37

stress, 23–24; and African-Caribbean British, 87–90, 94; and Alexandra (case 9), 142; in Ghana, 6, 8; and Meg (case 12), 184; in North India, 56, 209; and Poi (case 11), 172; and Priyanka (case 3), 56, 58, 60–61, 65; in Romania, 142; and Sita (case 6), 103–4; and social defeat, 198, 202, 209; in Thailand, 172; in United States, 160, 184; and Violet (case 5), 90, 94

structural violence, 198, 200–201

substance use/abuse, 98, 116, 154, 160–61, 189, 193–94, 233nn1–2. *See also* alcohol use/ alcoholism; drug use/abuse

sudoku, 165

suicide, 22, 66, 88, 98, 163, 183–84, 193, 199; attempted suicide, 170, 175, 214

Suicide (Durkheim), 5–6

Sunita (case 8), 127, 130–38, *132*, 209, 211, 213–15

supernatural forces, 4; in Accra (Ghana), 113–15, 118–122; and Alexandra (case 9), 140, 149, 151–52; in Balaji Temple (India), 129, 214; and Charles (case 7), 114–15, 118–122; and Hood, John (case 1), 30–31; in Romania, 140, 149, 151–52; and social defeat, 213–14; in South India, 64. *See also* God/Gods; spirits

Surinamese, 20

suspiciousness, 17; and Anisha (case 2), 45, 47; in North India, 45, 47, 56, 58–60, 62, 65; and Poi (case 11), 168, 173–74; and Priyanka (case 3), 58–60, 62, 65; in Thailand, 168, 173–74. *See also* paranoia

symbolic violence, 198, 200–201

symptoms, 1–2, 3, 8, 12, 223n3; in Accra (Ghana), 113, 119; and African Americans, 18; and African-Caribbean British, 87, 91, 94–97, 204; and Ahmed, Kemal (case 2), 50–52; and Alexandra (case 9), 140–42, 145, 152; and Anisha (case 2), 44–45, 47–50; in Balaji Temple (India), 134–35, 214; and Charles (case 7), 119; in Chennai (India), 100–102, 104–5, 111; and the Colonel (case 2),

symptoms (continued)
53; and DOSMeD, 21; and *DSM-III*, 14–15; and Hood, John (case 1), 28, 31; and ISoS study, 21–22; and Madhu (case 4), 76, 79–80; and Meg (case 12), 191–92, 194; in North India, 43–45, 47–53, 56, 62–63, 71, 134–5, 205, 210, 214; and Poi (case 11), 168–172, 174–75, 178; and pragmatic lessons, 218–19, 222; and Priyanka (case 3), 56, 71, 210; in Romania, 140–42, 145, 152; and Sita (case 6), 100–101, 104–5, 111, 205; and social defeat, 202–5, 207, 209–10, 214; and Sunita (case 8), 134–35, 214; in Thailand, 167–172, 174–75, 178; in United States, 18, 28, 31, 155, 163, 166, 167, 184–85, 191–94, 209, 218–19; and Veena (case 2), 43–44, 48–50; and Violet (case 5), 87, 91, 94–97, 204
Szasz, Thomas, 12–13, 223n3

Taco Bell, 39
Tallensi, 23
Tamil language, 110
Tamil Nadu (India), 110, 211. *See also* Chennai (India)
Tanacu Scandal, 149, 152
tantrik, 64
television, 37; in Accra (Ghana), 115; and African-Caribbean British, 96; and Alexandra (case 9), 140, 146–47, 235n12; and Charles (case 7), 115; and commanding voices, 115; in North India, 44; and Poi (case 11), 172; in Romania, 140, 146–47, 235n12; in Thailand, 172; in United States, 158, 181; and Veena (case 2), 44; and Violet (case 5), 96
temples: in Balaji (Mehndipur, India), 127–138, 211, 214; Hanuman temple (Allahabad, India), 64; and Madhu (case 4), 73, 77, 80–81, 84–85; and Poi (case 11), 170, 174, 176–77; and Priyanka (case 3), 64; Sholingur Temple, 112; and Sita (case 6), 106–8, 110–12; and social defeat, 211, 214; and Sunita (case 8), 127, 130–38, 132, 211, 214; temple healing, 127–29, 131, 133, 135, 137–38; temple myths, 128; in Thailand, 170, 174, 176–77
Teresa, Mother, 81
Thailand, 167–179, 171, 204, 208–9, 214–15
Tietze, Trude, 10–11
toughness, 12, 161–63, 166, 204, 212
tranquilizers, 176

trauma, 15, 194, 226n39
trespassing, 189, 199
Tristes Tropiques (Lévi-Strauss), 6
trust/distrust, 10, 13; and Alexandra (case 9), 149; in Chennai (India), 110; in Chicago (Ill.), 159, 164; and Poi (case 11), 173–74; in Romania, 149; and Sita (case 6), 110; in Thailand, 173–74
tuberculosis, 42
tulsi leaves, 103, 233n5
twin studies, 16, 231n7

unemployment, 94–95, 143, 183–85, 209, 225n27
Unitarian Church shelter, 187, 192, 194
United Kingdom, 6–7, 23, 225n23; and African-Caribbean British, 20, 86–98, 203–6, 208–9; and Hood, John (case 1), 28–29, 31; new therapeutic approaches in, 112; and pragmatic lessons, 218; and social defeat, 203–6, 208–9, 211, 215; and Violet (case 5), 86–87, 90–98, 204–5, 208–9
United States, 4, 9, 19–20; Chicago (Ill.), 153–166, 157, 201, 207, 211–12, 216–17, 225n29; and Hood, John (case 1), 9, 27–41, 32, 203–4, 211, 215; India compared to, 4, 99, 101, 103–5, 111, 203, 213, 221, 233n9; institutional circuits in, 4, 158, 186, 190, 192, 209, 211–12, 222; and Meg (case 12), 180–195, 207–9, 212; and NARP (non-affective remitting psychosis), 169–170; Norwegian immigrants to, 229n74; pragmatic lessons for, 216–222; and Recovery Movement, 19, 35, 206–7, 228n66; and social defeat, 199–200, 202–4, 206–9, 211–13, 215–16; and Zaney (case 10), 153–55, 157–59, 161–63, 162, 165–66, 201, 211–12, 216–17
University College (Ibadan, Nigeria), 8
upper class, 74–76. *See also* social class/status
urban living, 20, 21, 225n29, 227n58; in Accra (Ghana), 118; and African-Caribbean British, 88; in India, 22, 73, 82, 105, 225n29; and pragmatic lessons, 219–220; in Romania, 150; and social defeat, 202; in United States, 225n29
Uttar Pradesh (India), 58. *See also* North India

Varanasi (India), 56–71, 225n29, 230n4; Ghats of, 57

Veena (case 2), 43–44, 47–50, 54, 208, 231n7
violence, 8, 10; and African-Caribbean British, 92; and Ahmed, Kemal (case 2), 51; and Cornici, Irina, 152; and "distressing voices," 105; in North India, 51, 65; and pragmatic lessons, 221; in Romania, 152; and social defeat, 197–98, 200–201, 211; structural violence, 198, 200–201; symbolic violence, 198, 200–201; in United States, 38, 164–65, 211. *See also* domestic violence
Violet (case 5), 86–87, 90–98, 205, 208–9
viraha, 69
viral infections, 223n4, 231n7
voices, 1–2, 4, 8–9, 24, 226n39; in Accra (Ghana), 113–16, 118–126, 205–6, 215; and Alexandra (case 9), 140, 145–46, 150, 215; and Anisha (case 2), 47; in Balaji Temple (India), 127, 129, 131, 135–36, 138, 213–14; and Charles (case 7), 114–16, 118–126, 205–6, 215; in Chennai (India), 100–101, 104–12, 213; commanding voices, 99, 105, 107, 114, 121, 129, 213; and Cornici, Irina, 152; demonic voices, 113–15, 119, 122, 126; "distressing voices," 105; and *DSM-III*, 15; God's voice, 99, 108, 122–23, 131; and Hood, John (case 1), 30–31, 34; and Joan of Arc, 141–42; kind, admiring voices, 99, 107–9, 111, 123, 138, 213, 218; and Madhu (case 4), 76–80, 208, 214; mean, violent voices, 99, 105, 107–9, 111, 136, 153, 174, 213–14, 218; and Meg (case 12), 183, 191–92; more benign in India, 99, 213–14; murmuring voices, 84, 105, 213; and Poi (case 11), 173–74; and pragmatic lessons, 217–222; in Romania, 140, 145–46, 150, 152, 215; saying "thud," 12, 227n51; and Sita (case 6), 100–101, 104–12; and social defeat, 205–6, 208, 213–15; and Sunita (case 8), 127, 131, 133, 135–36, 138, 213–14; in Thailand, 173–74; in United States, 30–31, 34, 104–5, 107, 153–55, 165–66, 183, 191–92, 217–220; as vibrations, 106–7, 109; and Violet (case 5), 95; and Zaney (case 10), 153–55, 165–66
Volunteers for America, 39
vulnerability, 4, 25; and African-Caribbean British, 87, 90; and Alexandra (case 9), 142, 151; and Anisha (case 2), 50; in Balaji Temple (India), 127–28; and Cornici, Irina, 149; genetic vulnerability, 16–17, 87,

198, 202; and Madhu (case 4), 76–77; in North India, 43, 50, 56; and pragmatic lessons, 222; in Romania, 142, 149, 151; and social defeat, 197–99; in United States, 164–65, 199, 222; and Violet (case 5), 87, 90

Wanderling, Joe, 23
Waxler, Nancy, 23
West/Westerners, 3–4, 6–7, 9, 16, 21, 23; and catatonic schizophrenia, 48; descriptions of voices, 105, 107; and Field, M.J., 23, 121; India compared to, 4, 48, 101; and NARP (non-affective remitting psychosis), 8, 169; pragmatic lessons for, 221–22; and Romania, 139; and social defeat, 202–3, 209, 212–13. *See also names of Western countries*
whites/whiteness, 18–21; in Accra (Ghana), 122–23; in Chicago (Ill.), 153; in Great Britain, 86–87, 92, 96–98, 203; and social defeat, 197
Whitley, Rob, 5
WHO (World Health Organization) studies, 21–24, 169, 229n86
Wisconsin, 153
witches/witchcraft, 7; in Accra (Ghana), 113–16, 118–126, 206, 215, 234n14; and Charles (case 7), 113–16, 118–126, 205, 215; as demonic birds, 115; and social defeat, 205, 215
work, 17–19, 22–24; in Accra (Ghana), 115; and African-Caribbean British, 93–96, 208; and Alexandra (case 9), 142–44, 146; and Anisha (case 2), 44, 49–50, 54, 208; in Balaji Temple (India), 135–36, 138, 208–9; and Caterina (São Paulo, Brazil), 138; and Charles (case 7), 115; in Ghana, 225n27; and Hood, John (case 1), 28, 33, 35–38; industrial-age labor, 24; and Madhu (case 4), 73–78, 80–81, 83–84, 208, 214; and Meg (case 12), 182–86, 192–94, 207–8; in North India, 44, 46, 49–50, 53–54, 57, 59, 61–63, 65, 67, 135–6, 138, 208–9, 210; and Poi (case 11), 168–170, 172, 175, 208–9; and pragmatic lessons, 220; and Priyanka (case 3), 57, 59, 61–62, 65, 67, 210; in Romania, 142–44, 146; and Sita (case 6), 100–101, 111–12; and social defeat, 202–3, 206–10, 214; and Sunita (case 8), 135–36, 138, 208–9; in Thailand, 167–170, 172, 175,

work (*continued*)
208–9; in United States, 28, 33, 35–38, 154, 157, 182–86, 192–94, 206–8; and Violet (case 5), 93–96, 208; and Zaney (case 10), 154

Yale University, 181–82, 185, 189, 193, 207
Yoruba country, 8; Egba Yoruba, 16

Young, Neil, 29
Ypsilanti (Mich.), 141
Yupik-speaking Eskimos, 15–16

Zaney (case 10), 153–55, 157–59, 161–63, 162, 165–66, 201, 211–12, 216–17

CPSIA information can be obtained
at www.ICGtesting.com
Printed in the USA
LVHW092052221121
704128LV00012B/122

9 780520 291096